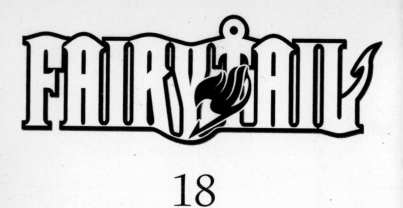

18

Hiro Mashima

Translated and adapted by William Flanagan
Lettered by AndWorld Design

KC
KODANSHA
COMICS

FROM HIRO MASHIMA

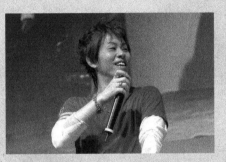

This is a photo of my Tokyo Game Show event. I go every year just to have fun, but this time I was a part of an event. It was a slightly surreal feeling.

I'm sure some of you out there are aware of it, but Fairy Tail will soon come out as a game. Its actually a lot of fun. I'm really looking forward to its release!!

Original Jacket Design: Hisao Ogawa

FAIRY TAIL

フェアリーテイル

18

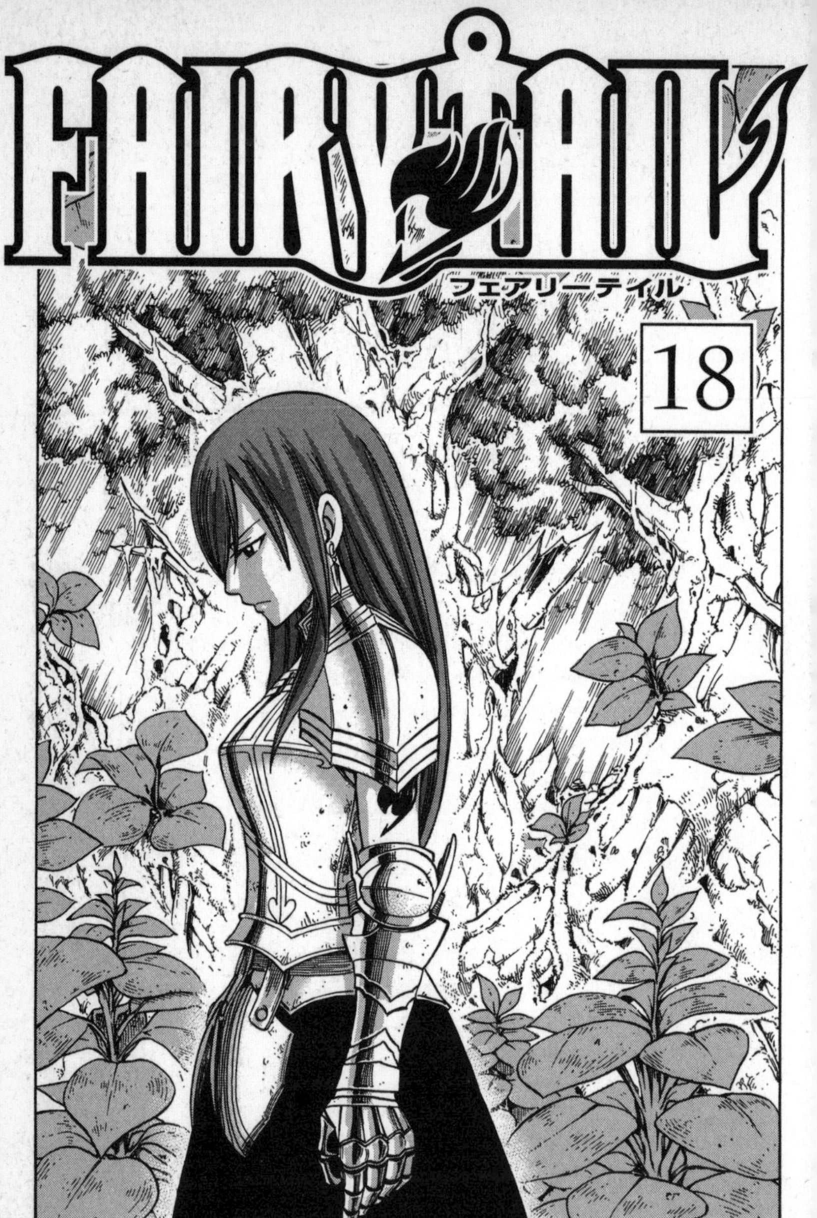

HIRO MASHIMA

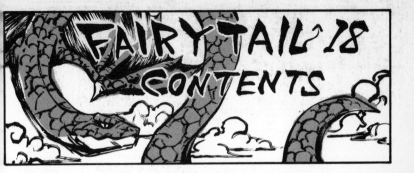

FAIRY TAIL 18
CONTENTS

Published in serial form by Weekly Shônen Magazine 2009 Volumes 34 - 42/43.

FAIRY TAIL

フェアリーテイル

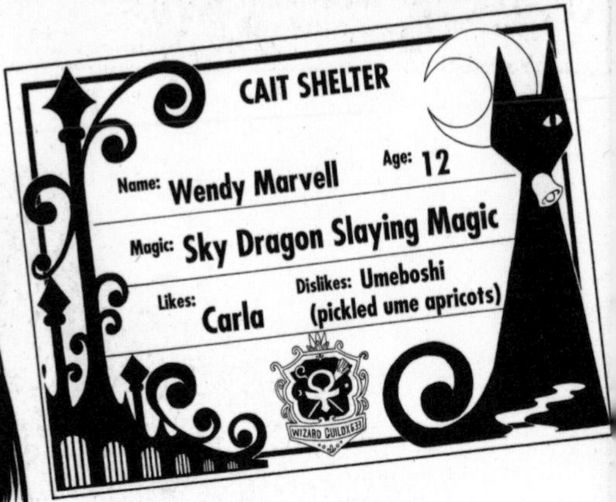
CAIT SHELTER
Name: Wendy Marvell
Age: 12
Magic: Sky Dragon Slaying Magic
Likes: Carla
Dislikes: Umeboshi (pickled ume apricots)
WIZARD GUILD

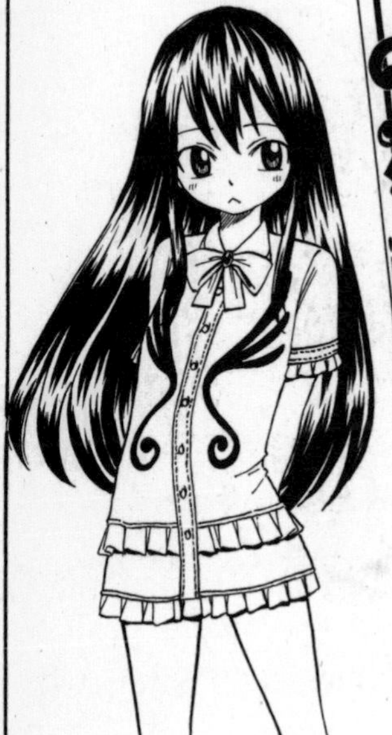

Remarks

This young member of the Cait Shelter Magical Guild is a Sky Dragon Slayer Wizard. She learned her ability to heal wounds from a dragon. Her magic comes from air; the cleaner the air, the stronger the magic. In polluted air, her magic doesn't work at all. Seven years ago, the dragon that raised her, Grandine, went missing, just like the dragons that trained Natsu and Gajeel. When she heard rumors of Natsu, she felt she needed to meet him, so she volunteered for this mission.

For Wendy, who is usually extremely shy, volunteering took a huge amount of courage.

Chapter 144, Pretty Voice

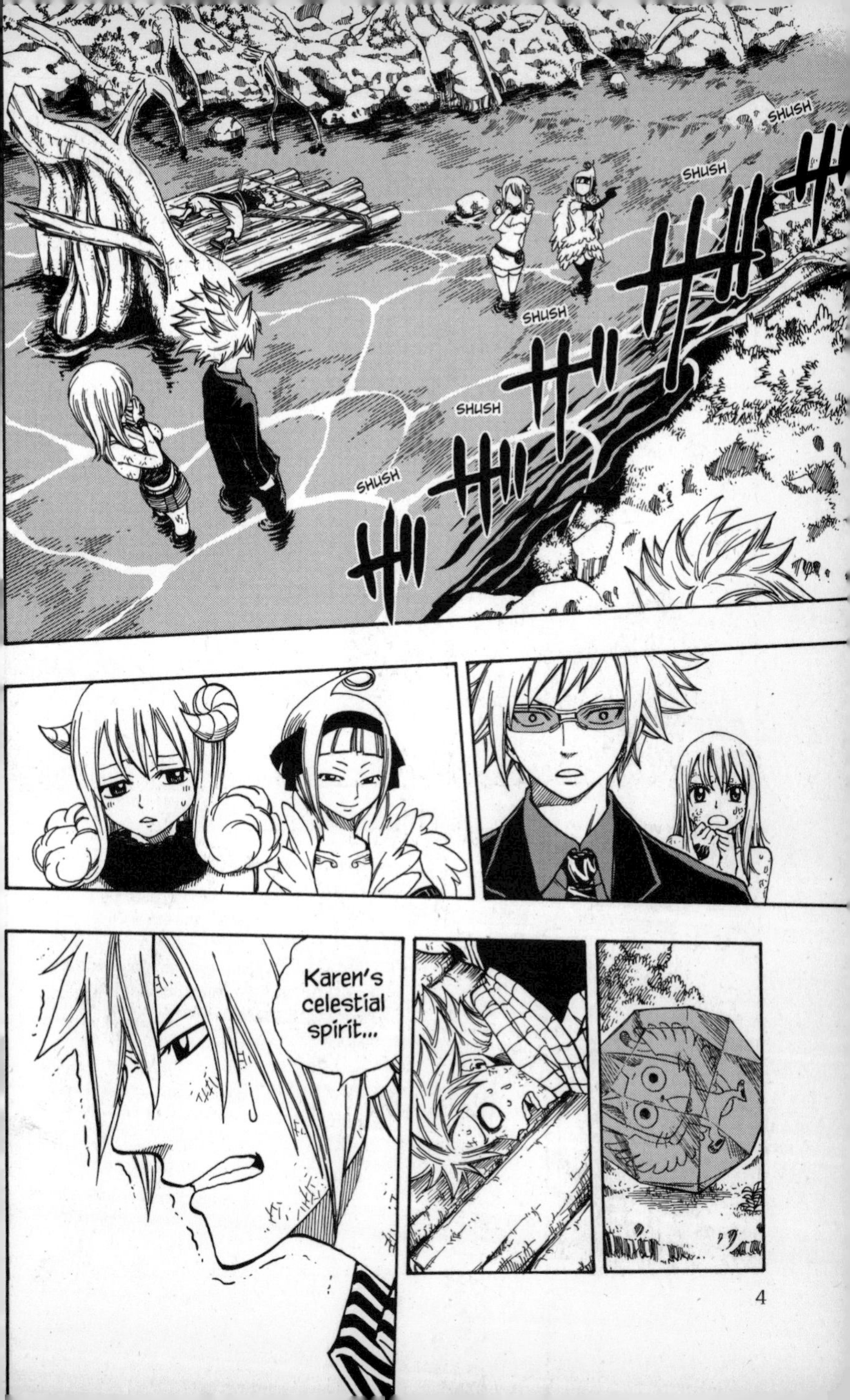
SHUSH
SHUSH
SHUSH
SHUSH
SHUSH
Karen's celestial spirit...

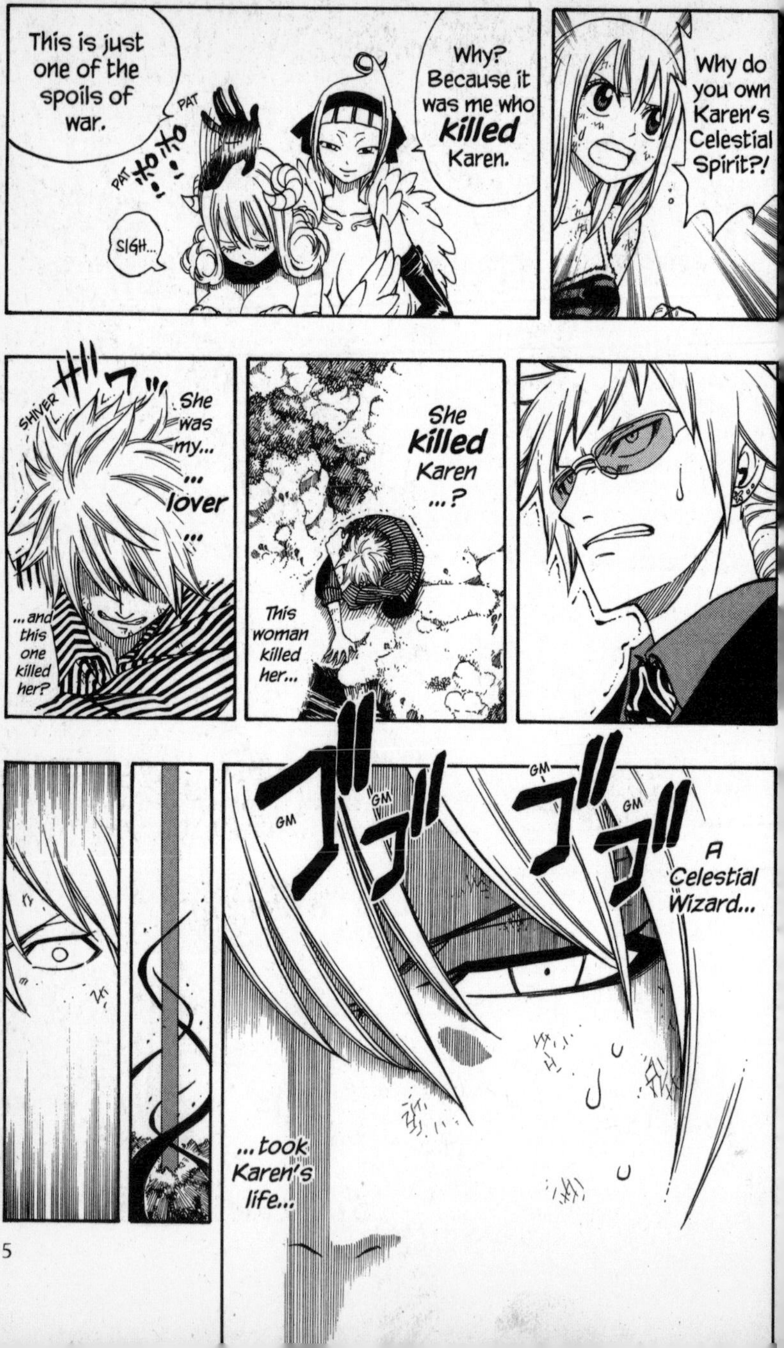
Why do you own Karen's Celestial Spirit?!
Why? Because it was me who **killed** Karen.
PAT
This is just one of the spoils of war.
PAT
SIGH...
She **killed** Karen ...?
This woman killed her...
She was my... ... **lover** ...
SHIVER
...and this one killed her?
GM
GM
GM
GM
A Celestial Wizard...
...took Karen's life...

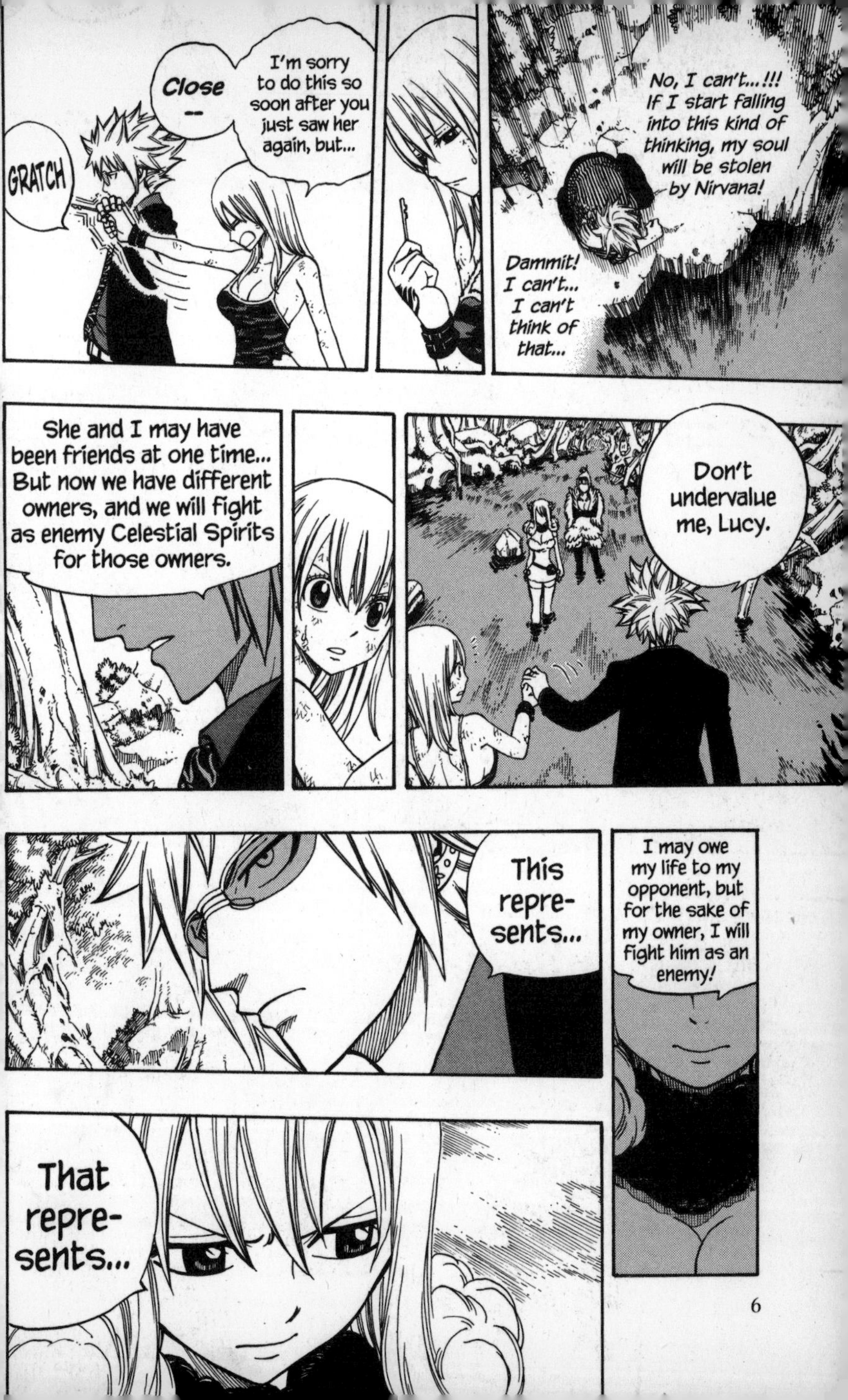
No, I can't...!!! If I start falling into this kind of thinking, my soul will be stolen by Nirvana!
Dammit! I can't... I can't think of that...
I'm sorry to do this so soon after you just saw her again, but...
Close --
GRATCH
Don't undervalue me, Lucy.
She and I may have been friends at one time... But now we have different owners, and we will fight as enemy Celestial Spirits for those owners.
I may owe my life to my opponent, but for the sake of my owner, I will fight him as an enemy!
This repre-sents...
That repre-sents...

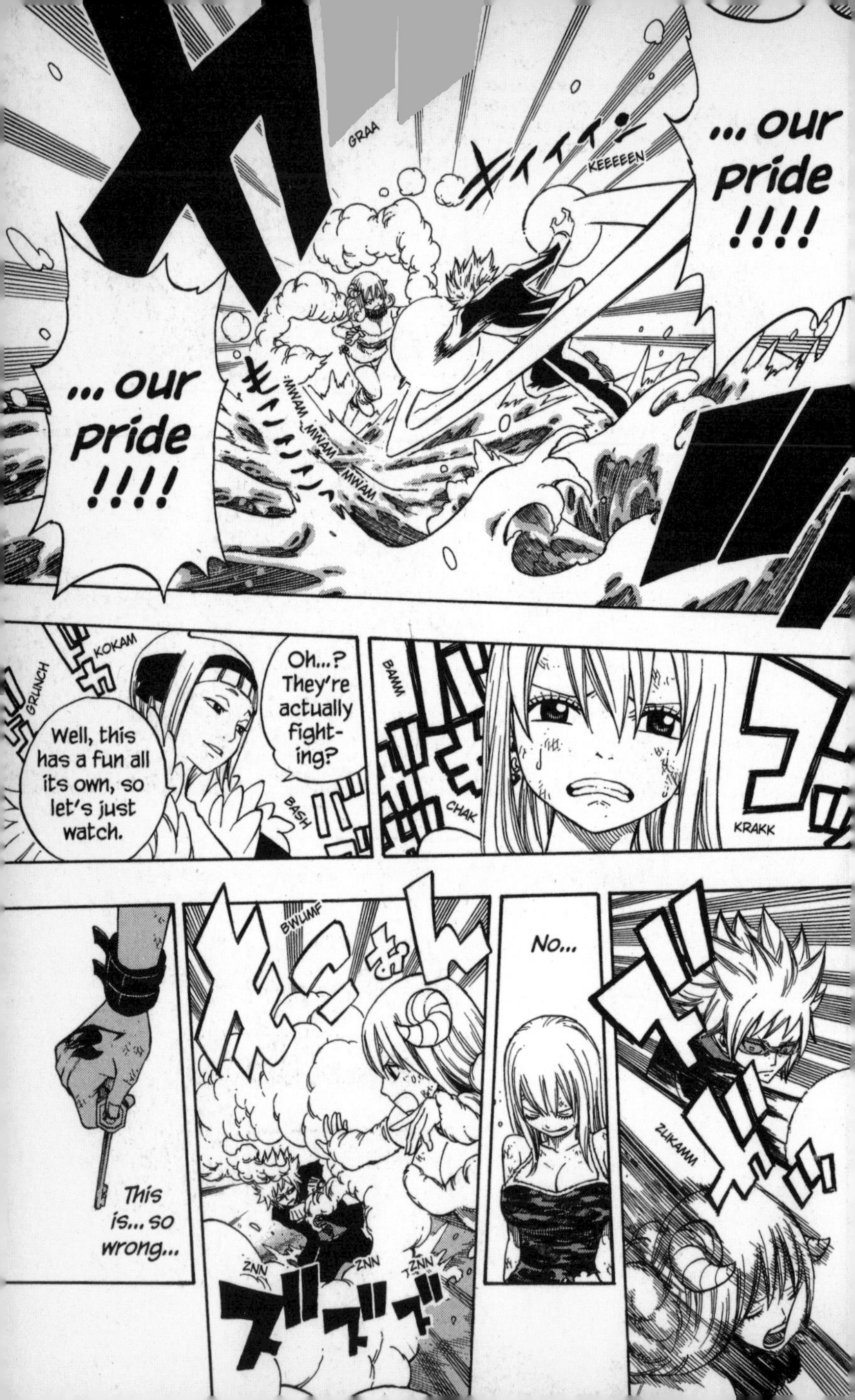

...our pride !!!!
KEEEEEN
GRAA
...our pride !!!!
MWAM MWAM MWAM
Oh...? They're actually fight-ing?
KRAKK
CHAK
BAMM
BASH
KOKAM
GRLINCH
Well, this has a fun all its own, so let's just watch.
ZUKAMM
No...
BWUMF
ZNN ZNN ZNN
This is... so wrong...

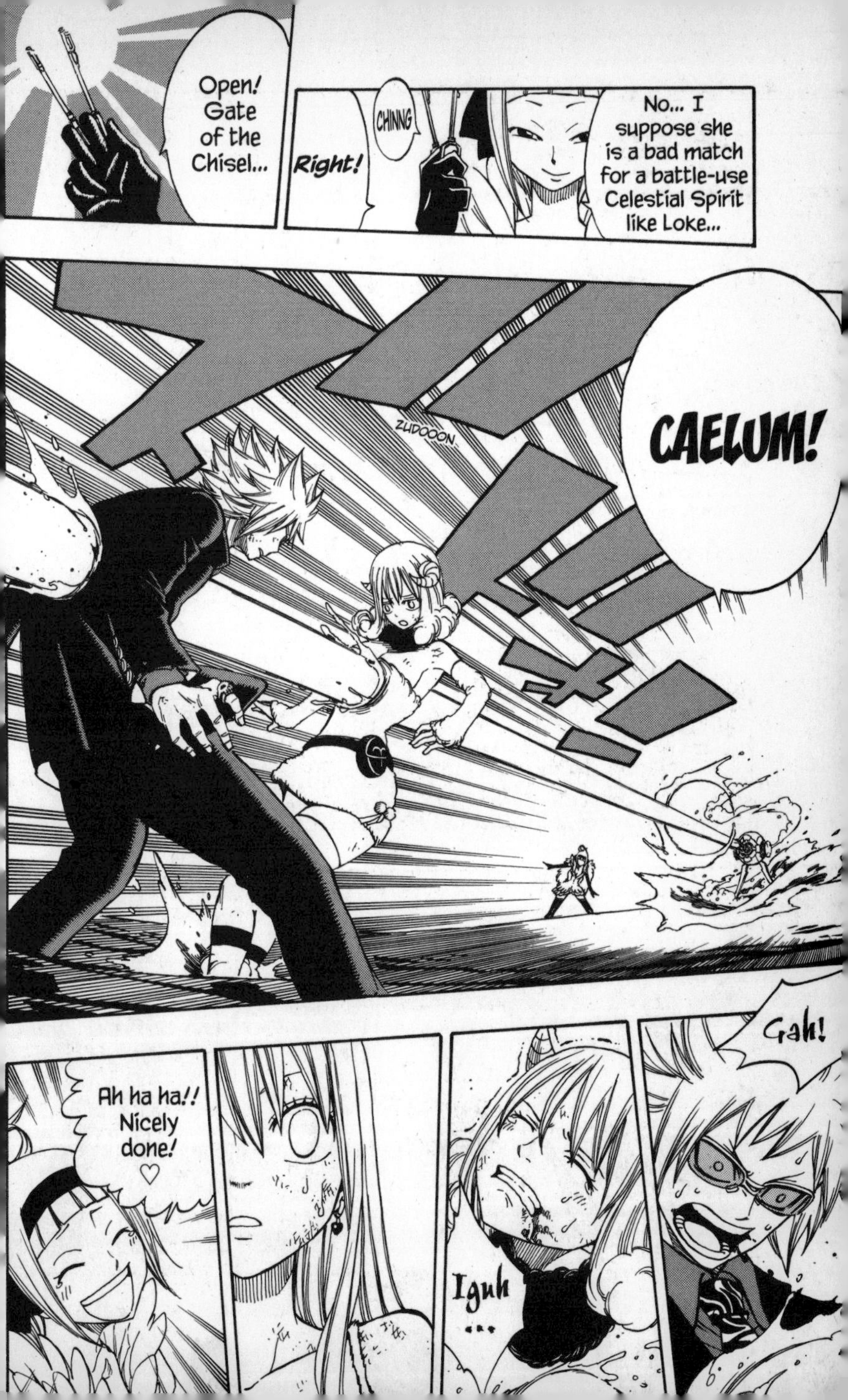
No... I suppose she is a bad match for a battle-use Celestial Spirit like Loke...
CHINNG
Right!
Open! Gate of the Chisel...
CAELUM!
ZUDOOON
Gah!
Iguh ...
Ah ha ha!! Nicely done! ♡

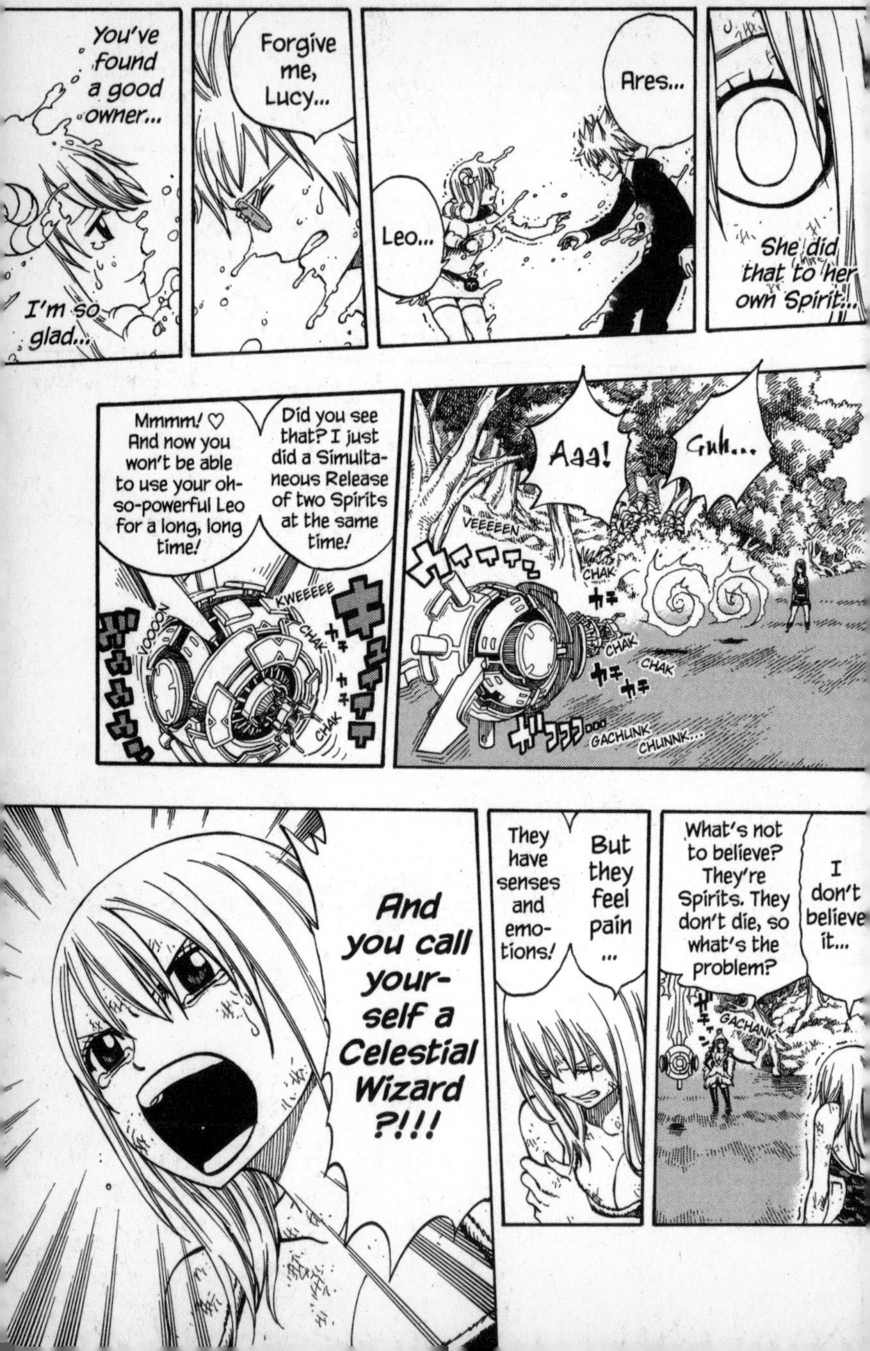
She did that to her own Spirit...
Ares...
Leo...
Forgive me, Lucy...
You've found a good owner...
I'm so glad...
Guh...
Aaa!
VEEEEEN
CHAK
CHAK
CHAK
GACHUNK
CHUNNK...
Did you see that? I just did a Simultaneous Release of two Spirits at the same time!
Mmmm! ♡ And now you won't be able to use your oh-so-powerful Leo for a long, long time!
KWEEEEE
CHAK
CHAK
VOOOON
I don't believe it...
What's not to believe? They're Spirits. They don't die, so what's the problem?
GACHANK
But they feel pain...
They have senses and emotions!
And you call yourself a Celestial Wizard?!!!

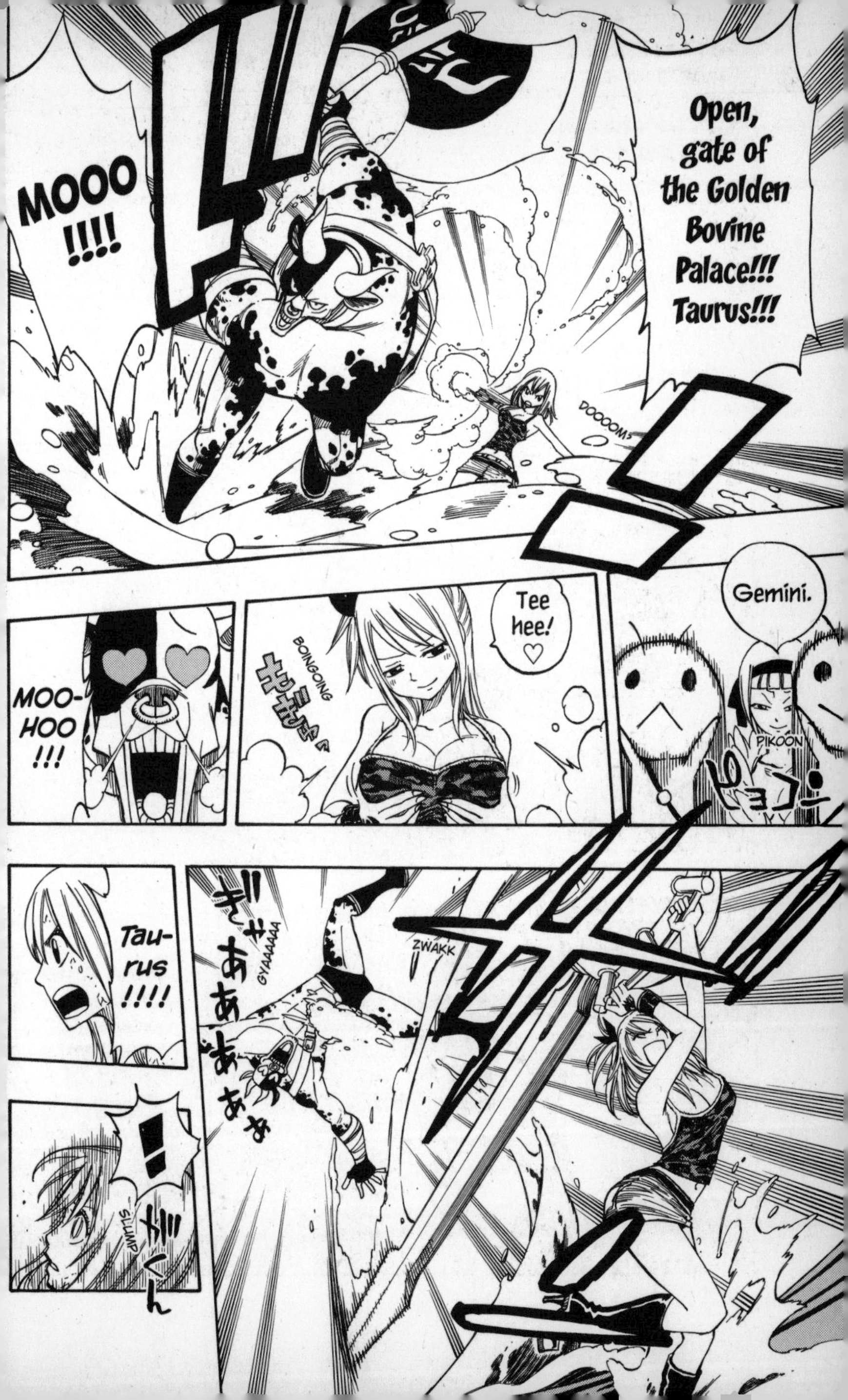
Open, gate of the Golden Bovine Palace!!! Taurus!!!
DOOOOM
MOOO!!!!
Gemini.
PIKOON
Tee hee! ♡
BOINGOING
MOO-HOO!!!
ZWAKK
GYAAAAAA
Tau-rus!!!!
!
SLUMP

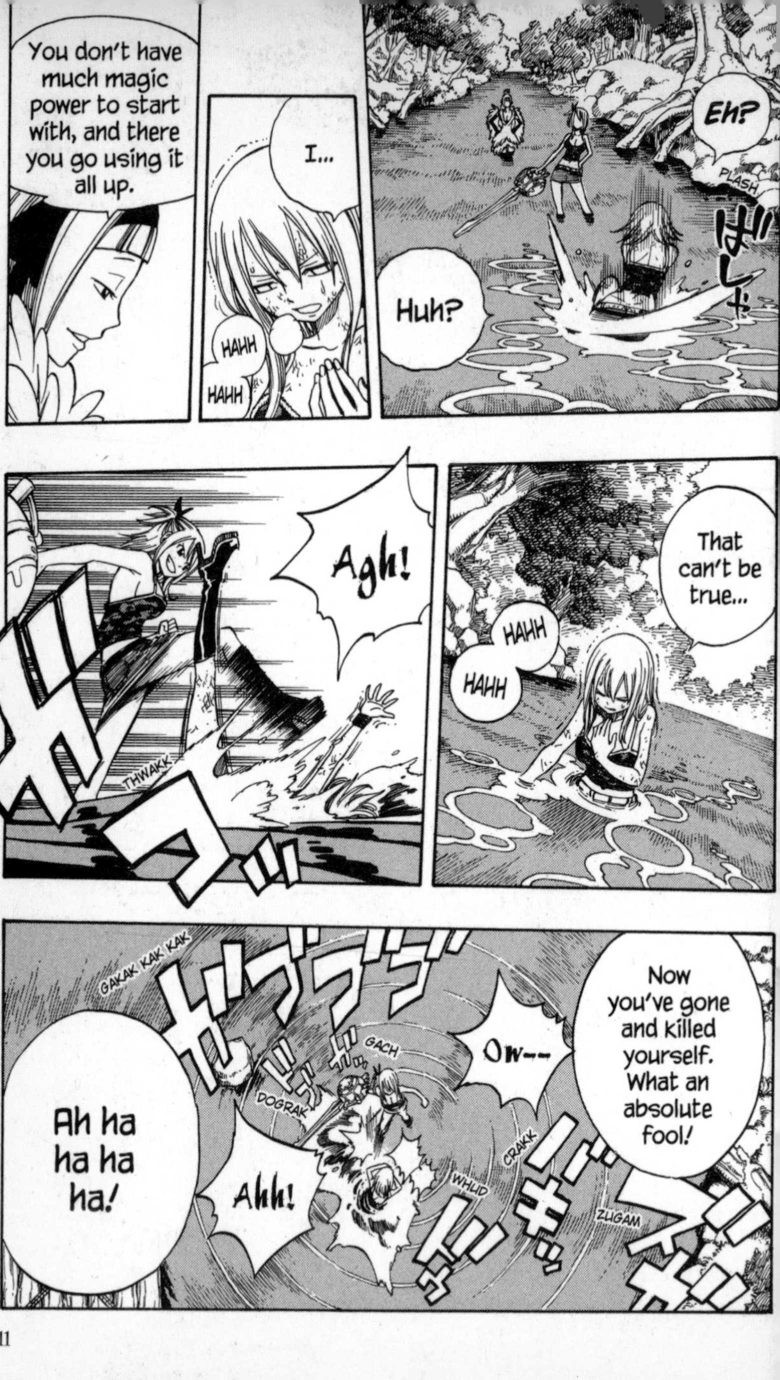
Eh?
PLASH
Huh?
I...
HAHH
HAHH
You don't have much magic power to start with, and there you go using it all up.
That can't be true...
HAHH
HAHH
Agh!
THWAKK
Now you've gone and killed yourself. What an absolute fool!
Ow--
ZUGAM
CRAKK
WHUD
GACH
DOGRAK
GAKAK KAK KAK
Ahh!
Ah ha ha ha ha!

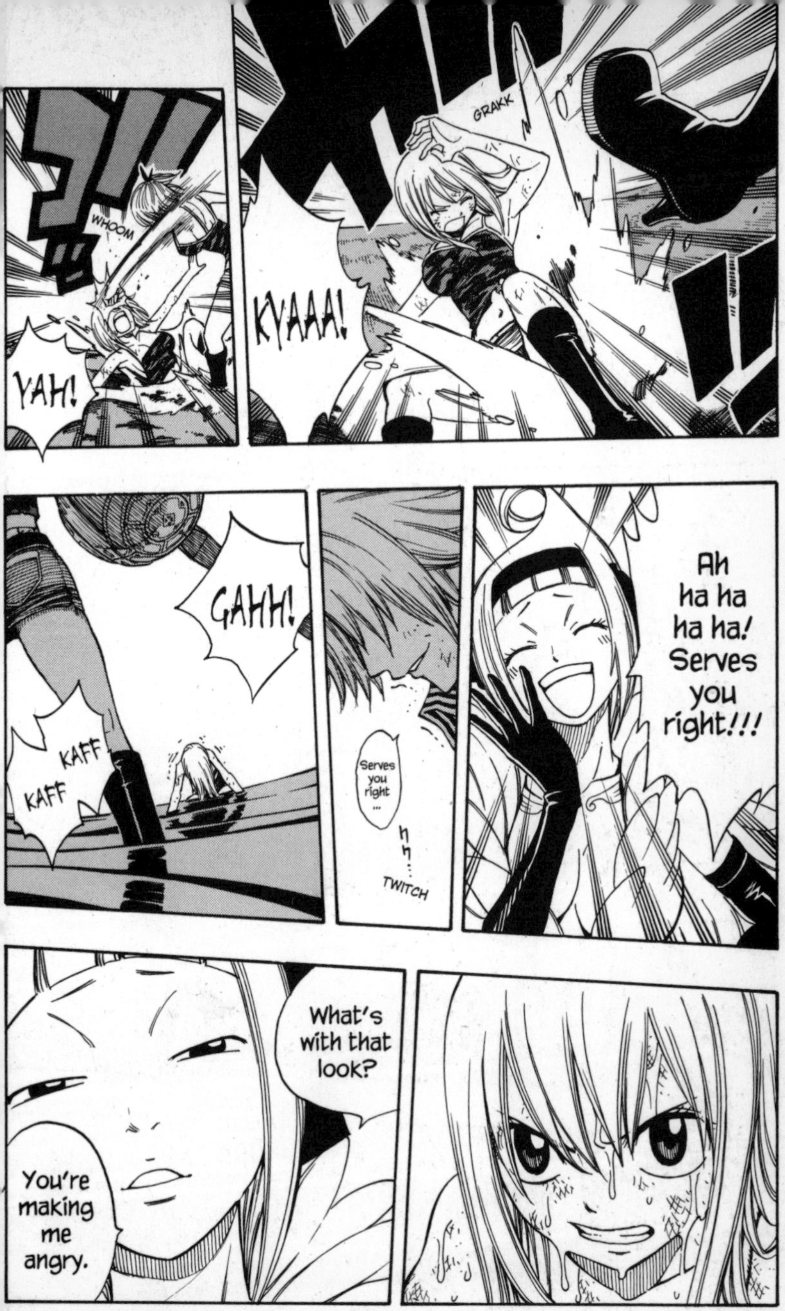
GRAKK
KYAAA!
WHOOM
YAH!
Ah ha ha ha ha! Serves you right!!!
Serves you right...
TWITCH
GAHH!
KAFF KAFF
What's with that look?
You're making me angry.

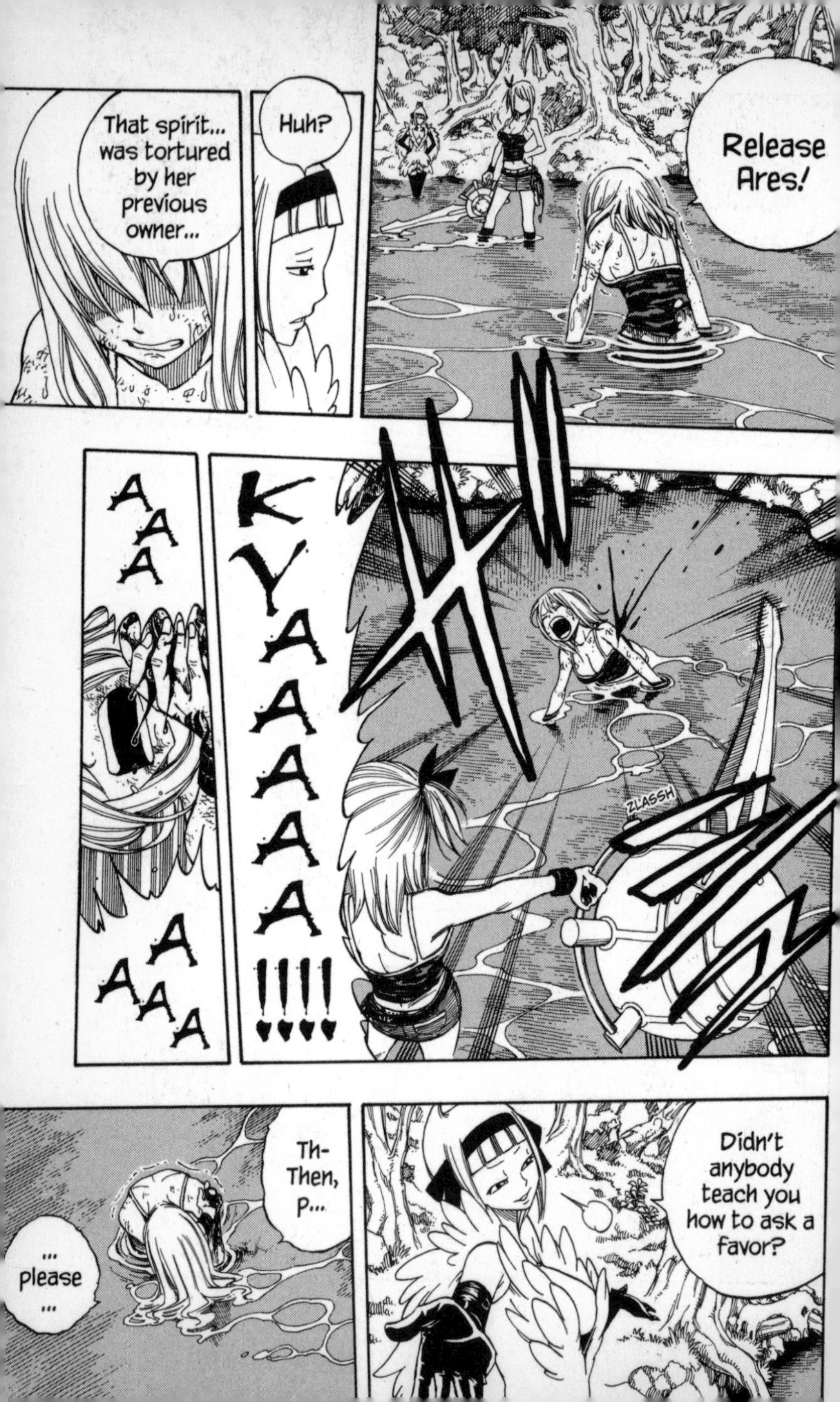
Release Ares!
Huh?
That spirit... was tortured by her previous owner...
KYAAAAA!!!!
ZLASSH
AAAAAAA
Didn't anybody teach you how to ask a favor?
Th- Then, p...
... please ...

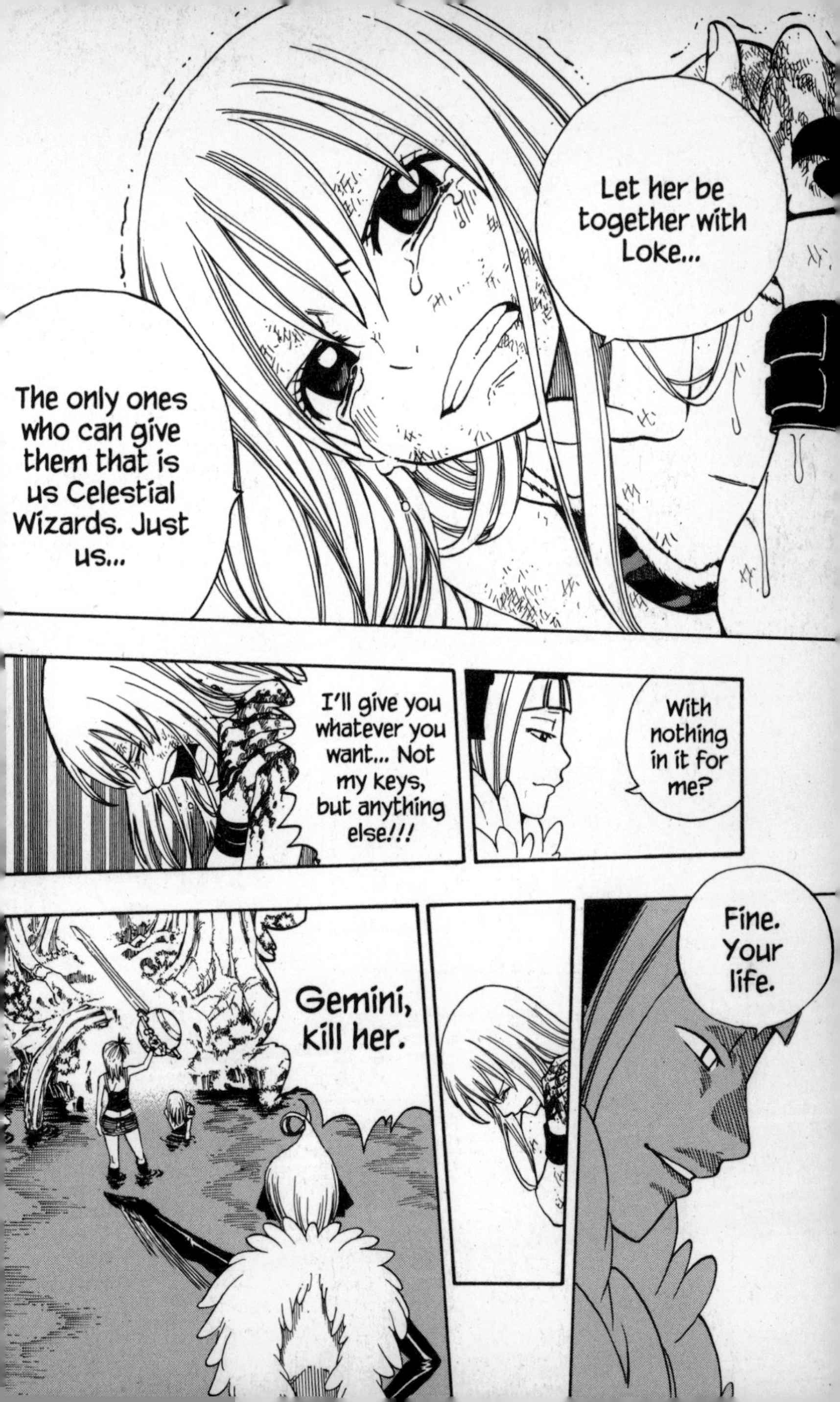
Let her be together with Loke...
The only ones who can give them that is us Celestial Wizards. Just us...
With nothing in it for me?
I'll give you whatever you want... Not my keys, but anything else!!!
Fine. Your life.
Gemini, kill her.

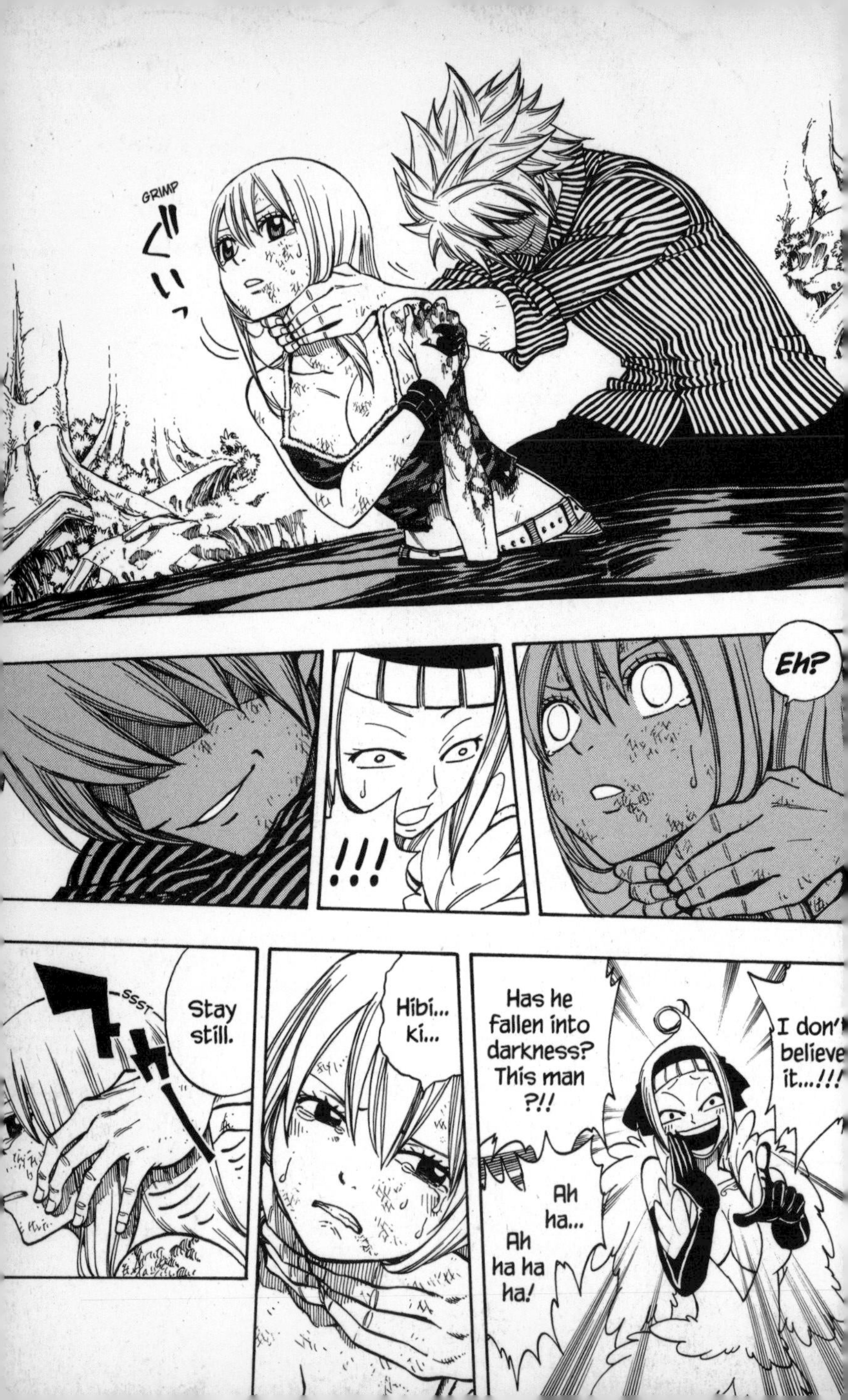
GRIMP
Eh?
!!!
I don't believe it...!!!
Has he fallen into darkness? This man ?!!
Ah ha...
Ah ha ha ha!
Hibi... ki...
Stay still.
SSST

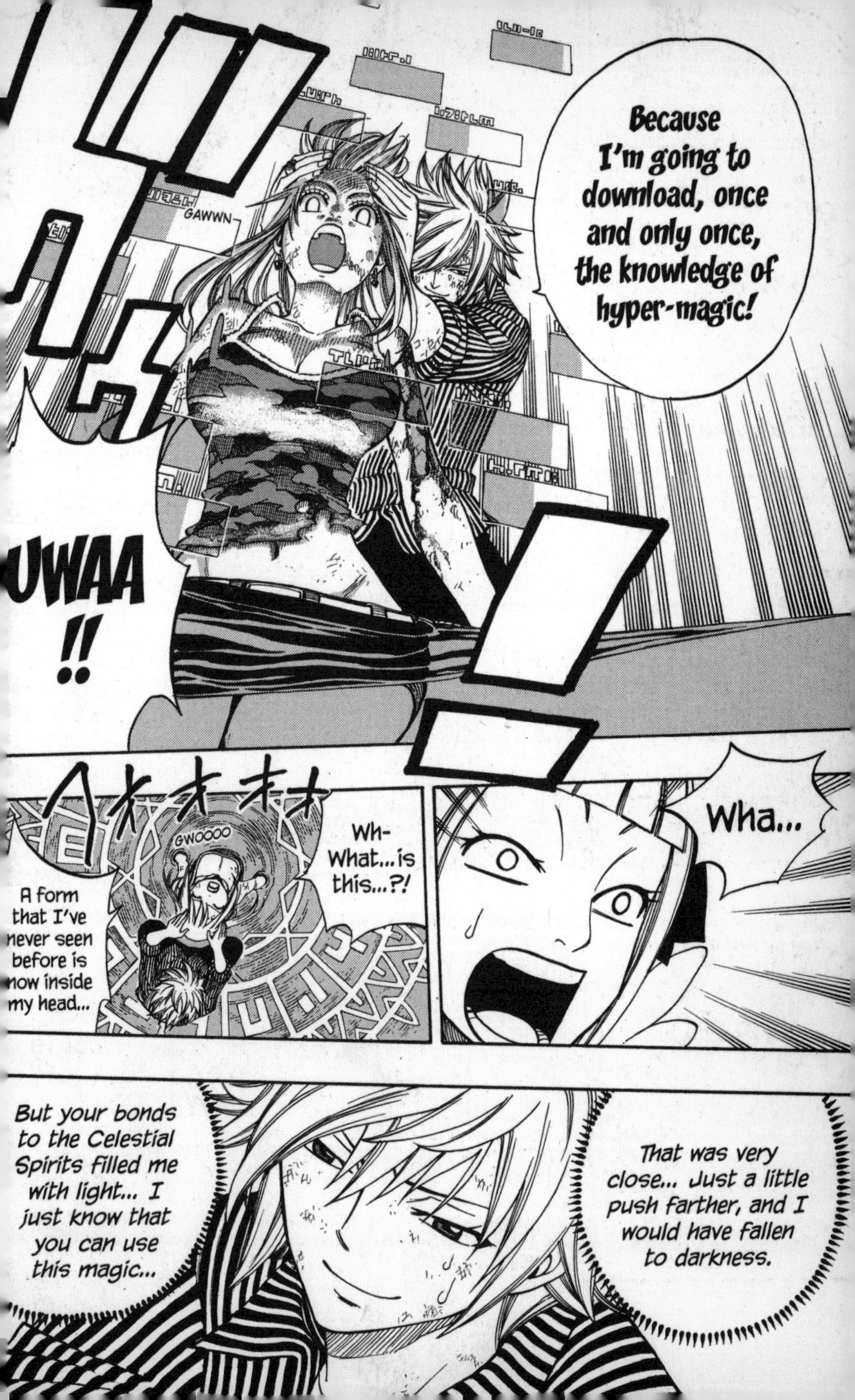
Because I'm going to download, once and only once, the knowledge of hyper-magic!
GAWWN
UWAA!!
Wha...
Wh- What...is this...?!
GWOOOO
A form that I've never seen before is now inside my head...
That was very close... Just a little push farther, and I would have fallen to darkness.
But your bonds to the Celestial Spirits filled me with light... I just know that you can use this magic...

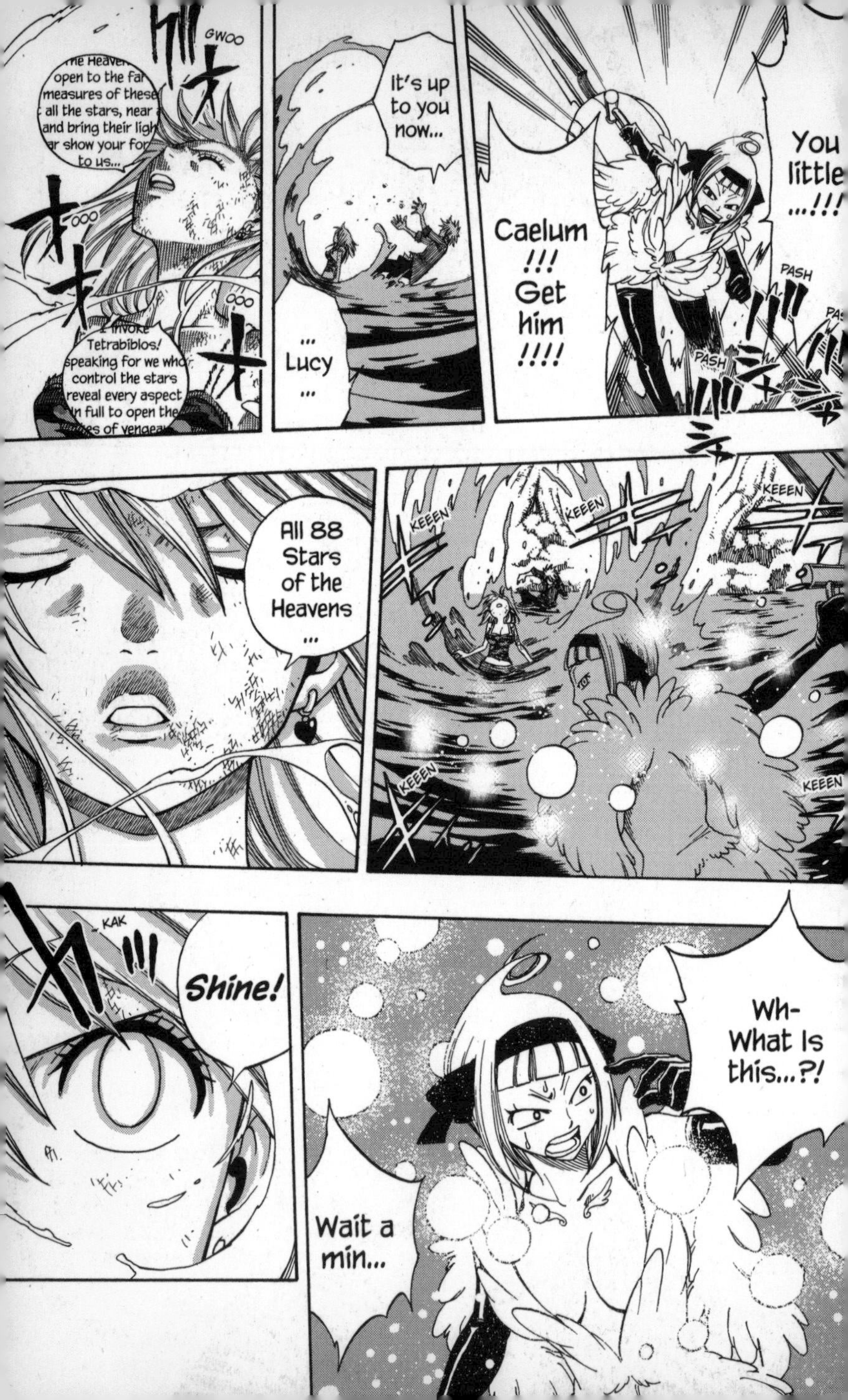
You little ...!!!
Caelum !!! Get him !!!!
PASH
PASH
PASH
It's up to you now...
... Lucy ...
GWOO
The Heaven open to the fa measures of these all the stars, near and bring their ligh ar show your fo to us...
OOO
OOO
I invoke Tetrabiblos! speaking for we who control the stars reveal every aspect in full to open the es of vengea
KEEEN
KEEEN
KEEEN
KEEEN
KEEEN
All 88 Stars of the Heavens ...
Wh- What is this...?!
Wait a min...
KAK
Shine!

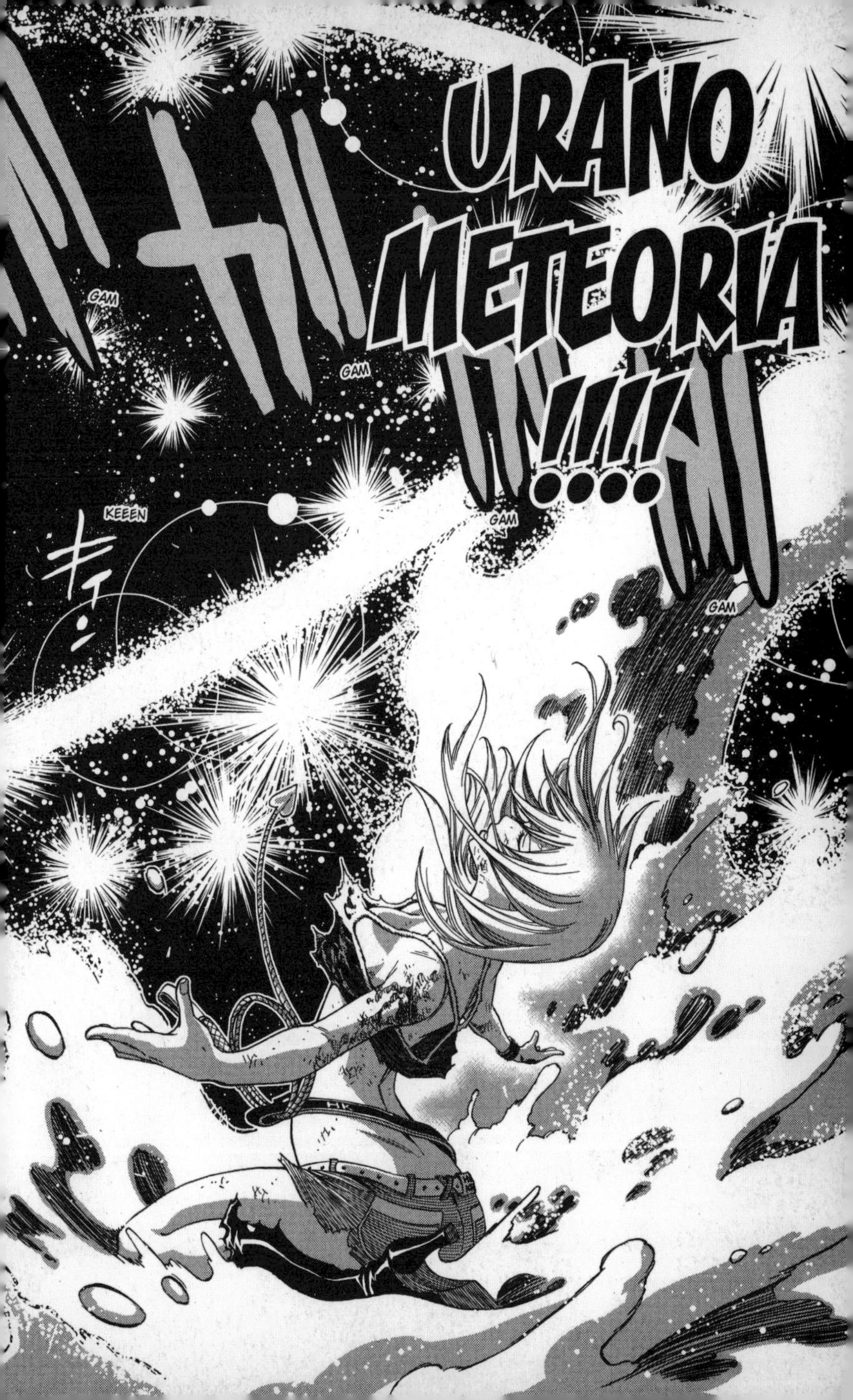
URANO METEORIA!!!!
GAM
GAM
GAM
GAM
KEEEN

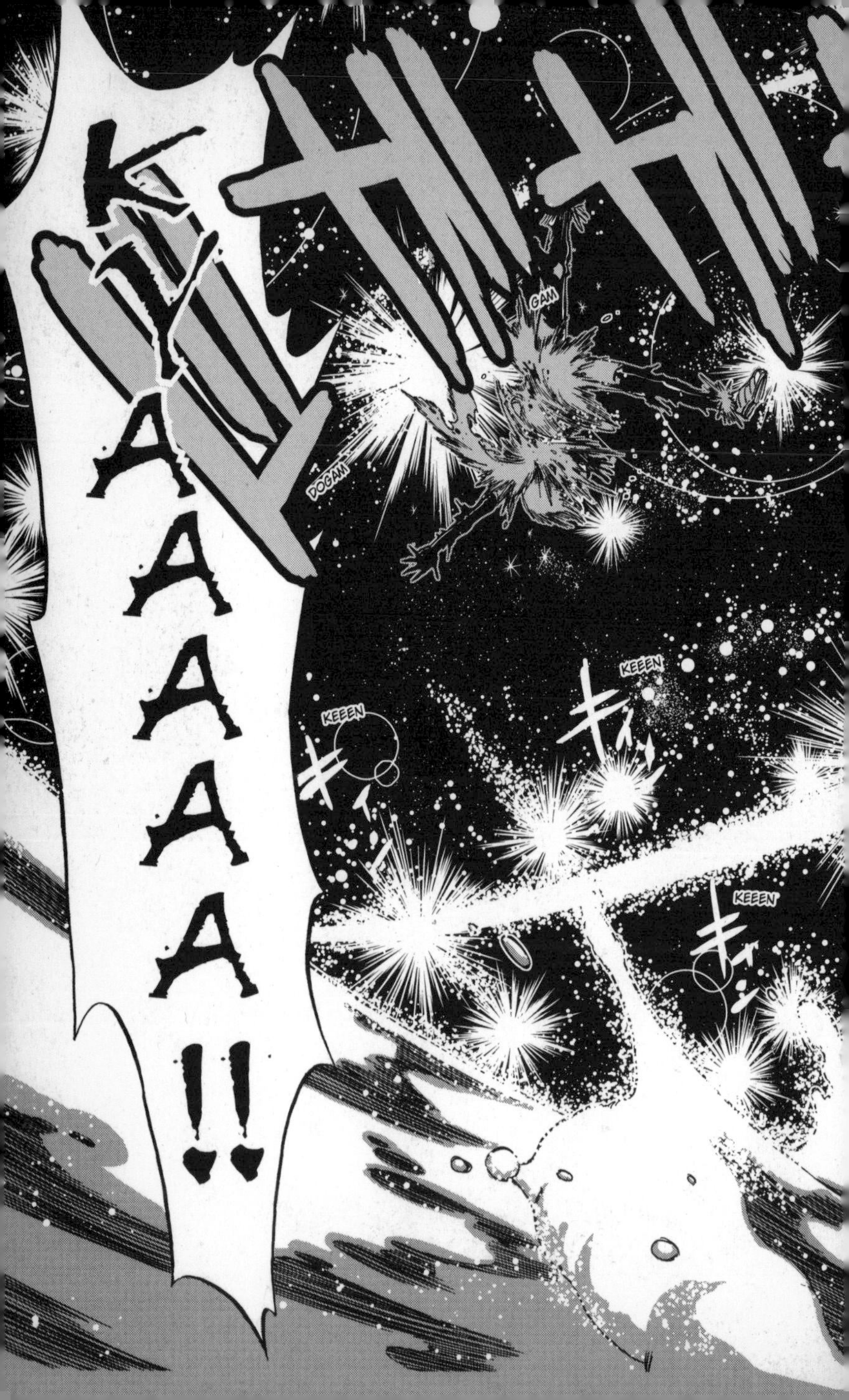
GAM
DOGAM
KYAAAAA!!
KEEEN
KEEEN
KEEEN

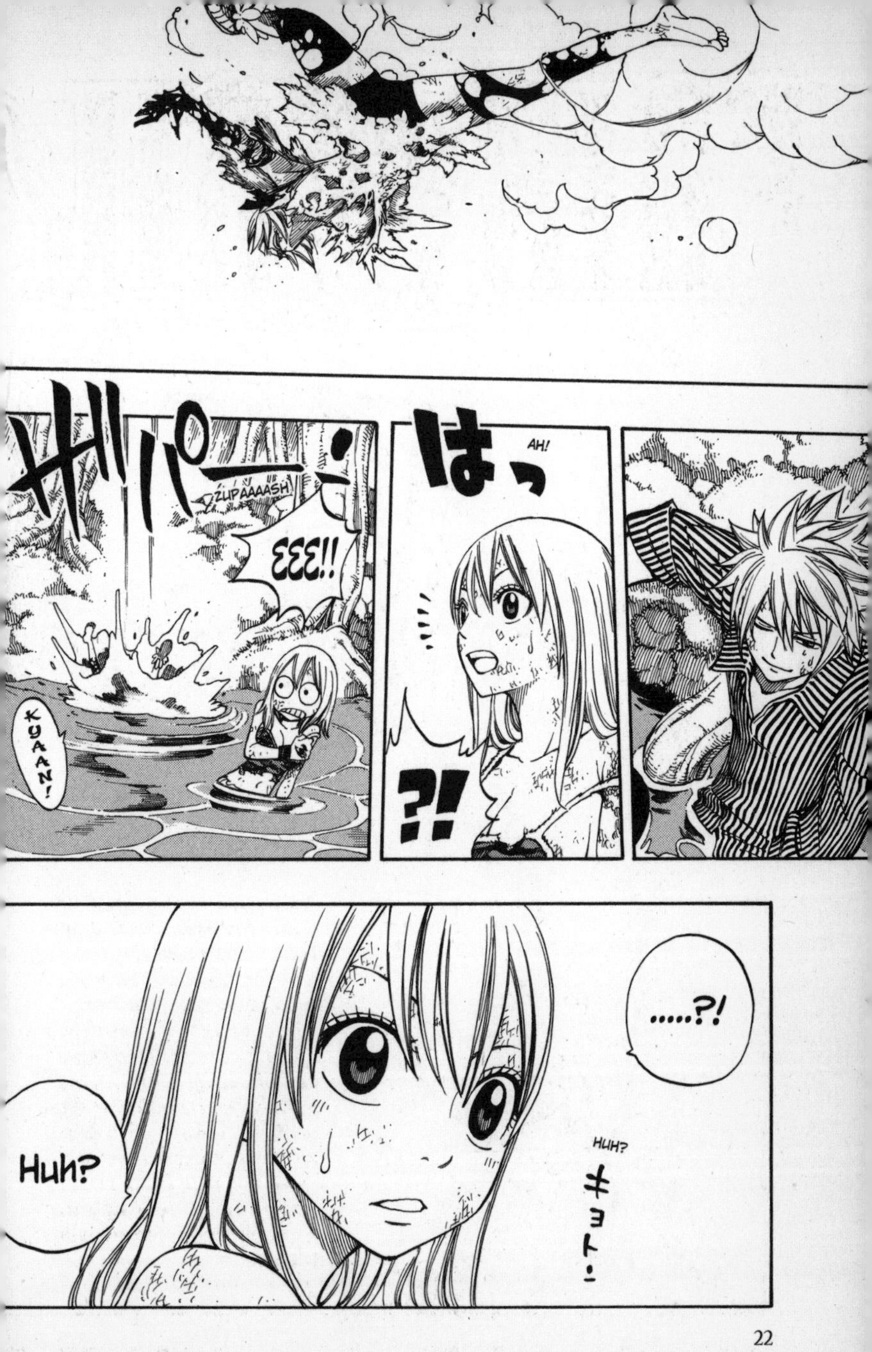
はっ
AH!
?!
ザパーン
ZUPAAAASH
EEE!!
KYAAN!
.....?!
HUH?
キョトン
Huh?

FAIRY TAIL

フェアリーテイル

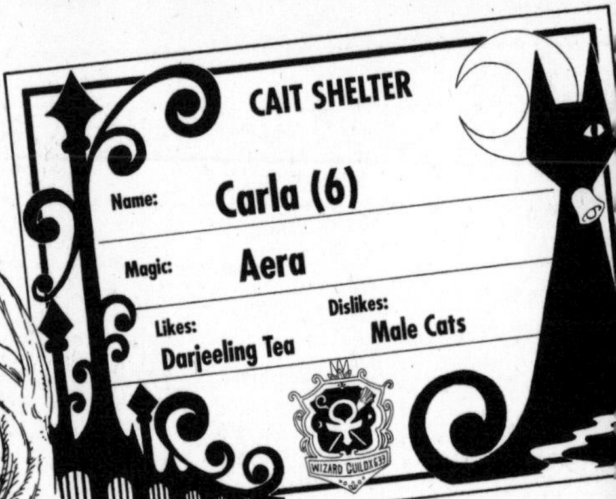
CAIT SHELTER
Name: Carla (6)
Magic: Aera
Likes: Darjeeling Tea
Dislikes: Male Cats
WIZARD GUILD X633

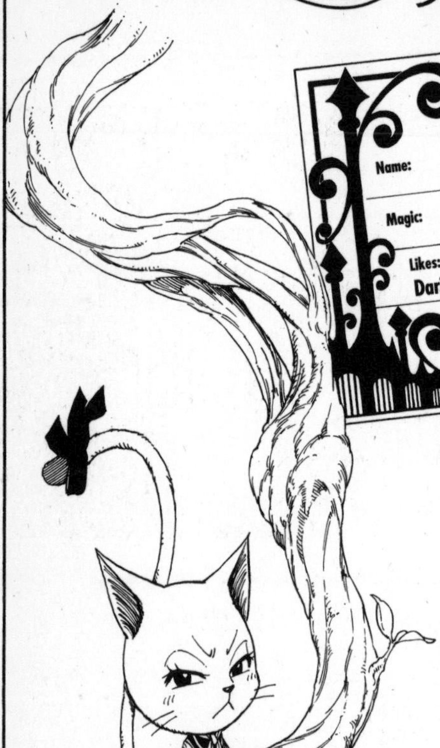

Remarks

A talking cat investigator of the Cait Shelter Guild. Unlike Happy, she wears clothes. She has appointed herself as Wendy's guardian, but it seems everyone around them thinks of her as Wendy's pet cat. Her magic, Aera, seems to be approximately the same as Happy's but beyond that the relationship between these two people (two cats?) is a mystery. One thing is for sure, she doesn't seem to like Happy...

Chapter 145, Memories of Jellal

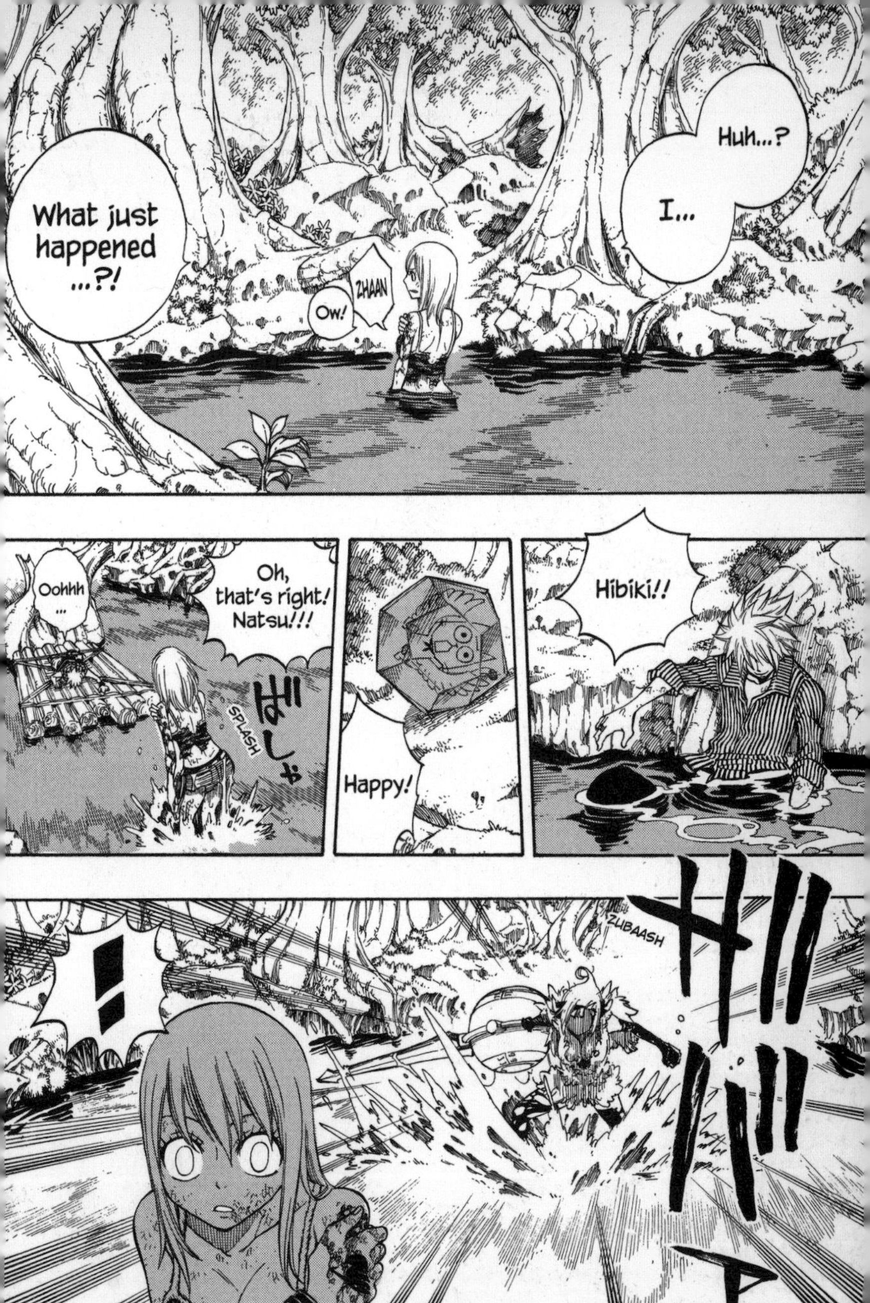
Huh...?
I...
ZHAAN
Ow!
What just happened ...?!
Hibiki!!
Happy!
Oh, that's right! Natsu!!!
ばしゃ
SPLASH
Oohhh ...
ザバア
ZUBAASH
!

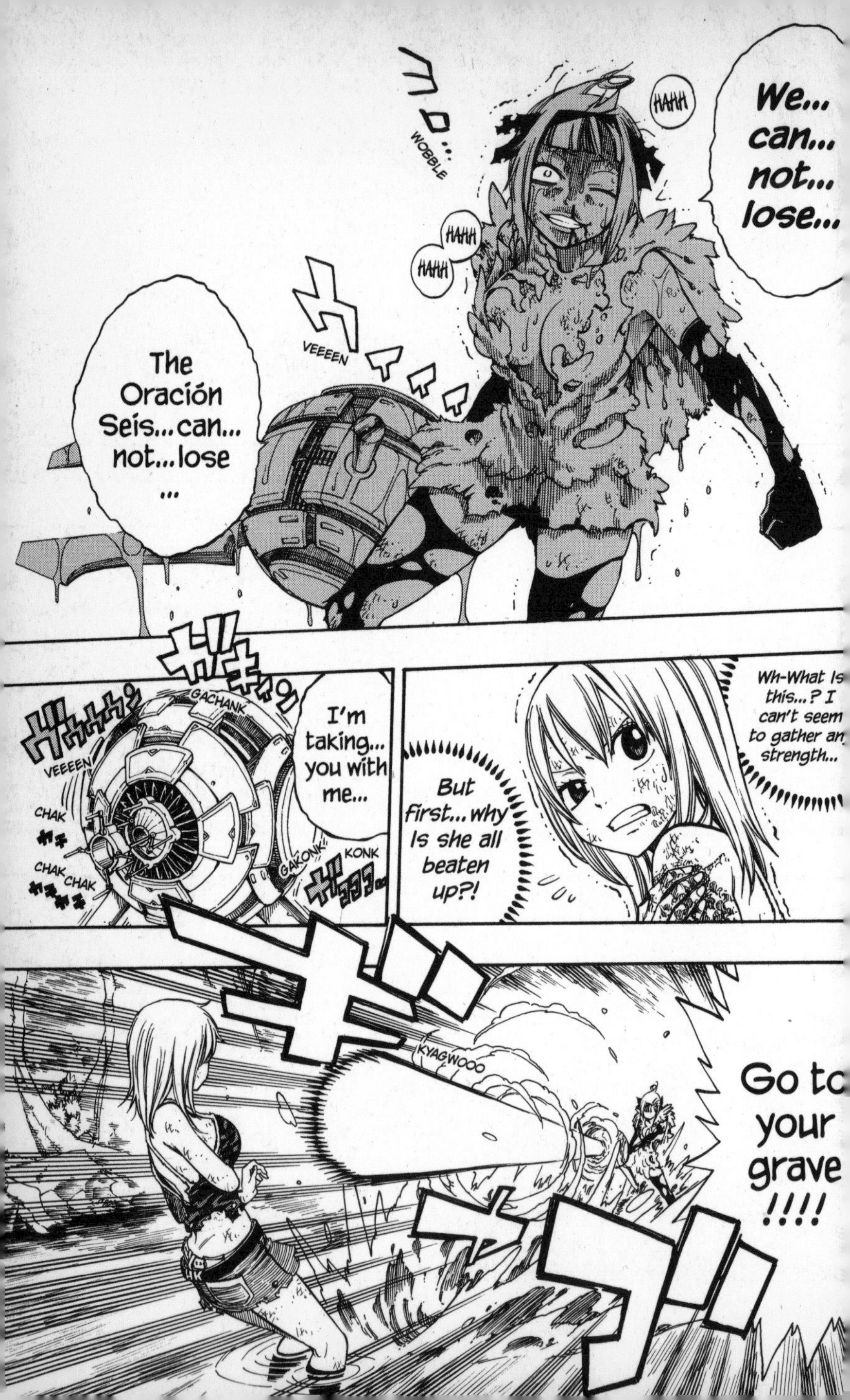
We... can... not... lose...
HAHH
WOBBLE
HAHH
HAHH
VEEEEN
The Oración Seis...can... not...lose ...
Wh-What is this...? I can't seem to gather any strength...
But first...why is she all beaten up?!
GACHANK
I'm taking... you with me...
VEEEEN
CHAK
CHAK CHAK
GAKONK
KONK
KYAGWOOO
Go to your grave !!!!

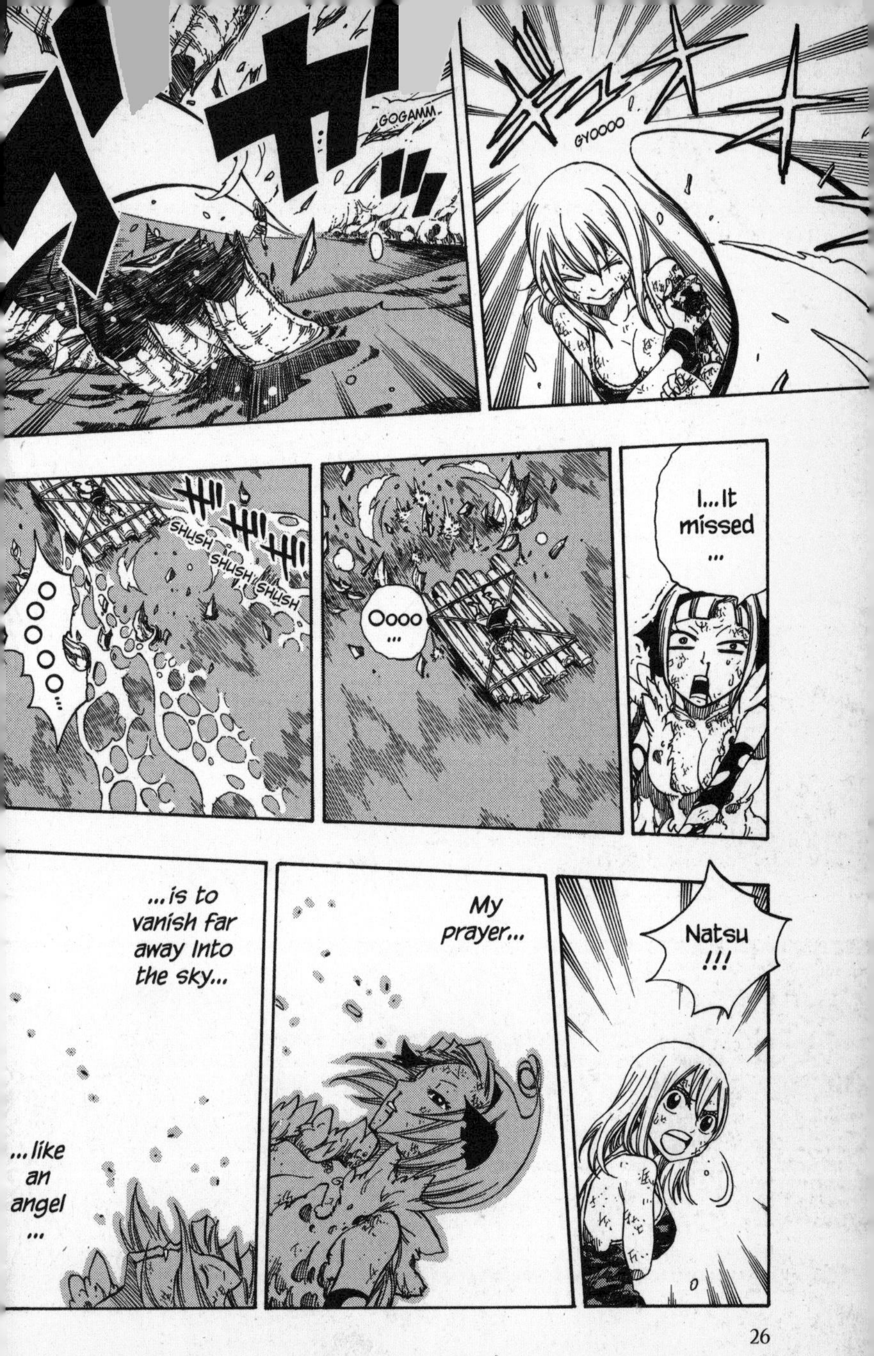
GYOOOO
GOGAMM
I...It missed ...
Oooo ...
SHUSH SHUSH SHUSH
OOOOOO...
Natsu !!!
My prayer...
...is to vanish far away into the sky...
...like an angel ...

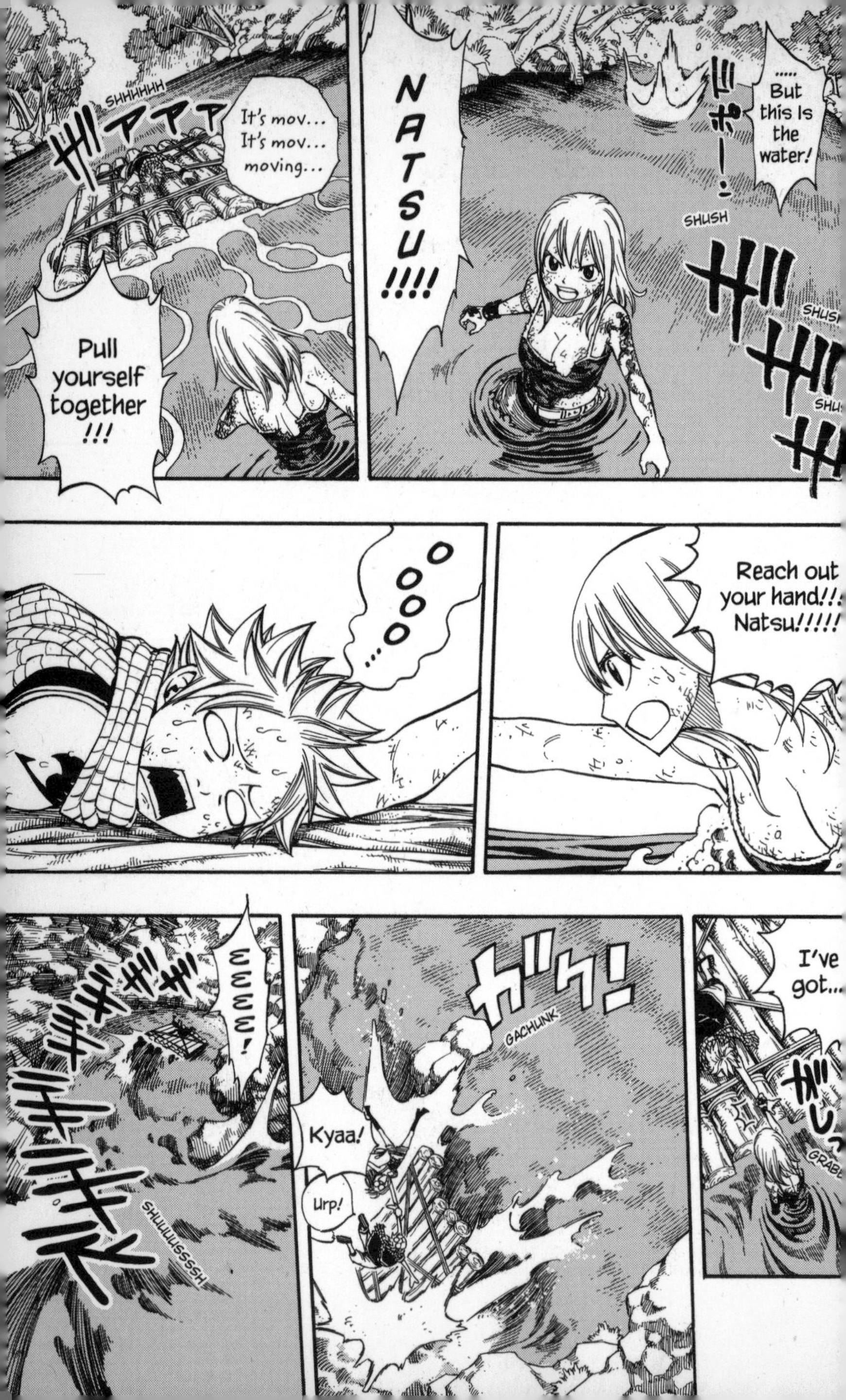
..... But this Is the water!
SHUSH
NATSU!!!!
It's mov... It's mov... moving...
SHHHHHH
Pull yourself together!!!
Reach out your hand!!! Natsu!!!!!
...oooo
I've got...
GACHUNK
Kyaa!
Urp!
SHUUUUSSSSH

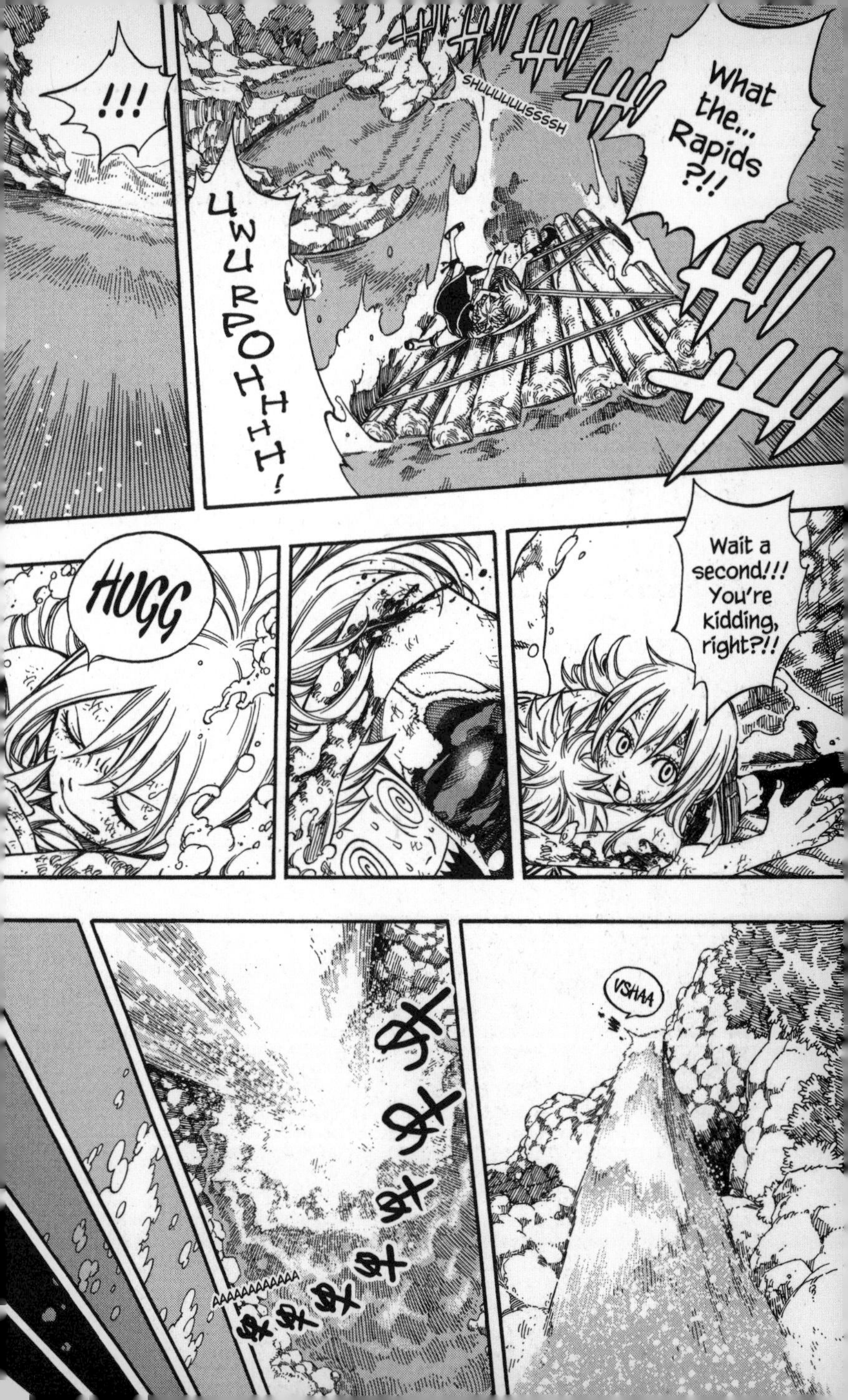
What the... Rapids?!!
SHUUUUUUUUSSSSH
UWURPOHHHH!
!!!
Wait a second!!! You're kidding, right?!!
HUGG
VSHAA
AAAAAAAAAAA

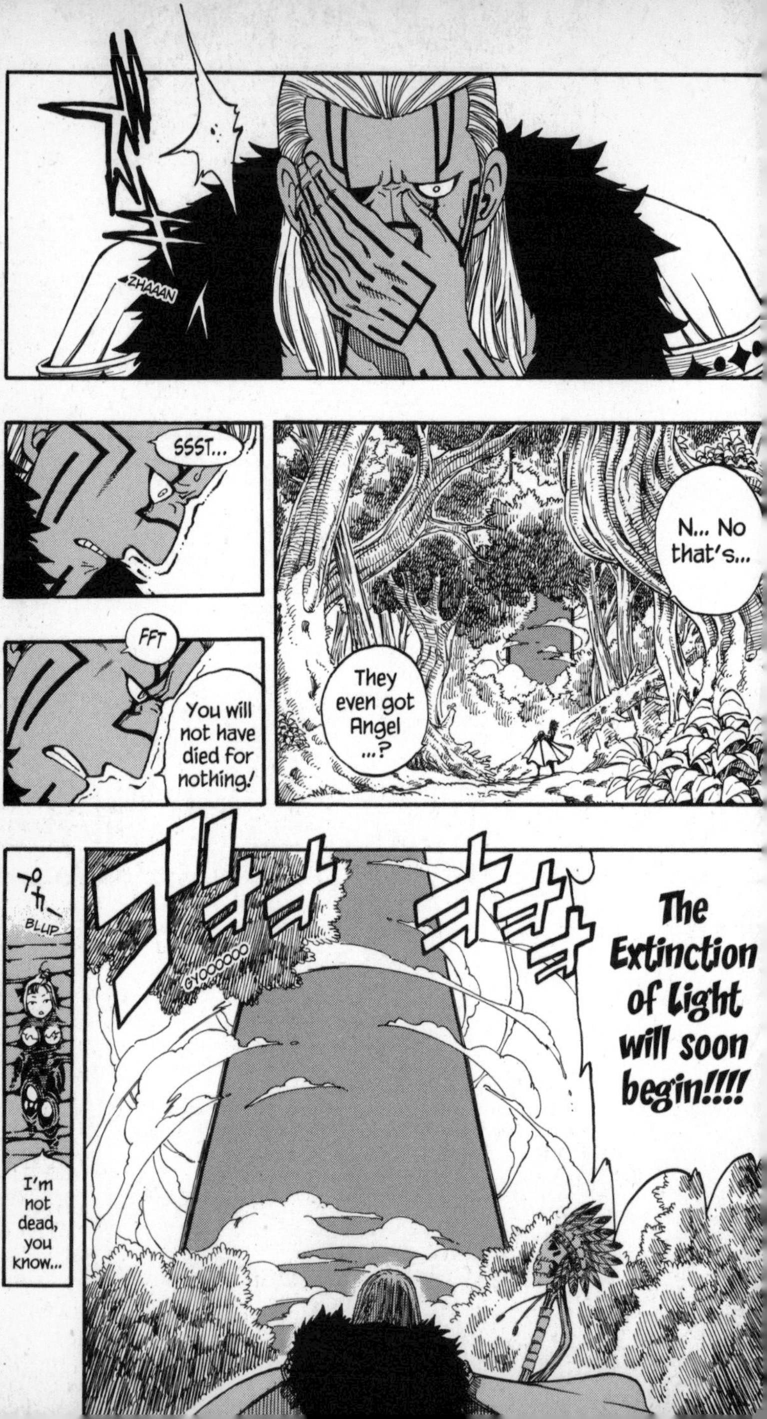
ZHAAAN
N... No that's...
They even got Angel ...?
SSST...
FFT
You will not have died for nothing!
GYOOOOOO
The Extinction of Light will soon begin!!!!
BLUP
I'm not dead, you know...

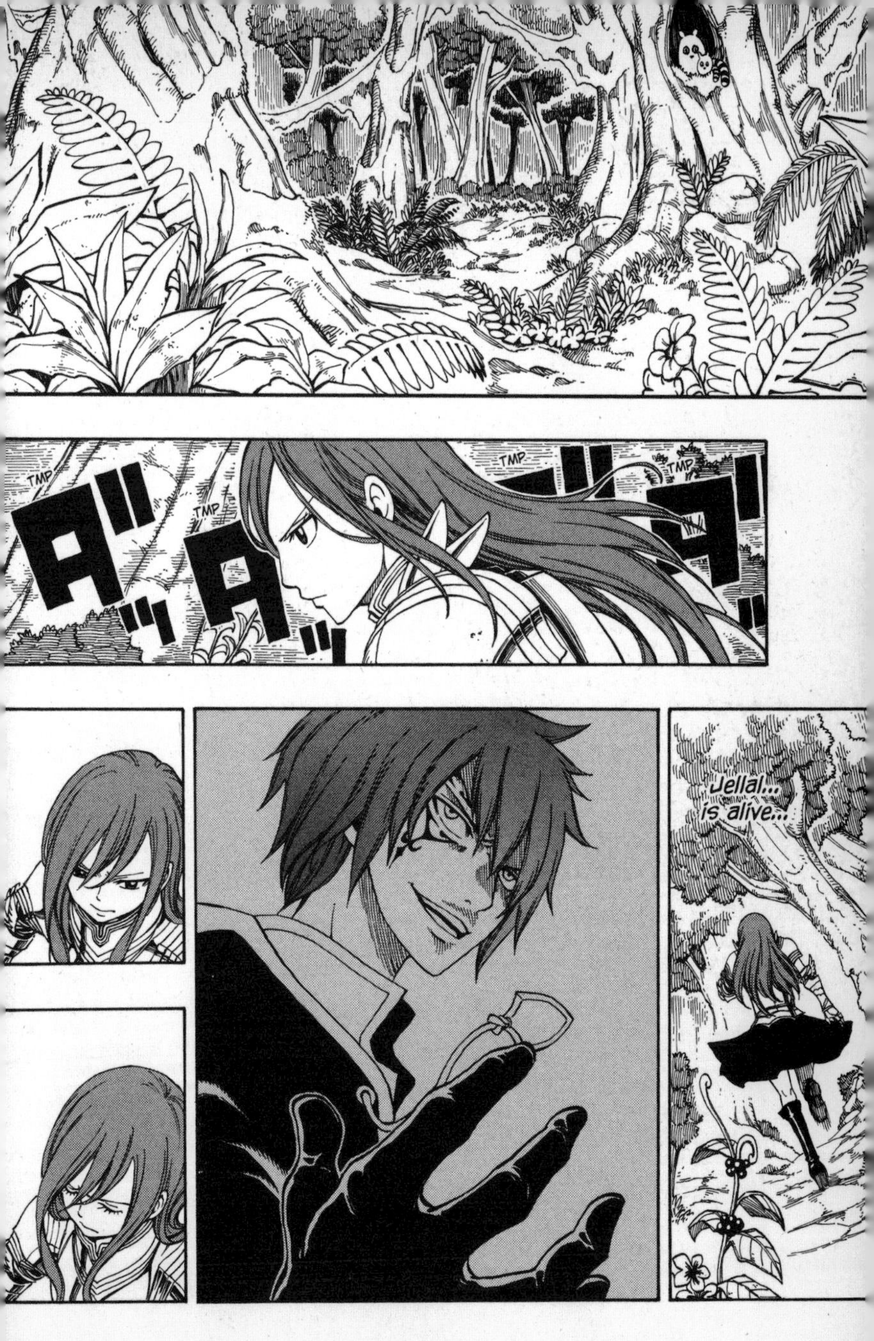
TMP
TMP
TMP
TMP
Jellal... is alive...

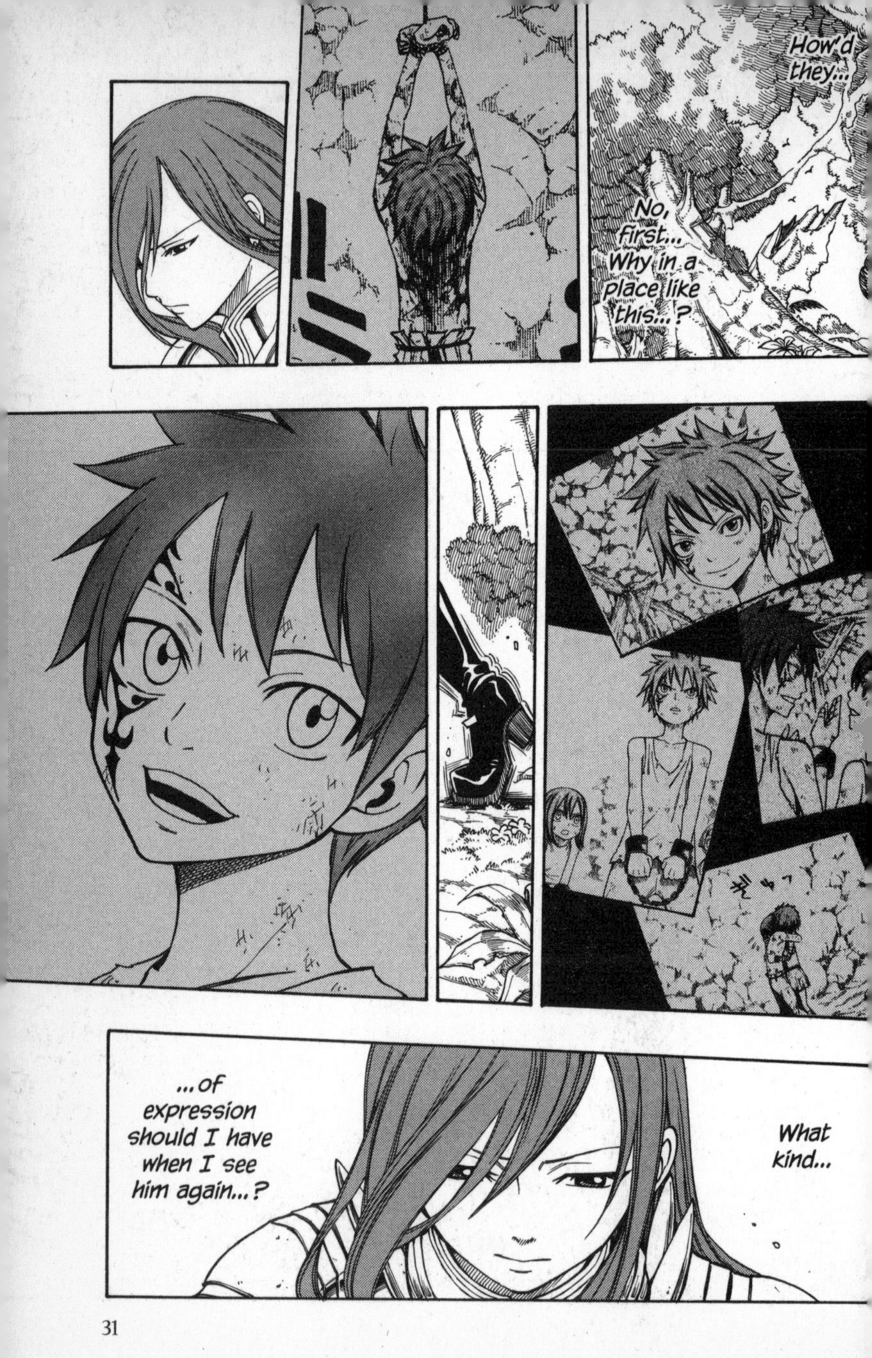
How'd they...
No, first... Why in a place like this...?
What kind...
...of expression should I have when I see him again...?

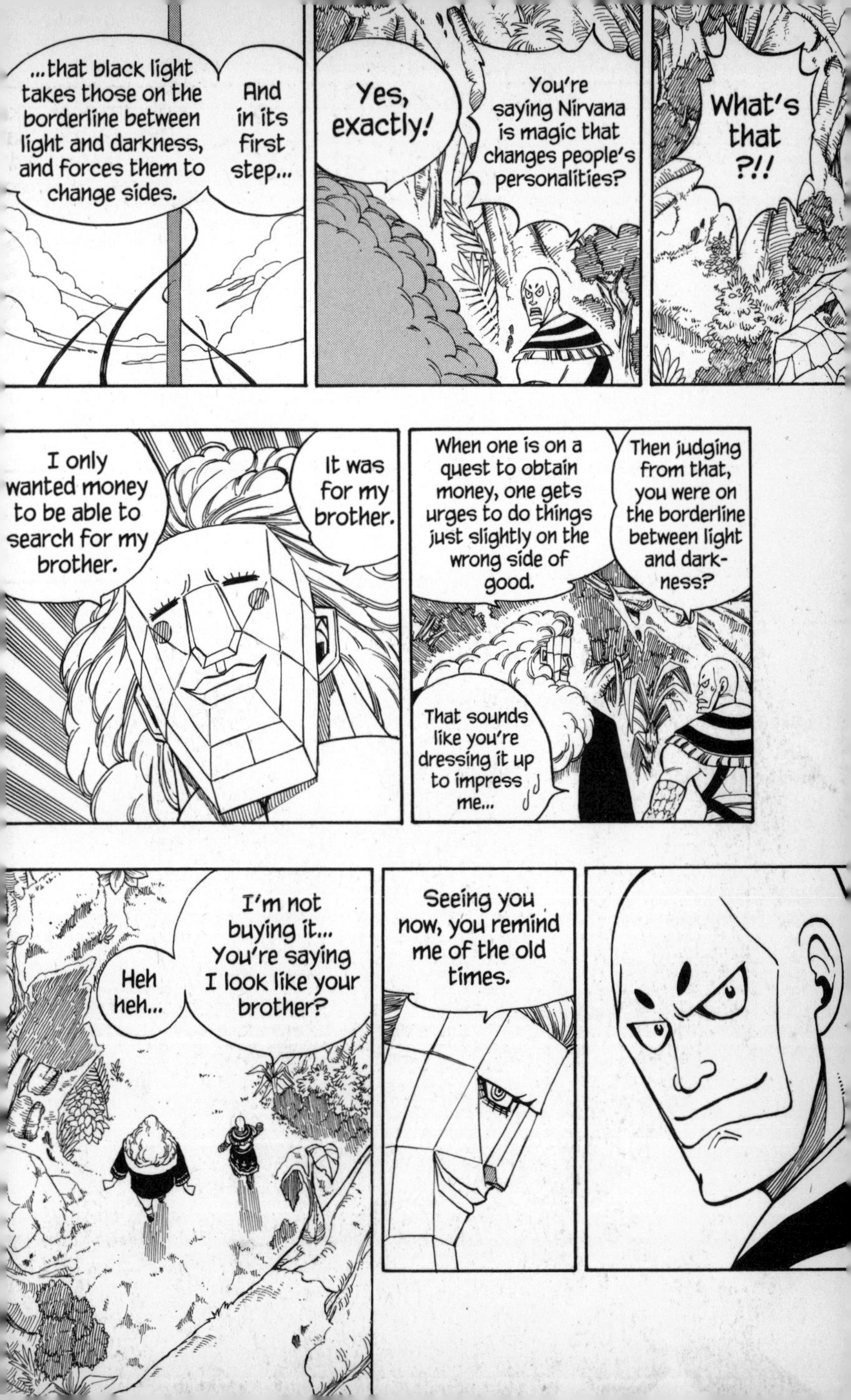
What's that ?!!
You're saying Nirvana is magic that changes people's personalities?
Yes, exactly!
And in its first step...
...that black light takes those on the borderline between light and darkness, and forces them to change sides.
Then judging from that, you were on the borderline between light and dark-ness?
When one is on a quest to obtain money, one gets urges to do things just slightly on the wrong side of good.
That sounds like you're dressing it up to impress me...
It was for my brother.
I only wanted money to be able to search for my brother.
Seeing you now, you remind me of the old times.
I'm not buying it... You're saying I look like your brother?
Heh heh...

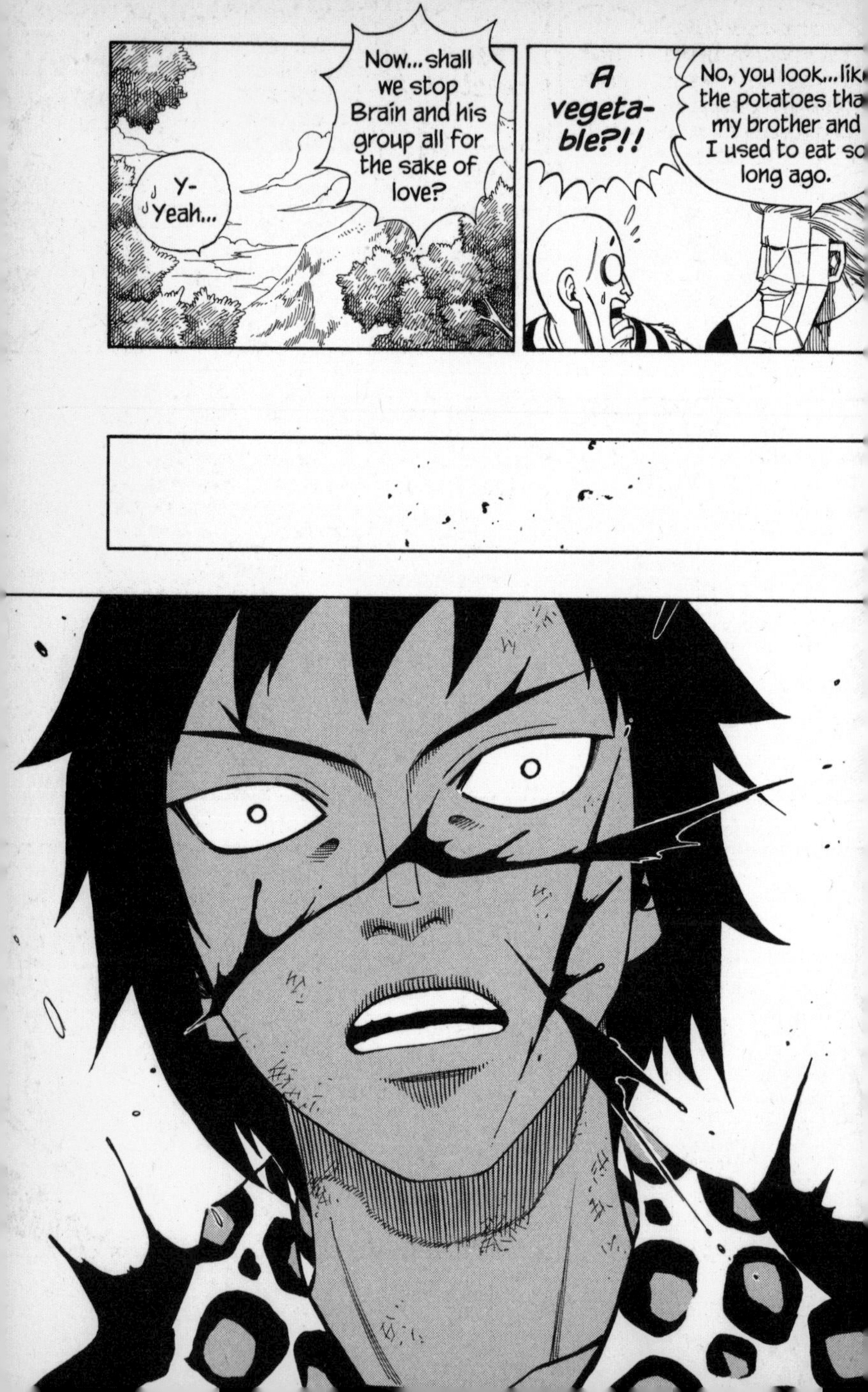

No, you look...lik
the potatoes tha
my brother and
I used to eat so
long ago.
A vegeta-ble?!!
Now...shall we stop Brain and his group all for the sake of love?
Y-Yeah...

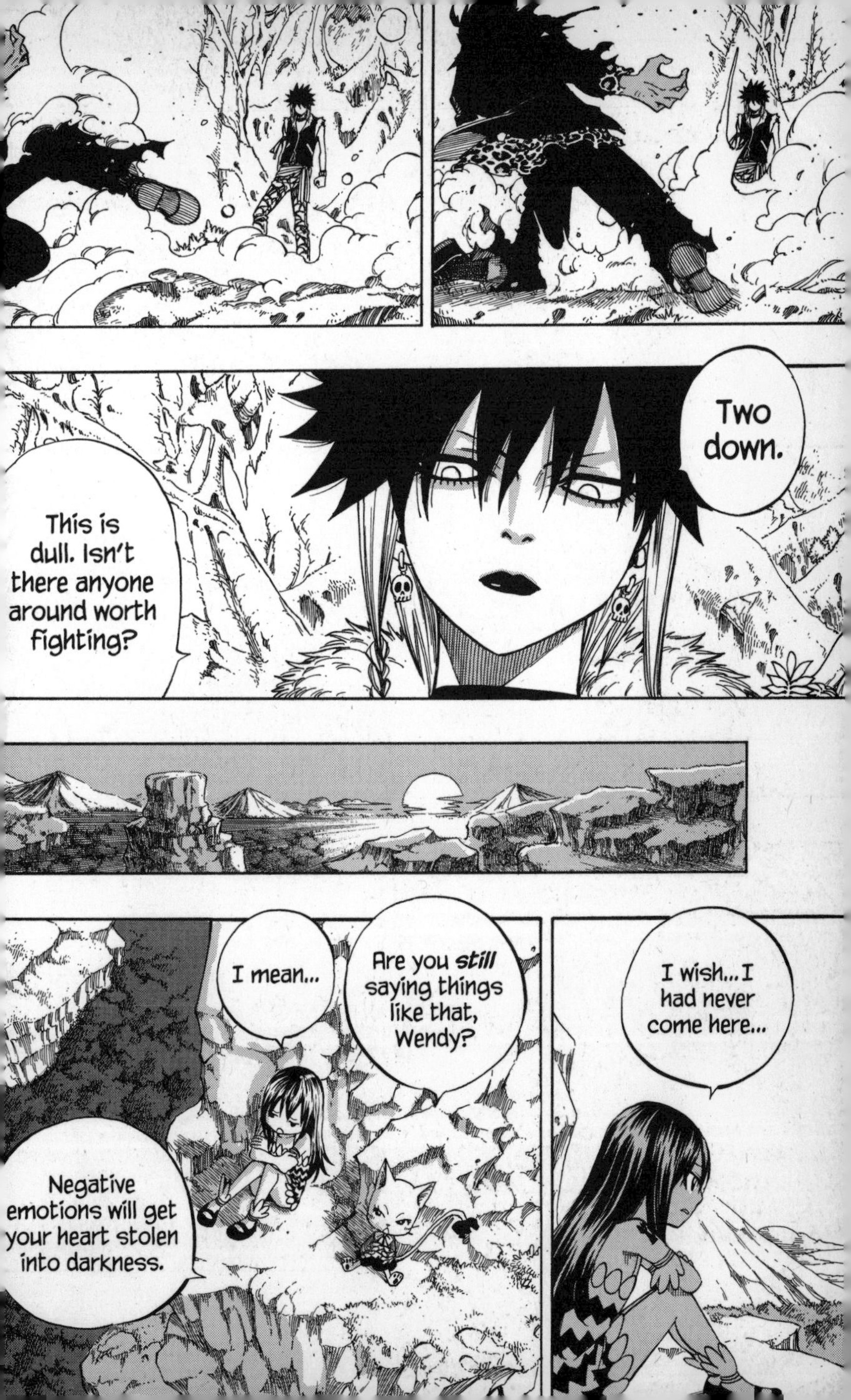

Two down.
This is dull. Isn't there anyone around worth fighting?
I wish...I had never come here...
Are you *still* saying things like that, Wendy?
I mean...
Negative emotions will get your heart stolen into darkness.

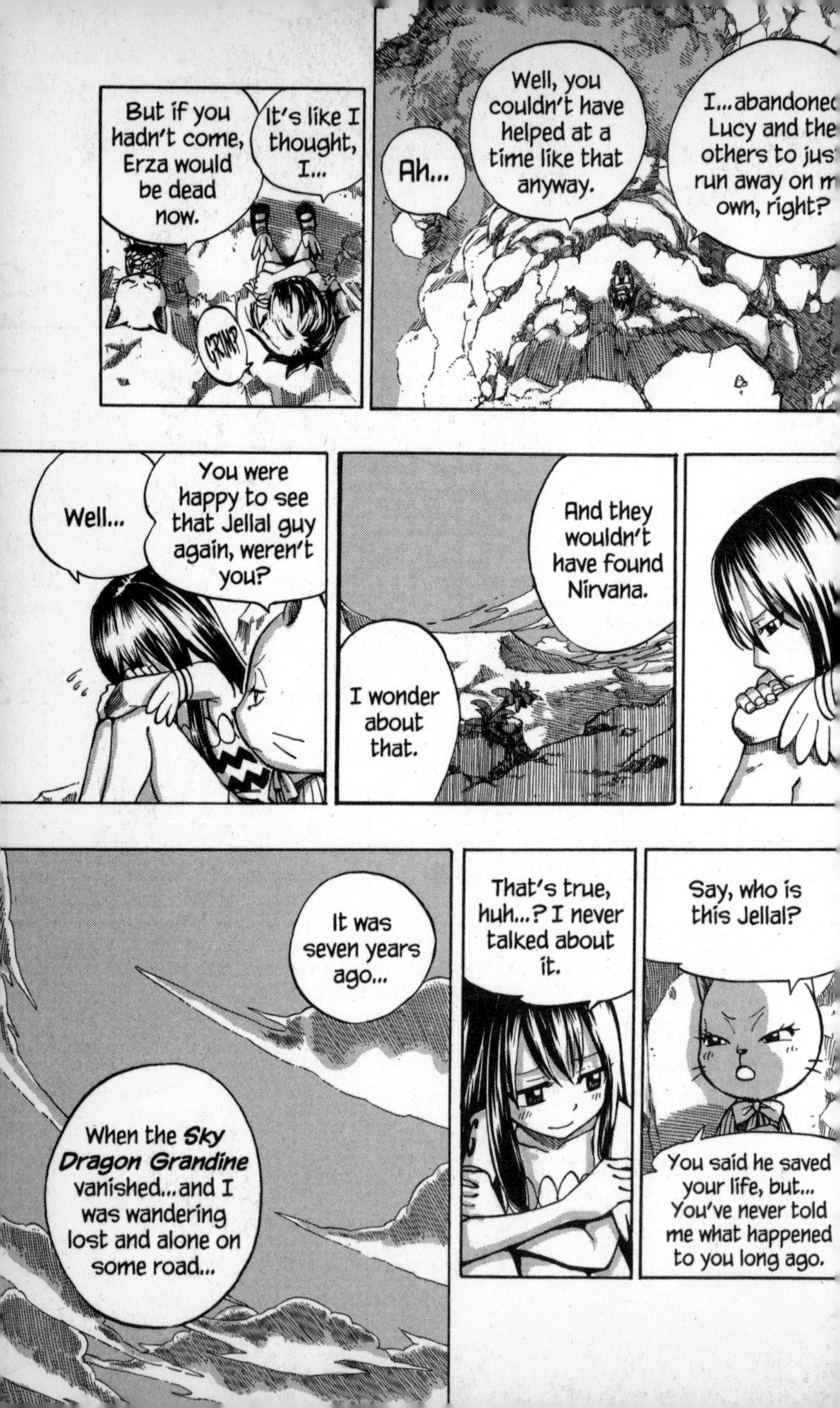
I...abandonec Lucy and the others to jus run away on m own, right?
Well, you couldn't have helped at a time like that anyway.
Ah...
It's like I thought, I...
But if you hadn't come, Erza would be dead now.
GRIN?
And they wouldn't have found Nirvana.
I wonder about that.
You were happy to see that Jellal guy again, weren't you?
Well...
Say, who is this Jellal?
You said he saved your life, but... You've never told me what happened to you long ago.
That's true, huh...? I never talked about it.
It was seven years ago...
When the *Sky Dragon Grandine* vanished...and I was wandering lost and alone on some road...

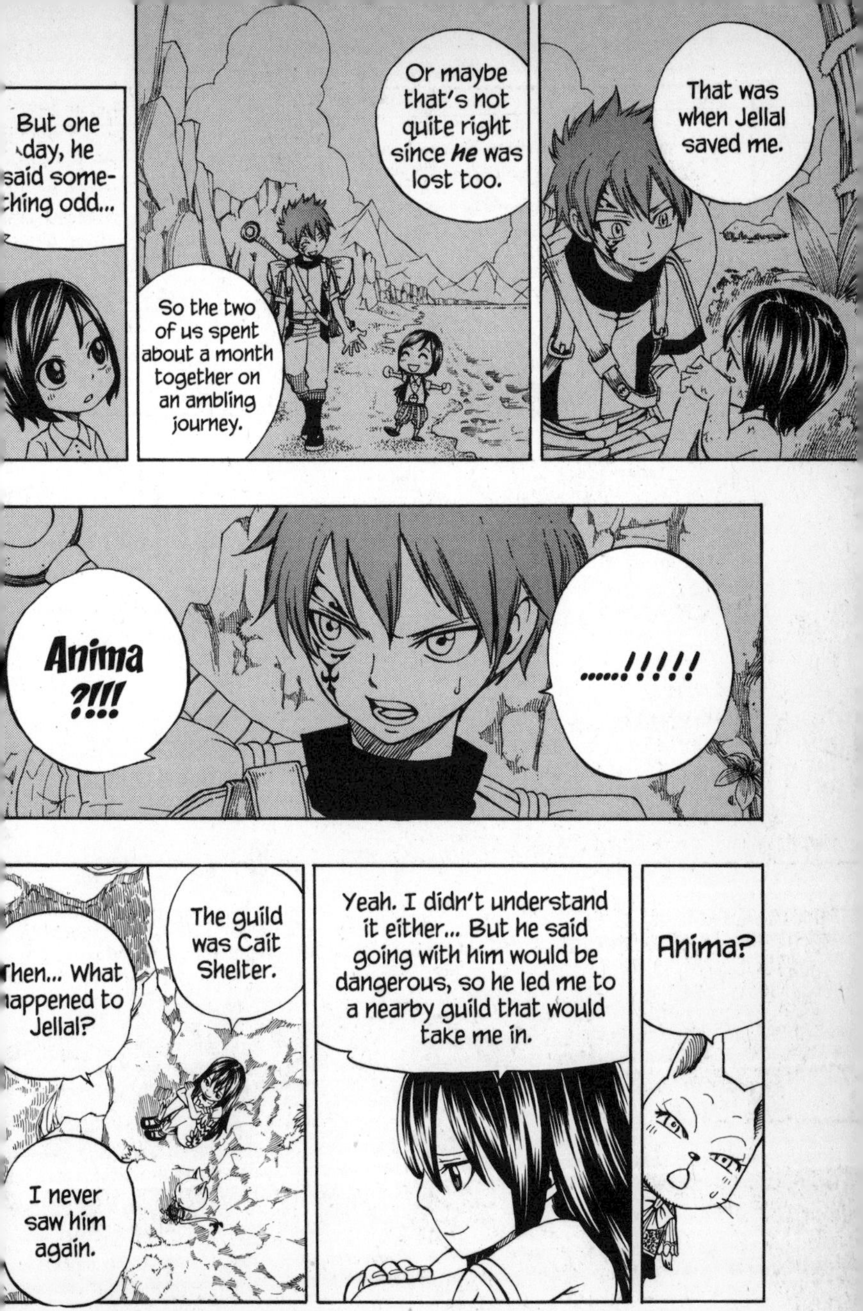
That was when Jellal saved me.
Or maybe that's not quite right since he was lost too.
So the two of us spent about a month together on an ambling journey.
But one day, he said some-thing odd...
......!!!!!
Anima ?!!!
Anima?
Yeah. I didn't understand it either... But he said going with him would be dangerous, so he led me to a nearby guild that would take me in.
The guild was Cait Shelter.
Then... What happened to Jellal?
I never saw him again.

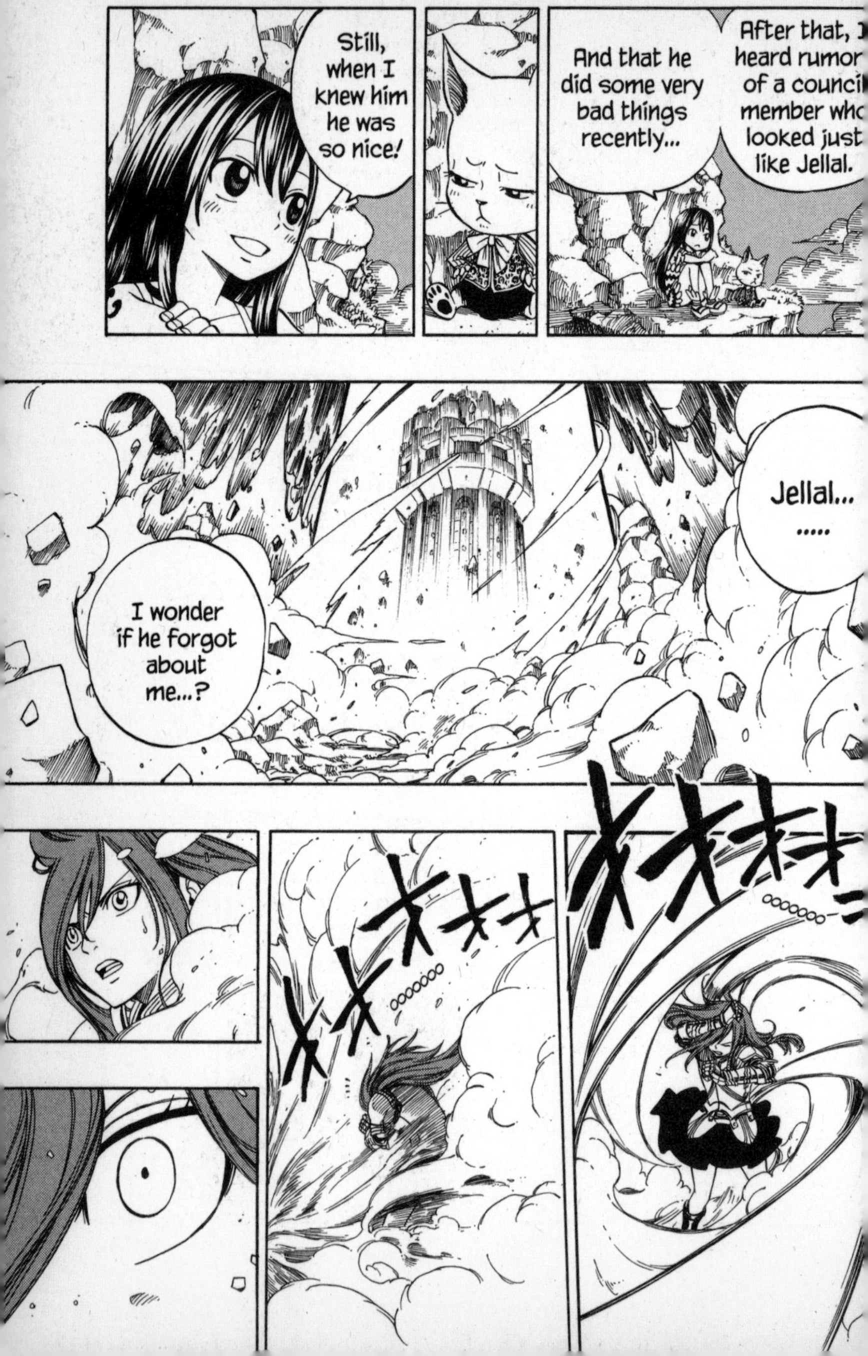
After that, I heard rumor of a council member who looked just like Jellal.
And that he did some very bad things recently...
Still, when I knew him he was so nice!
Jellal... .....
I wonder if he forgot about me...?

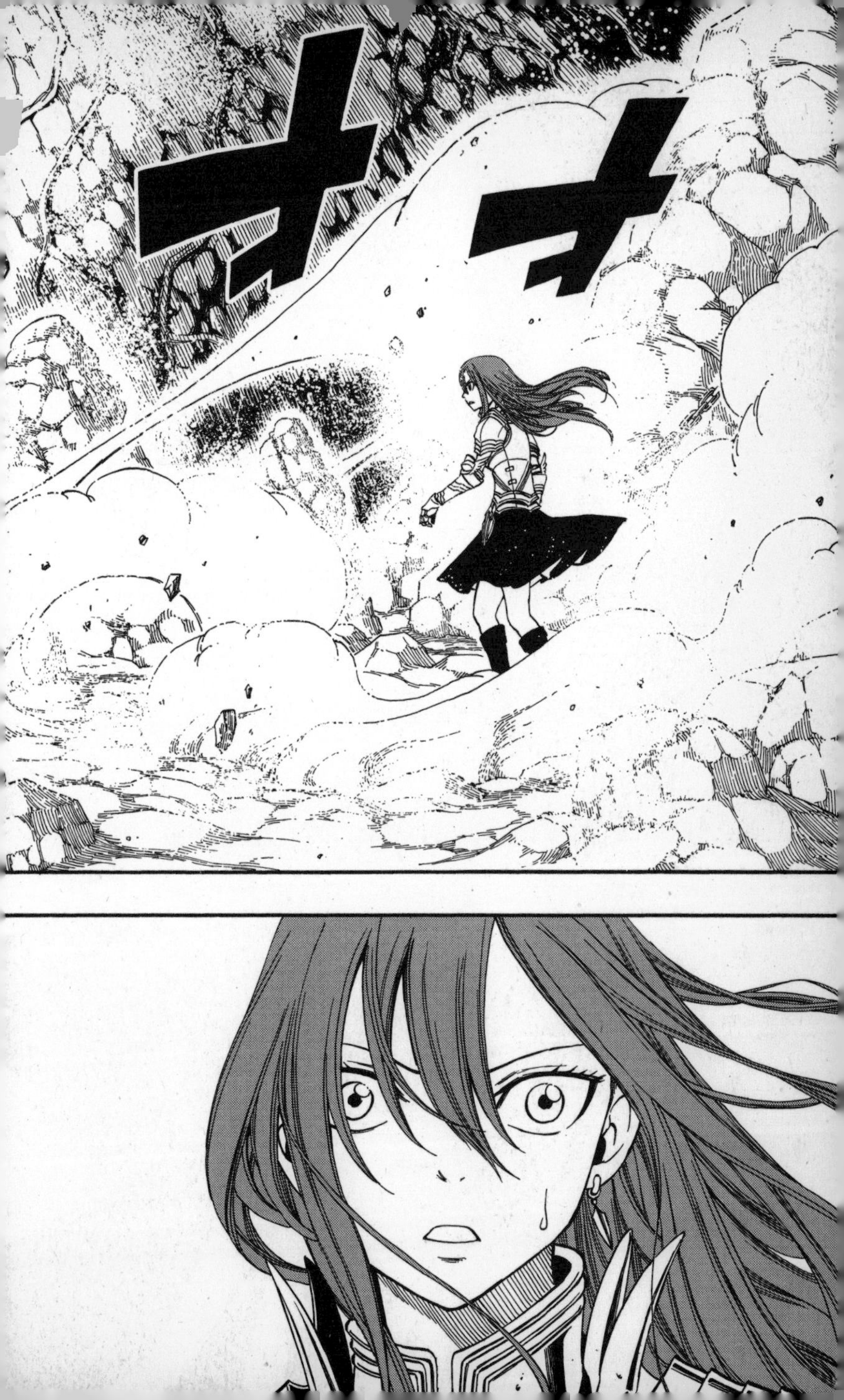

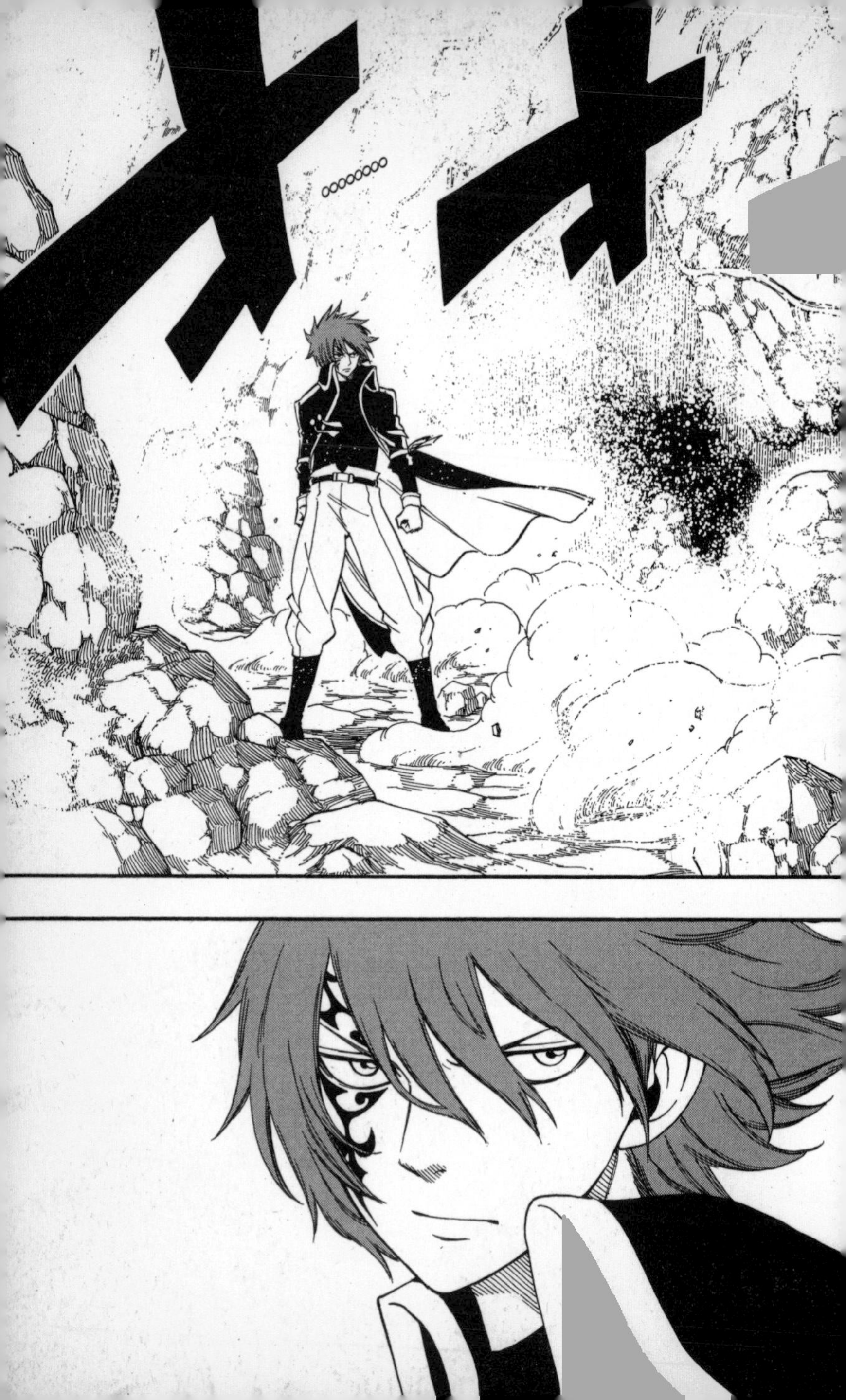
OOOOOOOO

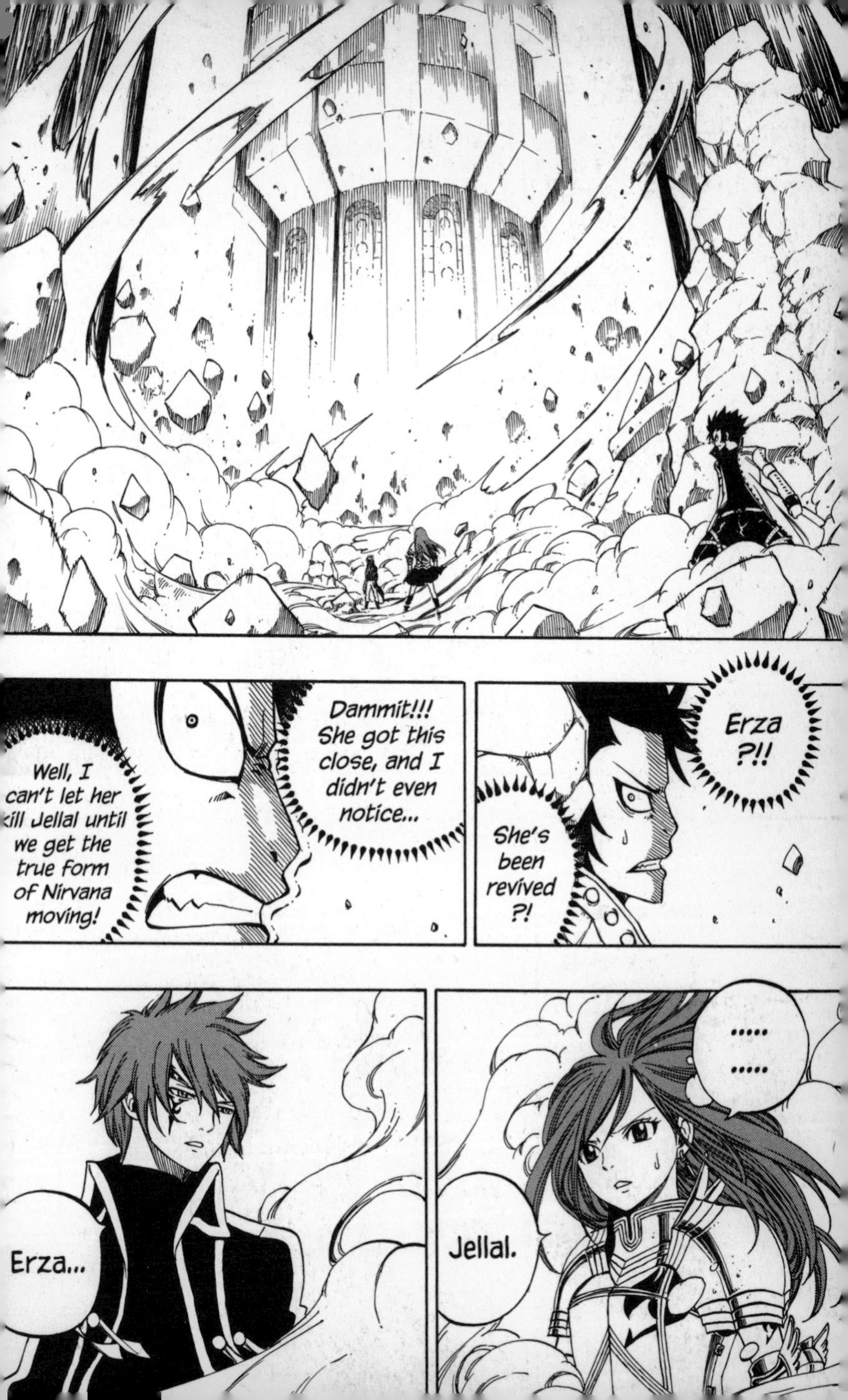
Erza ?!!
She's been revived ?!
Dammit!!! She got this close, and I didn't even notice...
Well, I can't let her kill Jellal until we get the true form of Nirvana moving!
....
Jellal.
Erza...

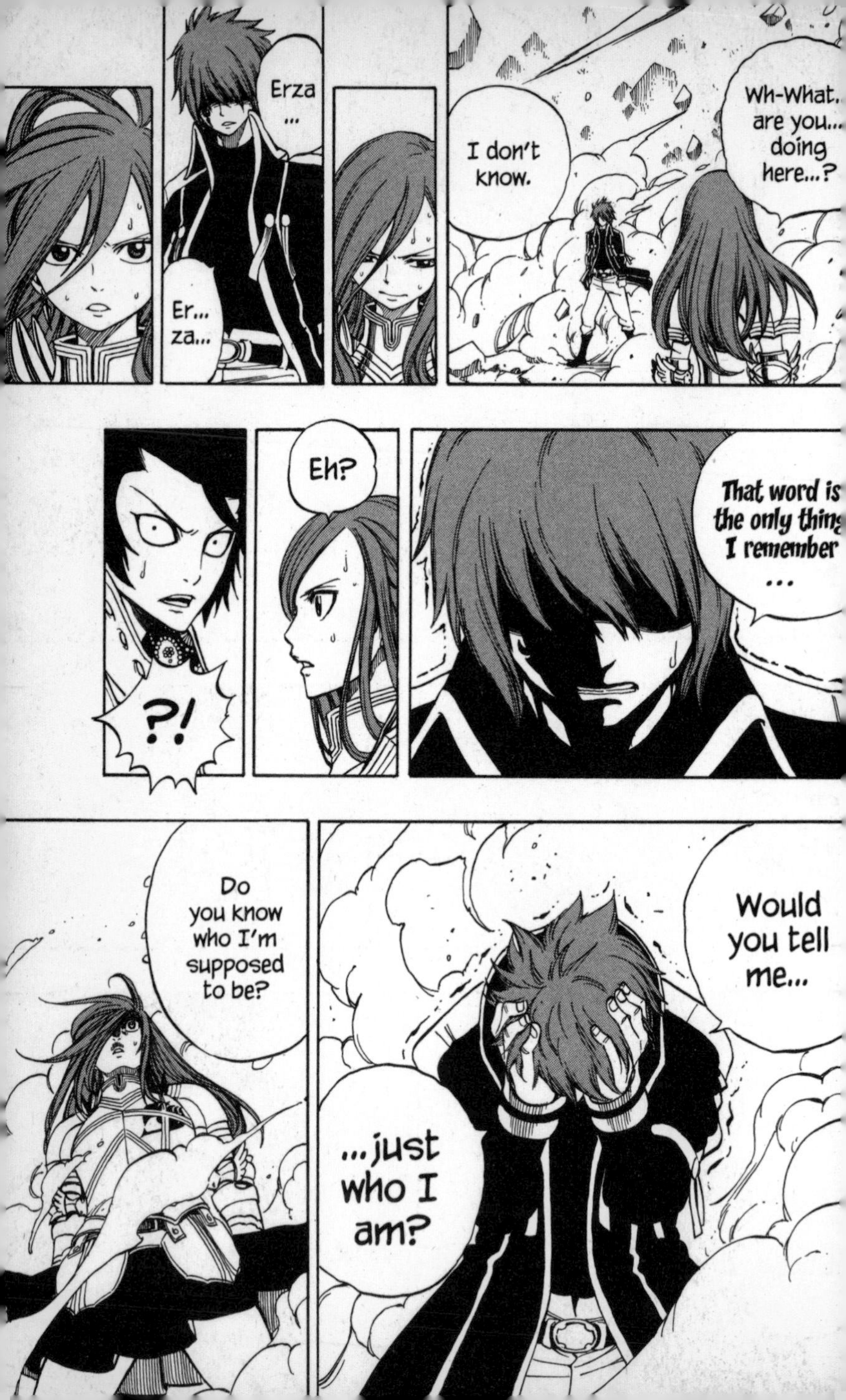
Wh-What. are you... doing here...?
I don't know.
Erza ...
Er... za...
That word is the only thing I remember ...
Eh?
?!
Would you tell me...
...just who I am?
Do you know who I'm supposed to be?

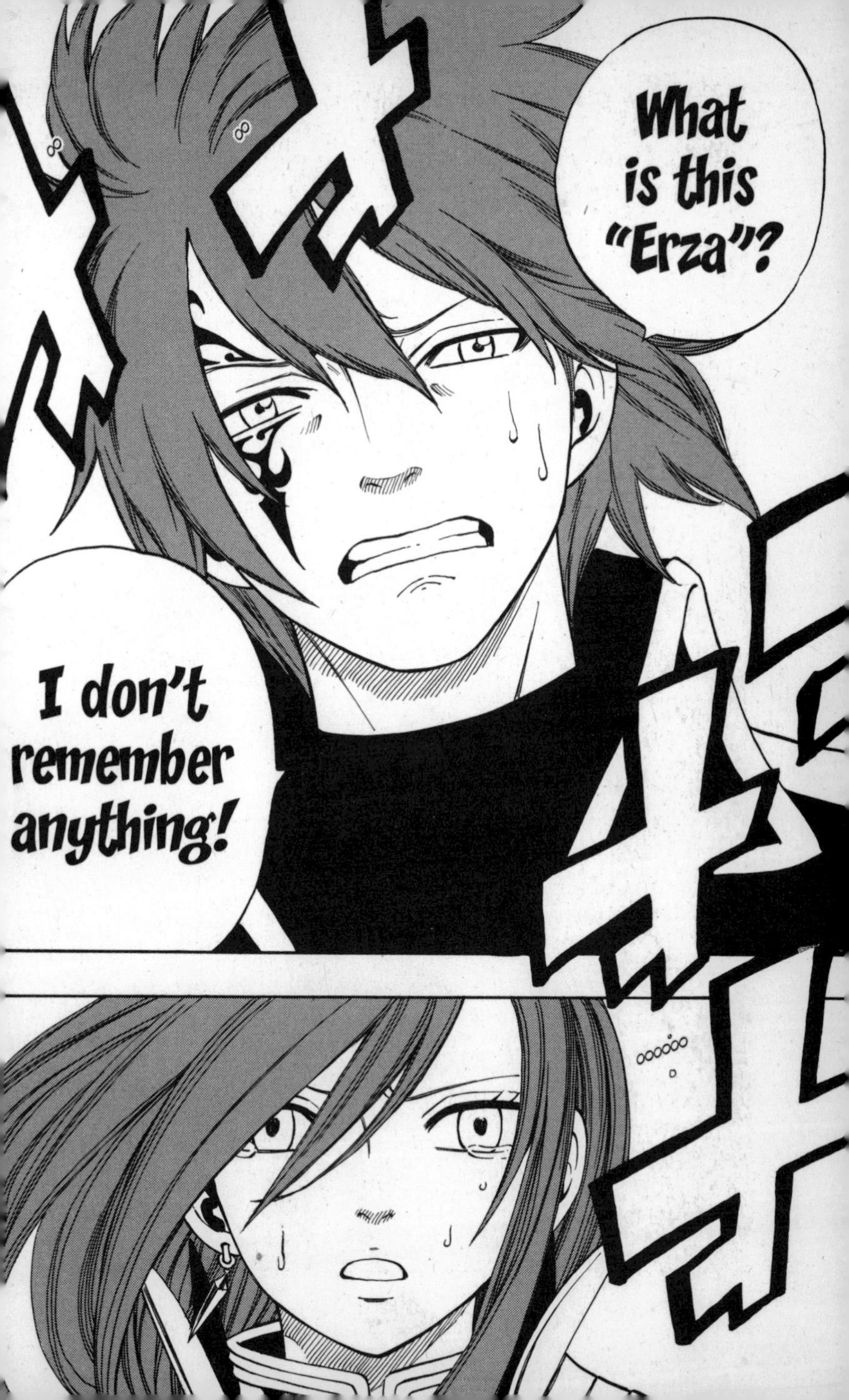
What is this "Erza"?
I don't remember anything!

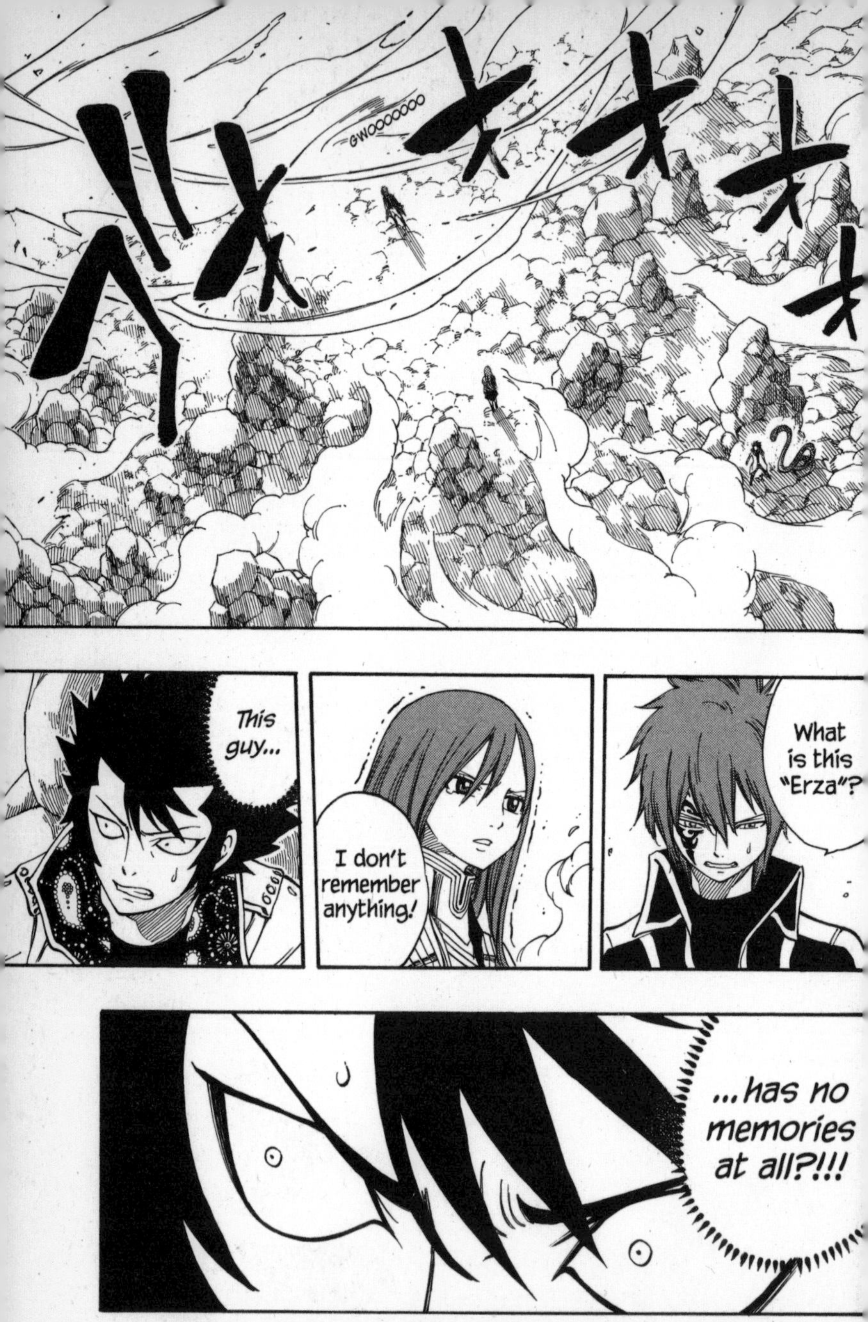
GWOOOOOOOO
What is this "Erza"?
I don't remember anything!
This guy...
...has no memories at all?!!!

Chapter 146, You Are Free

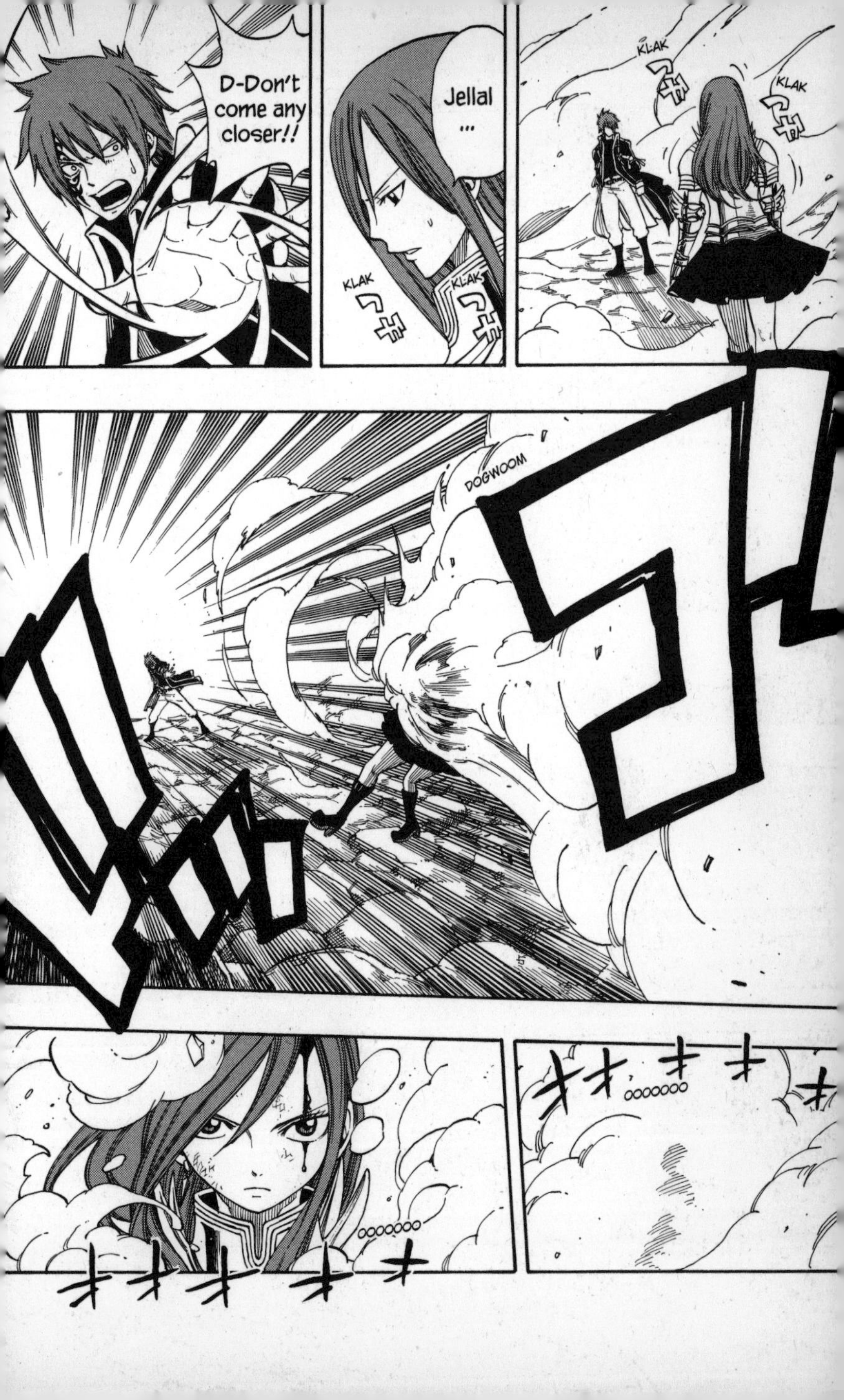
KLAK
KLAK
Jellal ...
KLAK
KLAK
D-Don't come any closer!!
DOGWOOM
OOOOOOO
OOOOOOO

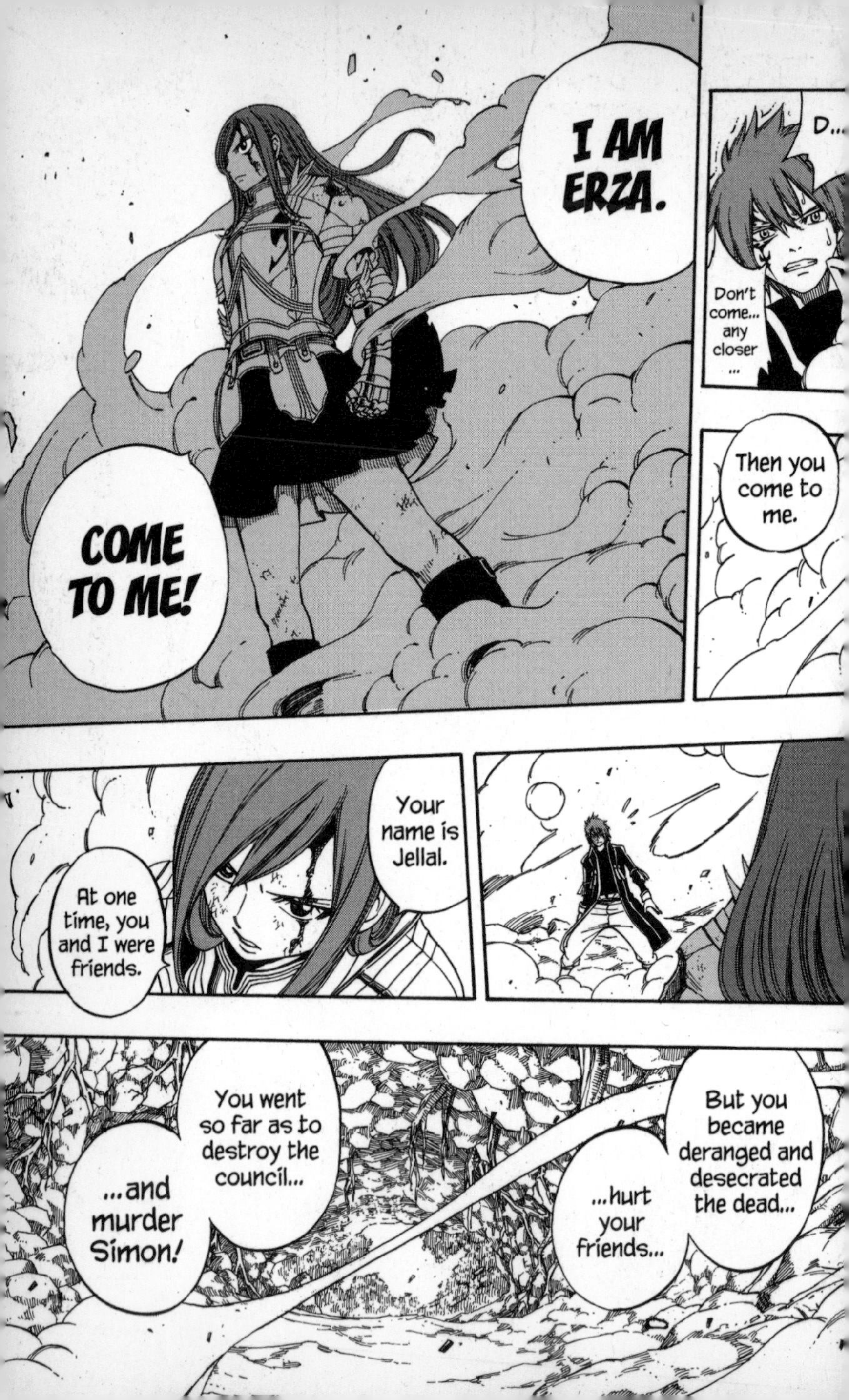
D...
Don't come... any closer ...
Then you come to me.
I AM ERZA.
COME TO ME!
Your name is Jellal.
At one time, you and I were friends.
But you became deranged and desecrated the dead...
...hurt your friends...
You went so far as to destroy the council...
...and murder Simon!

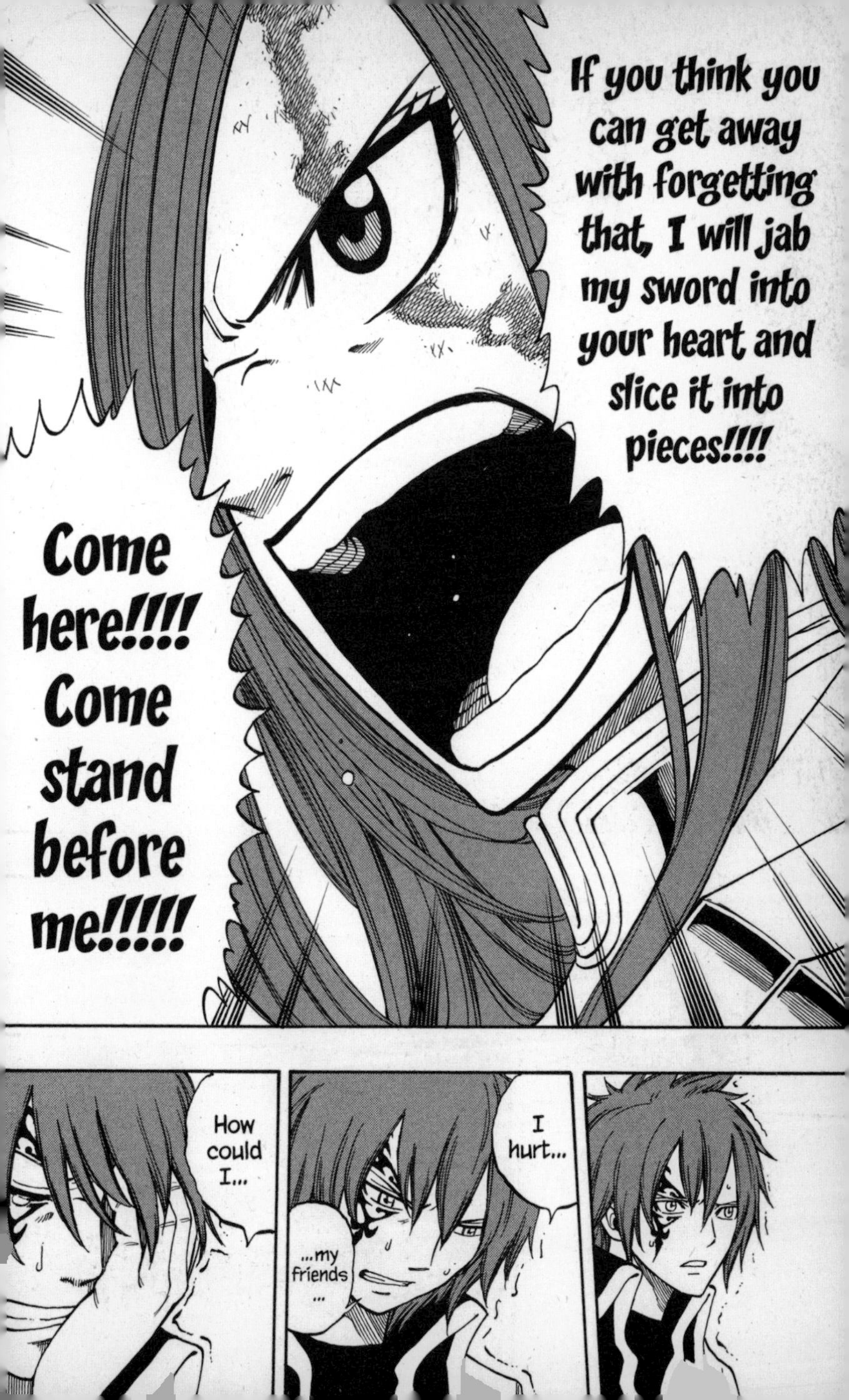
If you think you can get away with forgetting that, I will jab my sword into your heart and slice it into pieces!!!!
Come here!!!! Come stand before me!!!!!
I hurt...
...my friends...
How could I...

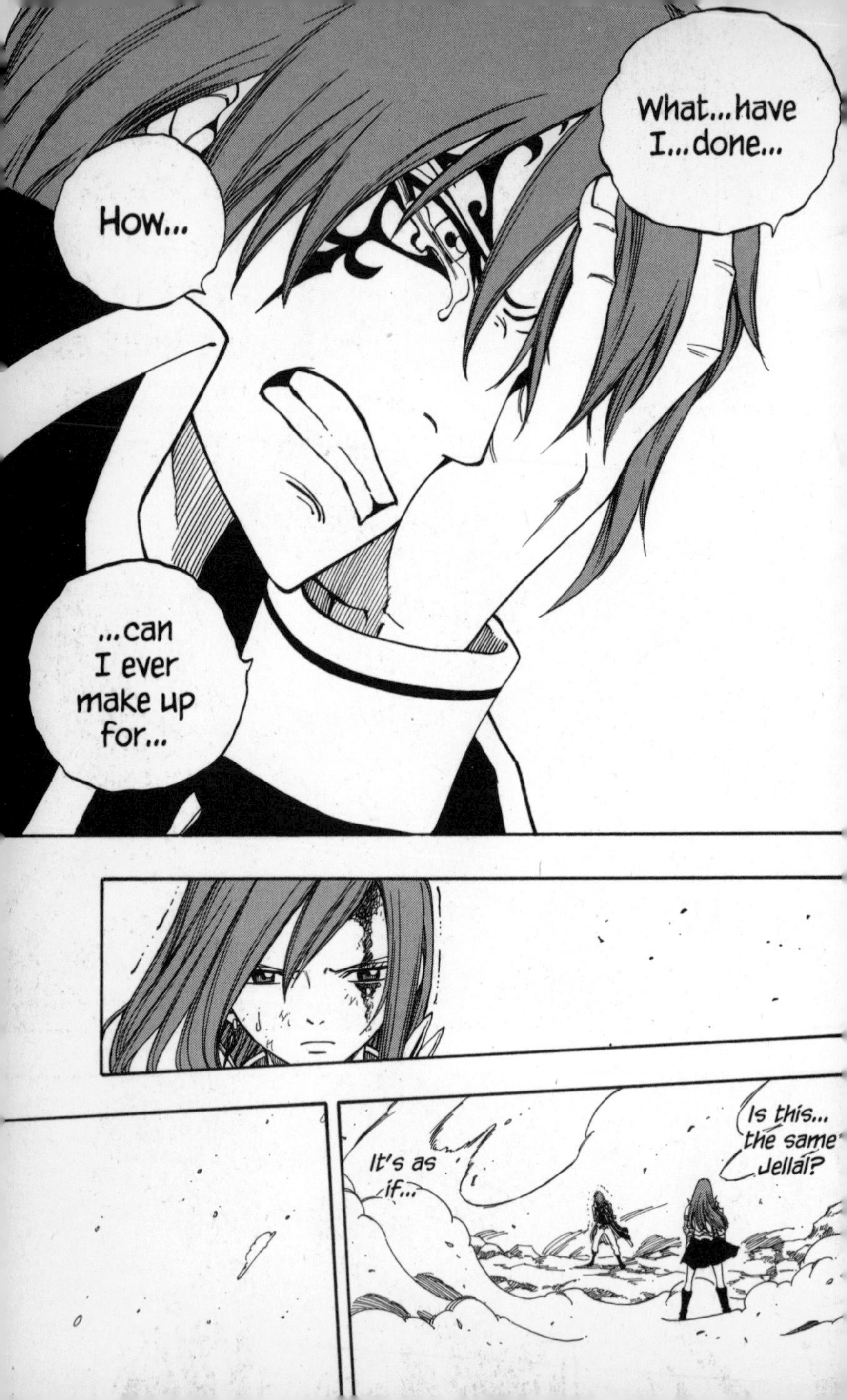
What...have I...done...
How...
...can I ever make up for...
Is this... the same Jellal?
It's as if...

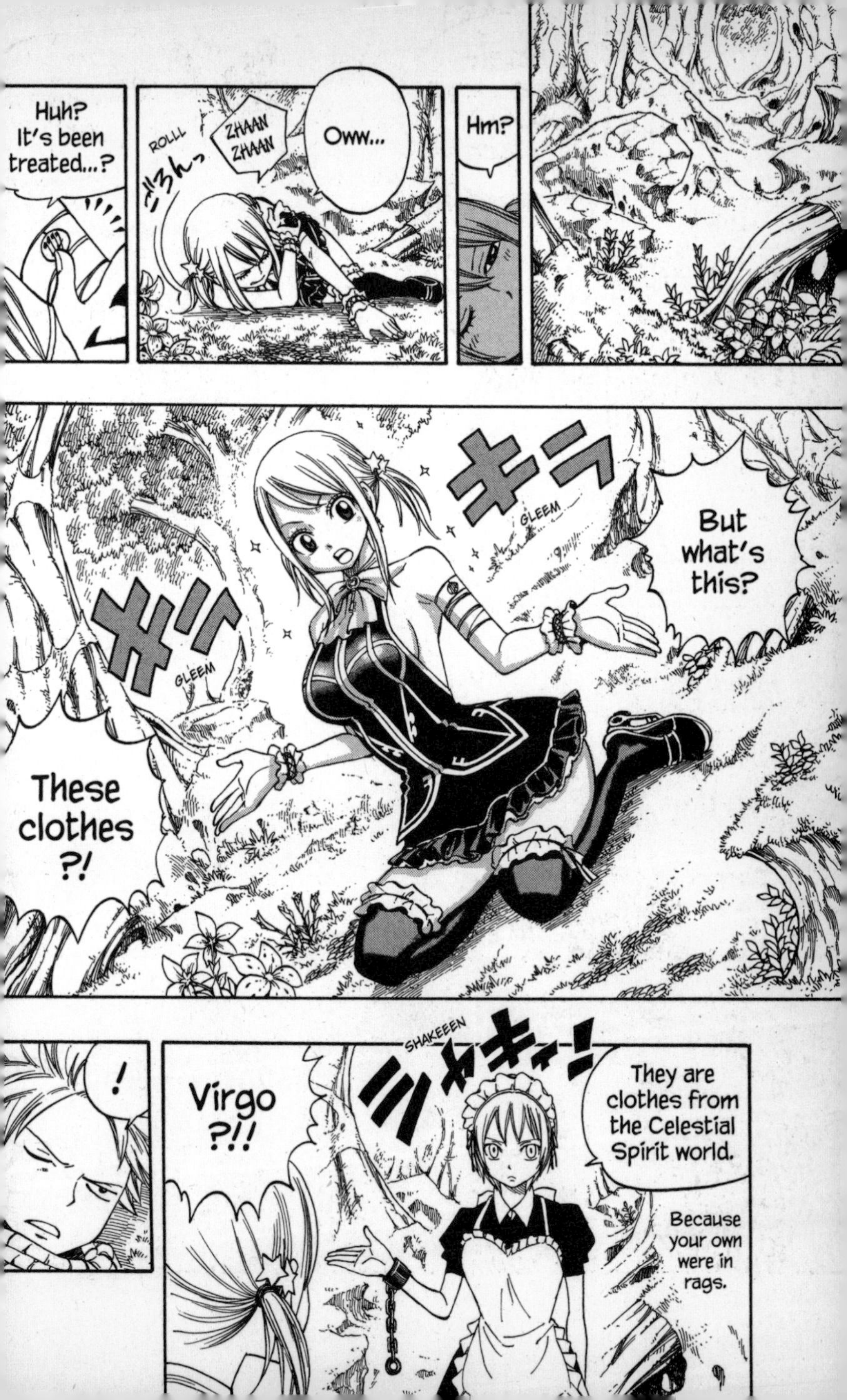

Hm?
Oww...
ZHAAN ZHAAN
ROLL
ごろんっ
Huh? It's been treated...?
But what's this?
GLEEM
GLEEM
These clothes ?!
SHAKEEEN
They are clothes from the Celestial Spirit world.
Because your own were in rags.
Virgo ?!!
!

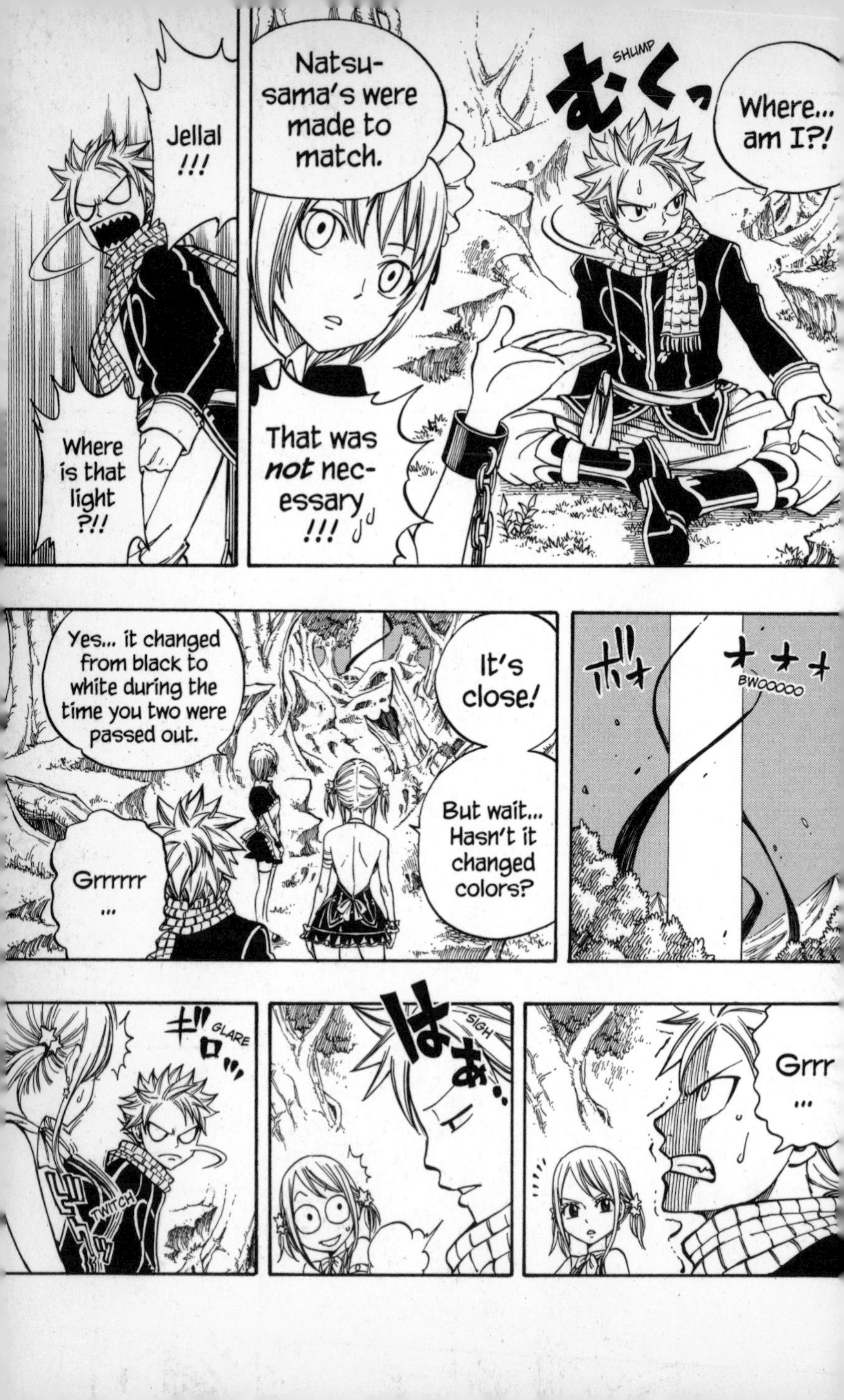
むくっ
SHUMP
Where... am I?!
Natsu-sama's were made to match.
That was *not* necessary!!!
Jellal!!!
Where is that light?!!
ボォォォ
BWOOOOO
It's close!
But wait... Hasn't it changed colors?
Yes... it changed from black to white during the time you two were passed out.
Grrrrr...
Grrr...
はぁ…
SIGH
ギロ
GLARE
TWITCH

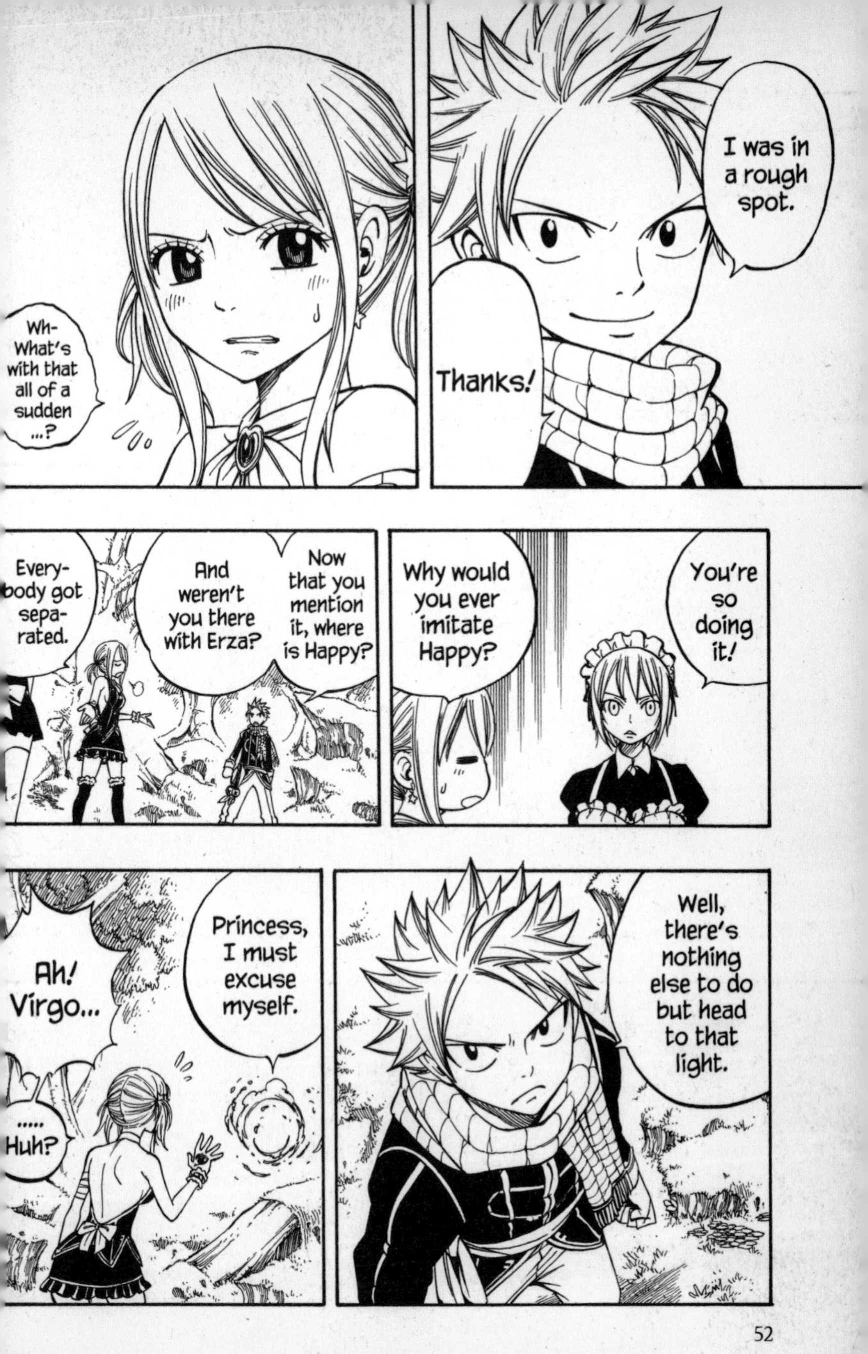
I was in a rough spot.
Thanks!
Wh- What's with that all of a sudden ...?
You're so doing it!
Why would you ever imitate Happy?
Now that you mention it, where is Happy?
And weren't you there with Erza?
Every-body got sepa-rated.
Well, there's nothing else to do but head to that light.
Princess, I must excuse myself.
Ah! Virgo...
..... Huh?

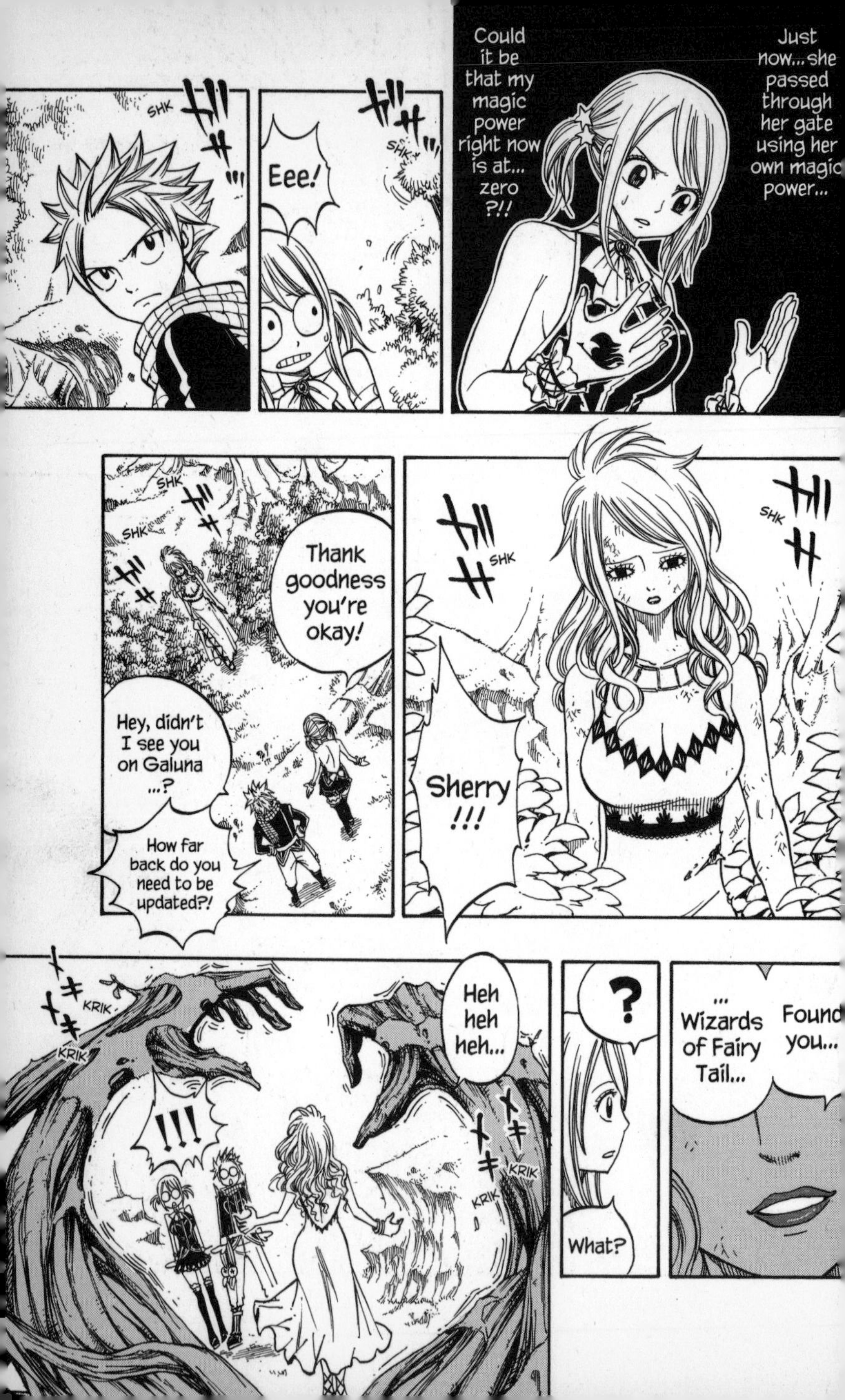
Just now...she passed through her gate using her own magic power...
Could it be that my magic power right now is at... zero ?!!
SHK
Eee!
SHK
SHK
Sherry !!!
SHK
SHK
SHK
Thank goodness you're okay!
Hey, didn't I see you on Galuna ...?
How far back do you need to be updated?!
Found you...
... Wizards of Fairy Tail...
?
What?
Heh heh heh...
KRIK
KRIK
!!!
KRIK
KRIK

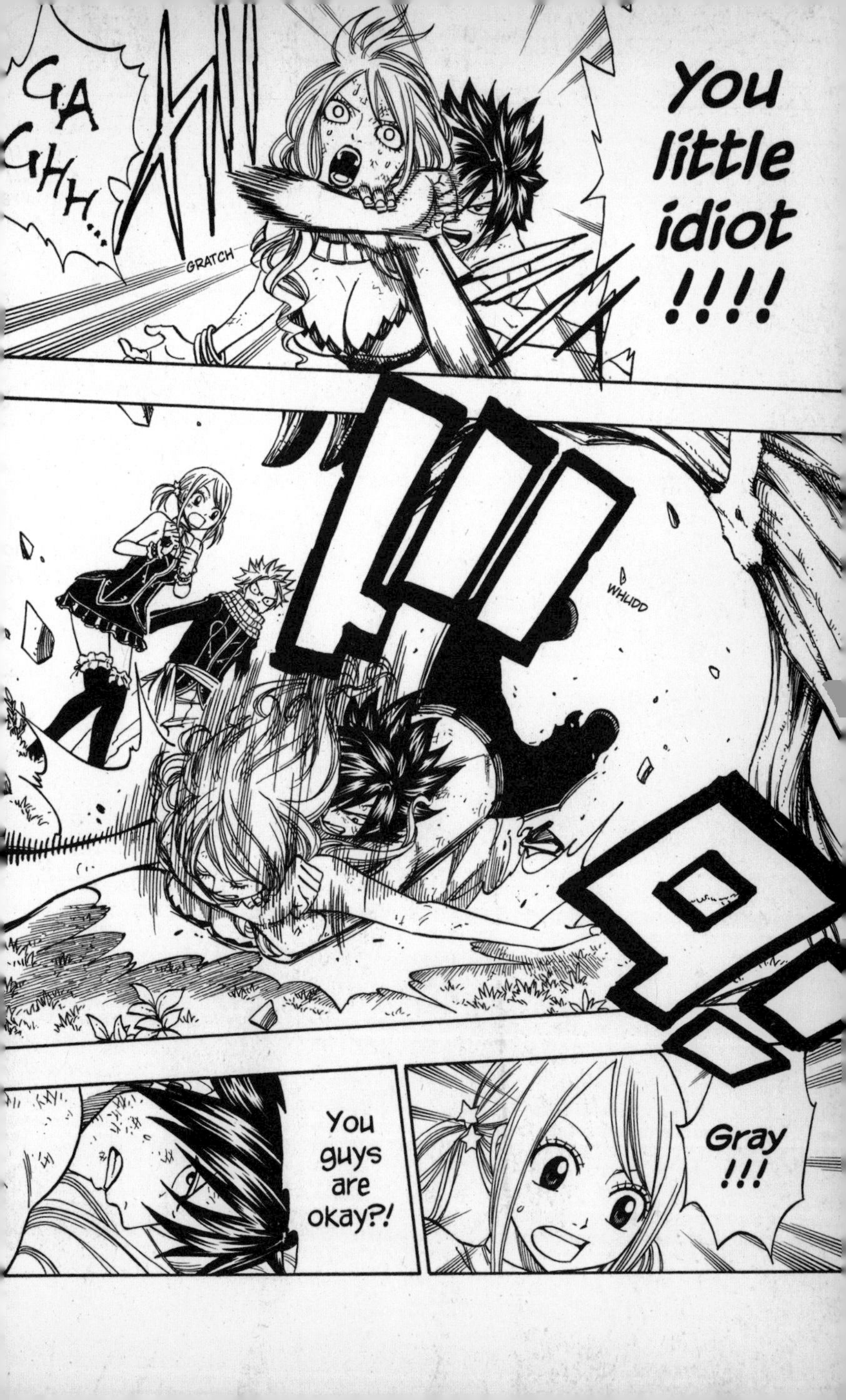
You little idiot!!!!
GAGHH...
GRATCH
WHUDD
Gray!!!
You guys are okay?!

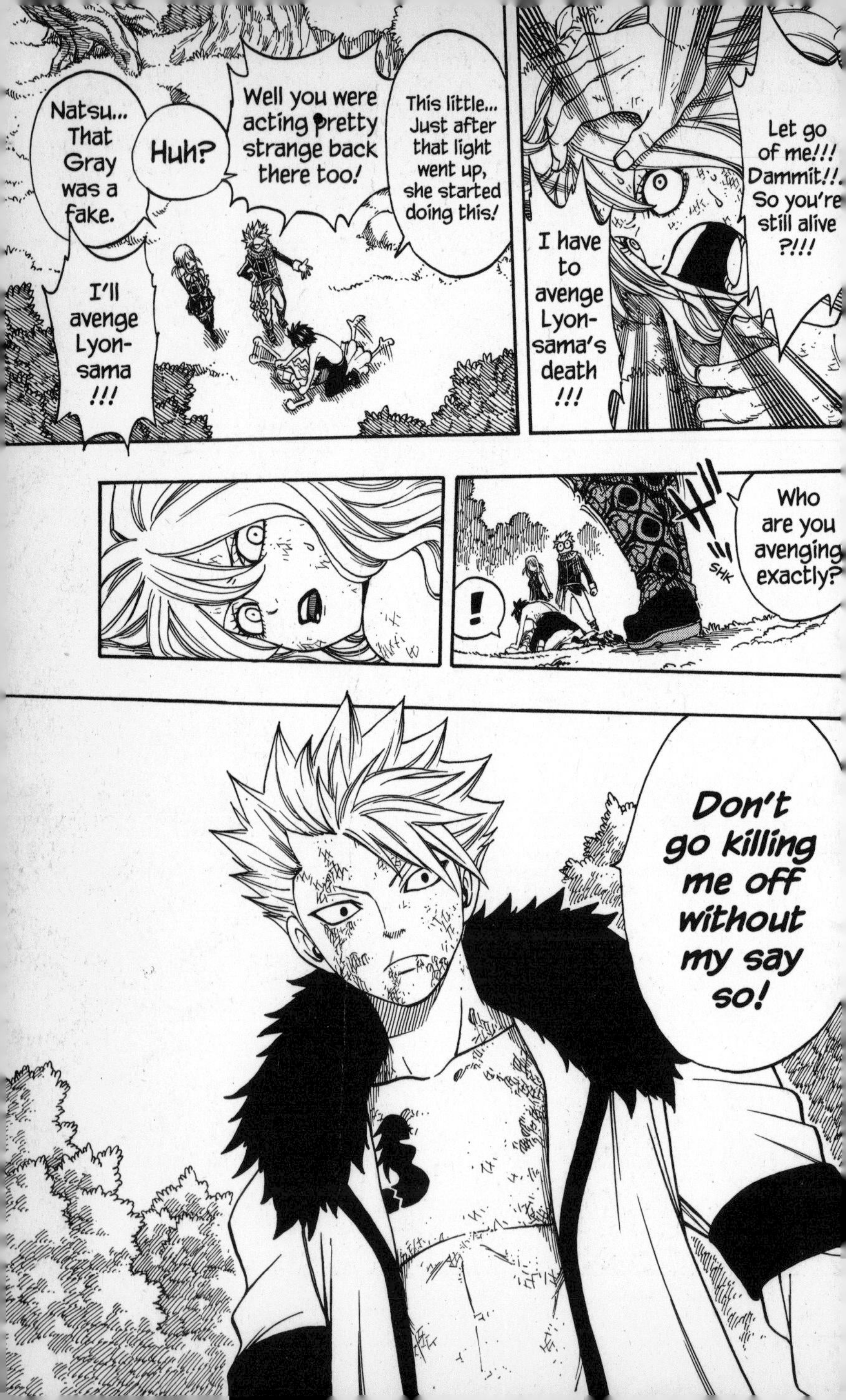
Let go of me!!! Dammit!!. So you're still alive ?!!!
I have to avenge Lyon-sama's death !!!
This little... Just after that light went up, she started doing this!
Well you were acting pretty strange back there too!
Huh?
Natsu... That Gray was a fake.
I'll avenge Lyon-sama !!!
Who are you avenging exactly?
SHK
!
Don't go killing me off without my say so!

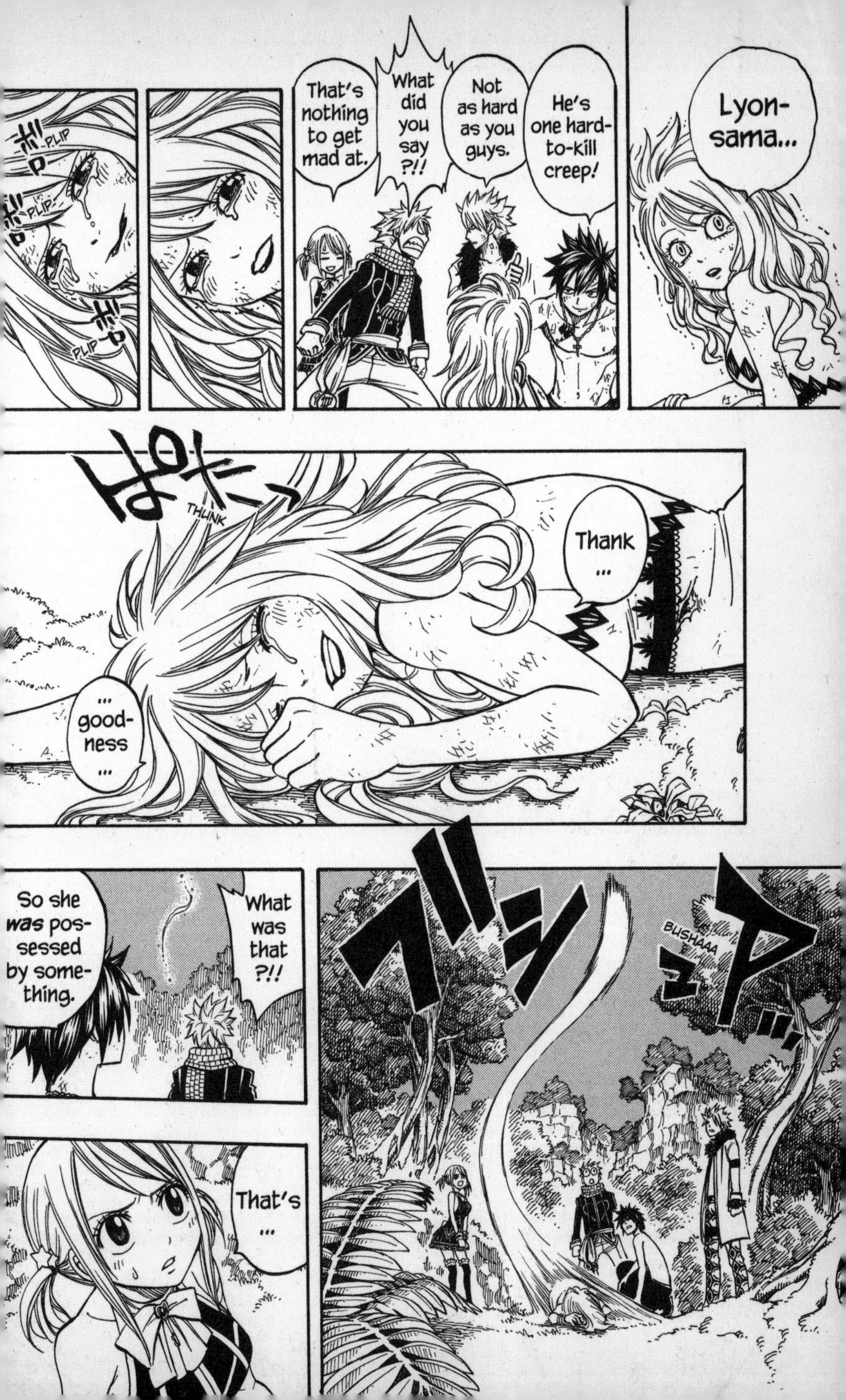

Lyon-sama...
He's one hard-to-kill creep!
Not as hard as you guys.
What did you say?!!
That's nothing to get mad at.
PLIP
PLIP
PLIP
THUNK
Thank...
...goodness...
BUSHAAA
What was that?!!
So she *was* possessed by something.
That's...

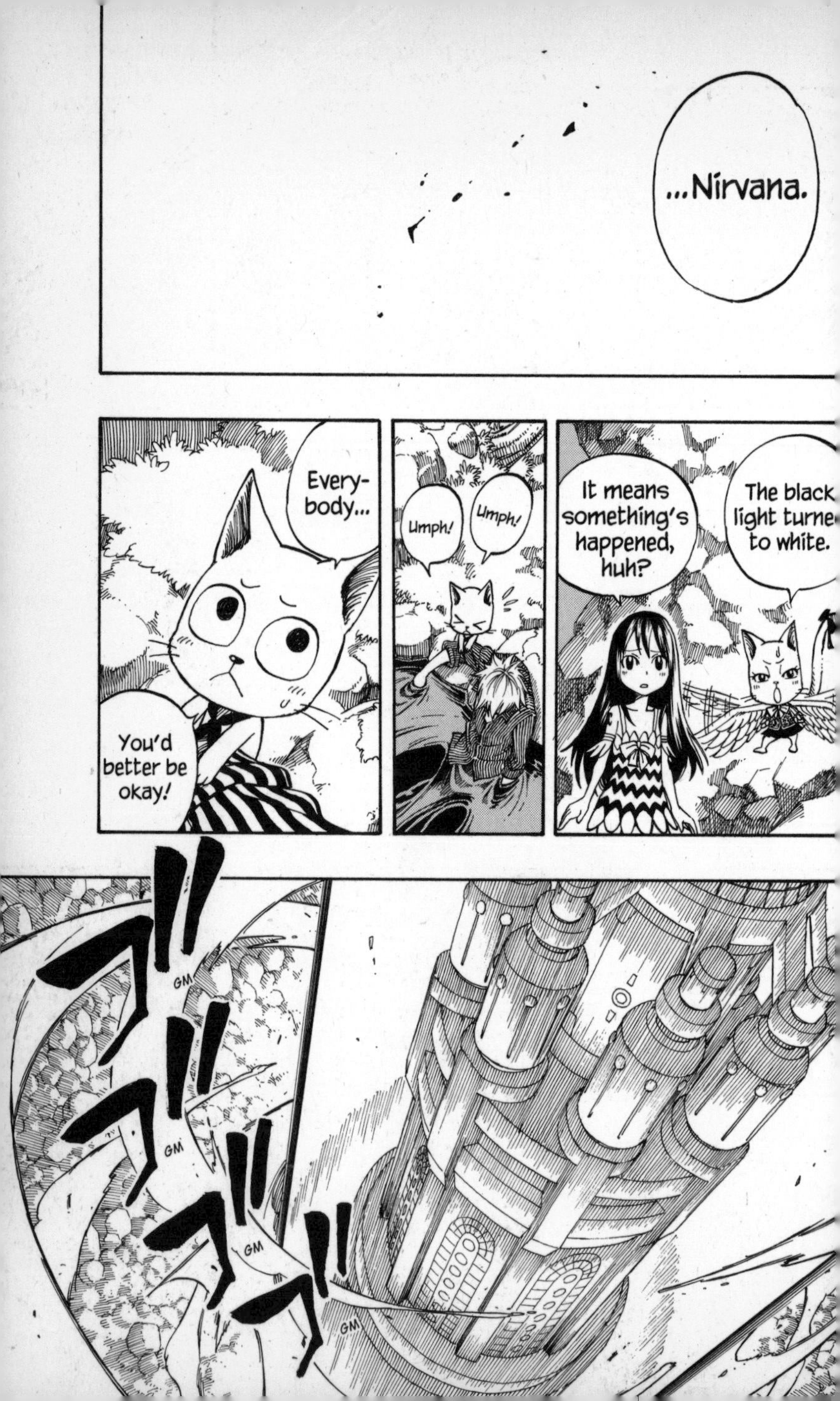
...Nirvana.
The black light turne to white.
It means something's happened, huh?
Umph!
Umph!
Every-body...
You'd better be okay!
GM
GM
GM
GM

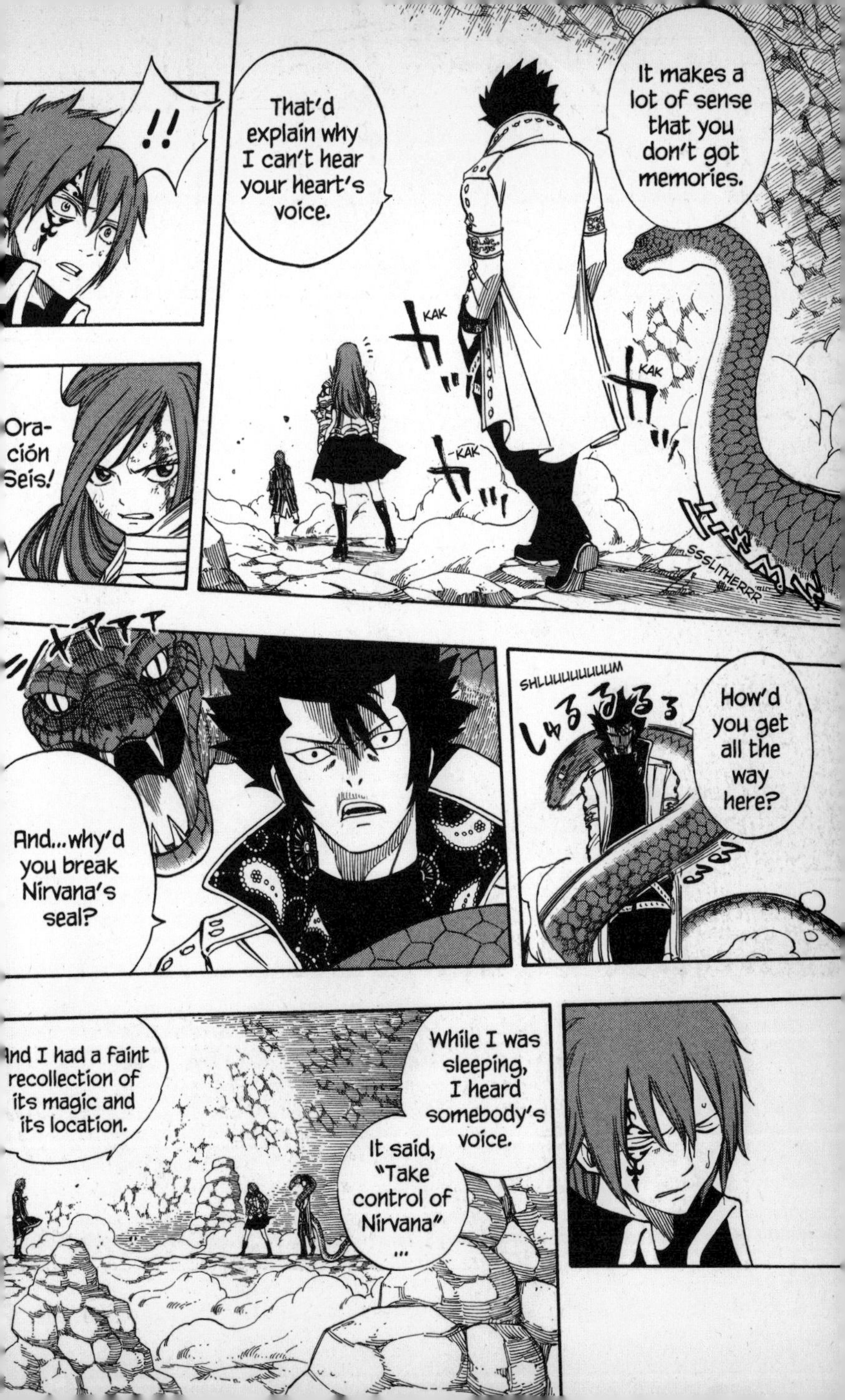
It makes a lot of sense that you don't got memories.
That'd explain why I can't hear your heart's voice.
KAK
KAK
-KAK
SSSLITHERRR
!!
Oración Seis!
SHLUUUUUUUUUM
How'd you get all the way here?
And...why'd you break Nirvana's seal?
While I was sleeping, I heard somebody's voice.
It said, "Take control of Nirvana"...
And I had a faint recollection of its magic and its location.

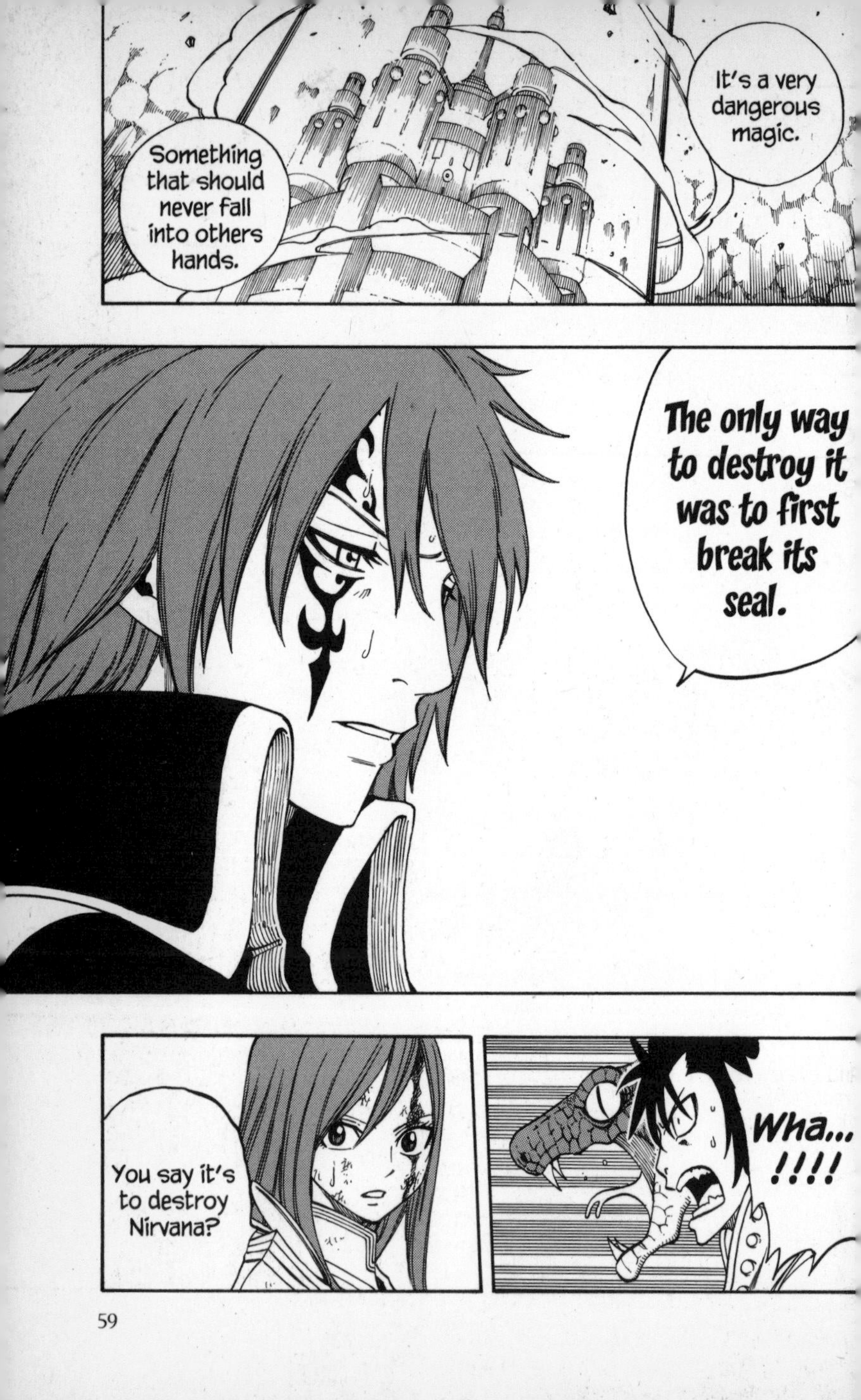
It's a very dangerous magic.
Something that should never fall into others hands.
The only way to destroy it was to first break its seal.
Wha... !!!!
You say it's to destroy Nirvana?

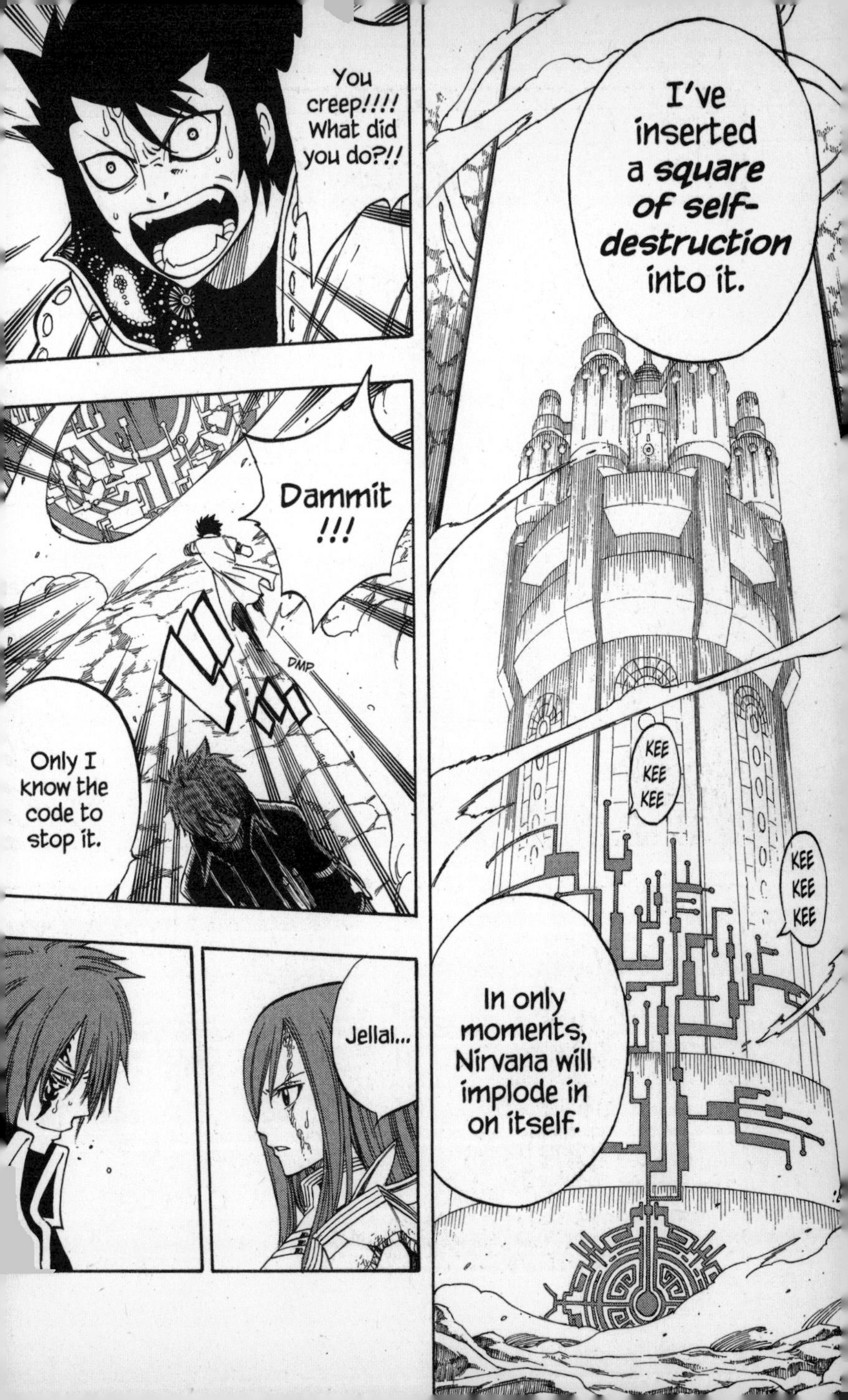
I've inserted a *square of self-destruction* into it.
KEE KEE KEE
KEE KEE KEE
In only moments, Nirvana will implode in on itself.
You creep!!!! What did you do?!!
Dammit!!!
DMP
Only I know the code to stop it.
Jellal...

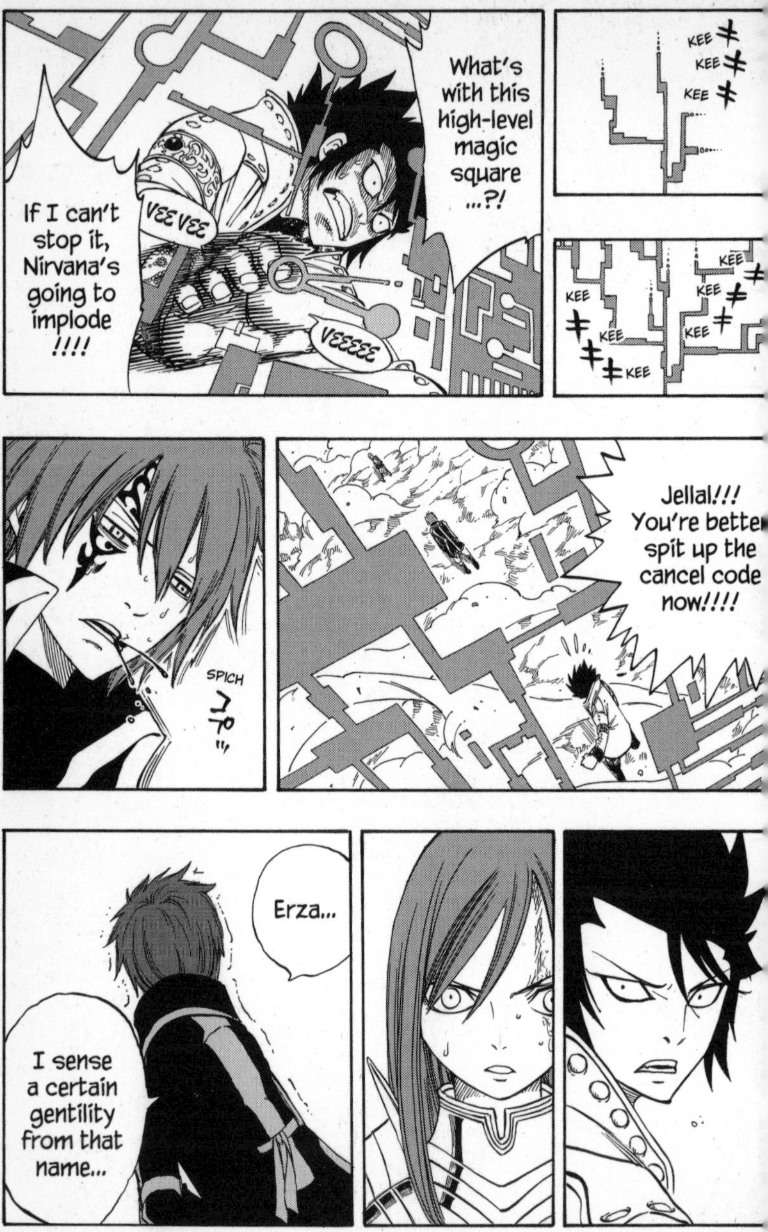
KEE KEE KEE
KEE KEE KEE KEE KEE KEE
What's with this high-level magic square ...?!
VEE VEE
VEEEEE
If I can't stop it, Nirvana's going to implode !!!!
Jellal!!! You're bette spit up the cancel code now!!!!
SPICH
Erza...
I sense a certain gentility from that name...

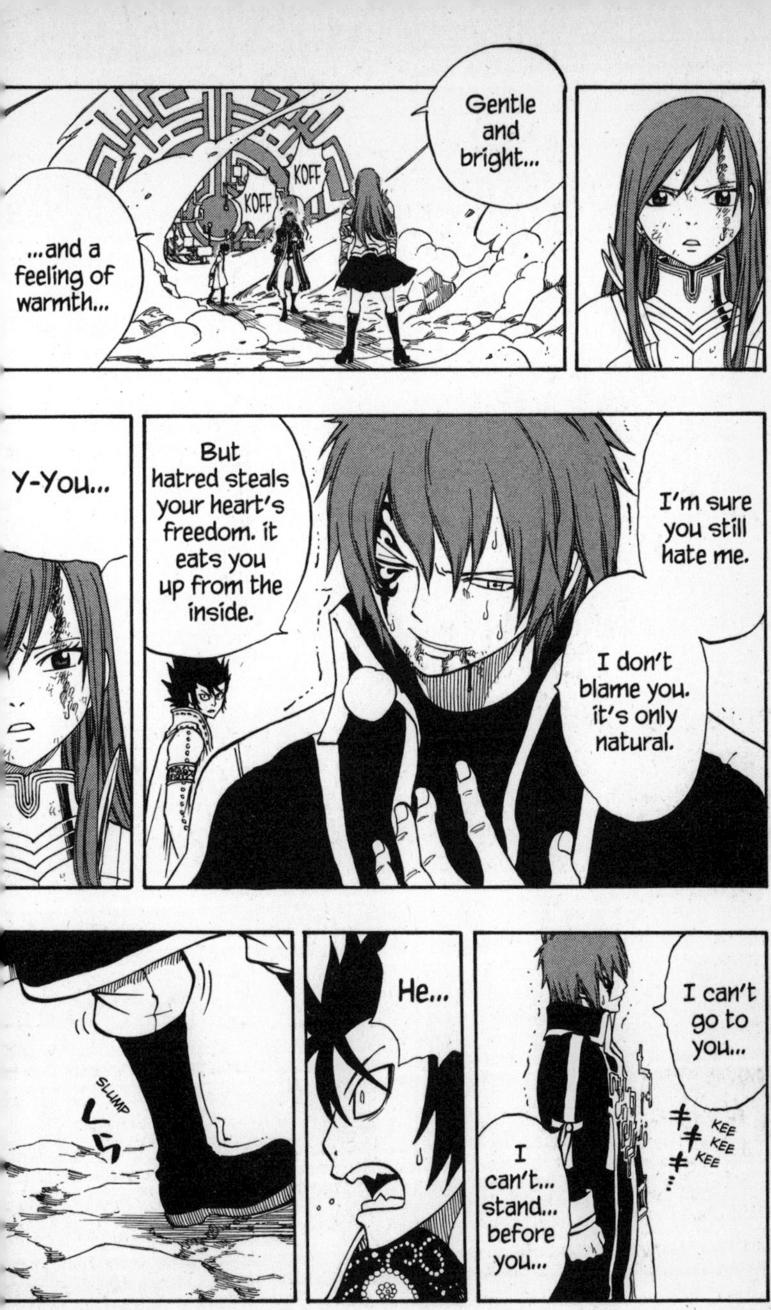
Gentle and bright...
KOFF
KOFF
...and a feeling of warmth...
I'm sure you still hate me.
I don't blame you. it's only natural.
But hatred steals your heart's freedom. it eats you up from the inside.
Y-You...
I can't go to you...
KEE KEE KEE
I can't... stand... before you...
He...
SLUMP

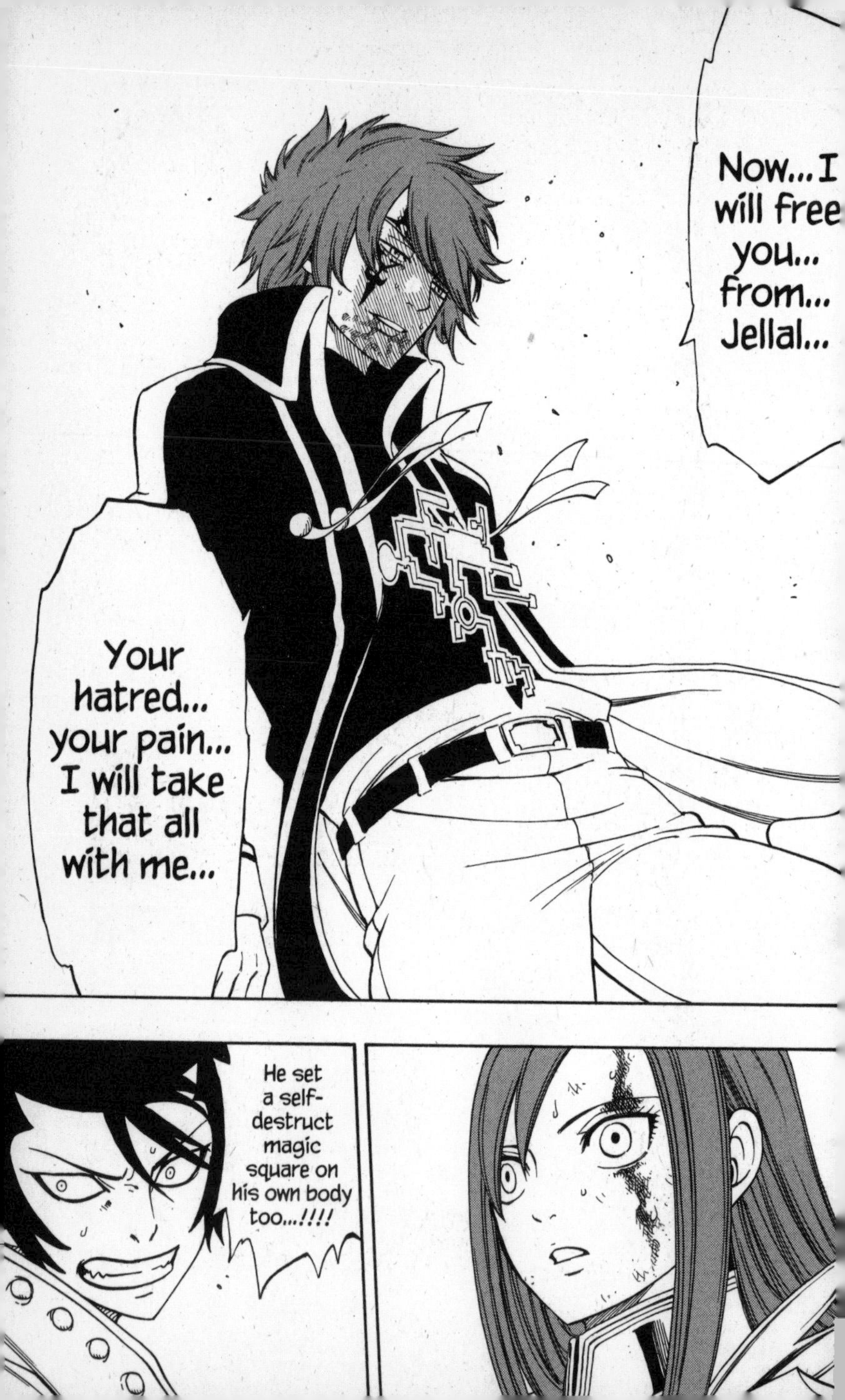
Now...I will free you... from... Jellal...
Your hatred... your pain... I will take that all with me...
He set a self-destruct magic square on his own body too...!!!!

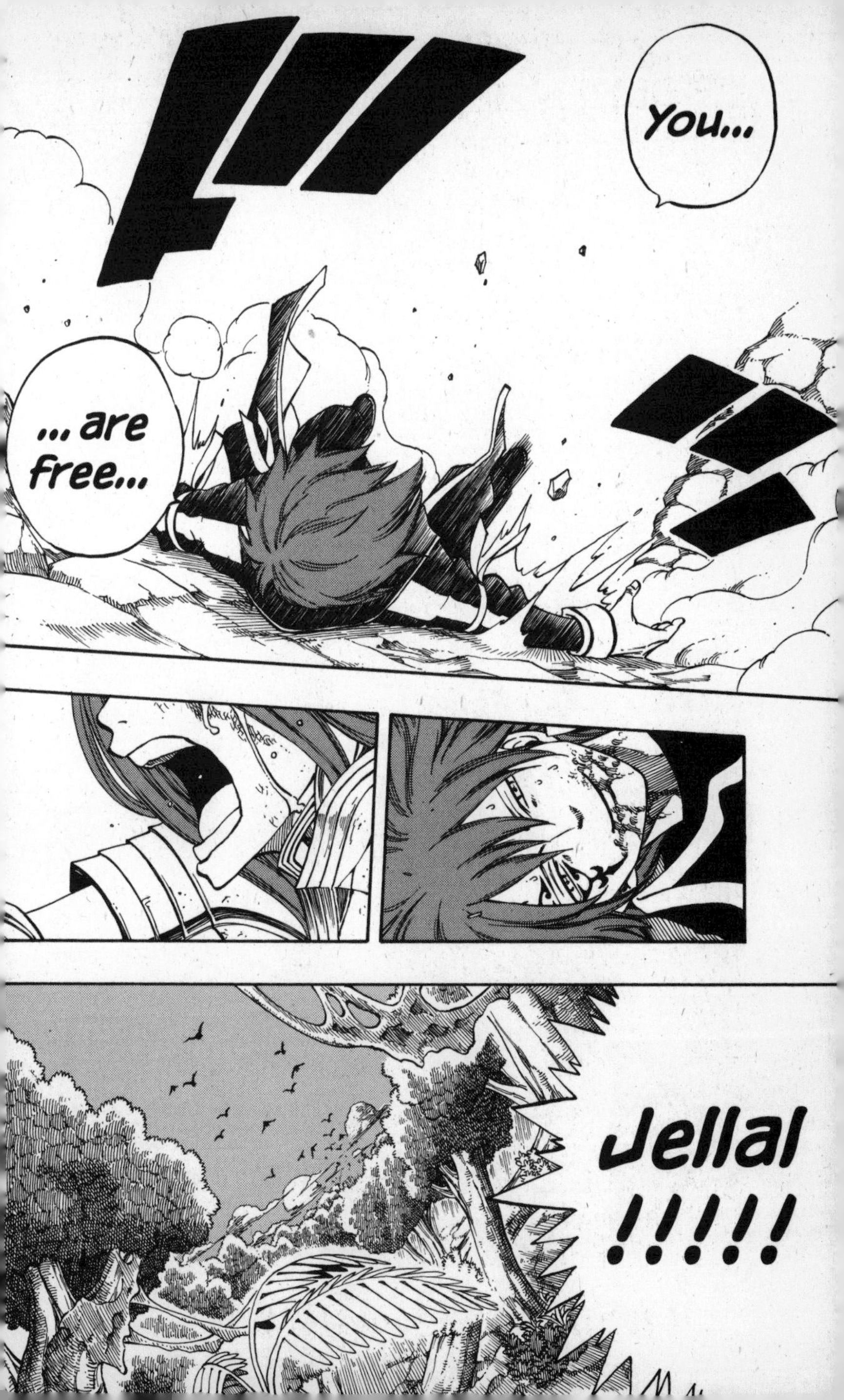
You...
...are free...
Jellal !!!!!

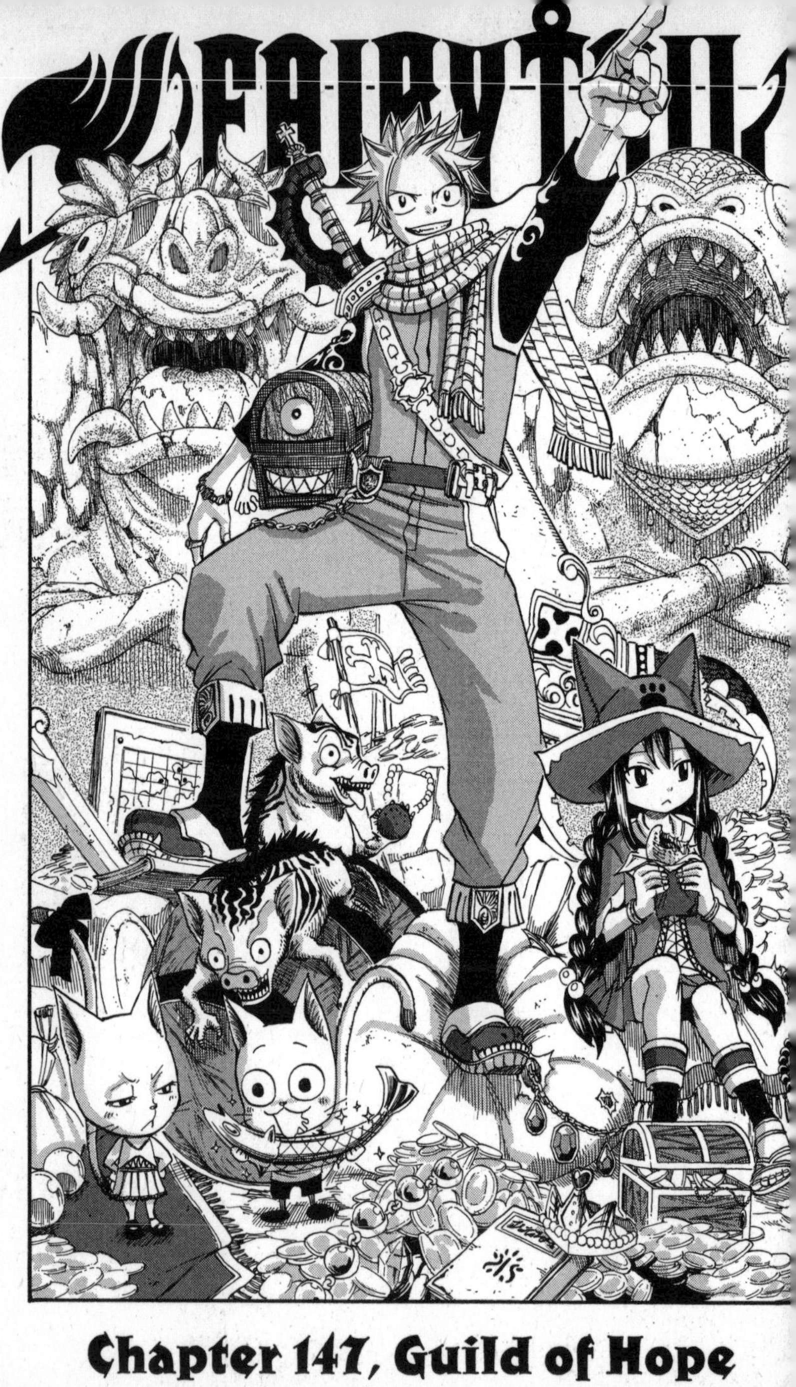

Chapter 147, Guild of Hope

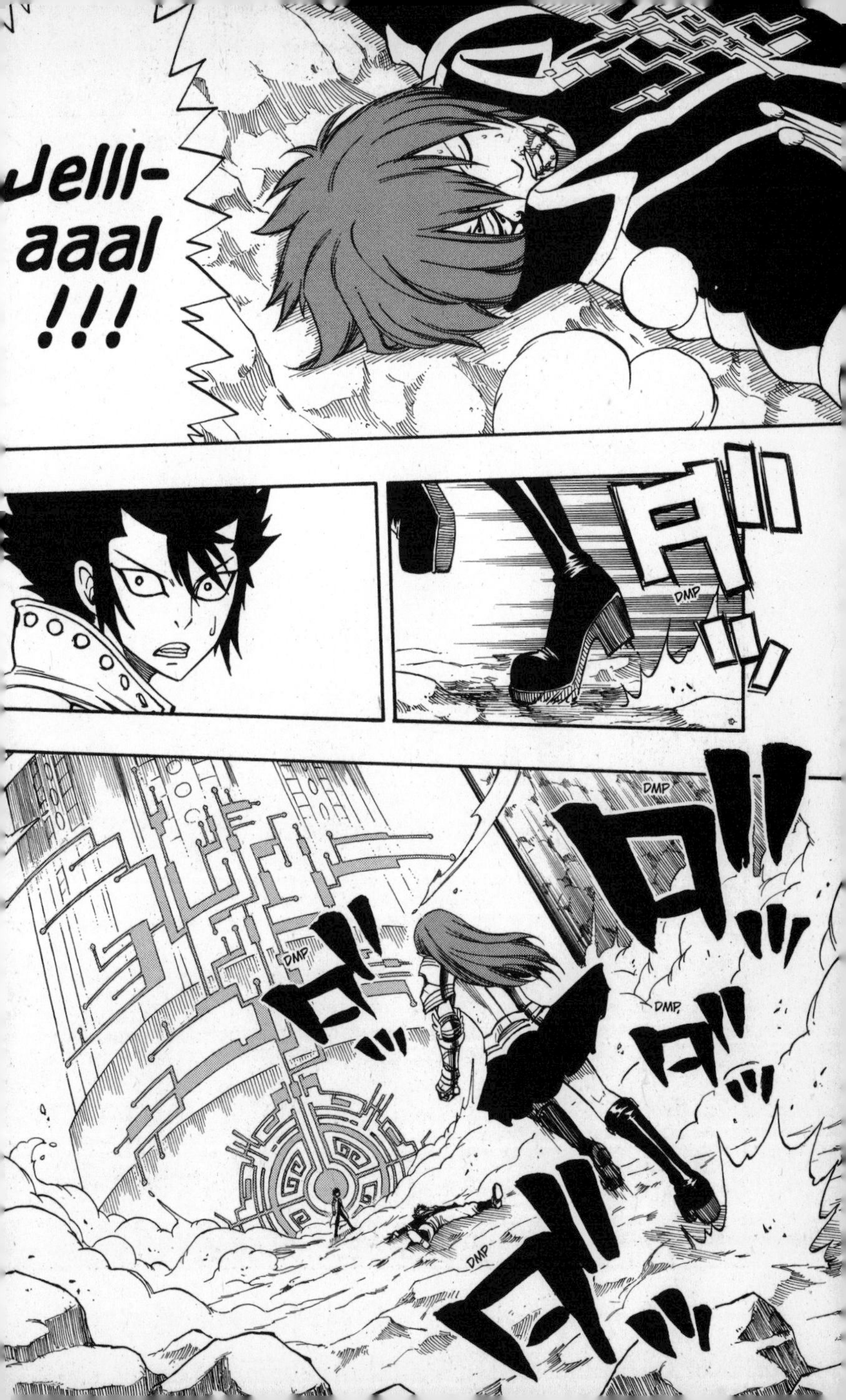
Jelll-
aaal
!!!
DMP
DMP
DMP
DMP
DMP

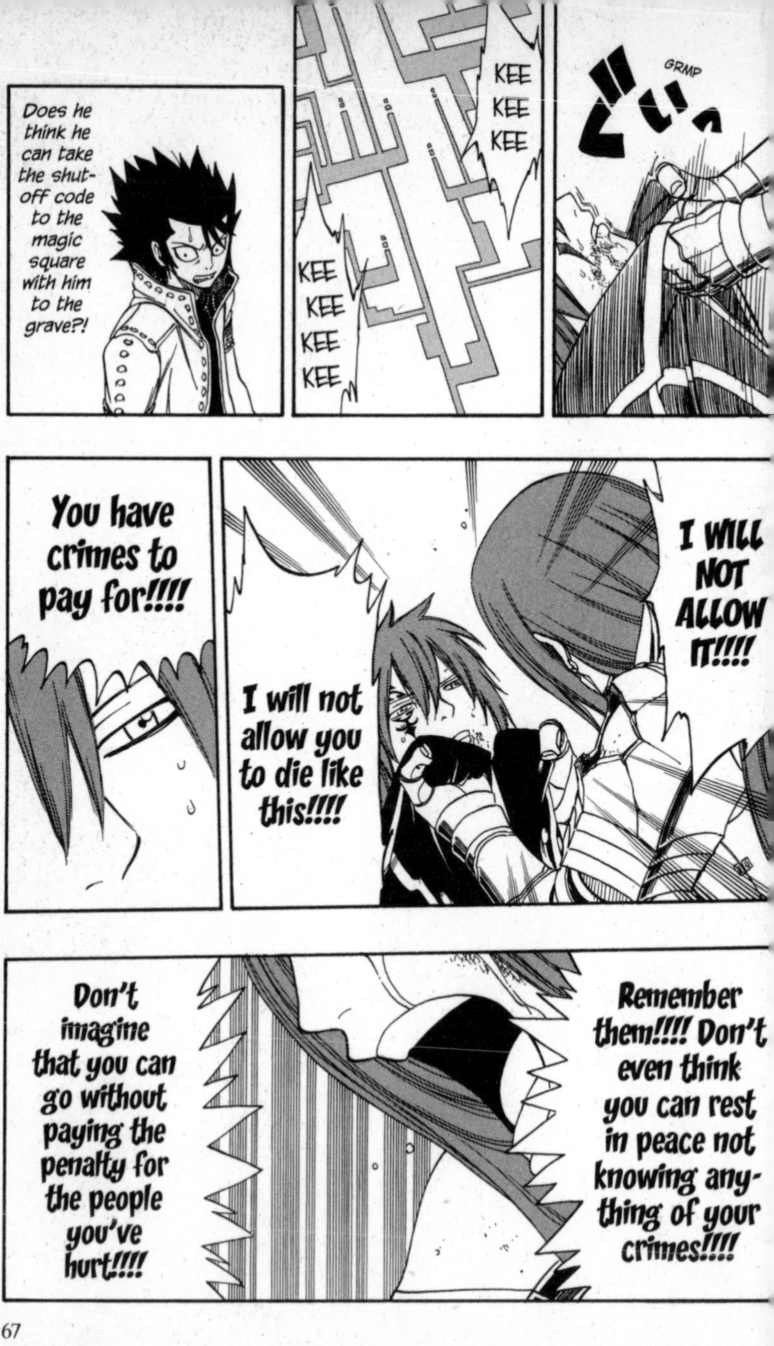
GRMP
KEE KEE KEE
KEE KEE KEE KEE
Does he think he can take the shut-off code to the magic square with him to the grave?!
I WILL NOT ALLOW IT!!!!
I will not allow you to die like this!!!!
You have crimes to pay for!!!!
Remember them!!!! Don't even think you can rest in peace not knowing anything of your crimes!!!!
Don't imagine that you can go without paying the penalty for the people you've hurt!!!!

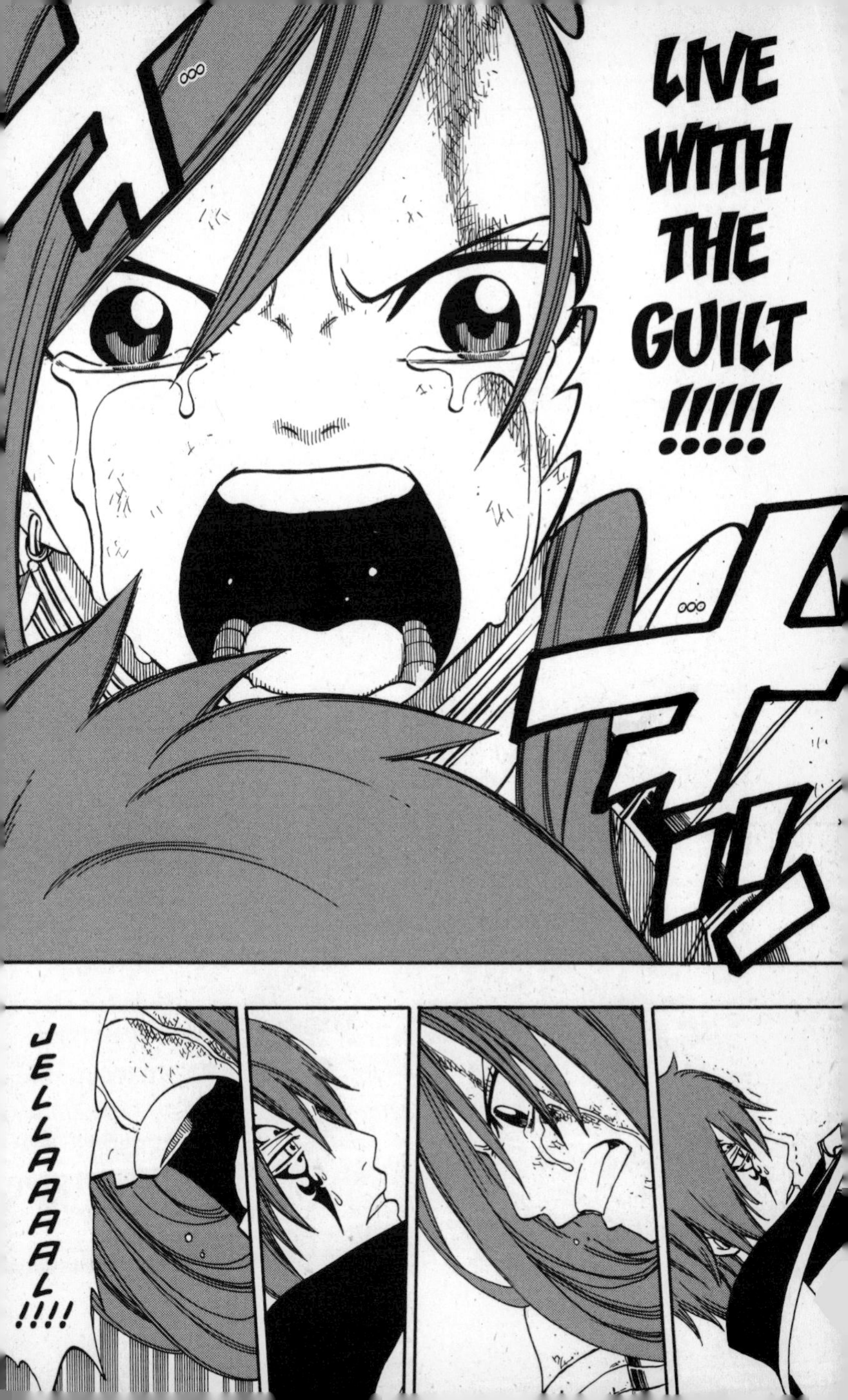
LIVE WITH THE GUILT!!!!!
JELLAAAAAL!!!!

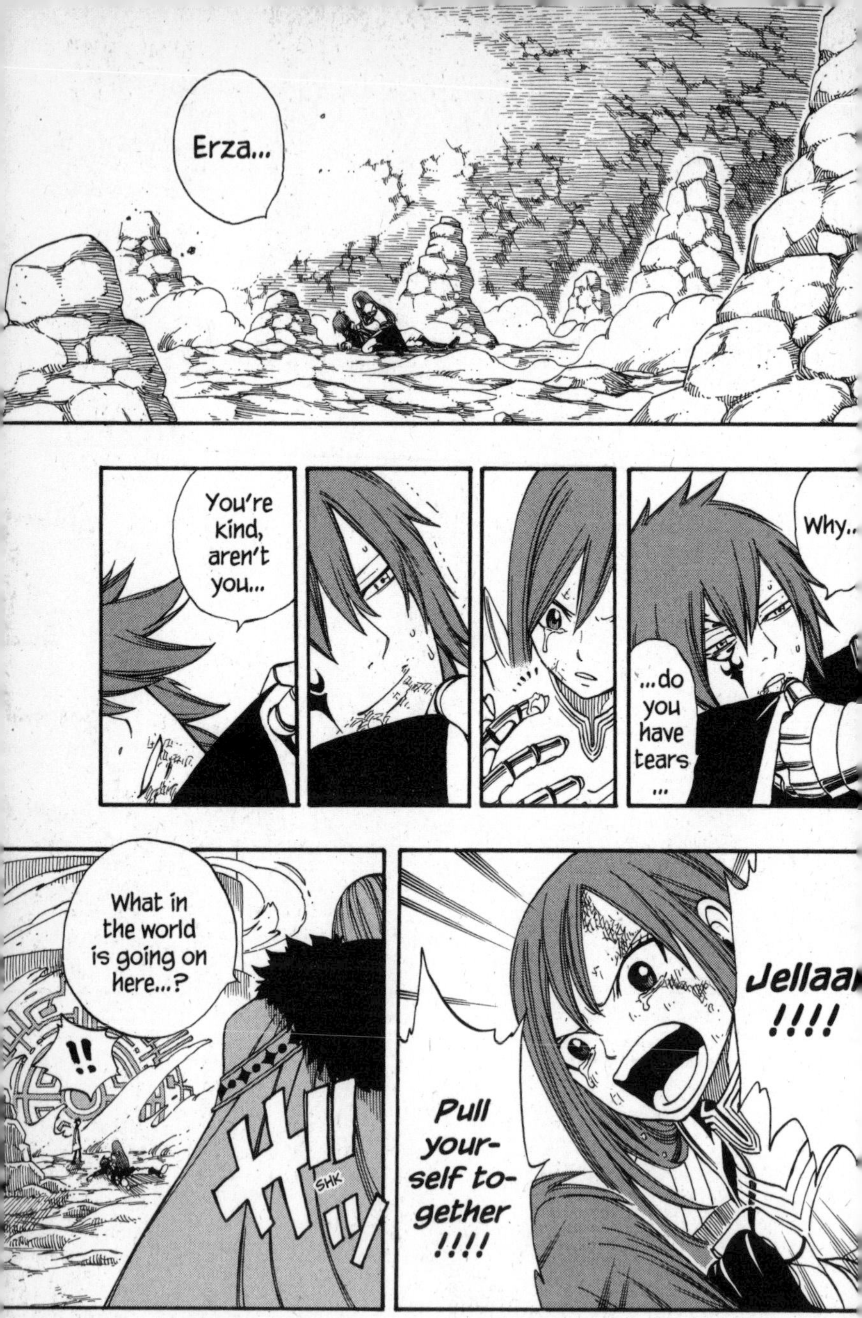
Erza...
Why...
...do you have tears ...
You're kind, aren't you...
Jellaa
!!!!
Pull yourself together !!!!
What in the world is going on here...?
!!
SHK

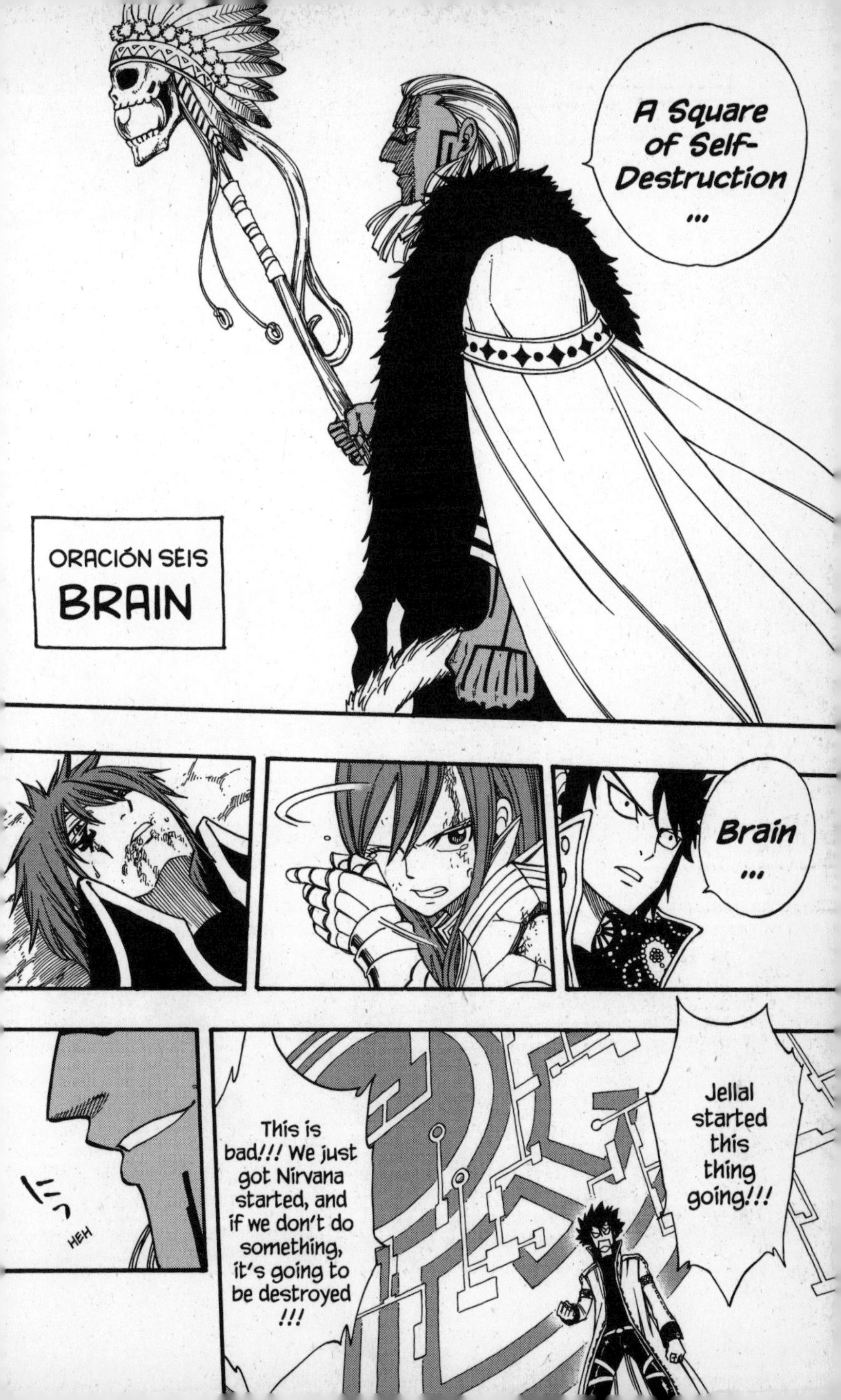
A Square of Self-Destruction ...
ORACIÓN SEIS
BRAIN
Brain ...
Jellal started this thing going!!!
This is bad!!! We just got Nirvana started, and if we don't do something, it's going to be destroyed !!!
HEH

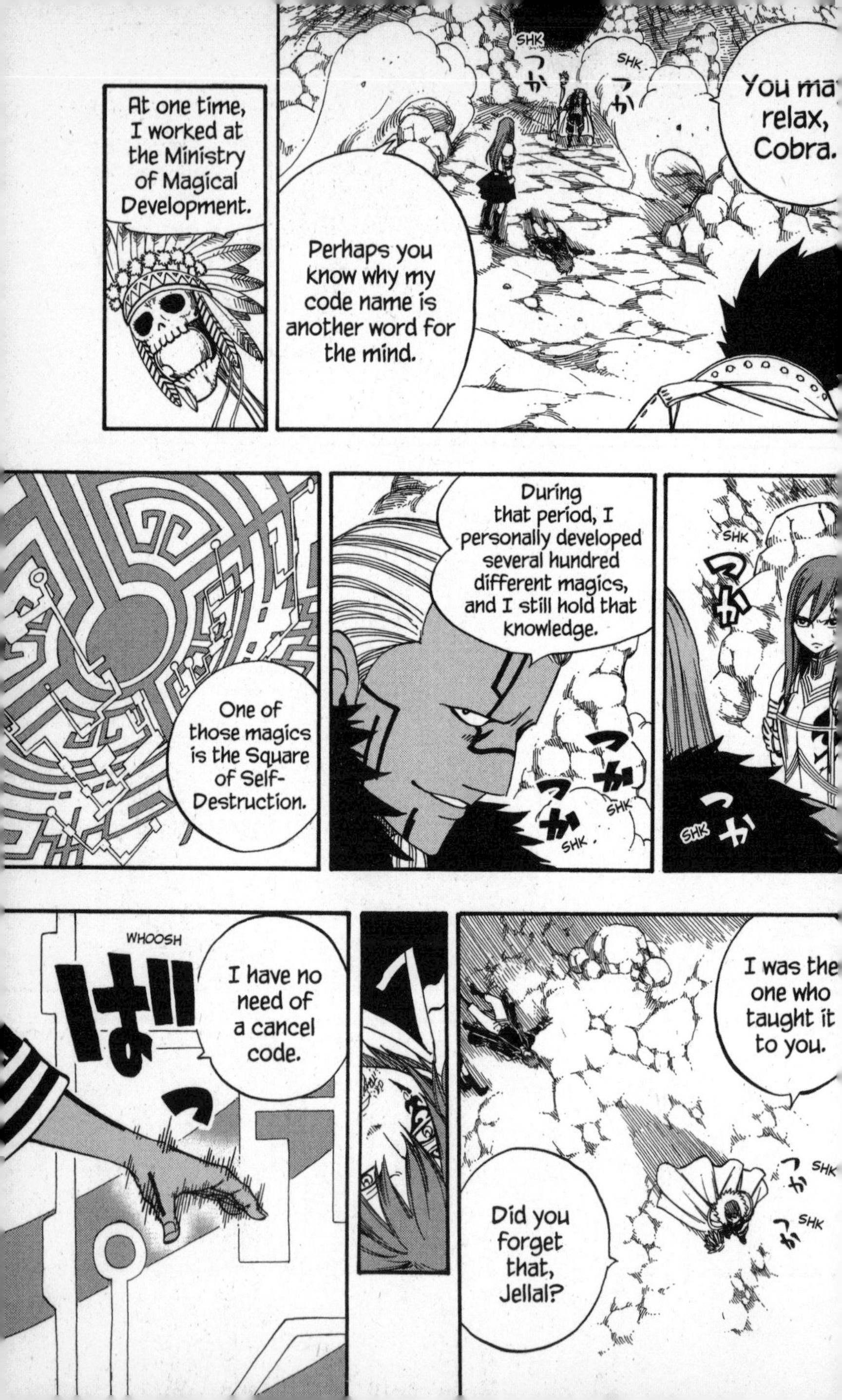
SHK
SHK
You ma relax, Cobra.
Perhaps you know why my code name is another word for the mind.
At one time, I worked at the Ministry of Magical Development.
SHK
SHK
During that period, I personally developed several hundred different magics, and I still hold that knowledge.
SHK
SHK
One of those magics is the Square of Self-Destruction.
I was the one who taught it to you.
SHK
SHK
Did you forget that, Jellal?
WHOOSH
I have no need of a cancel code.

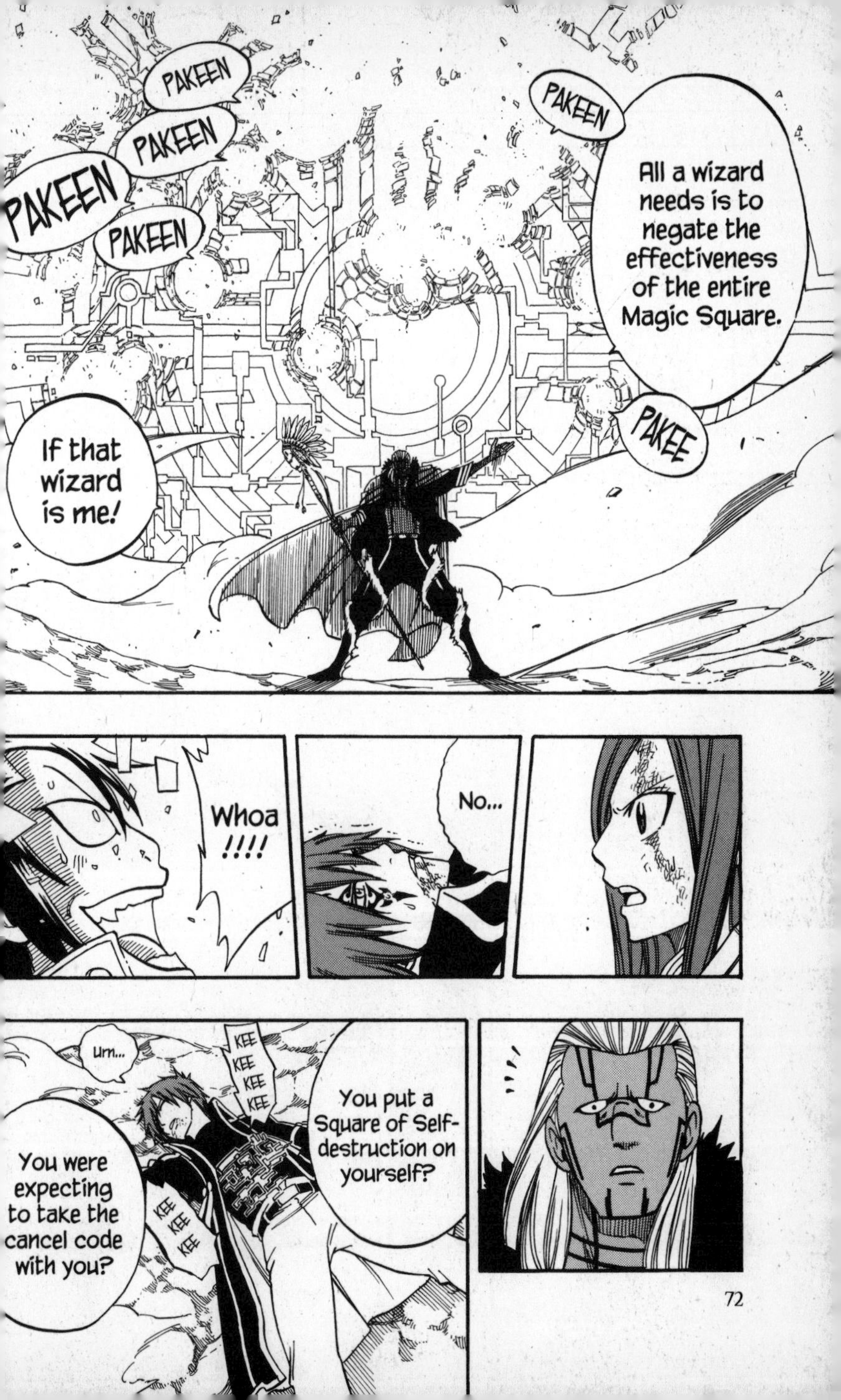
PAKEEN
All a wizard needs is to negate the effectiveness of the entire Magic Square.
PAKEE
PAKEEN
PAKEEN
PAKEEN
PAKEEN
If that wizard is me!
No...
Whoa !!!!
You put a Square of Self-destruction on yourself?
KEE KEE KEE KEE
um...
KEE KEE KEE
You were expecting to take the cancel code with you?

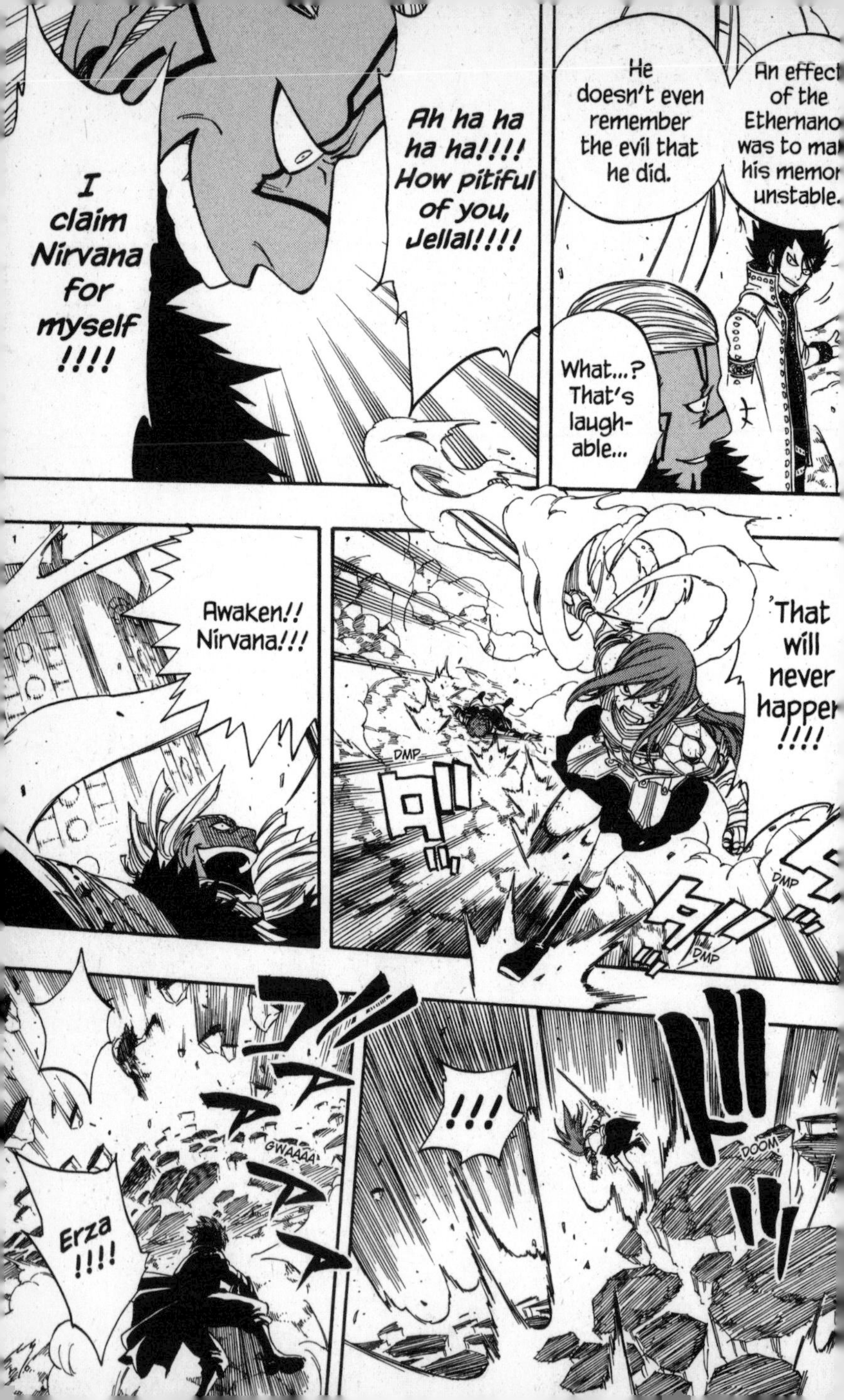

An effec of the Ethernano was to ma his memor unstable.
He doesn't even remember the evil that he did.
What...? That's laugh-able...
Ah ha ha ha ha!!!! How pitiful of you, Jellal!!!!
I claim Nirvana for myself!!!!
That will never happe !!!!
DMP
DMP
DMP
Awaken!! Nirvana!!!
DOOM
!!!
GWAAAA
Erza!!!!

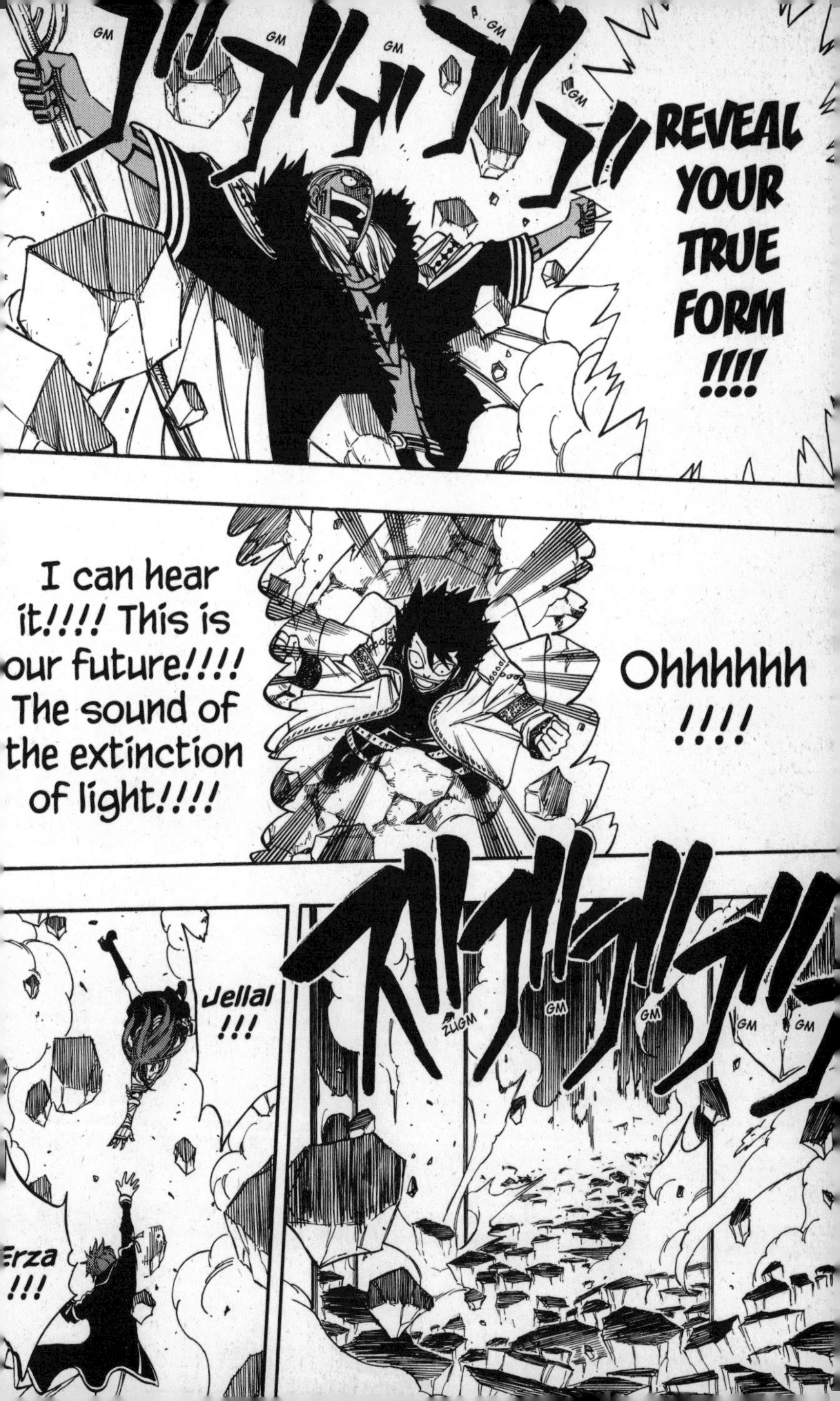
GM
GM
GM
GM
GM
REVEAL YOUR TRUE FORM !!!!
Ohhhhhh !!!!
I can hear it!!!! This is our future!!!! The sound of the extinction of light!!!!
GM
GM
GM
GM
ZUGM
Jellal !!!
Erza !!!

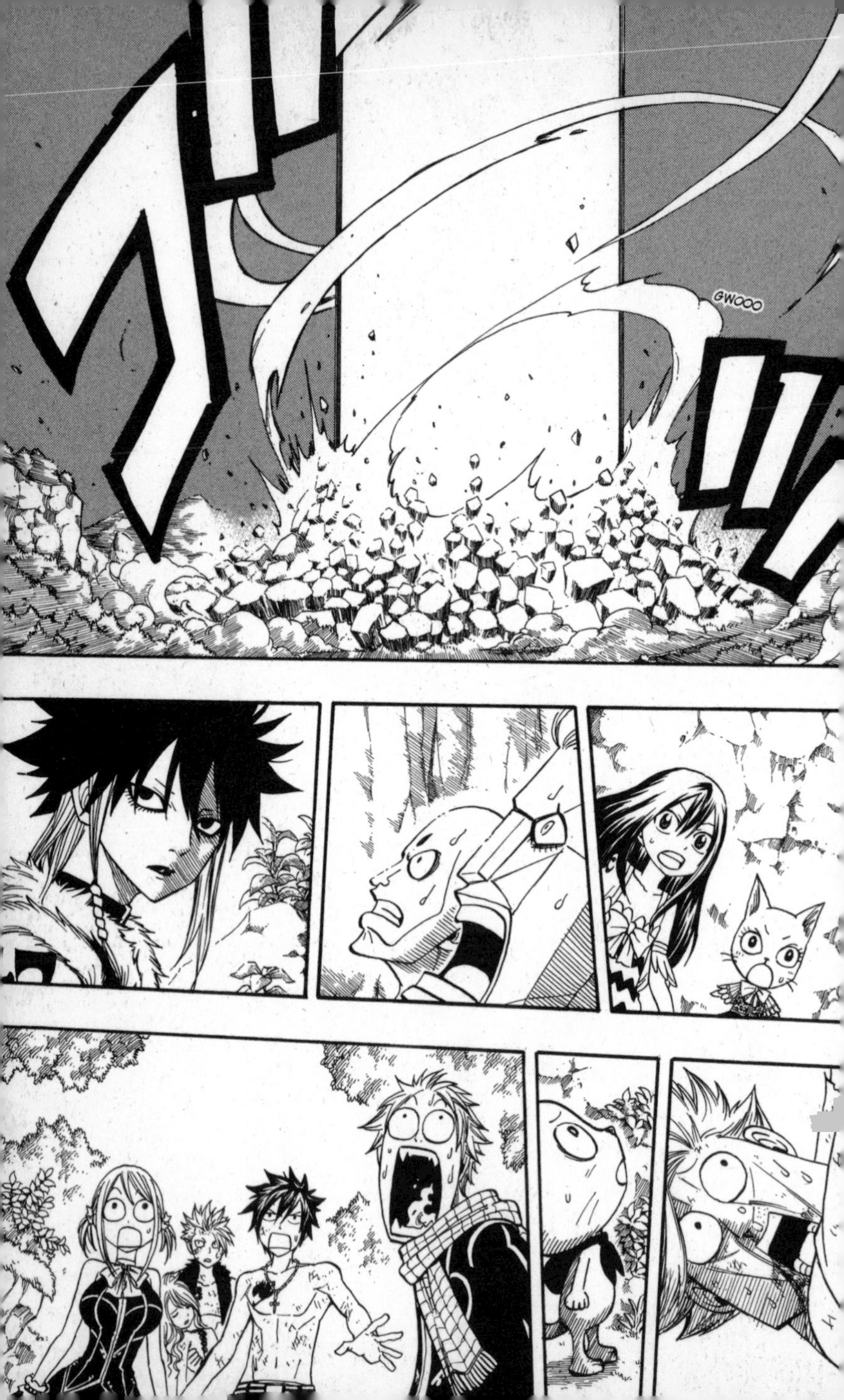
GWOOO

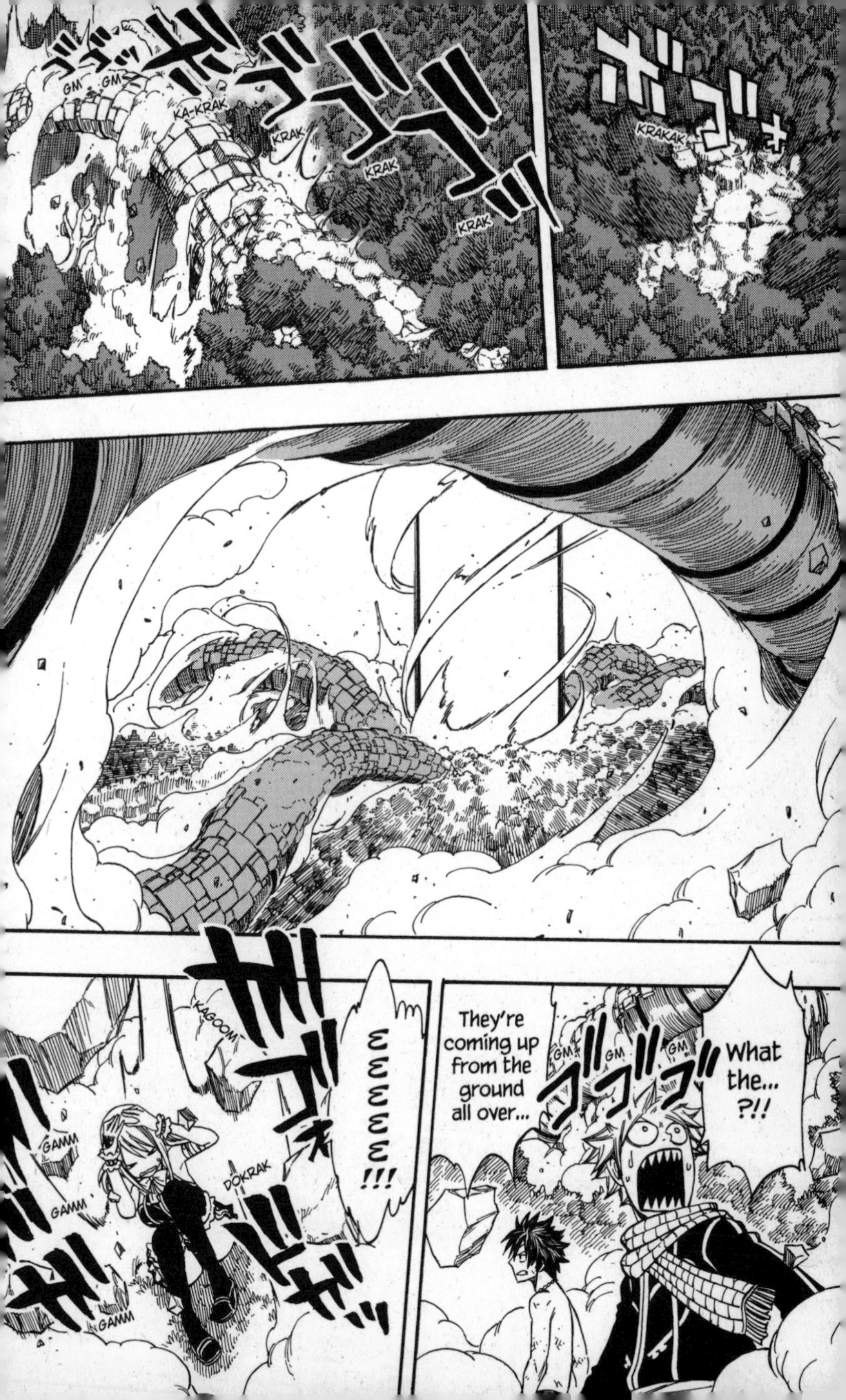
KRAKAK
GM
GM
KA-KRAK
KRAK
KRAK
KRAK
What the...?!!
GM
GM
GM
They're coming up from the ground all over...
KAGOOM
EEEEE!!!
GAMM
DOKRAK
GAMM
GAMM

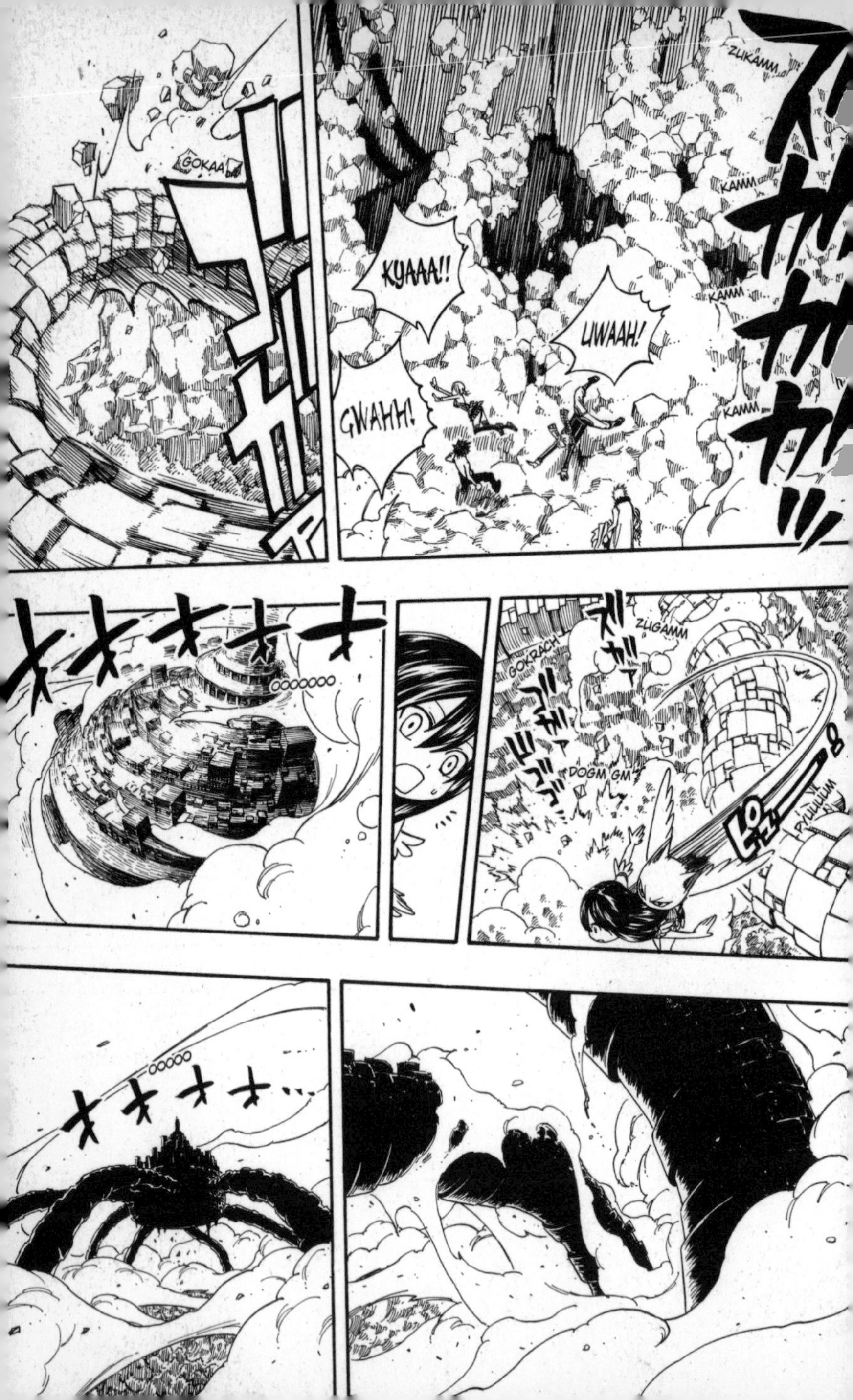
ZUKAMM
KAMM
KAMM
KAMM
UWAAH!
KYAAA!!
GWAHH!
GOKAA
ZUGAMM
GOKRACH
DOGM GM
PYUUUUM
OOOOOOO
OOOOO

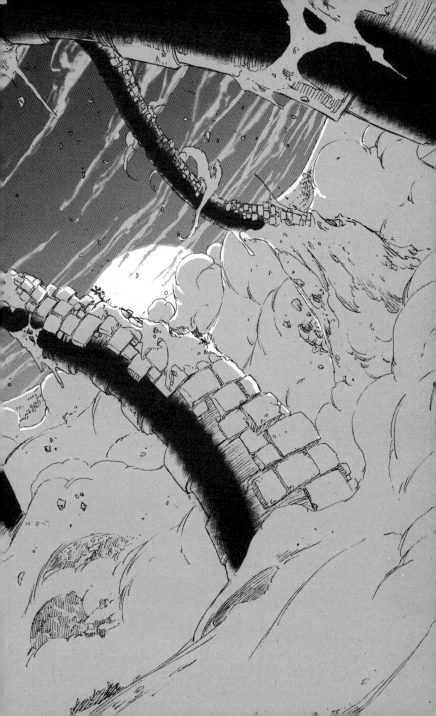

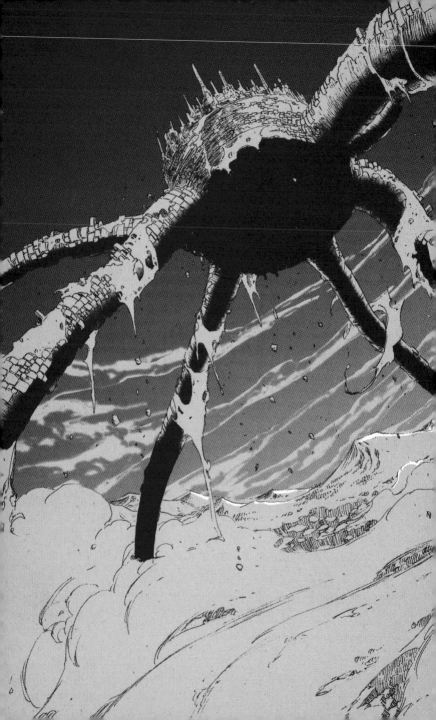

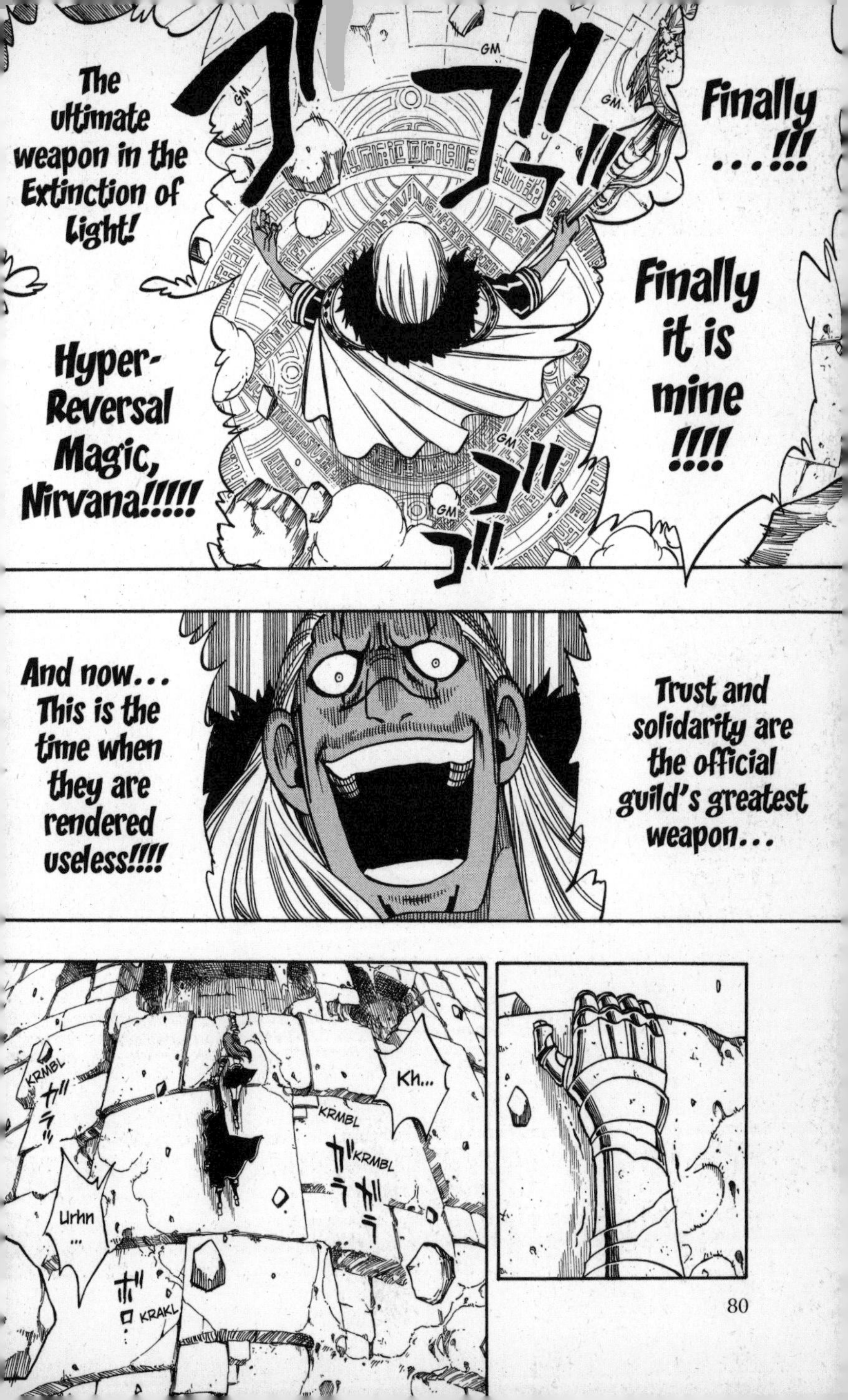
GM
GM
GM
Finally ...!!!
Finally it is mine!!!!
The ultimate weapon in the Extinction of Light!
Hyper-Reversal Magic, Nirvana!!!!!
GM
GM
Trust and solidarity are the official guild's greatest weapon...
And now... This is the time when they are rendered useless!!!!
Kh...
KRMBL
KRMBL
KRMBL
Urhn ...
KRAKL

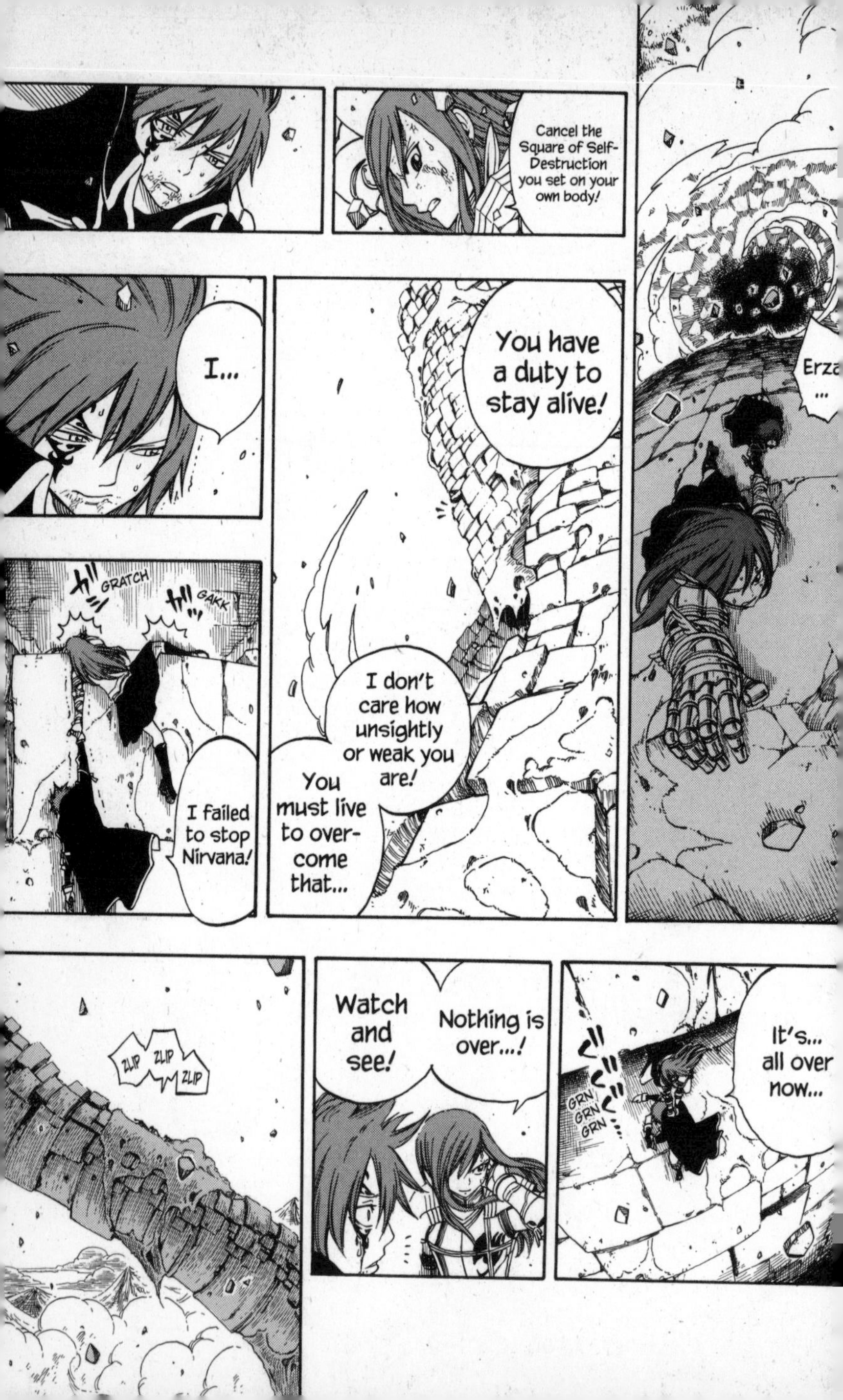
Erza
...
Cancel the Square of Self-Destruction you set on your own body!
You have a duty to stay alive!
I don't care how unsightly or weak you are!
You must live to overcome that...
I...
GRATCH
GAKK
I failed to stop Nirvana!
It's... all over now...
GRN GRN GRN
Nothing is over...!
Watch and see!
ZLIP ZLIP ZLIP

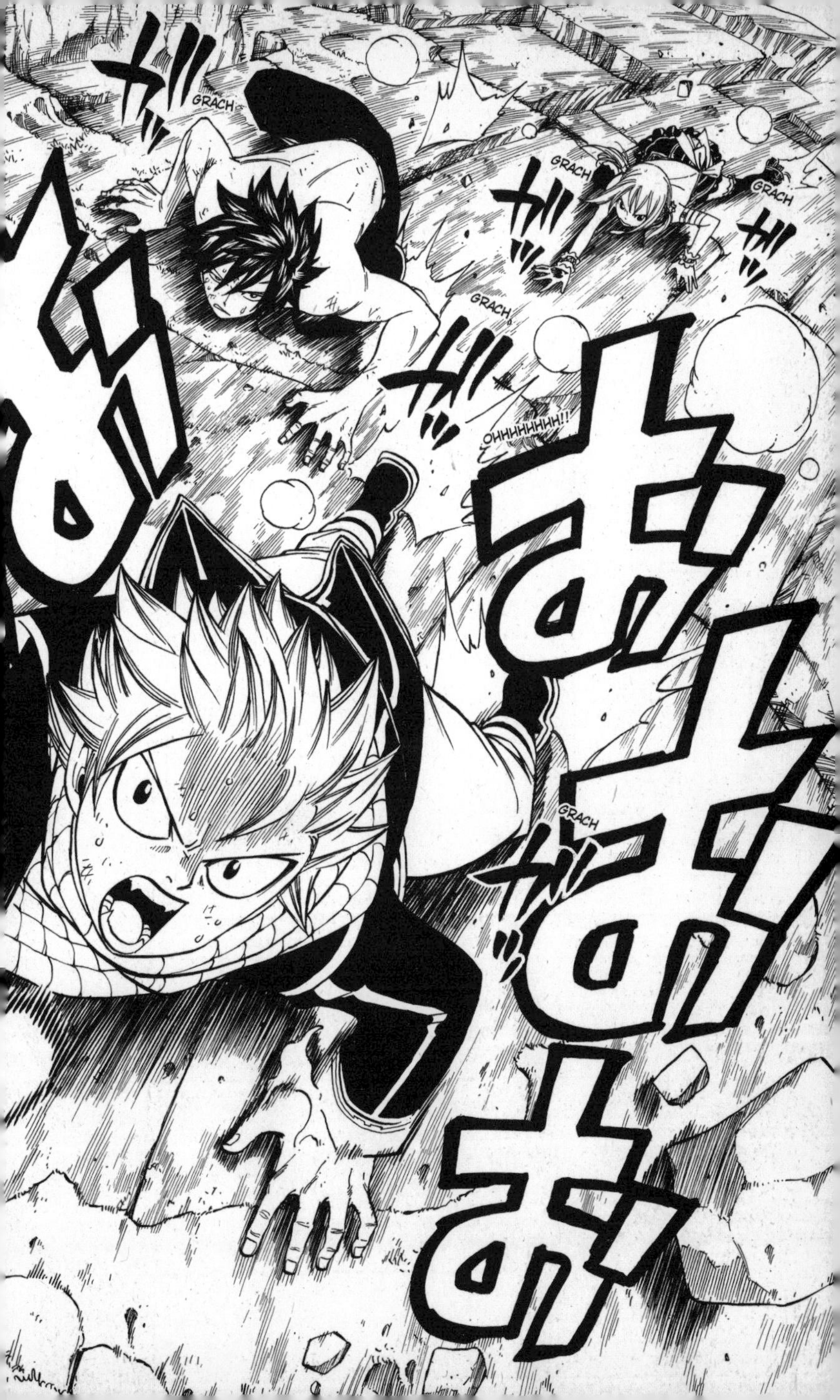

GRACH
GRACH
GRACH
GRACH
OHHHHHHHH!!
GRACH

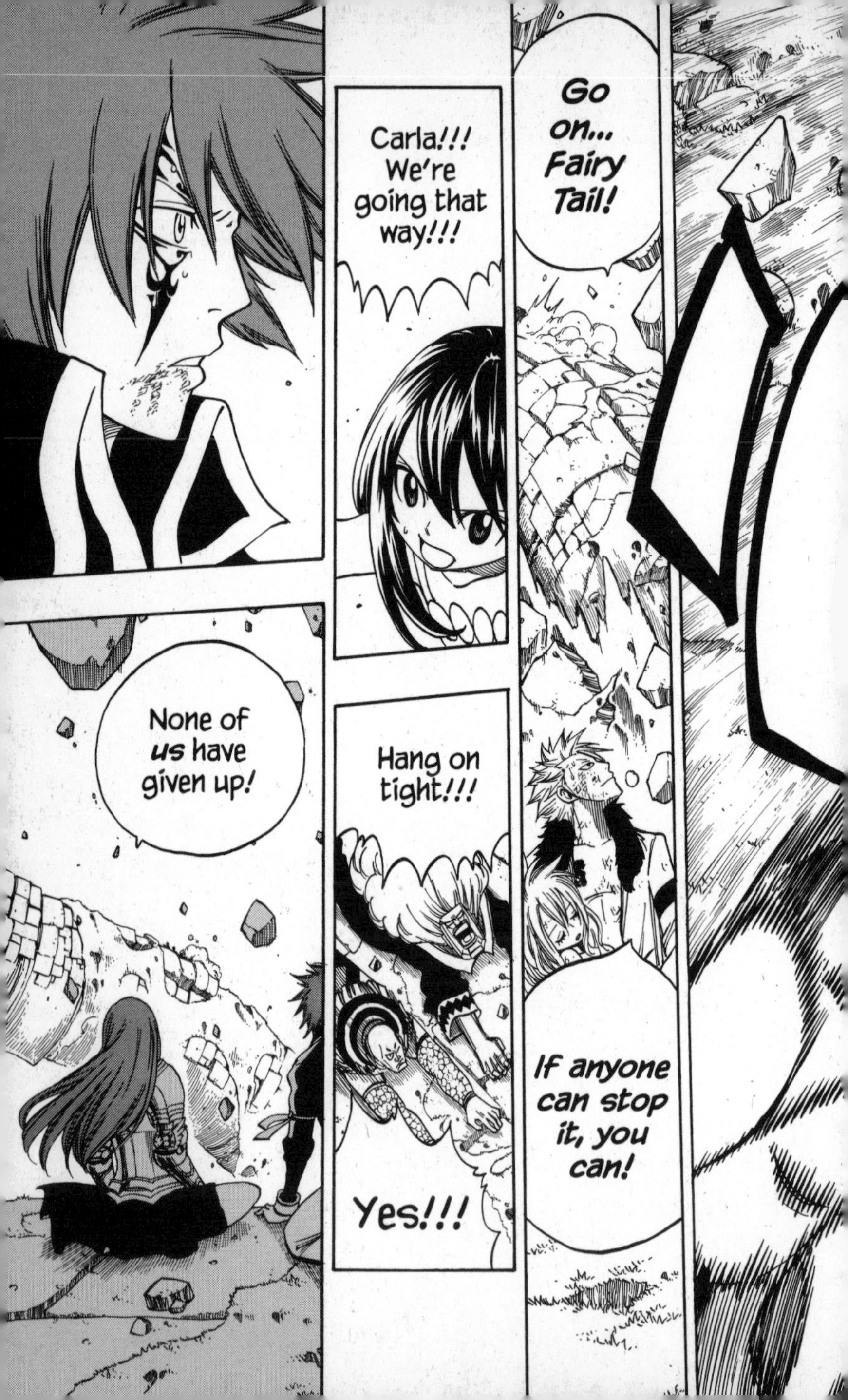
Go on... Fairy Tail!
If anyone can stop it, you can!
Carla!!! We're going that way!!!
Hang on tight!!!
Yes!!!
None of us have given up!

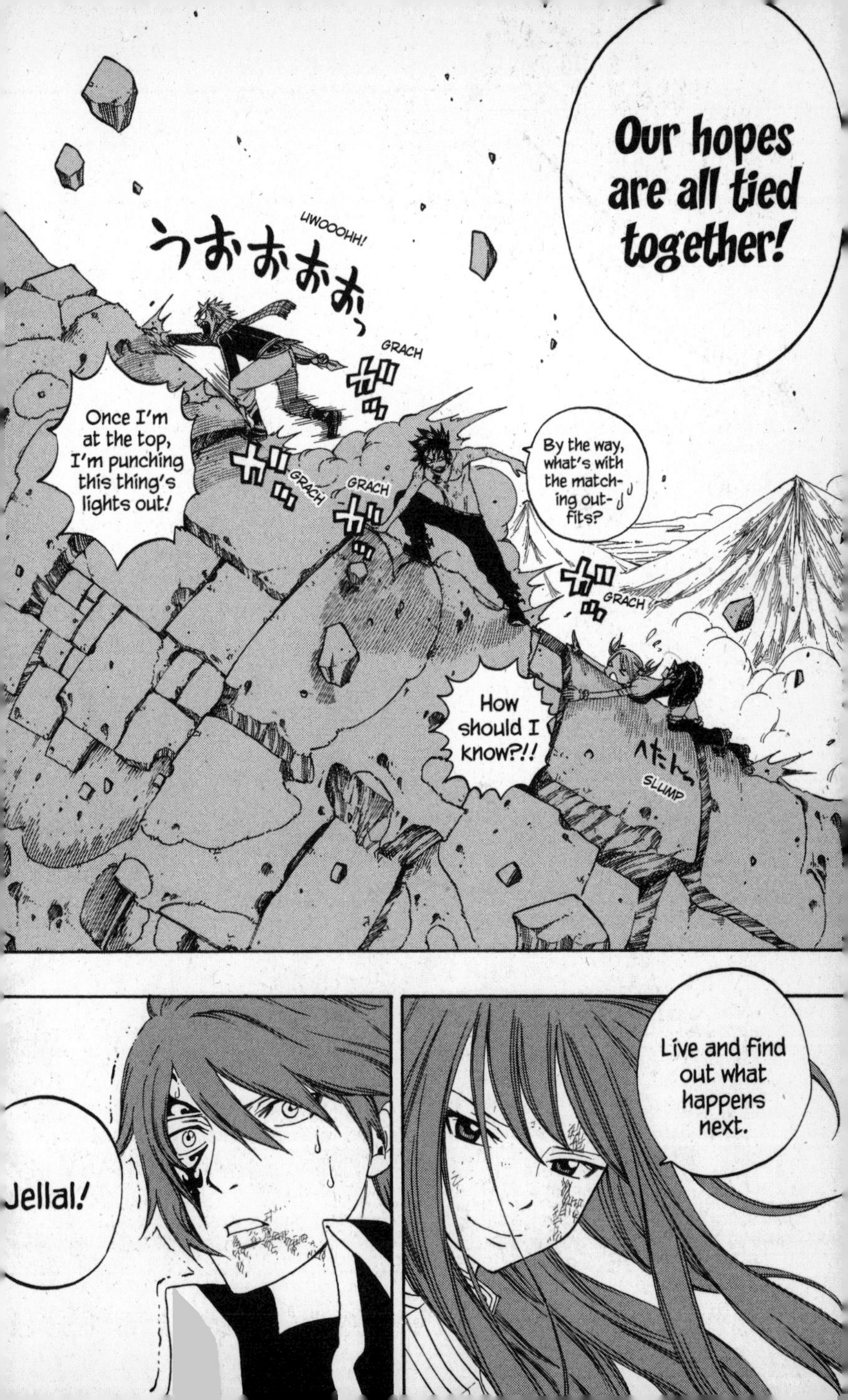
Our hopes are all tied together!
By the way, what's with the matching outfits?
GRACH
うおおおおっ
UWOOOHH!
GRACH
Once I'm at the top, I'm punching this thing's lights out!
GRACH
GRACH
How should I know?!!
へたん
SLUMP
Live and find out what happens next.
Jellal!

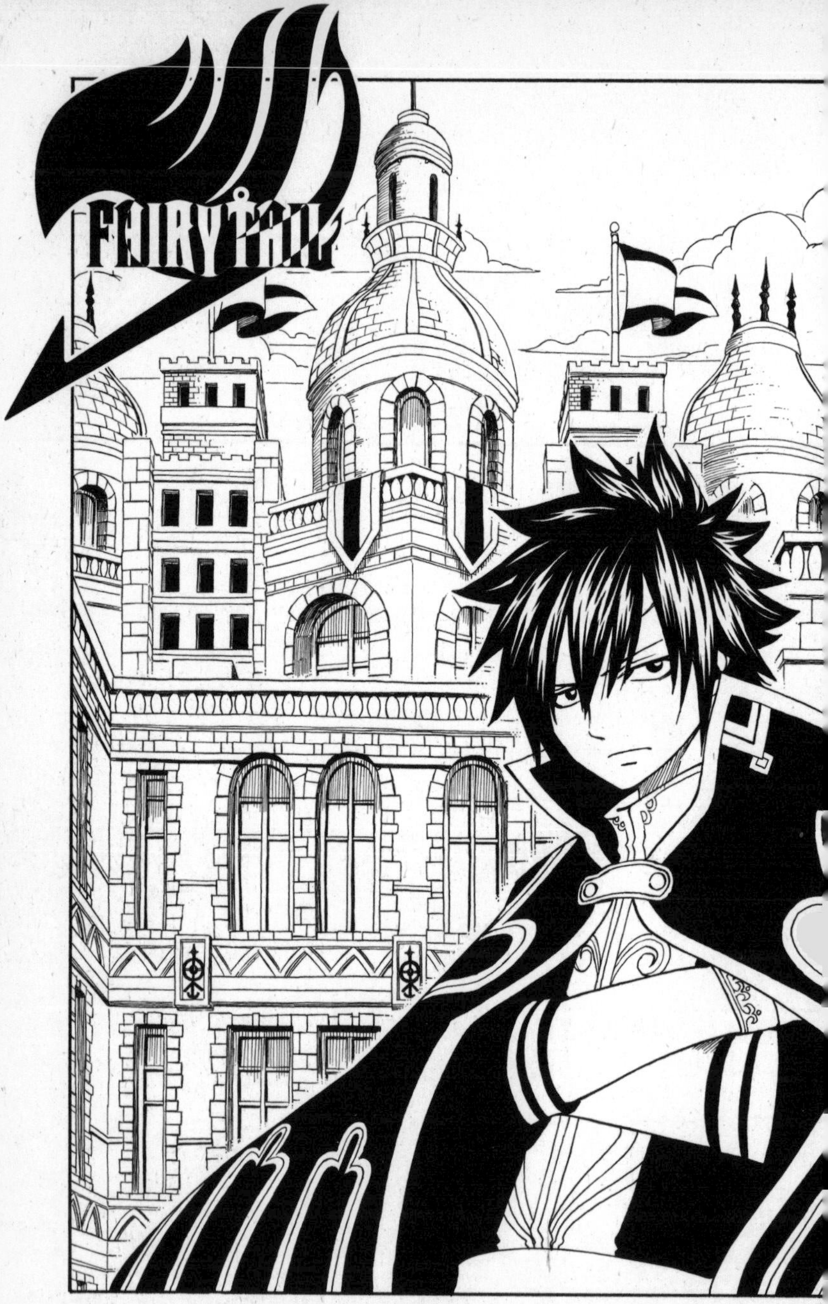
FAIRY TAIL

Chapter 148, March of Destruction

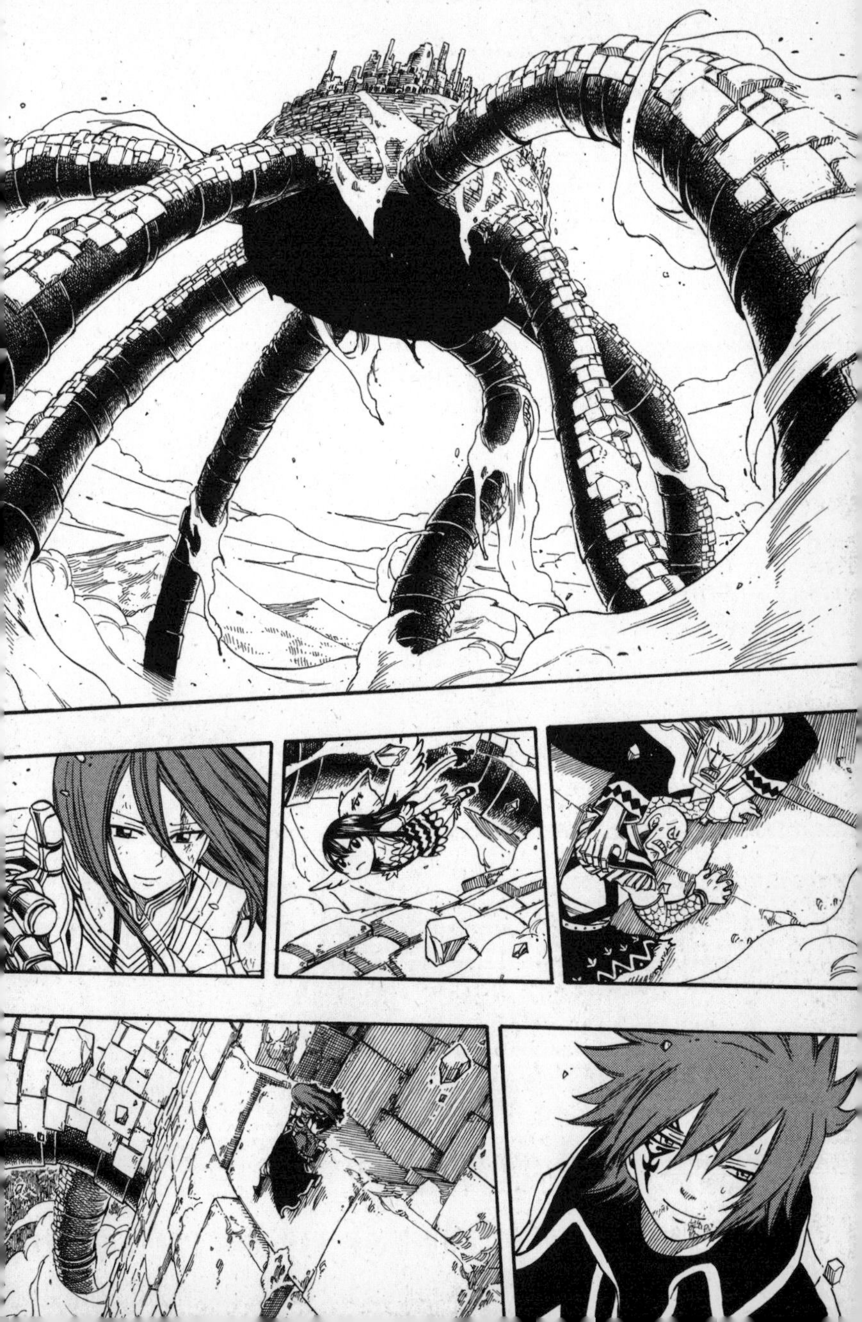

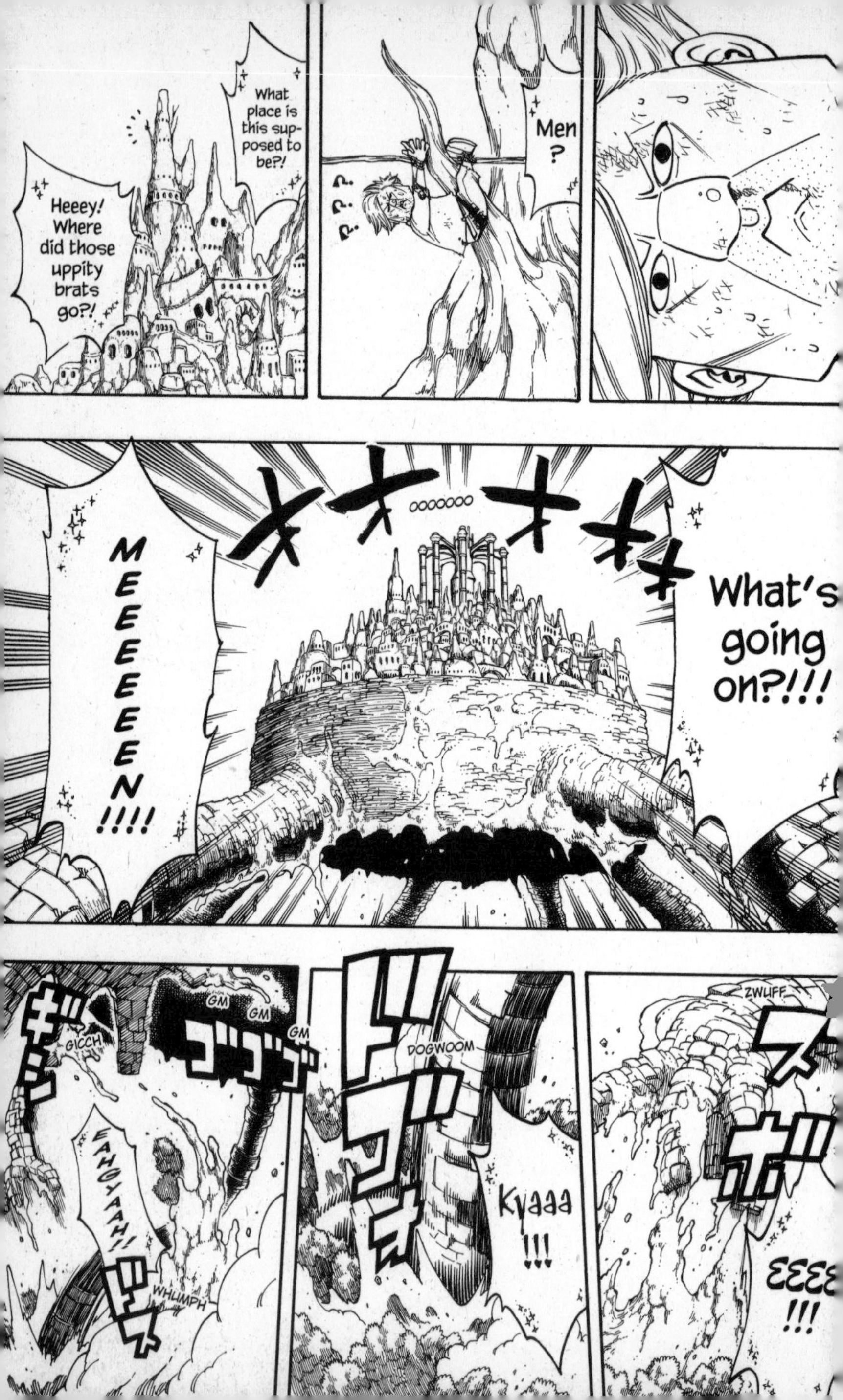
Men ?
What place is this sup-posed to be?!
Heeey! Where did those uppity brats go?!
What's going on?!!!
OOOOOOO
MEEEEEEEN !!!!
ZWUFF
EEEE !!!
DOGWOOM
Kyaaa !!!
GM
GM
GM
GICCH
EAHGYAAH!!
WHUMPH

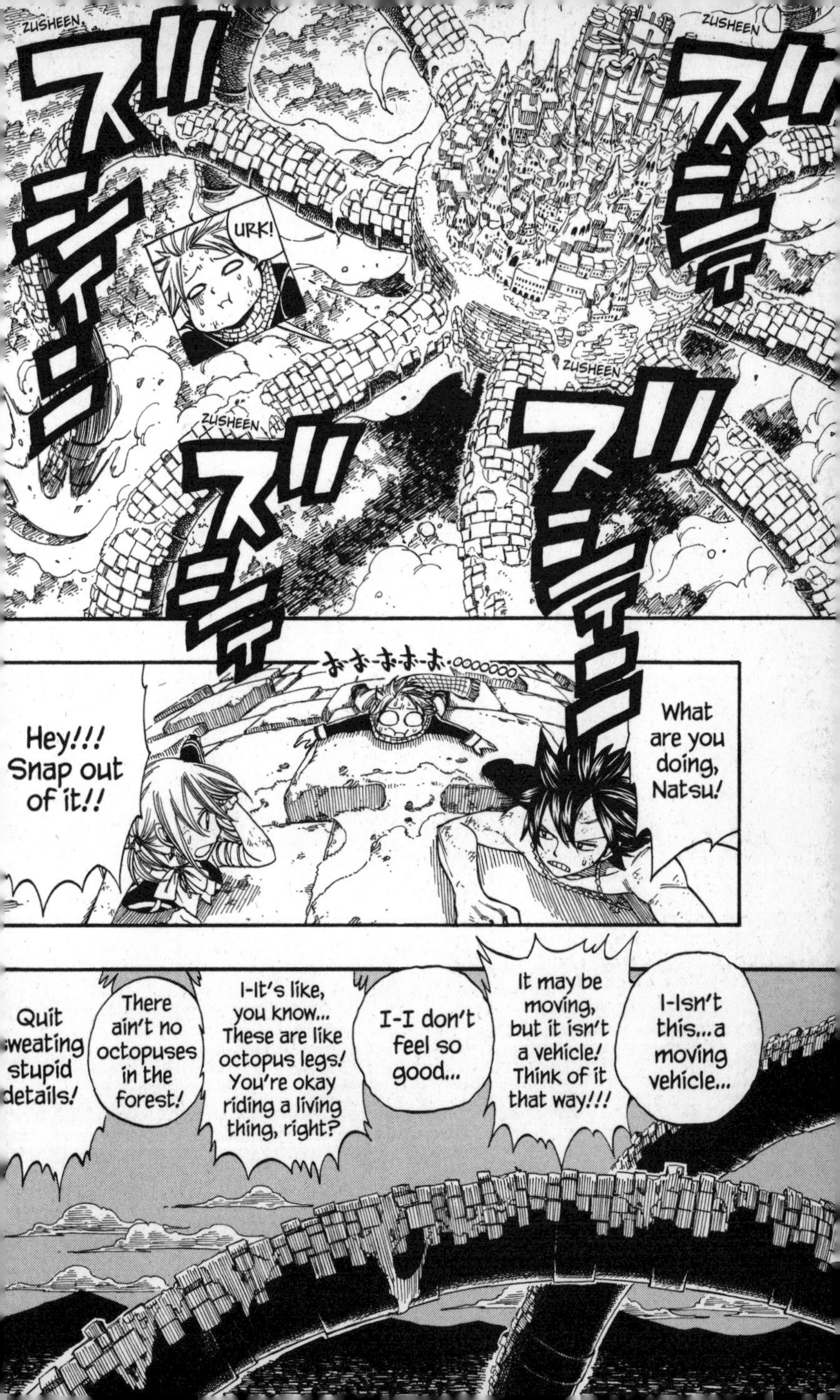
ZUSHEEN
ZUSHEEN
URK!
ZUSHEEN
ZUSHEEN
What are you doing, Natsu!
Hey!!! Snap out of it!!
I-Isn't this...a moving vehicle...
It may be moving, but it isn't a vehicle! Think of it that way!!!
I-I don't feel so good...
I-It's like, you know... These are like octopus legs! You're okay riding a living thing, right?
There ain't no octopuses in the forest!
Quit sweating stupid details!

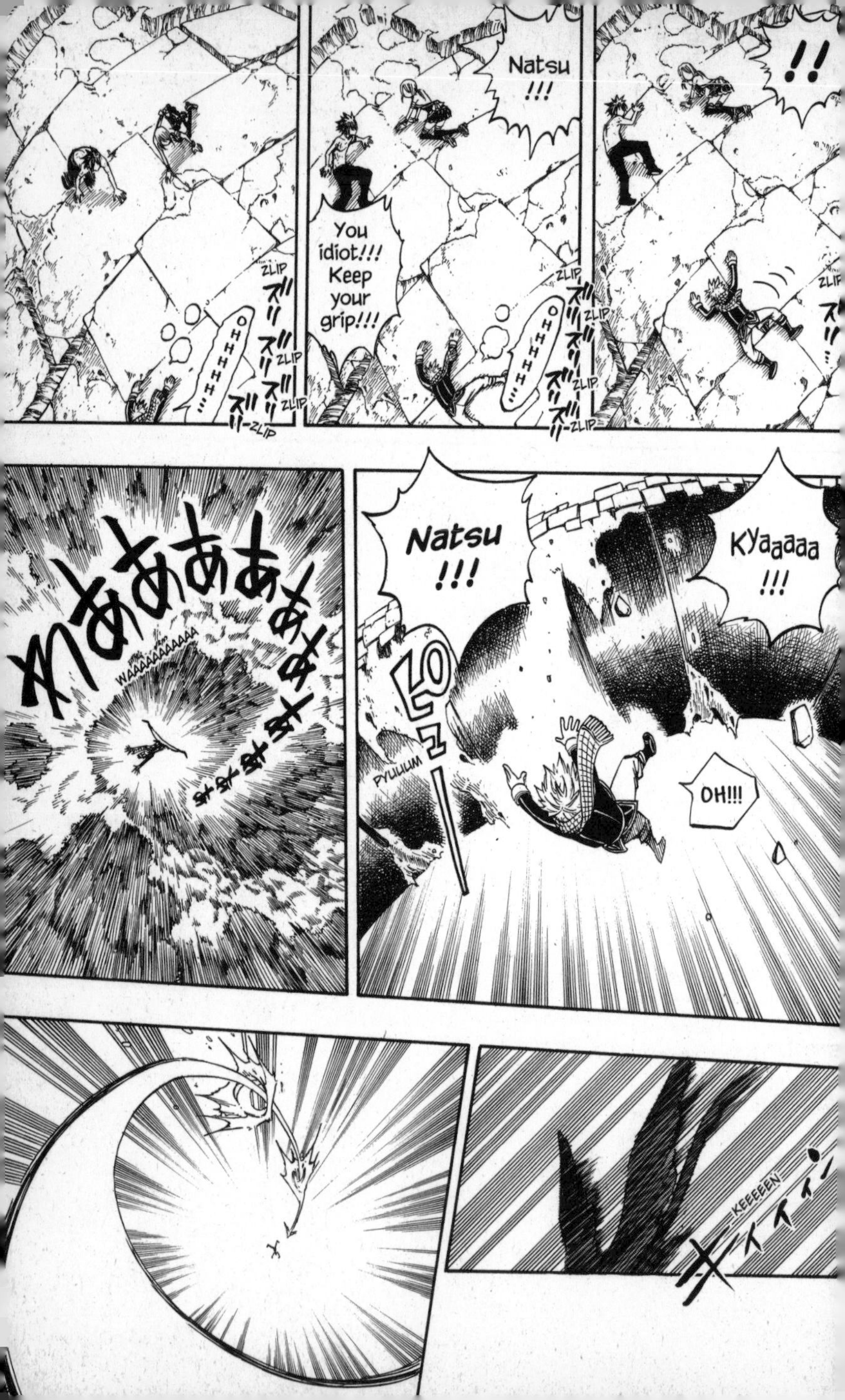

!!
ZLIP
Natsu !!!
You idiot!!! Keep your grip!!!
OHHHHHH...!!
ZLIP
ZLIP
OHHHHHH...!!
ZLIP
ZLIP
Kyaaaaa !!!
Natsu !!!
OH!!!
PYUUUM
WAAAAAAAAAAA
KEEEEEN

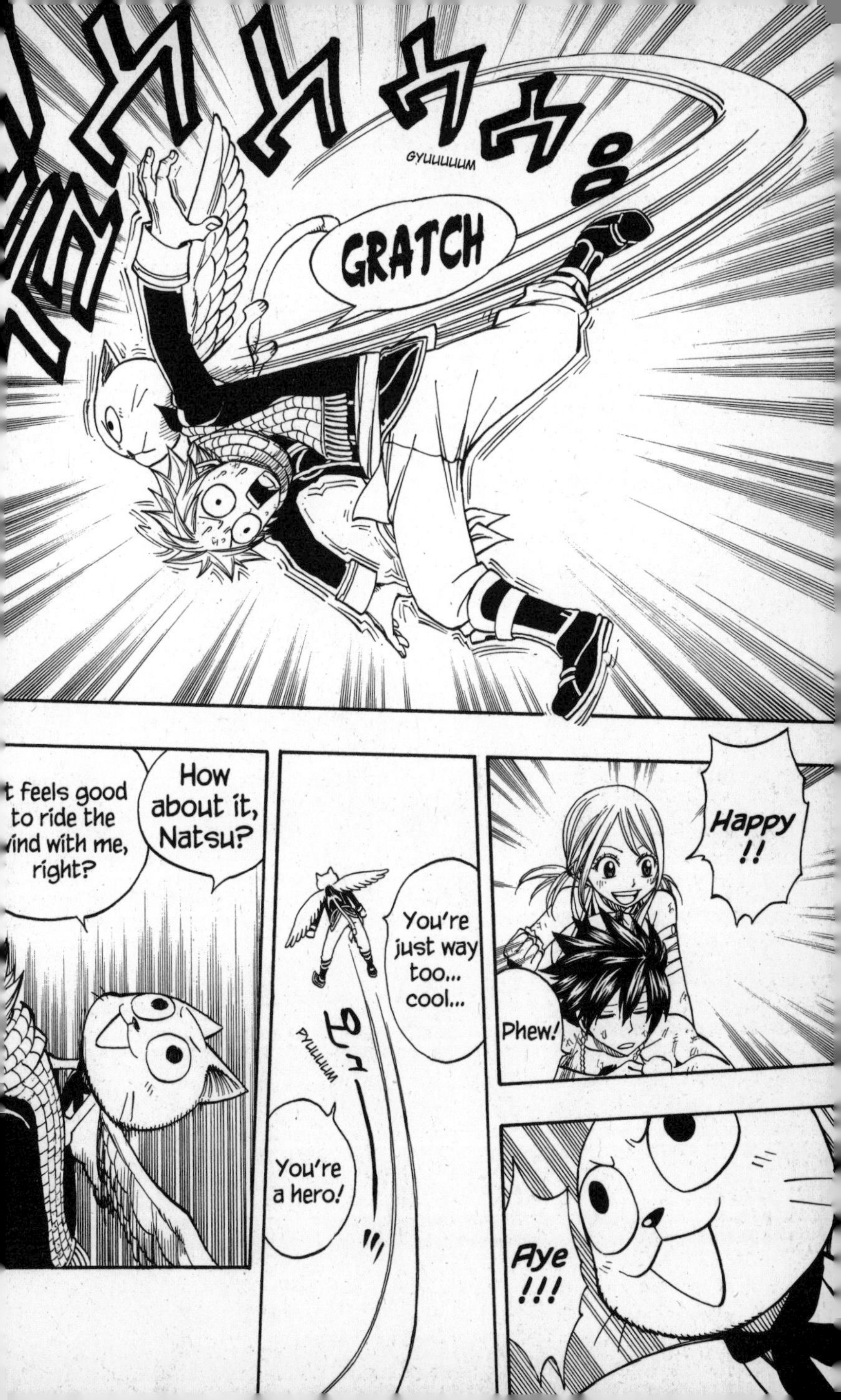
GYUUUUUUM
GRATCH
Happy!!
Phew!
Aye!!!
You're just way too... cool...
PYUUUUM
You're a hero!
How about it, Natsu?
t feels good to ride the wind with me, right?

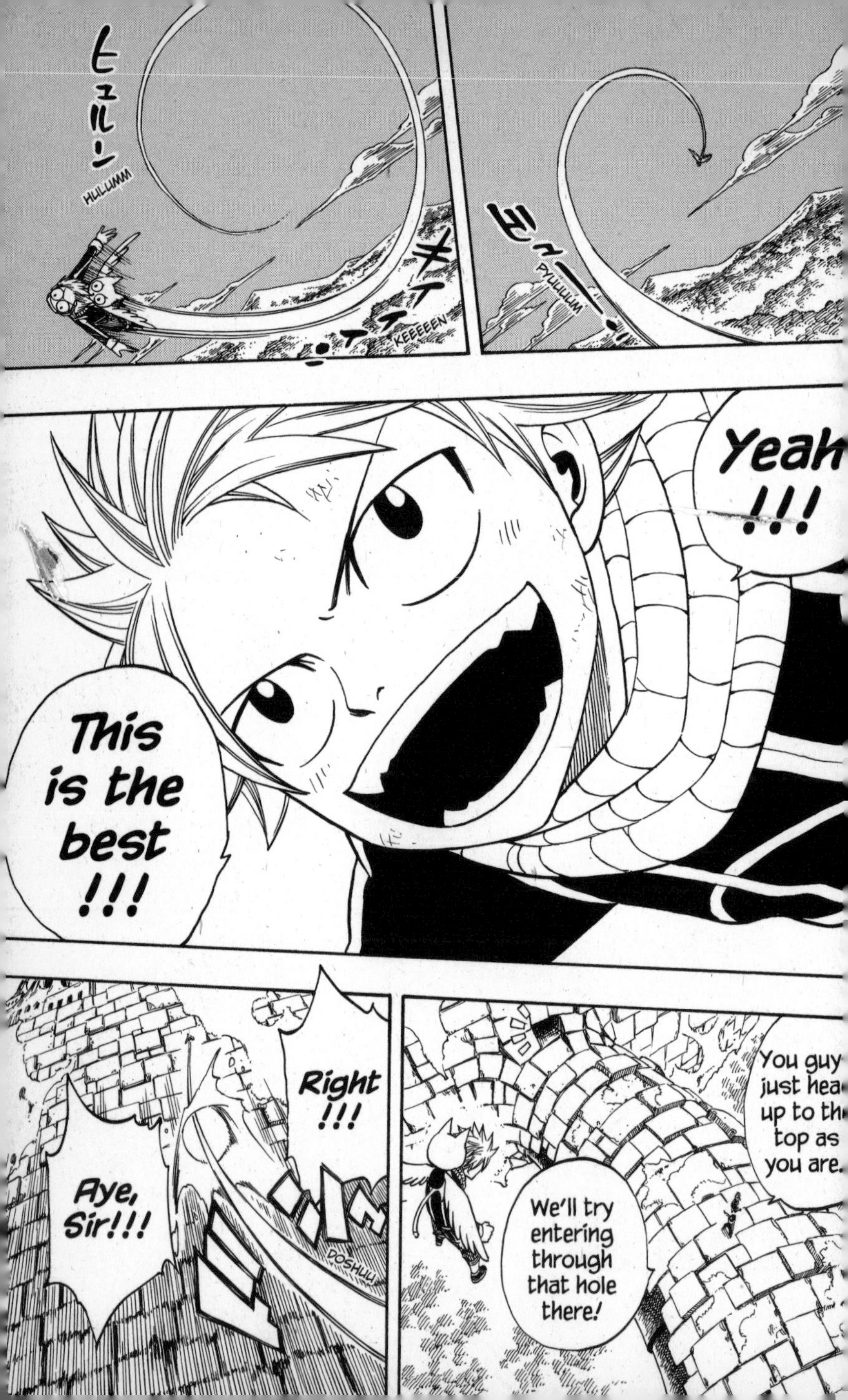
PYUUUUM
KEEEEEN
HULUMM
Yeah!!!
This is the best!!!
You guy just hea up to th top as you are.
We'll try entering through that hole there!
Right!!!
Aye, Sir!!!
DOSHUU

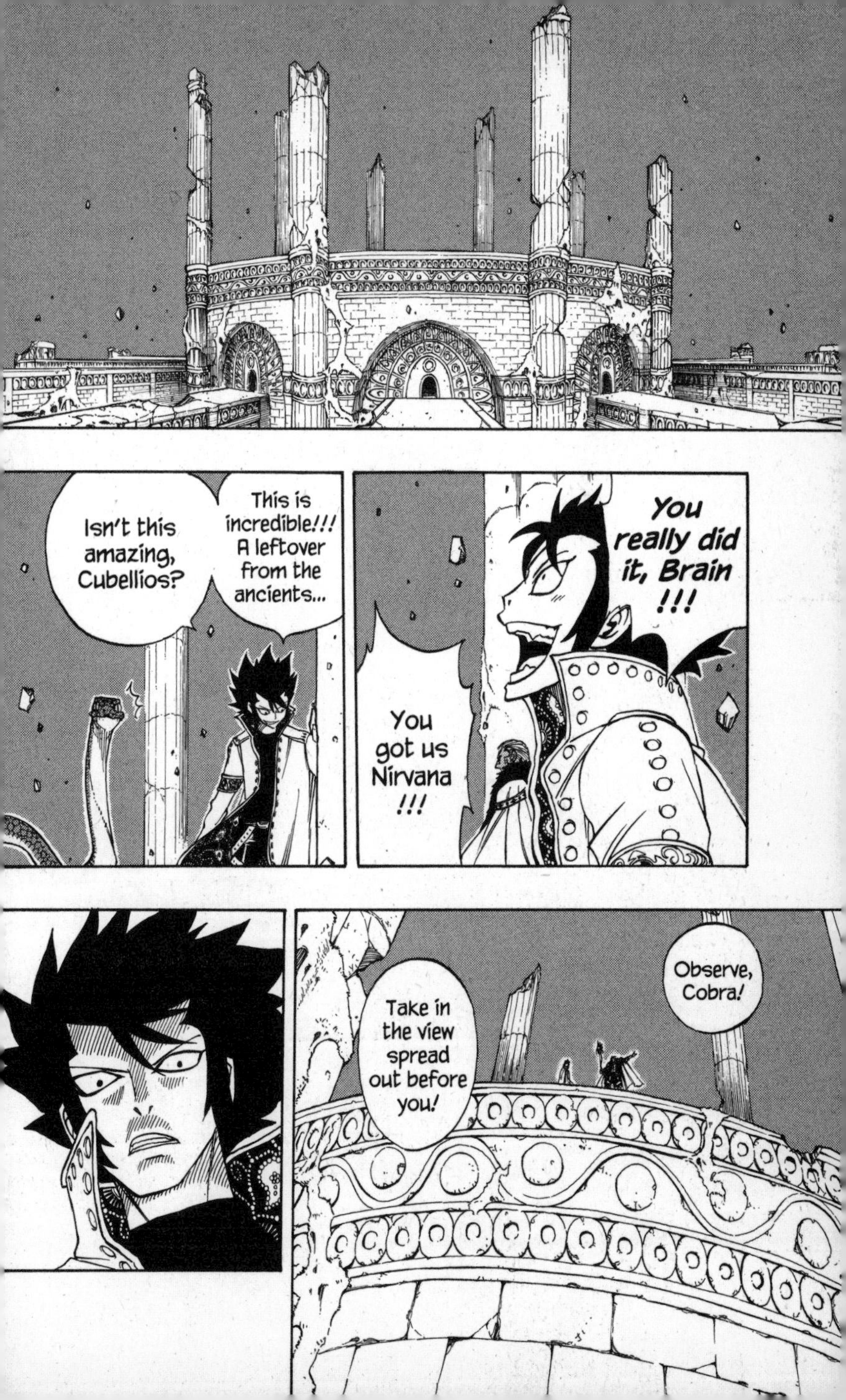
You really did it, Brain!!!
You got us Nirvana!!!
This is incredible!!! A leftover from the ancients...
Isn't this amazing, Cubellios?
Observe, Cobra!
Take in the view spread out before you!

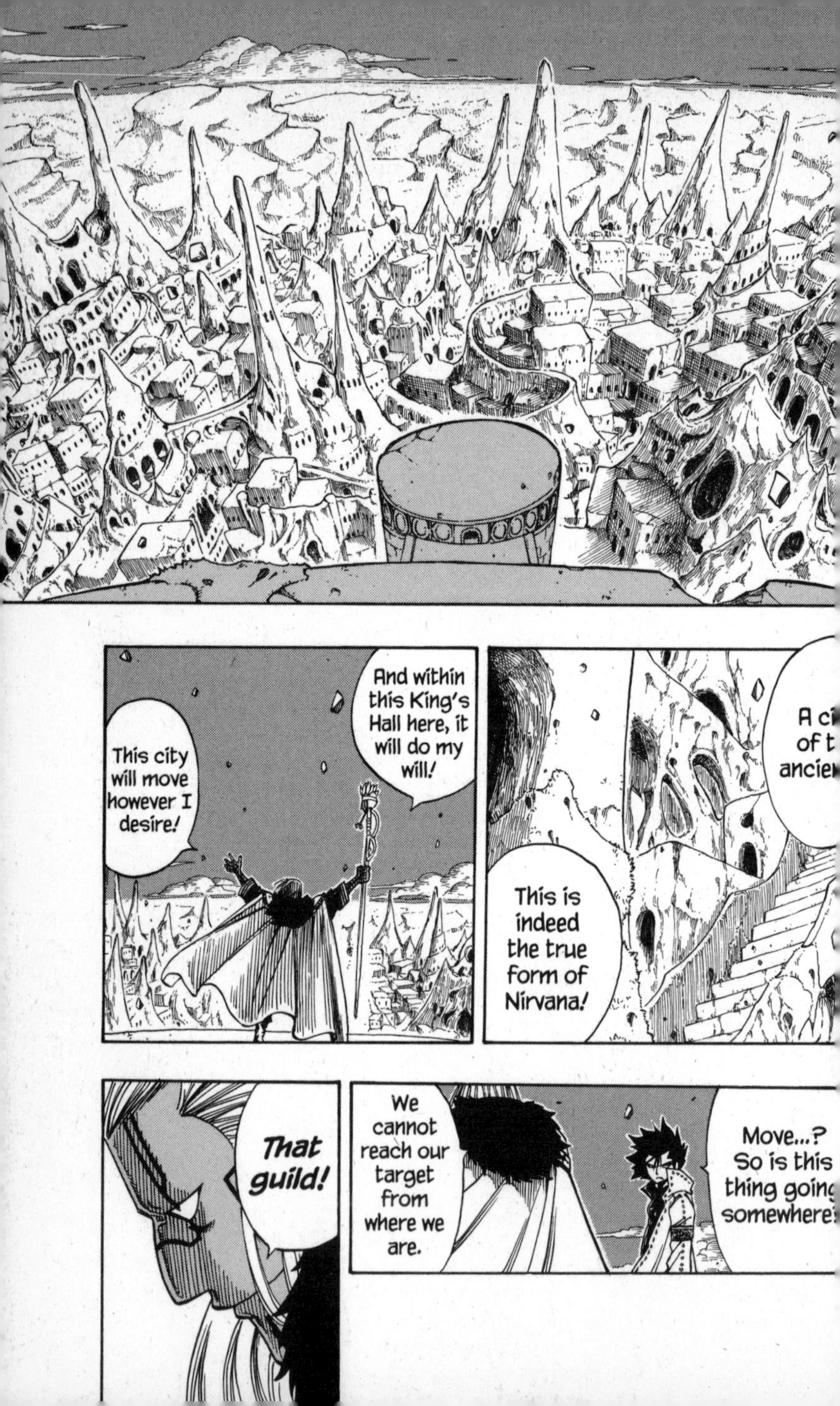
This is indeed the true form of Nirvana!
And within this King's Hall here, it will do my will!
This city will move however I desire!
Move...? So is this thing going somewhere
We cannot reach our target from where we are.
That guild!

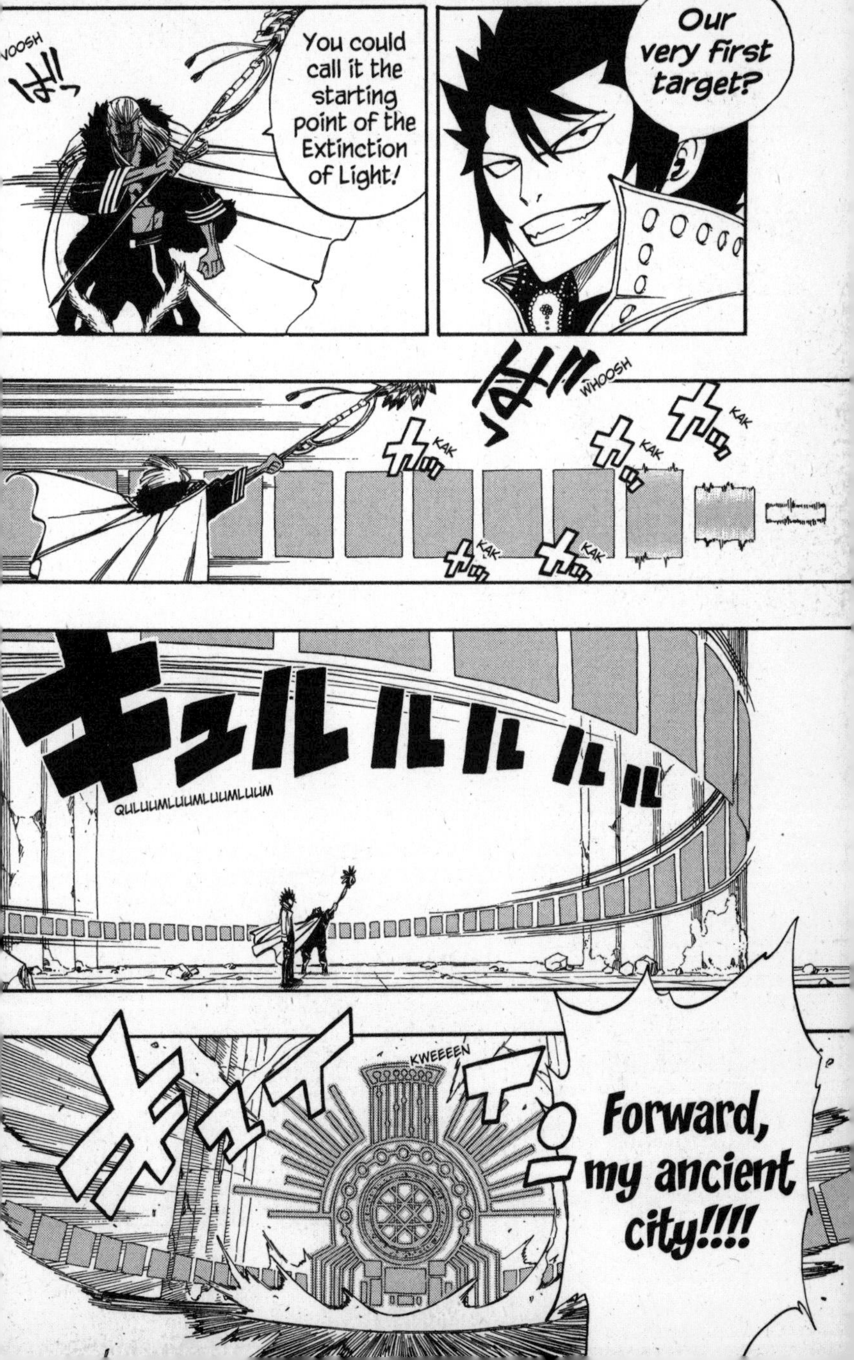
Our very first target?
You could call it the starting point of the Extinction of Light!
VOOSH
WHOOSH
KAK
KAK
KAK
KAK
KAK
QULUUMLUUMLUUMLUUM
KWEEEEN
Forward, my ancient city!!!!

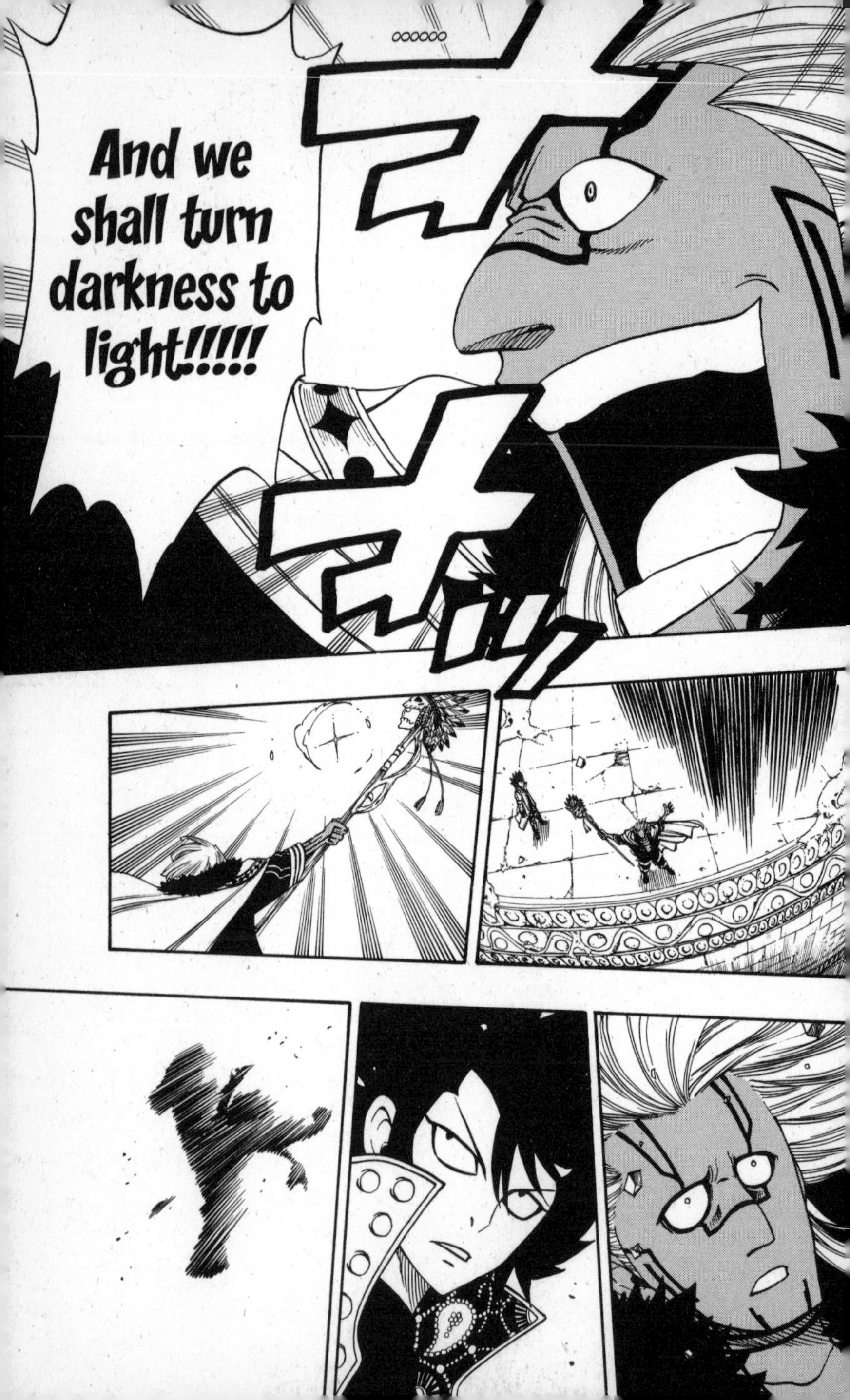
And we shall turn darkness to light!!!!!

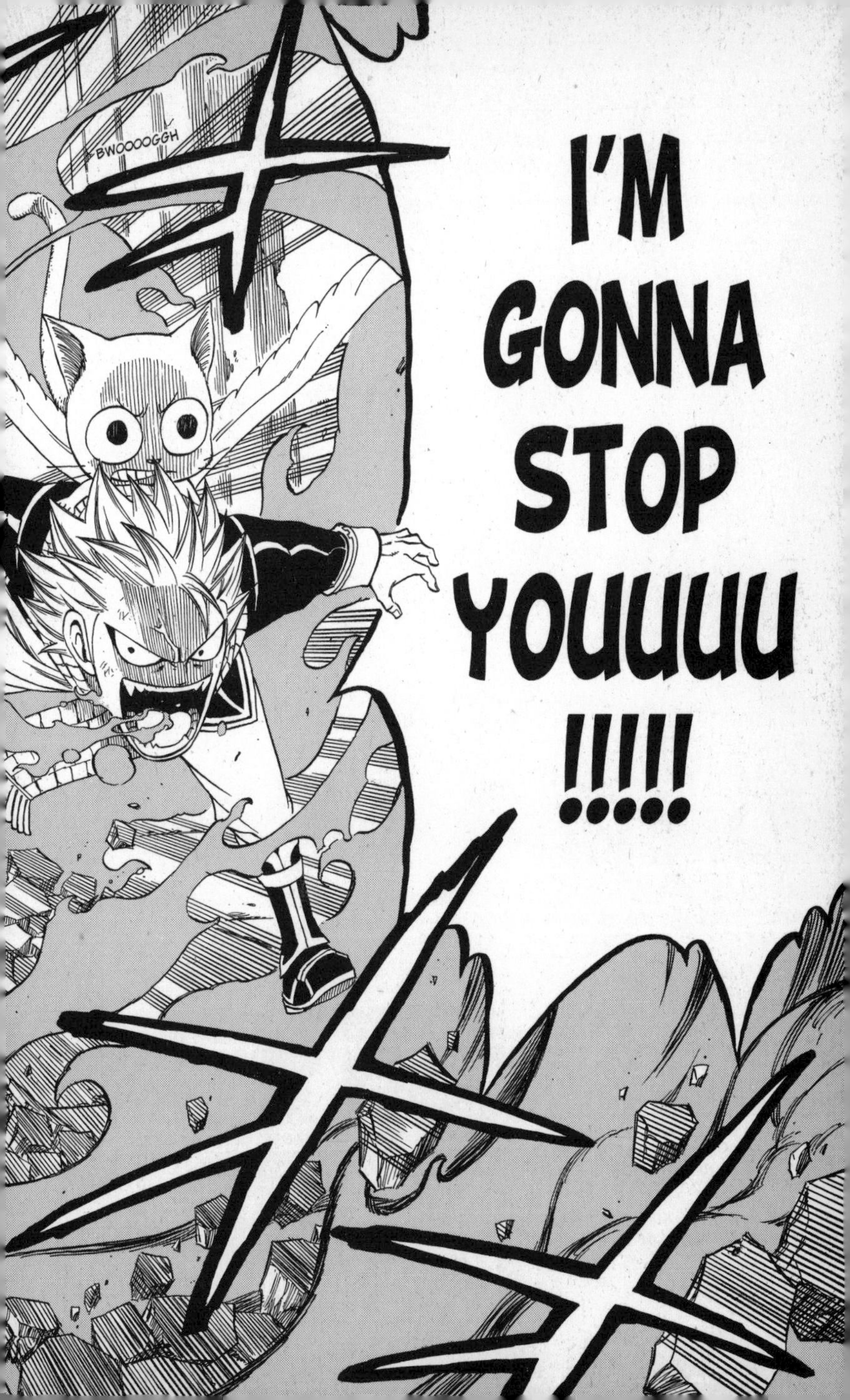
BWOOOOGGH
I'M GONNA STOP YOUUUU !!!!!

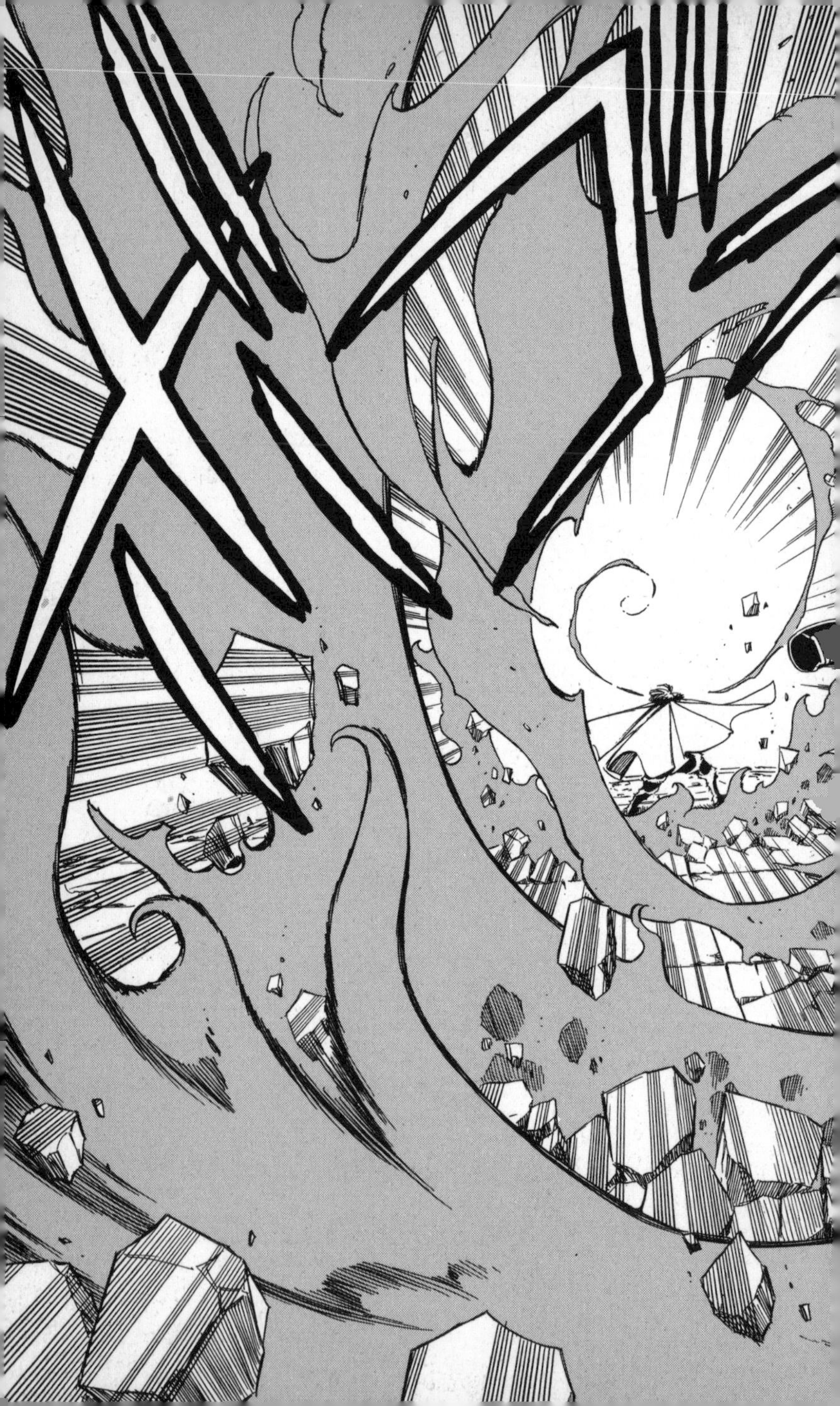

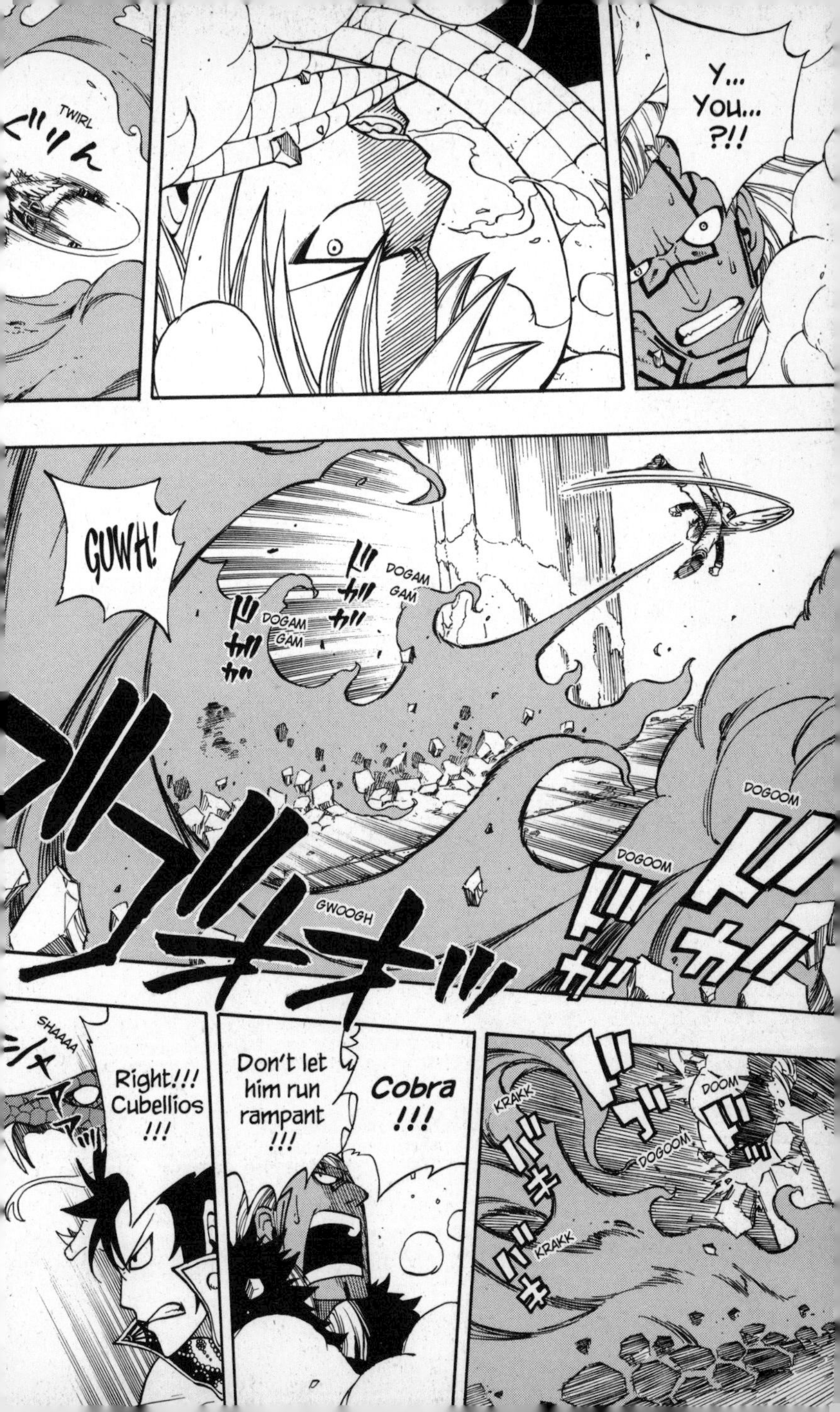

Y... YOU... ?!!
TWIRL
DOGAM GAM
GUWH!
DOGAM GAM
DOGOOM
DOGOOM
GWOOGH
DOOM
KRAKK
DOGOOM
KRAKK
Cobra!!!
Don't let him run rampant!!!
SHAAAA
Right!!! Cubellios!!!

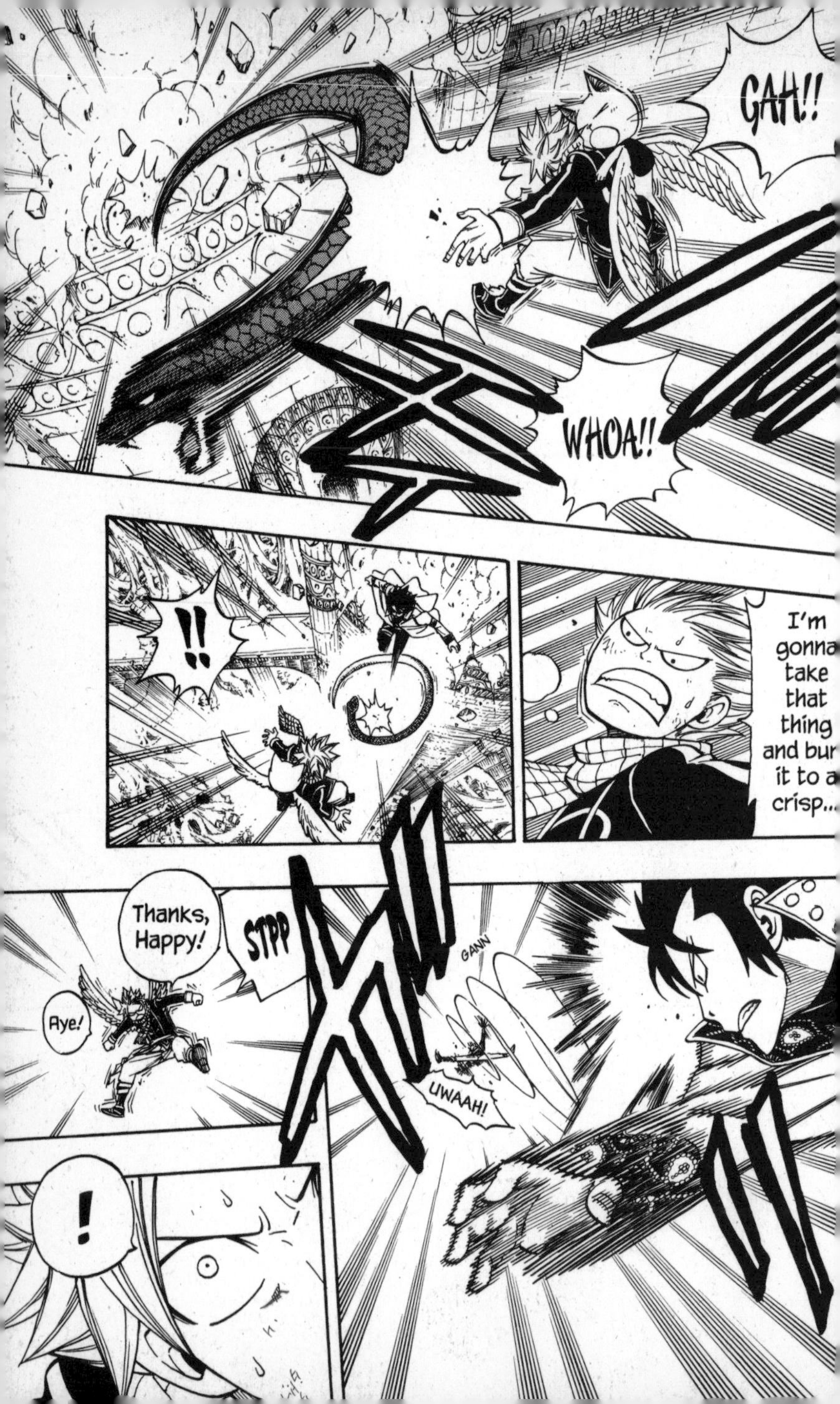
GAH!!
WHOA!!
I'm gonna take that thing and bur it to a crisp...
!!
GANN
UWAAH!
STPP
Thanks, Happy!
Aye!
!

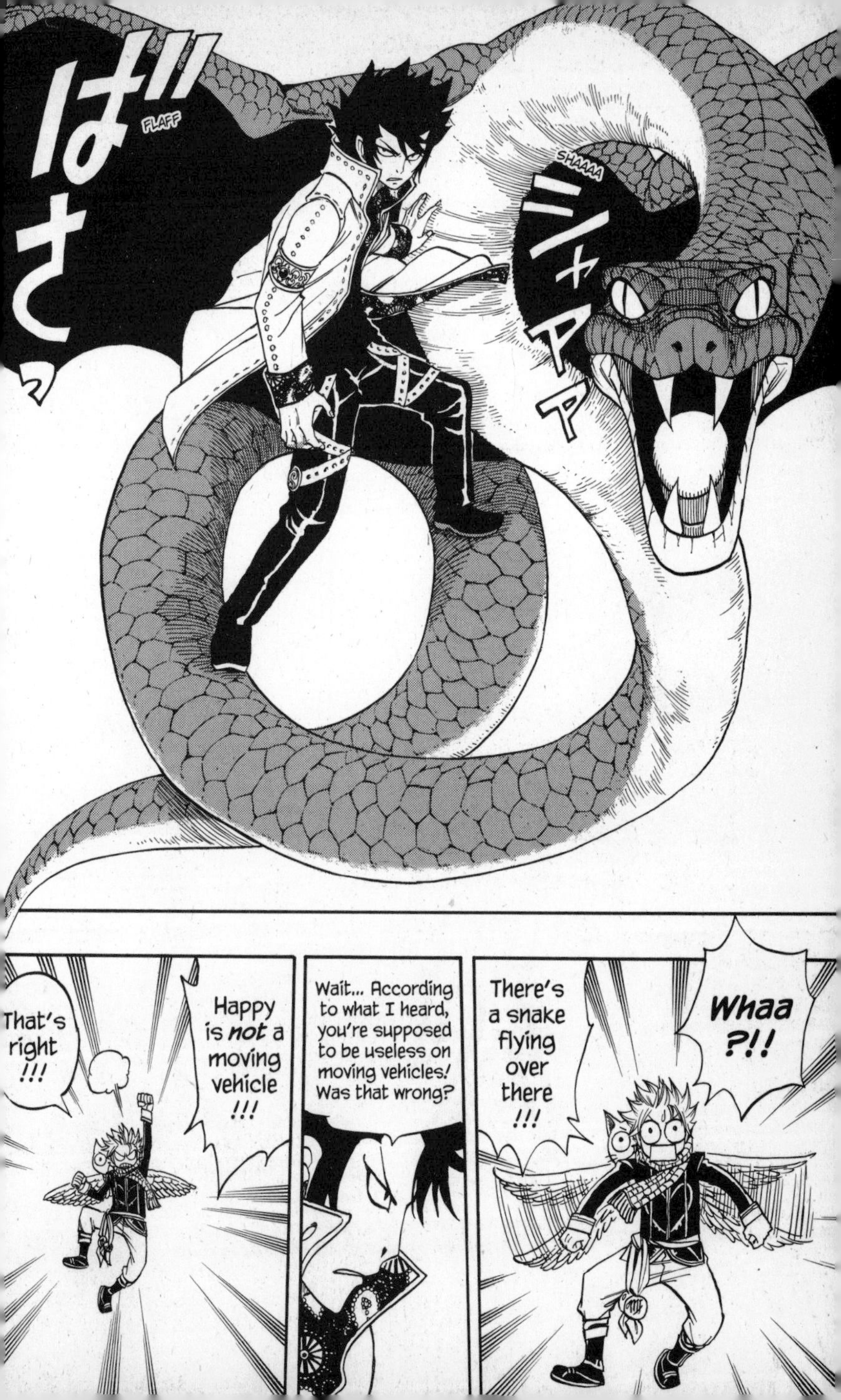

シャアア
SHAAAA
ばさっ
FLAFF
Whaa ?!!
There's a snake flying over there !!!
Wait... According to what I heard, you're supposed to be useless on moving vehicles! Was that wrong?
Happy is ***not*** a moving vehicle !!!
That's right !!!

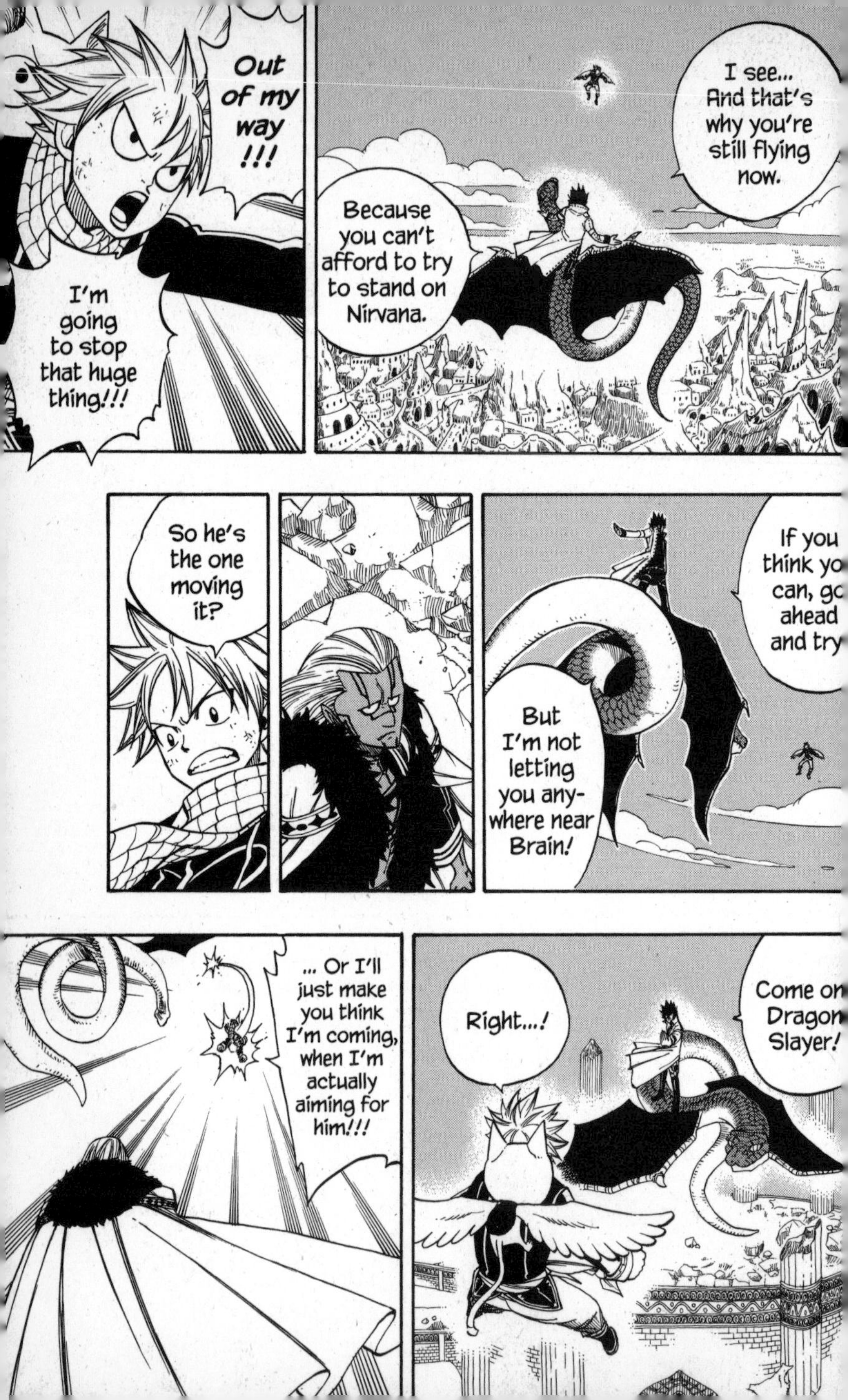
I see... And that's why you're still flying now.
Because you can't afford to try to stand on Nirvana.
Out of my way!!!
I'm going to stop that huge thing!!!
If you think yo can, go ahead and try
But I'm not letting you any-where near Brain!
So he's the one moving it?
Come on Dragon Slayer!
Right...!
... Or I'll just make you think I'm coming, when I'm actually aiming for him!!!

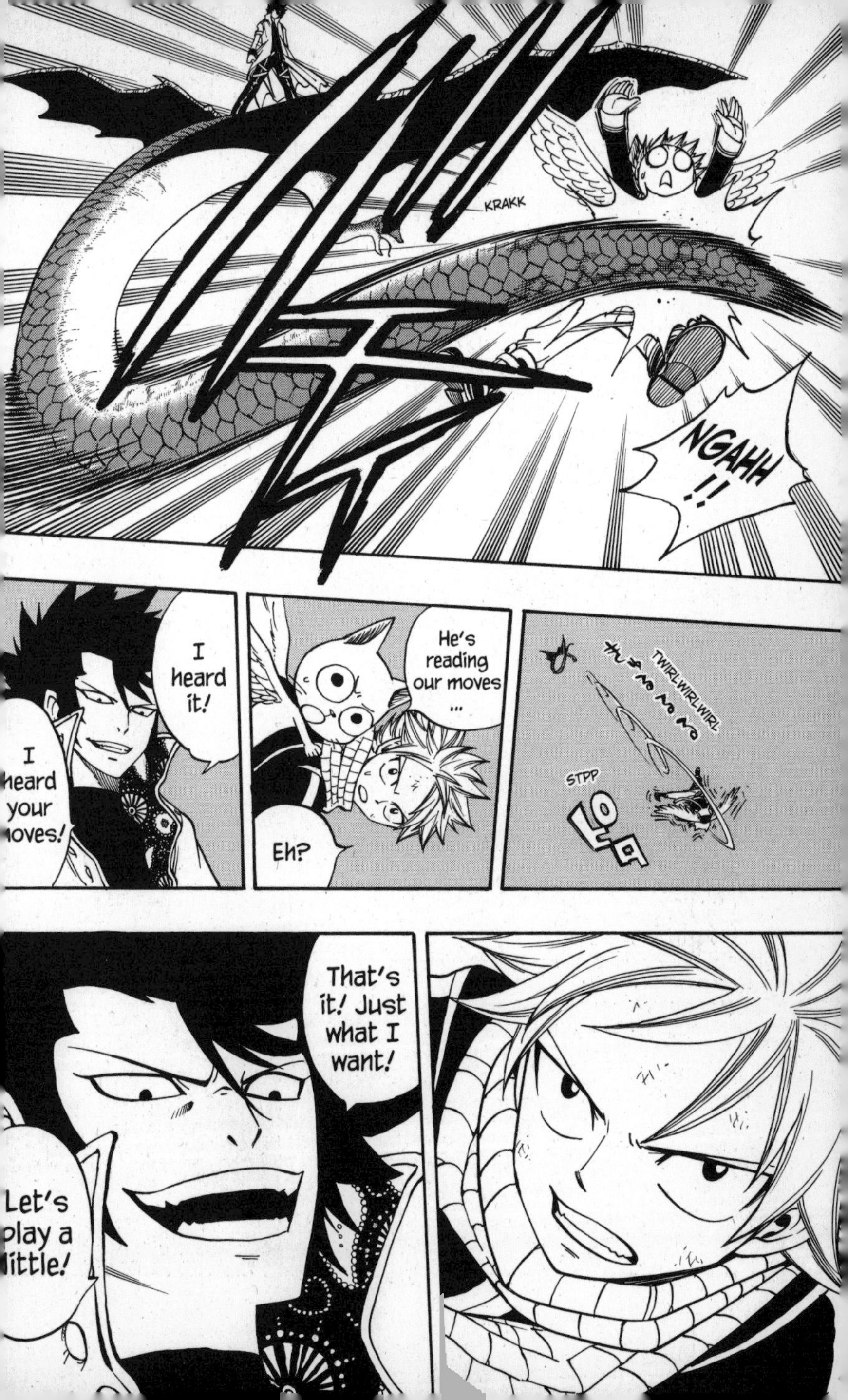
KRAKK
NGAHH!!
TWIRLWIRLWIRL
STPP
He's reading our moves ...
Eh?
I heard it!
I heard your moves!
That's it! Just what I want!
Let's play a little!

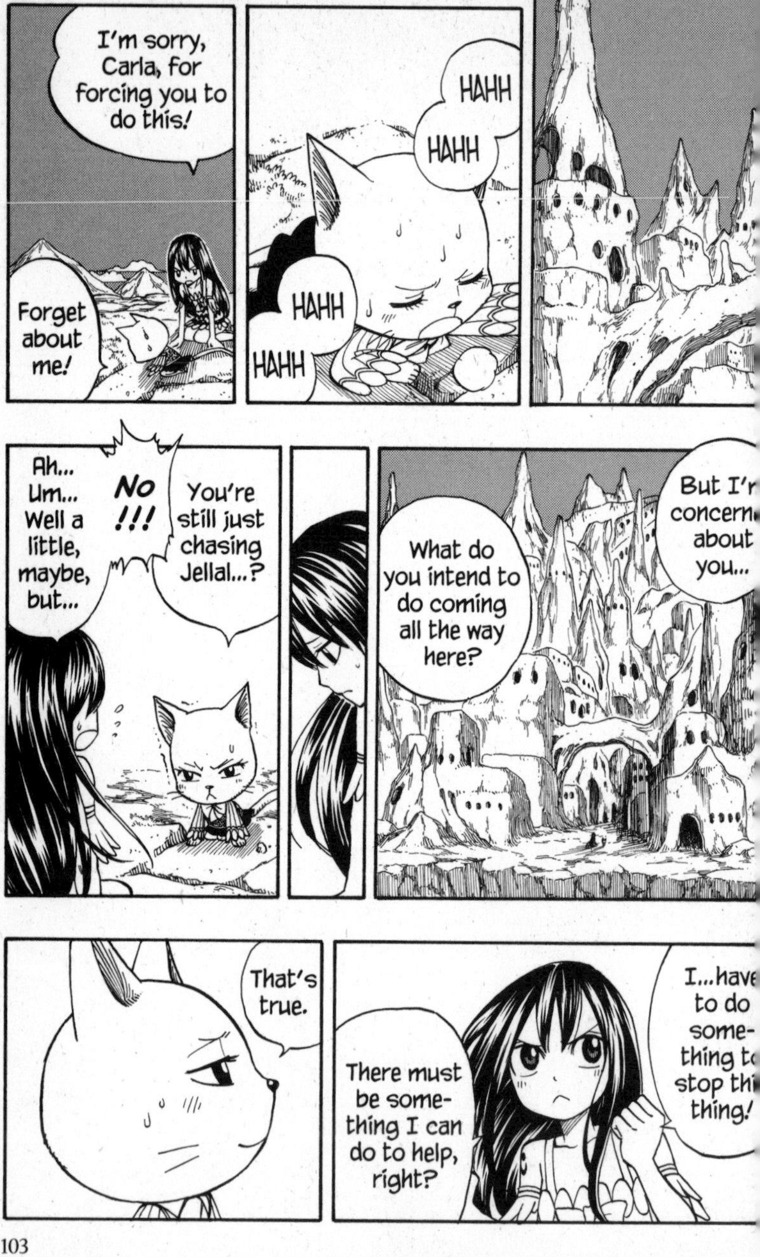
HAHH
HAHH
HAHH
HAHH
I'm sorry, Carla, for forcing you to do this!
Forget about me!
But I'r concern about you...
What do you intend to do coming all the way here?
You're still just chasing Jellal...?
No !!!
Ah... Um... Well a little, maybe, but...
I...have to do some- thing t stop thi thing!
There must be some- thing I can do to help, right?
That's true.

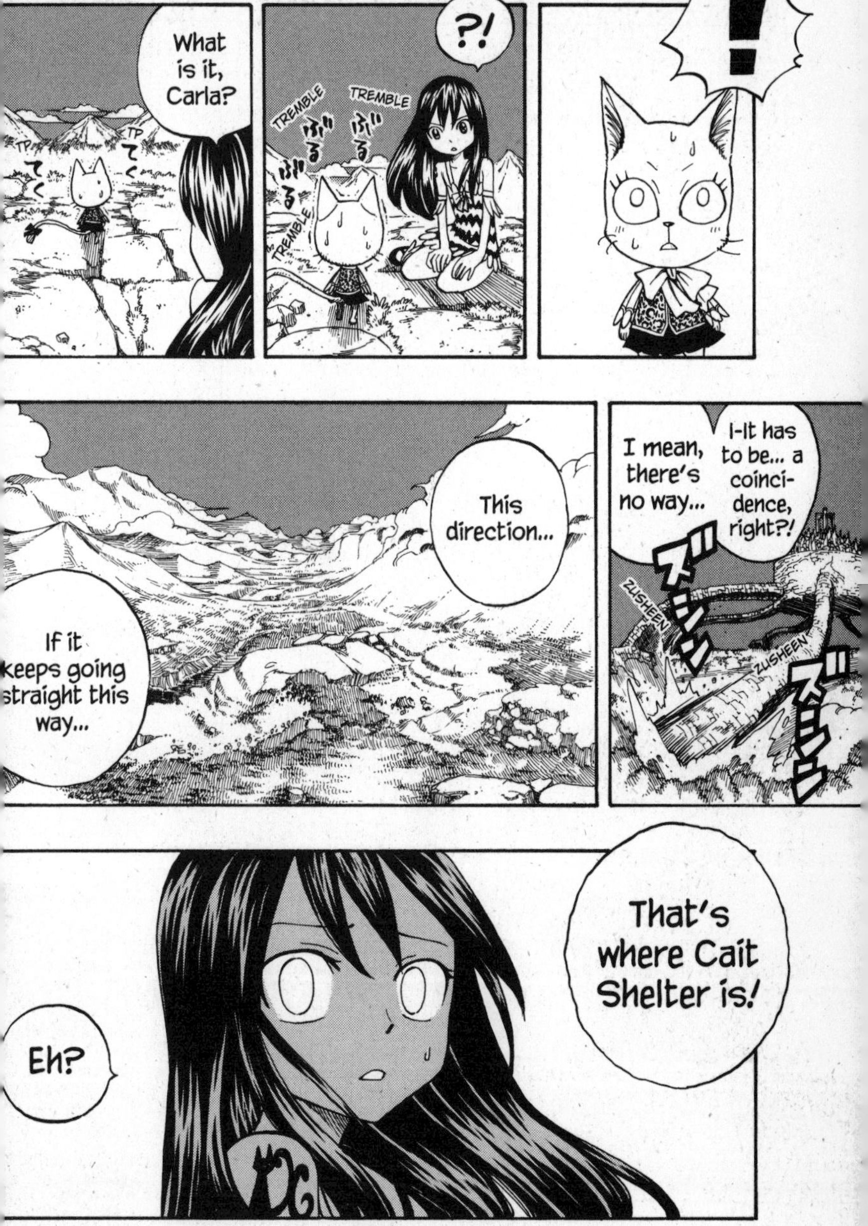
!
?!
TREMBLE
ぶる
TREMBLE
ぶる
TREMBLE
ぶる
What is it, Carla?
TP
てく
TP
てく
I-It has to be... a coincidence, right?!
I mean, there's no way...
ZUSHEEN
ズシン
ZUSHEEN
ズシン
This direction...
If it keeps going straight this way...
That's where Cait Shelter is!
Eh?

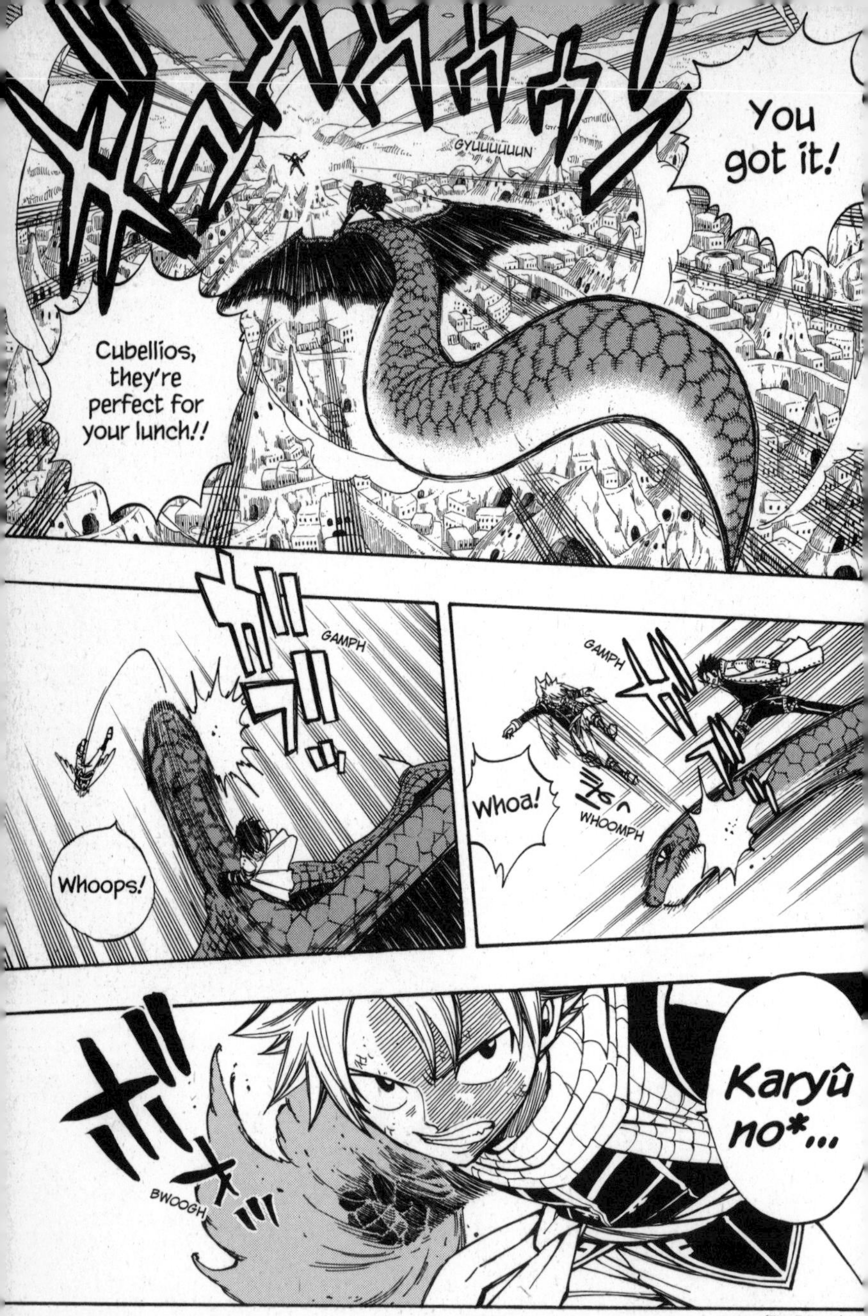
You got it!
GYUUUUUUN
Cubellios, they're perfect for your lunch!!
GAMPH
Whoa!
WHOOMPH
GAMPH
Whoops!
Karyû no*...
BWOOGH

*Fire Dragon's...

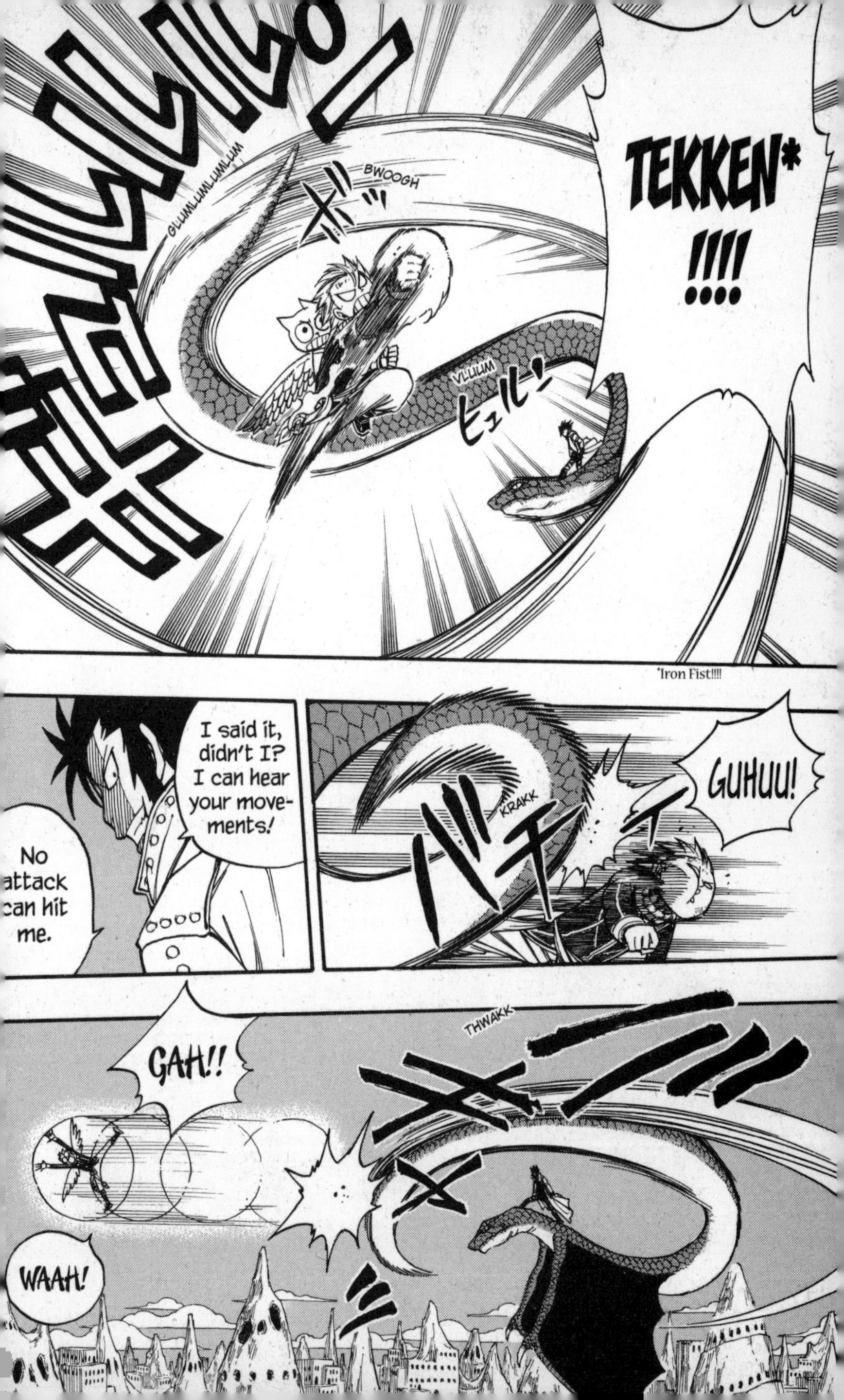
TEKKEN*!!!!
BWOOGH
GLUMLUMLUMLUM
VLUUM
GUHUU!
KRAKK
I said it, didn't I? I can hear your movements!
No attack can hit me.
GAH!!
THWAKK
WAAH!

*Iron Fist!!!!

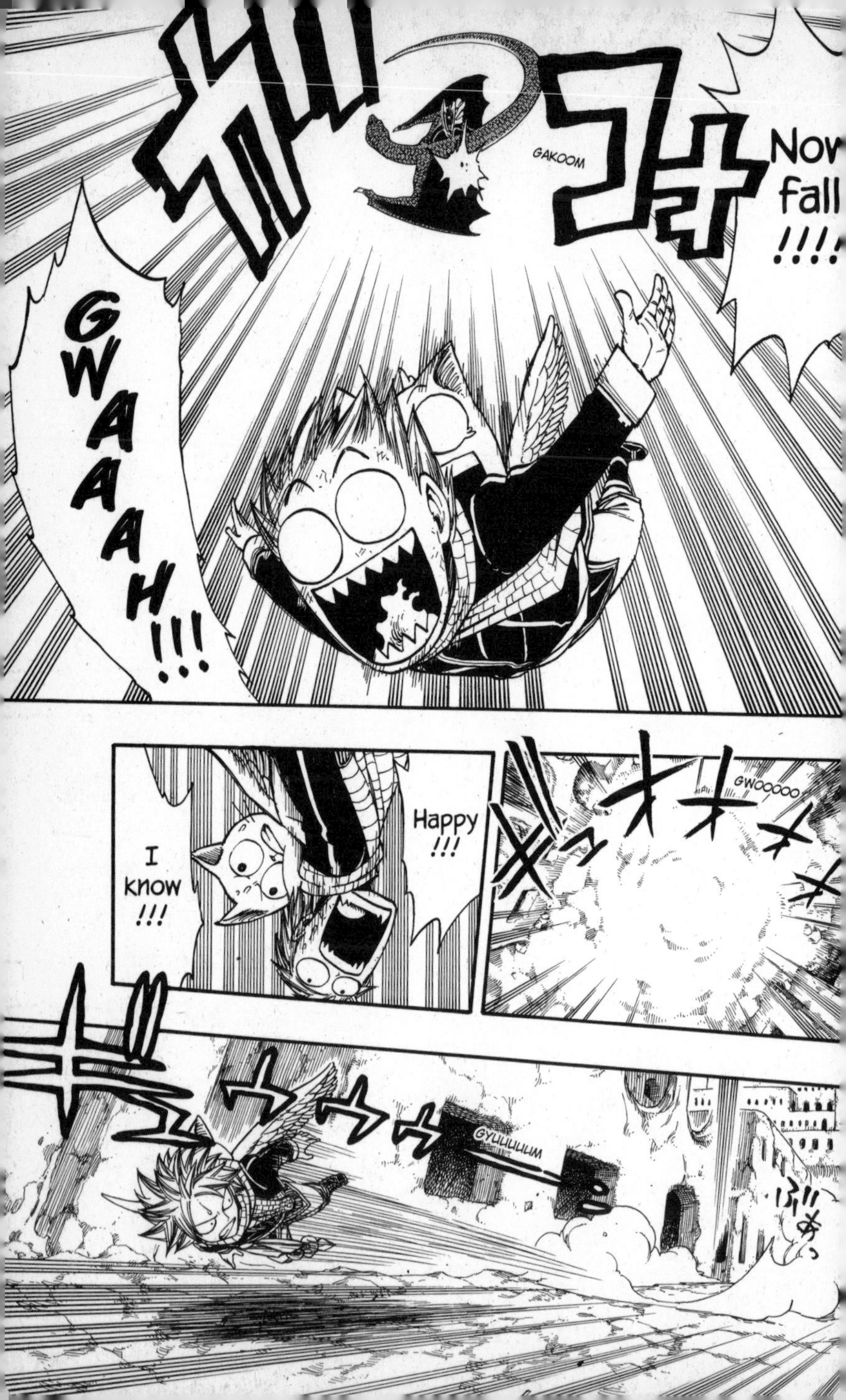
GAKOOM
Now fall!!!!
GWAAAAH!!!
GWOOOOO
Happy!!!
I know!!!
GYUUUUUUM

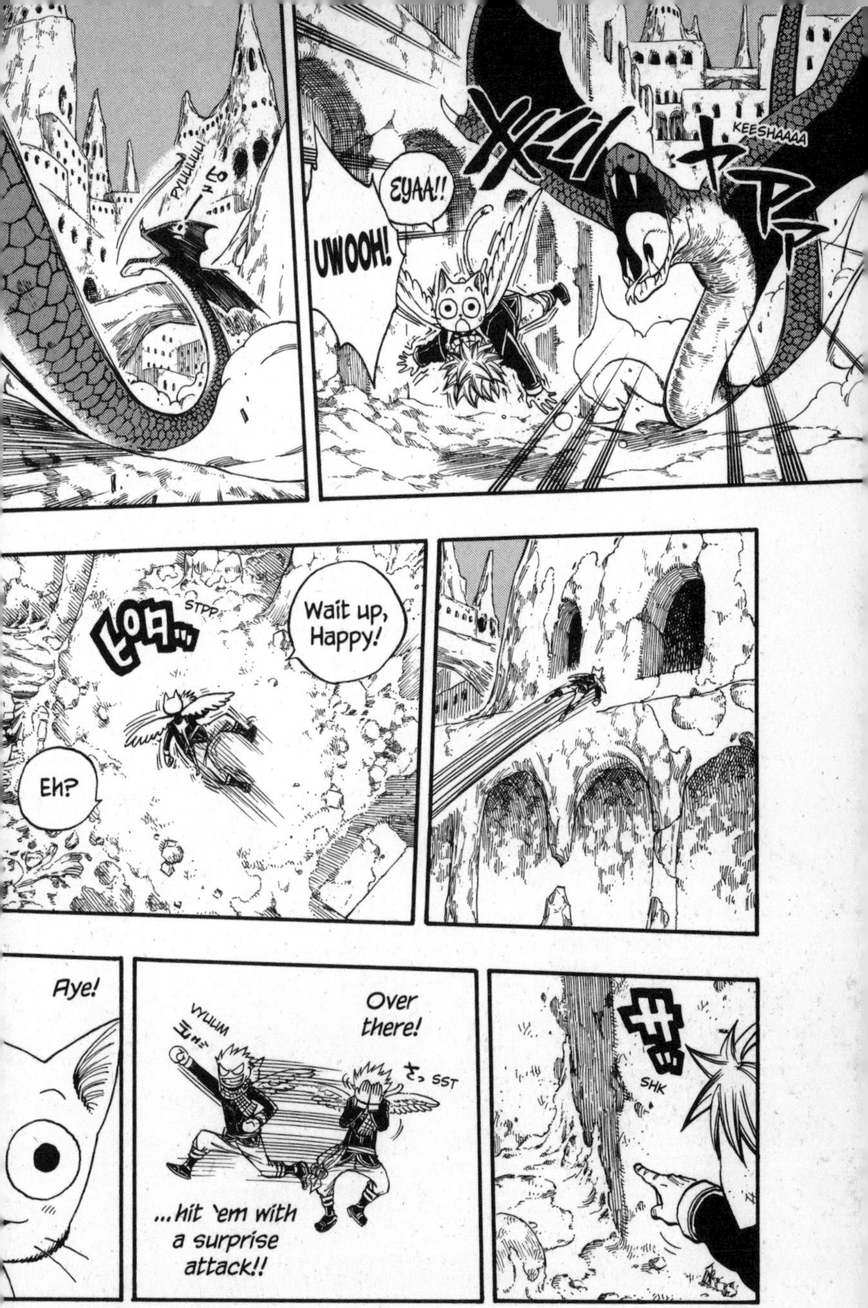
KEESHAAAA
ΣYAA!!
UWOOH!
PYUUUUU
Wait up, Happy!
STPP
Eh?
SHK
Over there!
SST
VYUUM
...hit 'em with a surprise attack!!
Aye!

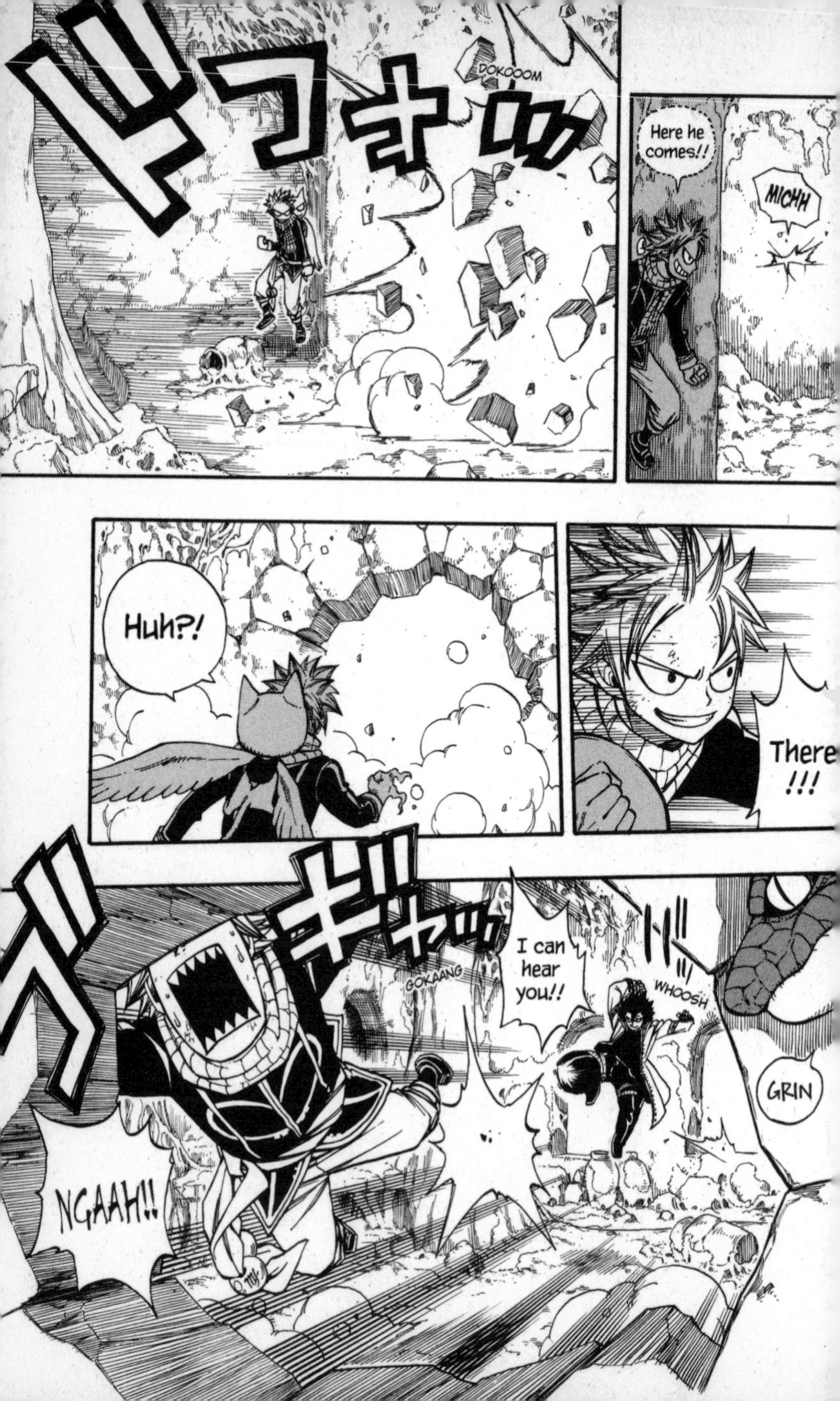

Here he comes!!
MICHH
DOKOOOM
There!!!
Huh?!
GRIN
WHOOSH
I can hear you!!
GOKAANG
NGAAH!!

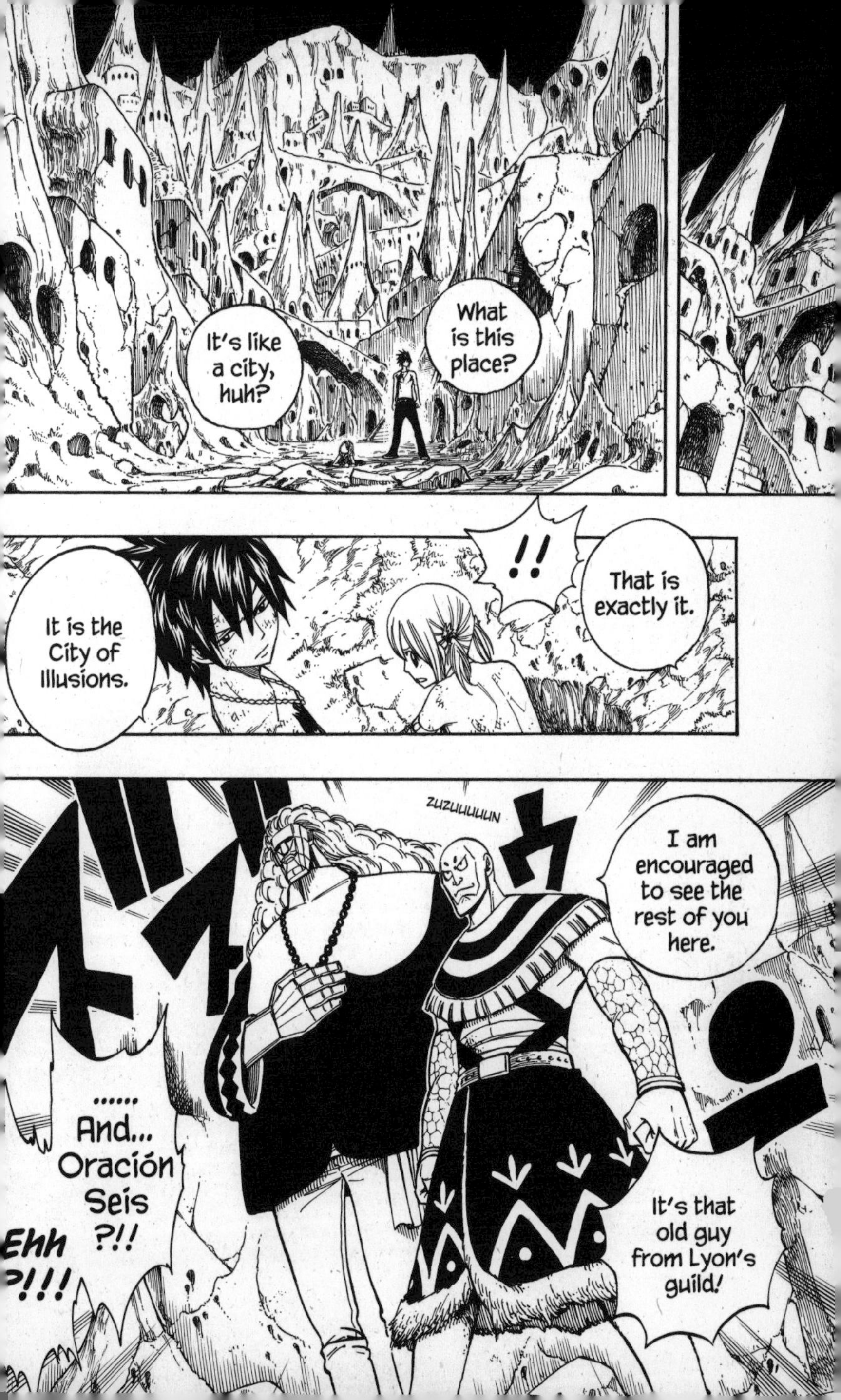
What is this place?
It's like a city, huh?
!!
That is exactly it.
It is the City of Illusions.
ZUZUUUUUN
I am encouraged to see the rest of you here.
It's that old guy from Lyon's guild!
...... And... Oración Seis ?!!
Ehh ?!!!

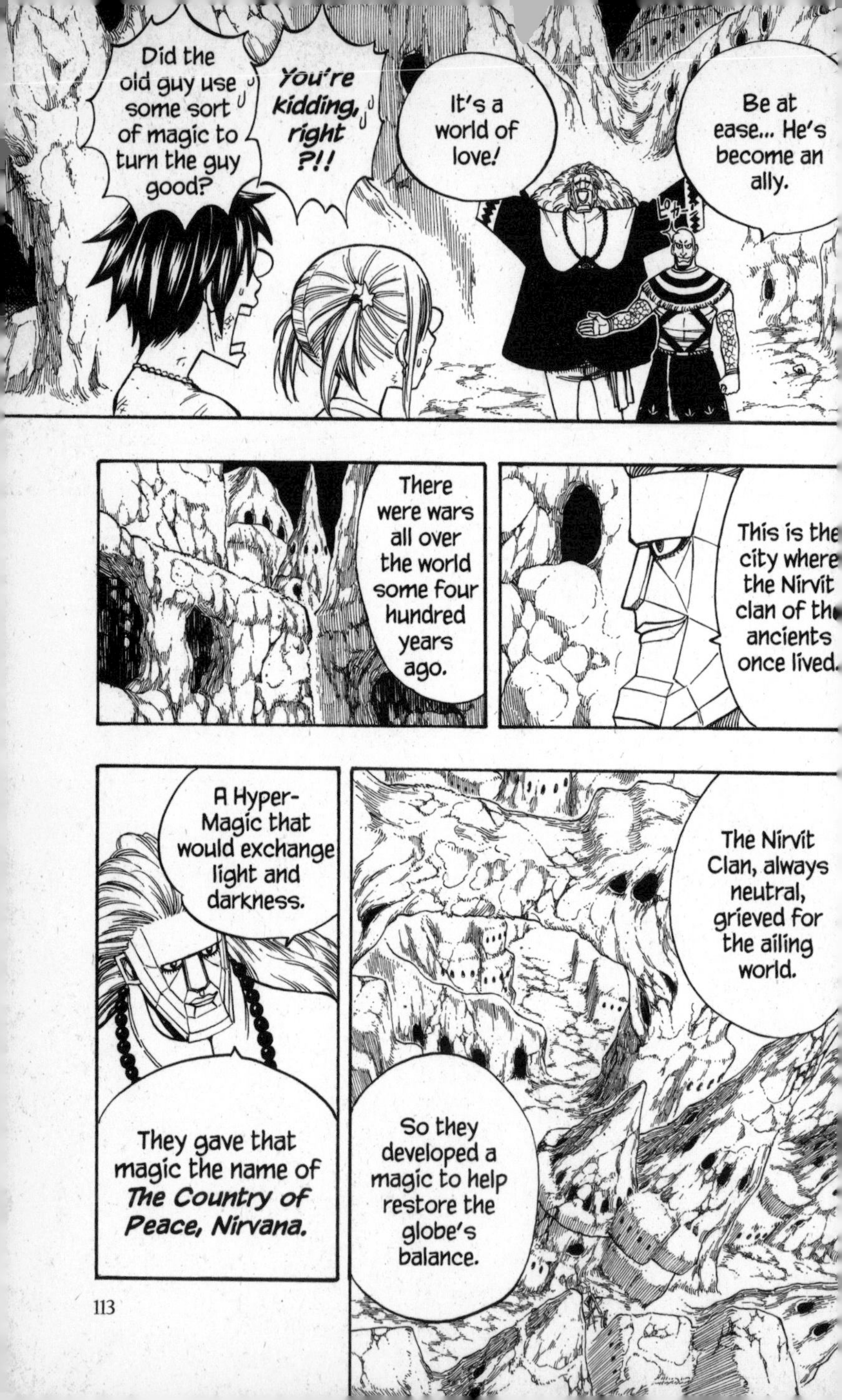
Be at ease... He's become an ally.
It's a world of love!
You're kidding, right?!!
Did the old guy use some sort of magic to turn the guy good?
This is the city where the Nirvit clan of the ancients once lived.
There were wars all over the world some four hundred years ago.
The Nirvit Clan, always neutral, grieved for the ailing world.
So they developed a magic to help restore the globe's balance.
A Hyper-Magic that would exchange light and darkness.
They gave that magic the name of ***The Country of Peace, Nirvana.***

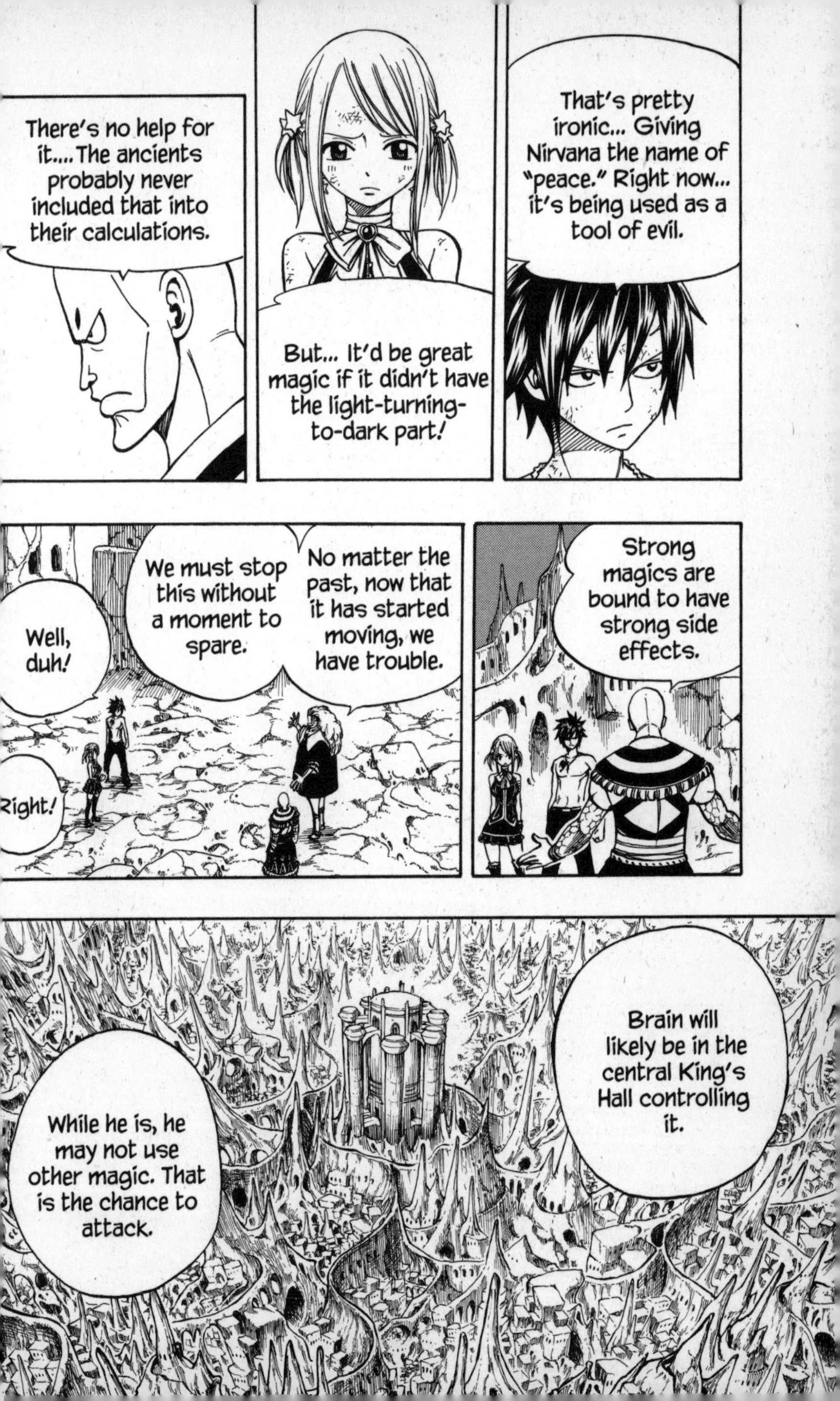

That's pretty ironic... Giving Nirvana the name of "peace." Right now... it's being used as a tool of evil.
But... It'd be great magic if it didn't have the light-turning-to-dark part!
There's no help for it.... The ancients probably never included that into their calculations.
Strong magics are bound to have strong side effects.
No matter the past, now that it has started moving, we have trouble.
We must stop this without a moment to spare.
Well, duh!
Right!
Brain will likely be in the central King's Hall controlling it.
While he is, he may not use other magic. That is the chance to attack.

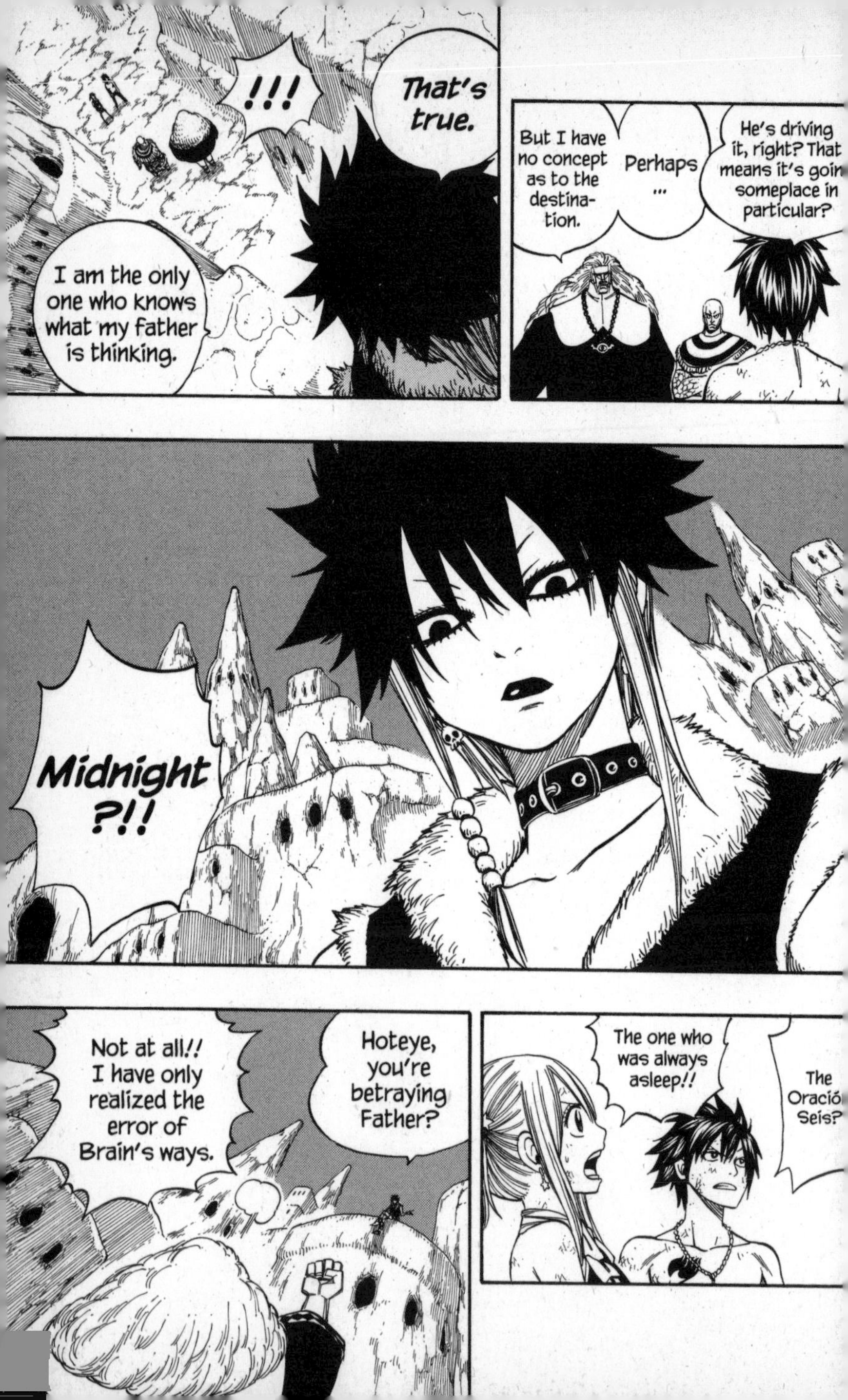
He's driving it, right? That means it's goin someplace in particular?
Perhaps ...
But I have no concept as to the destina-tion.
That's true.
!!!
I am the only one who knows what my father is thinking.
Midnight ?!!
The Oració Seis?
The one who was always asleep!!
Hoteye, you're betraying Father?
Not at all!! I have only realized the error of Brain's ways.

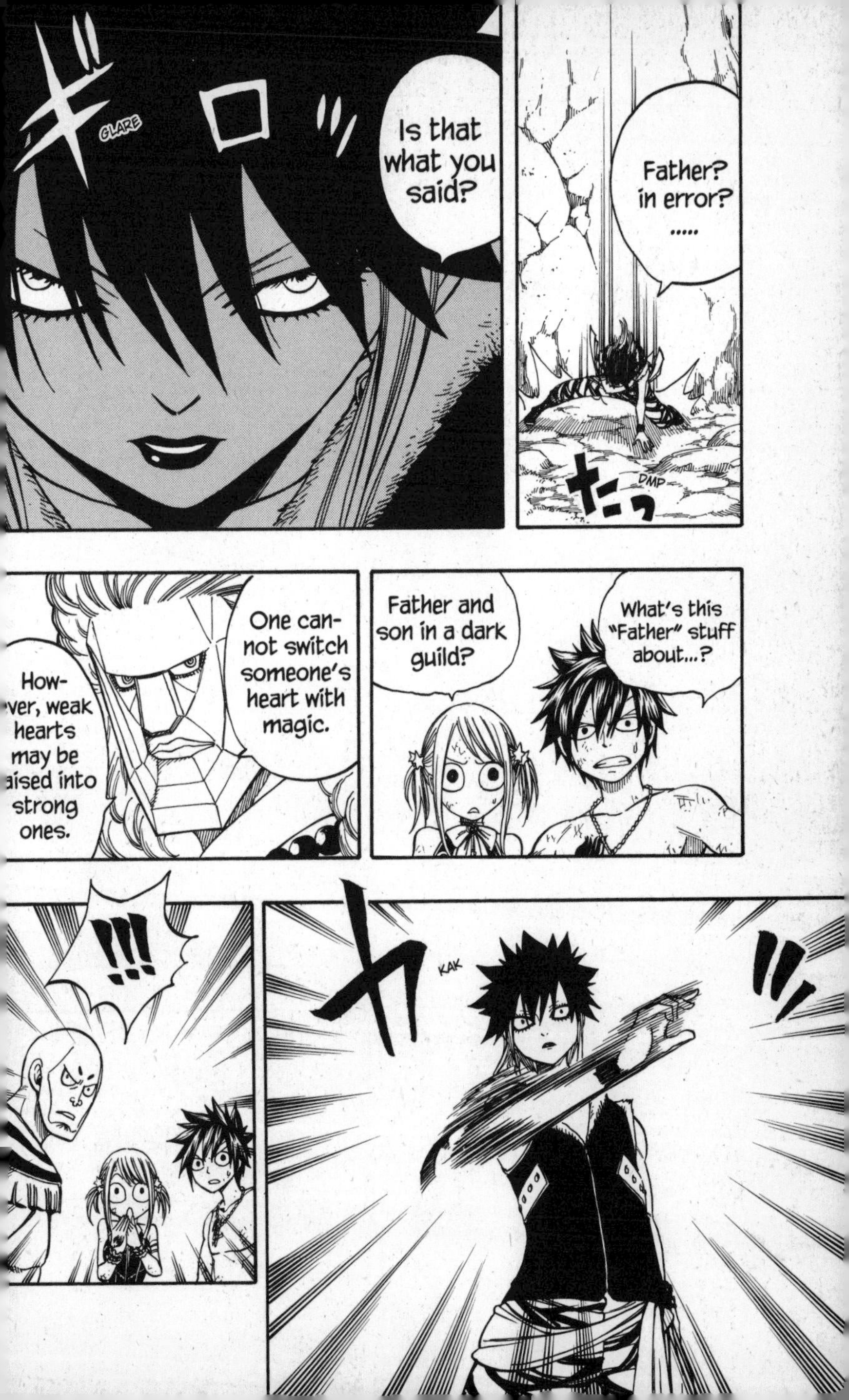
Father? in error? .....
DMP
GLARE
Is that what you said?
What's this "Father" stuff about...?
Father and son in a dark guild?
One can-not switch someone's heart with magic.
How- ver, weak hearts may be aised into strong ones.
KAK
!!!

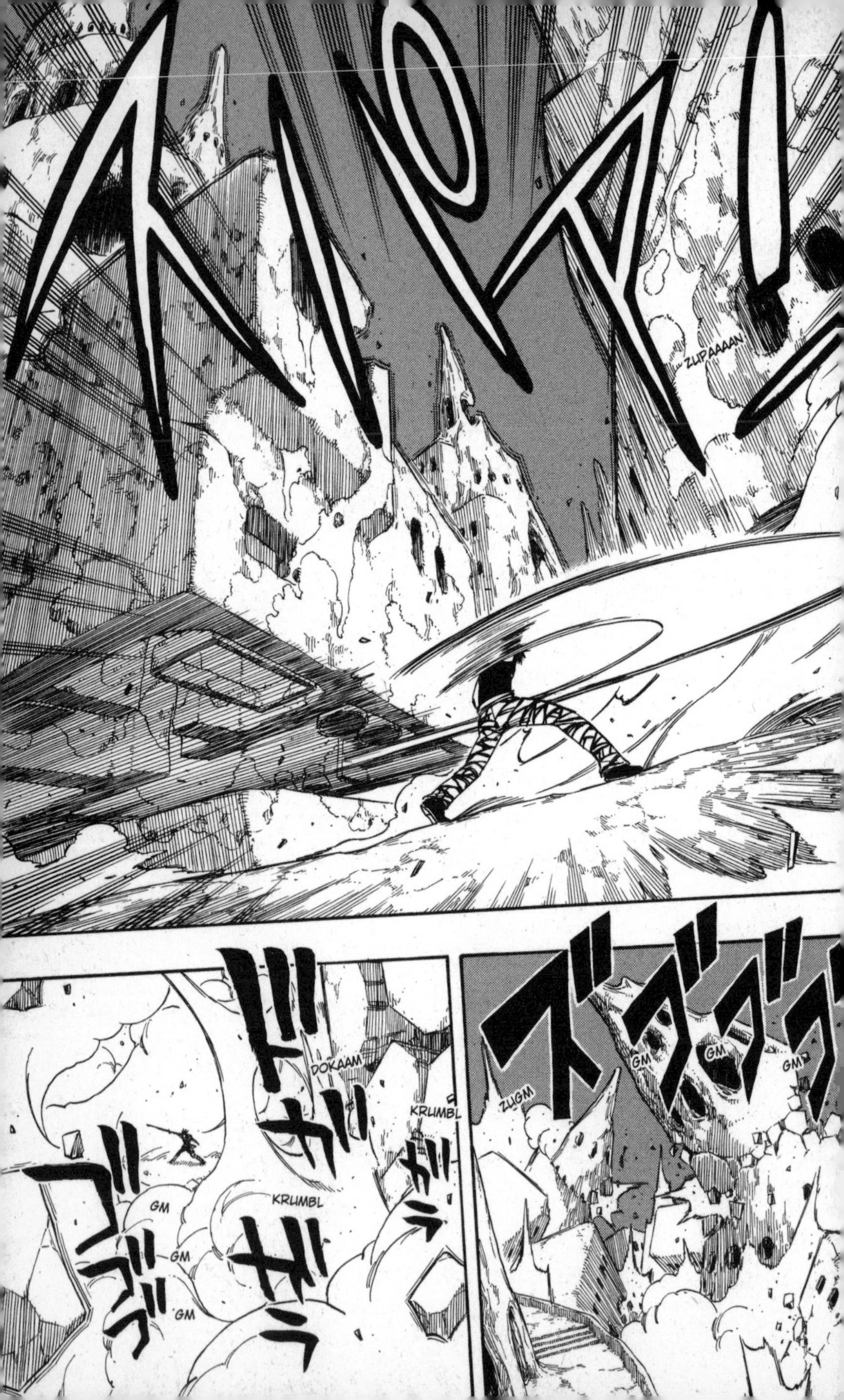
ZUPAAAAN
GM
GM
GM
ZUGM
DOKAAM
KRUMBL
KRUMBL
GM
GM
GM

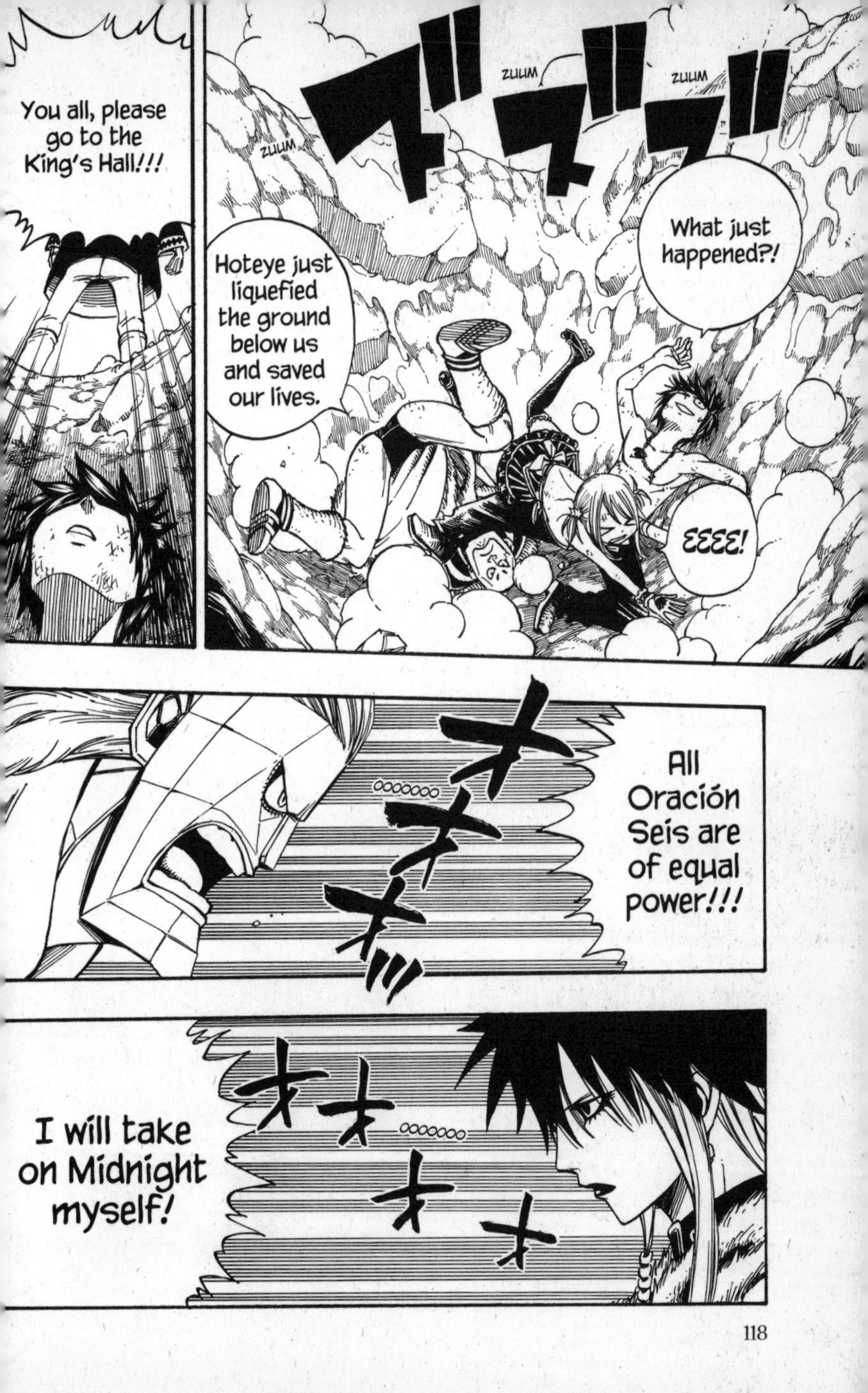
ZUUM
ZUUM
ZUUM
What just happened?!
Hoteye just liquefied the ground below us and saved our lives.
EEEE!
You all, please go to the King's Hall!!!
ooooooo
All Oración Seis are of equal power!!!
ooooooo
I will take on Midnight myself!

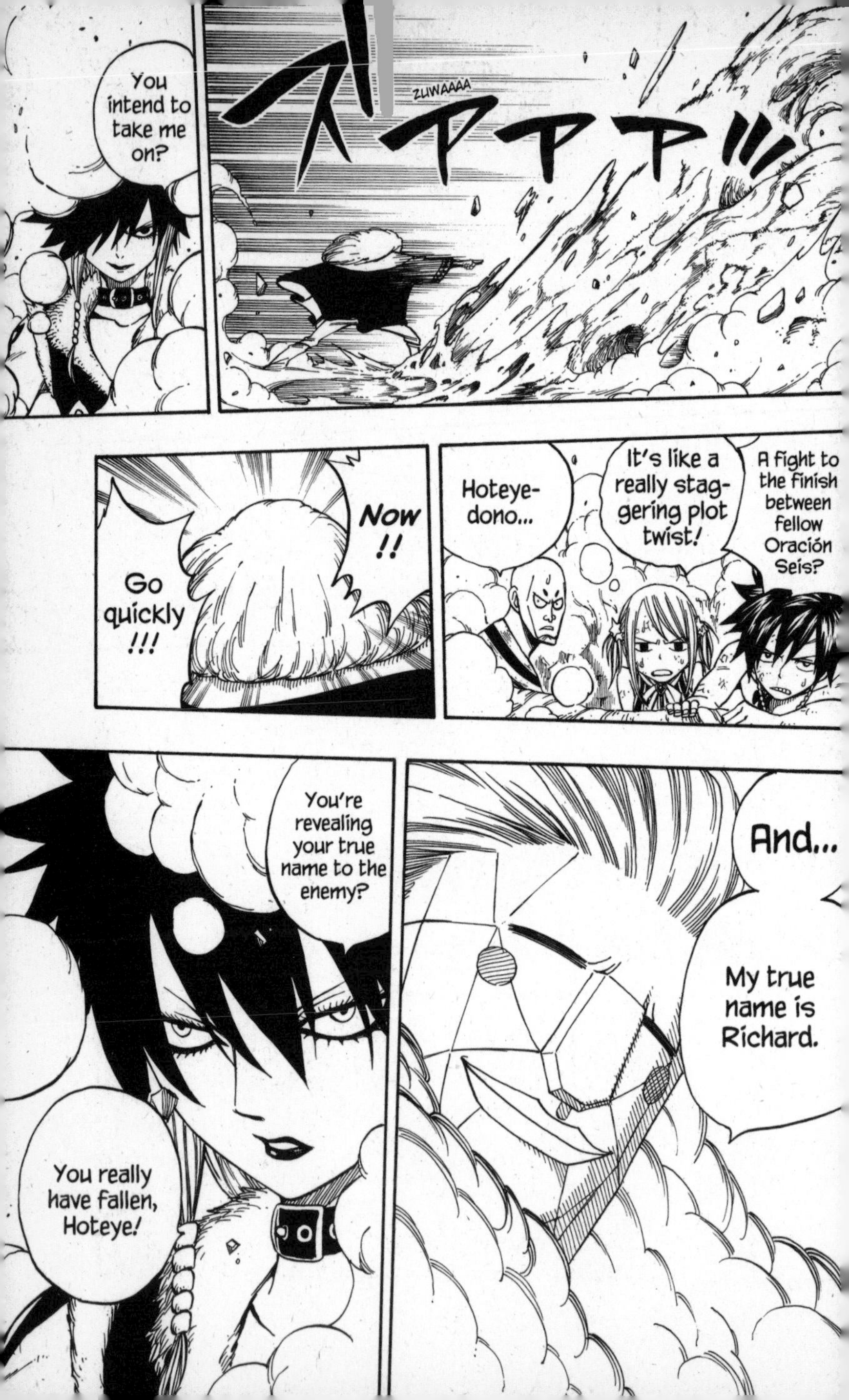
ZUWAAAA
You intend to take me on?
A fight to the finish between fellow Oración Seis?
It's like a really staggering plot twist!
Hoteye-dono...
Now!!
Go quickly!!!
And...
My true name is Richard.
You're revealing your true name to the enemy?
You really have fallen, Hoteye!

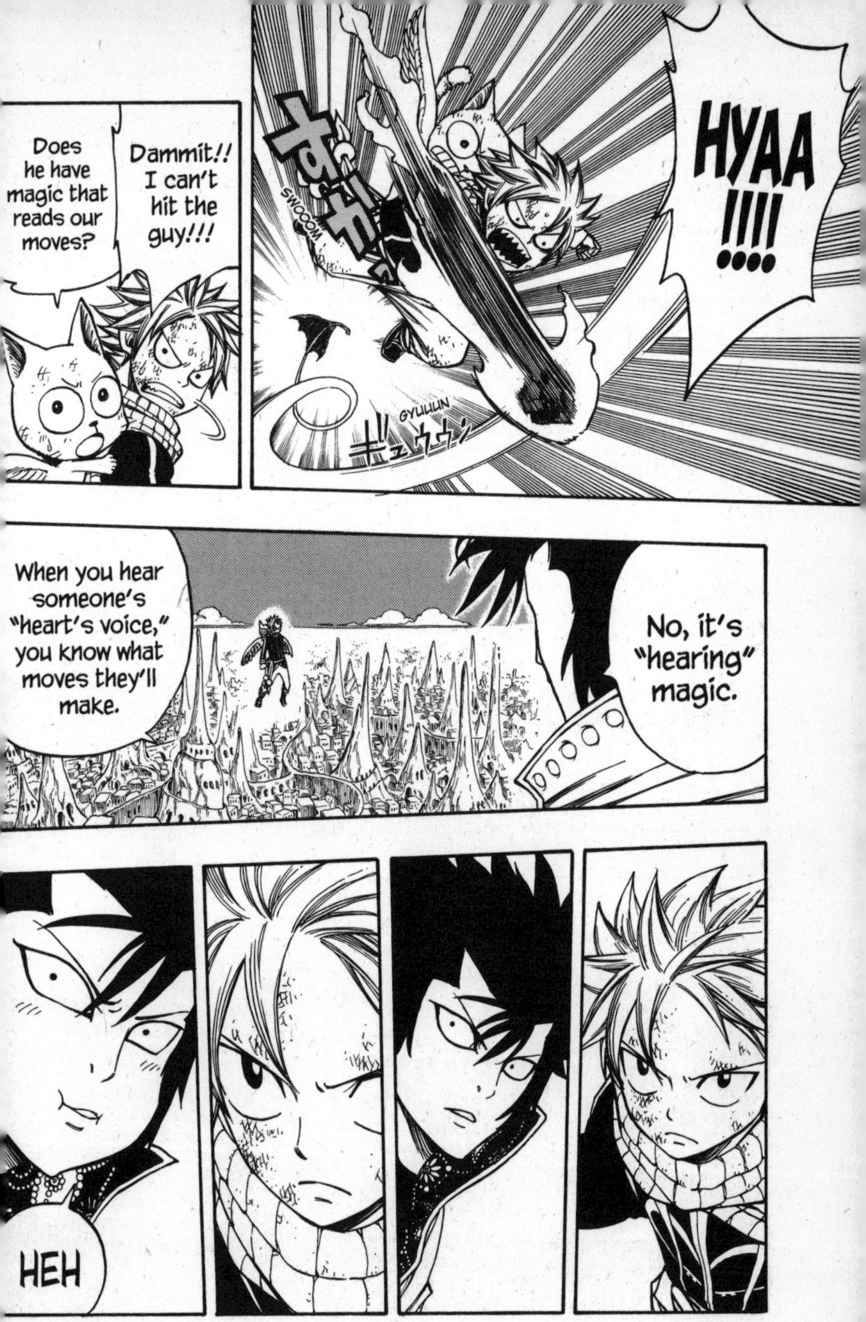
HYAA!!!!....
SWOOOM
GYUUUN
ギュウウン
Dammit!! I can't hit the guy!!!
Does he have magic that reads our moves?
No, it's "hearing" magic.
When you hear someone's "heart's voice," you know what moves they'll make.
HEH

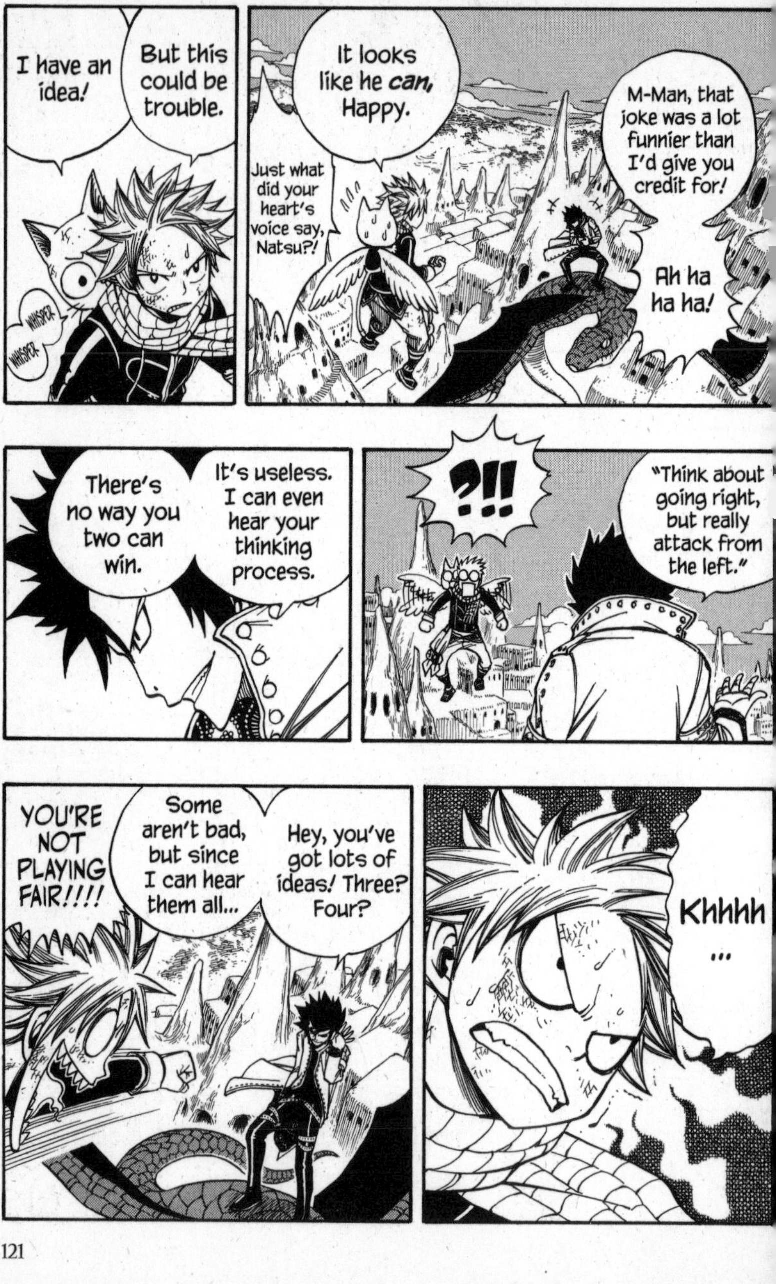
M-Man, that joke was a lot funnier than I'd give you credit for!
It looks like he *can,* Happy.
Just what did your heart's voice say, Natsu?!
Ah ha ha ha!
But this could be trouble.
I have an idea!
WHISPER
WHISPER
"Think about going right, but really attack from the left."
?!!
It's useless. I can even hear your thinking process.
There's no way you two can win.
Khhhh ...
Hey, you've got lots of ideas! Three? Four?
Some aren't bad, but since I can hear them all...
YOU'RE NOT PLAYING FAIR!!!!

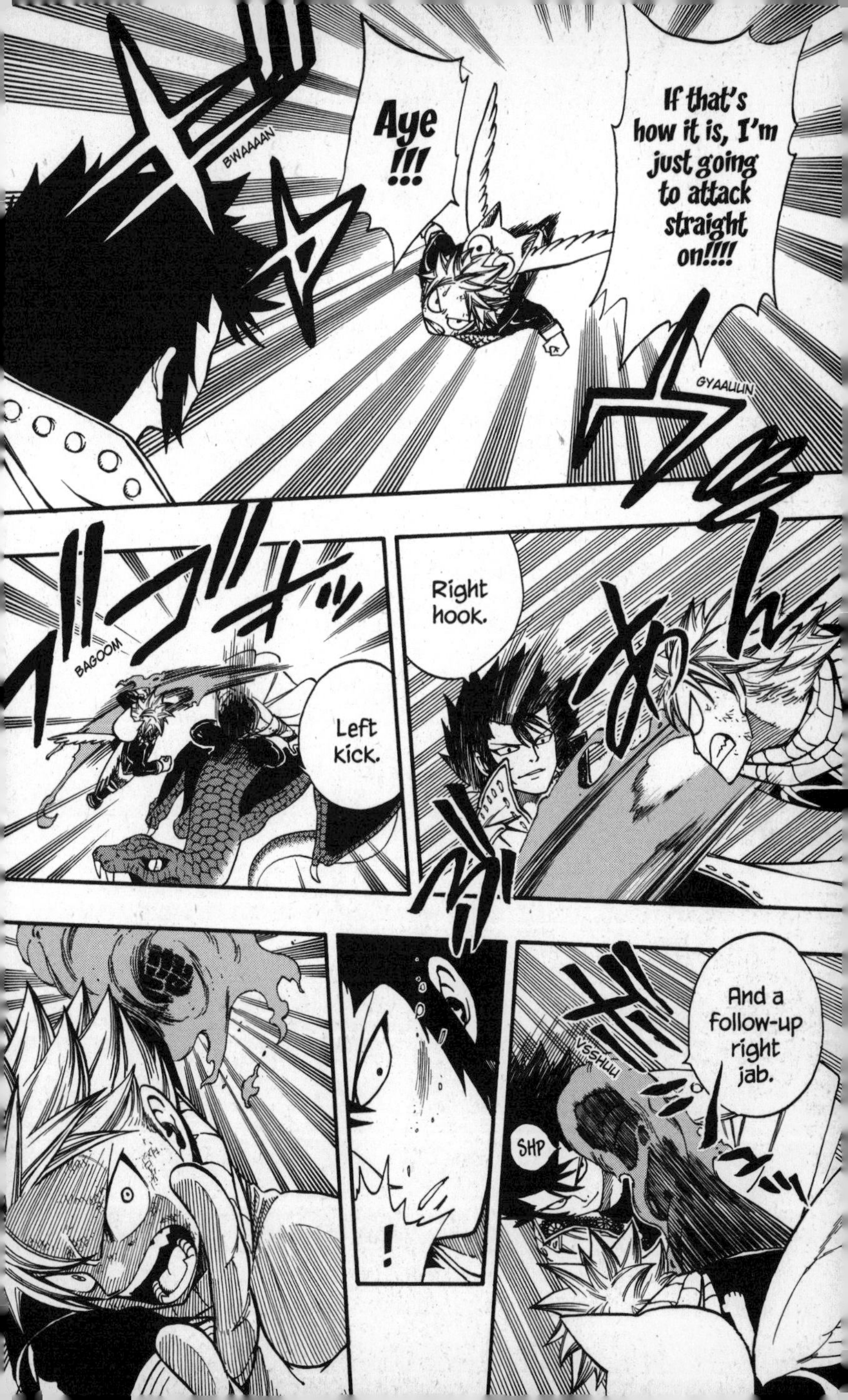
If that's how it is, I'm just going to attack straight on!!!!
Aye !!!
BWAAAAN
GYAAUUN
Right hook.
Left kick.
BAGOOM
And a follow-up right jab.
VSSHUU
SHP
!

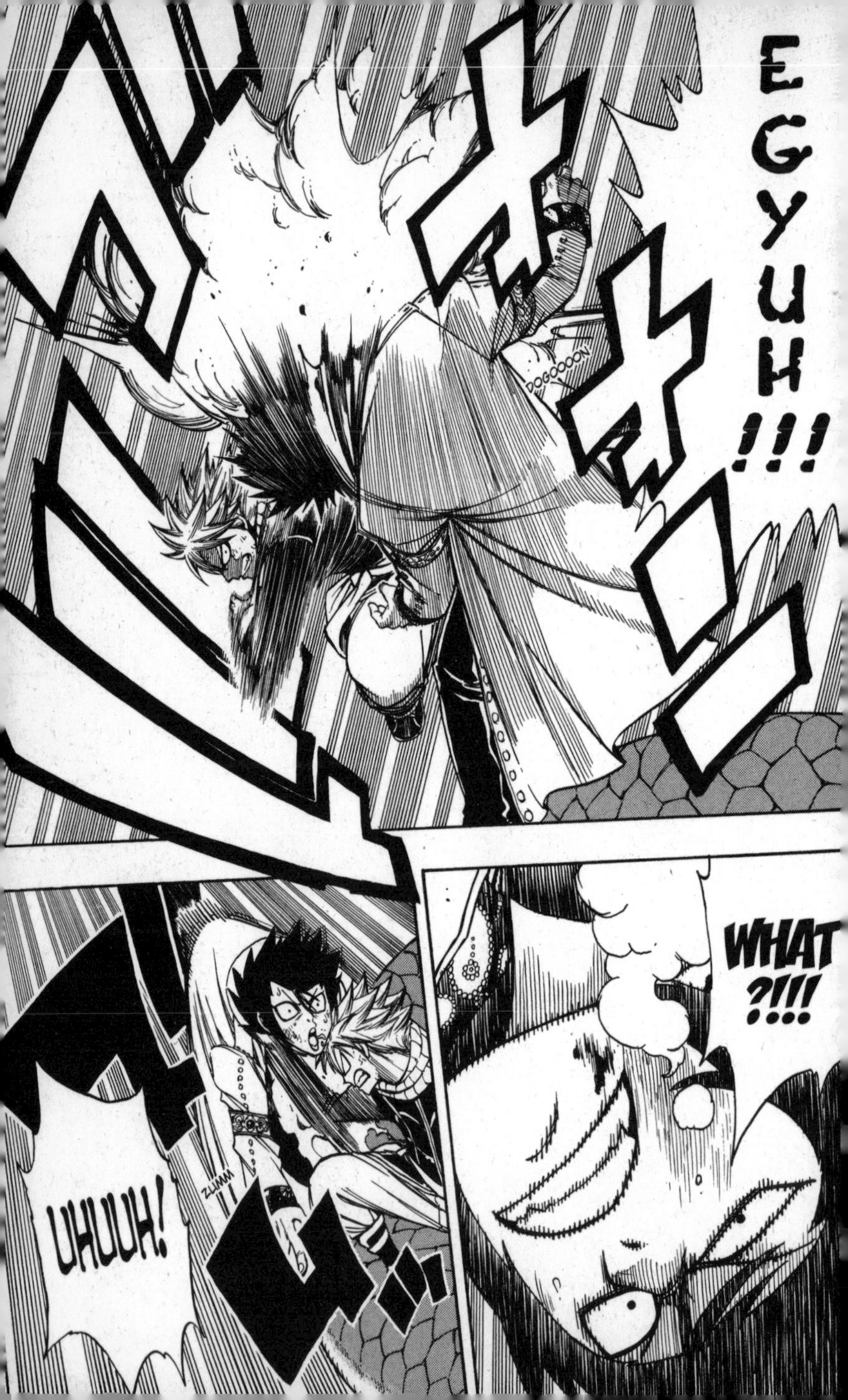
EGYUH!!!
DOGOOOON
WHAT?!!!
ZUMM
UHUUH!

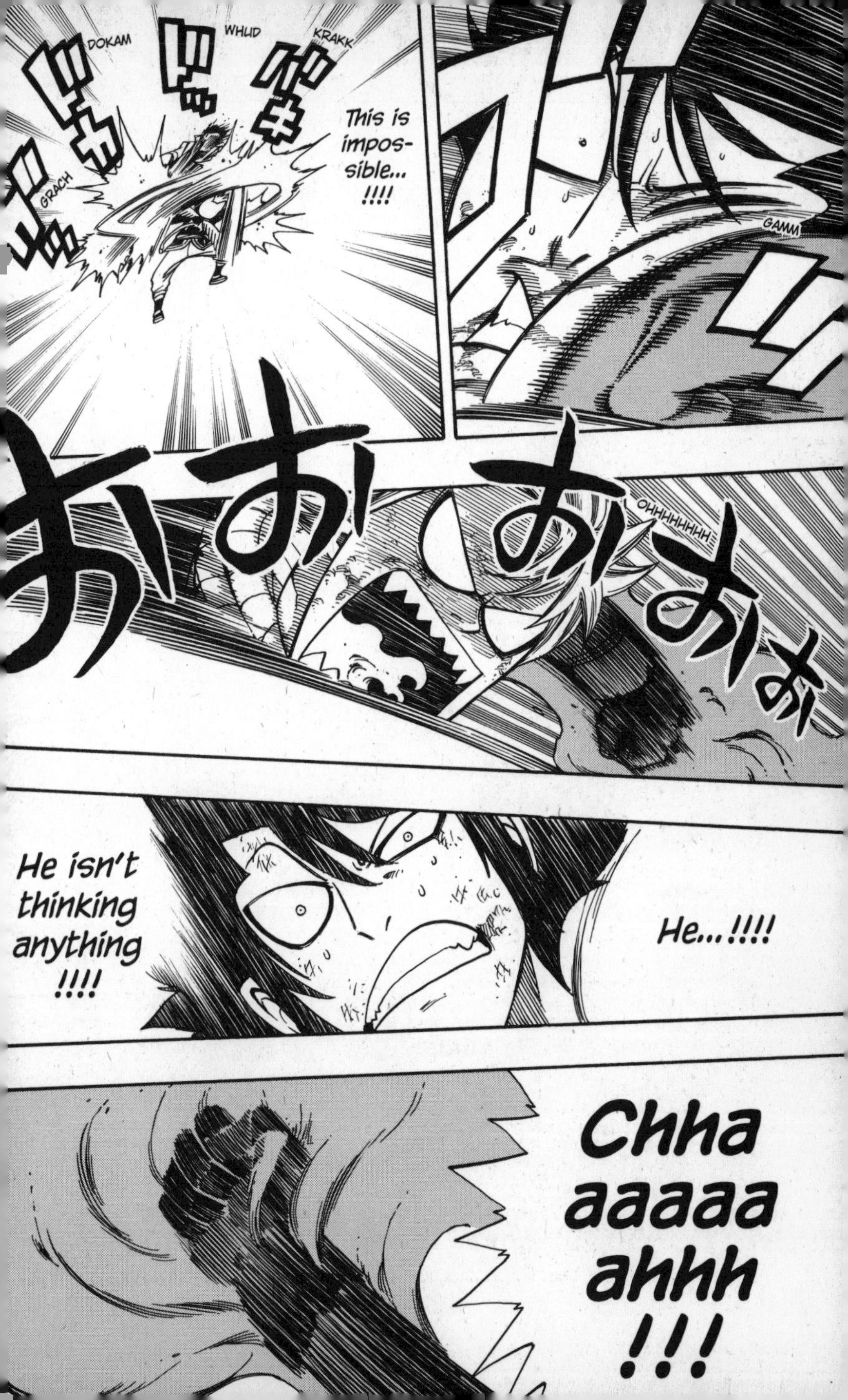

GAMM
This is impos-sible...!!!!
KRAKK
WHUD
DOKAM
GRACH
OHHHHHHHH
He...!!!!
He isn't thinking anything !!!!
Chhaaaaaaahhh !!!

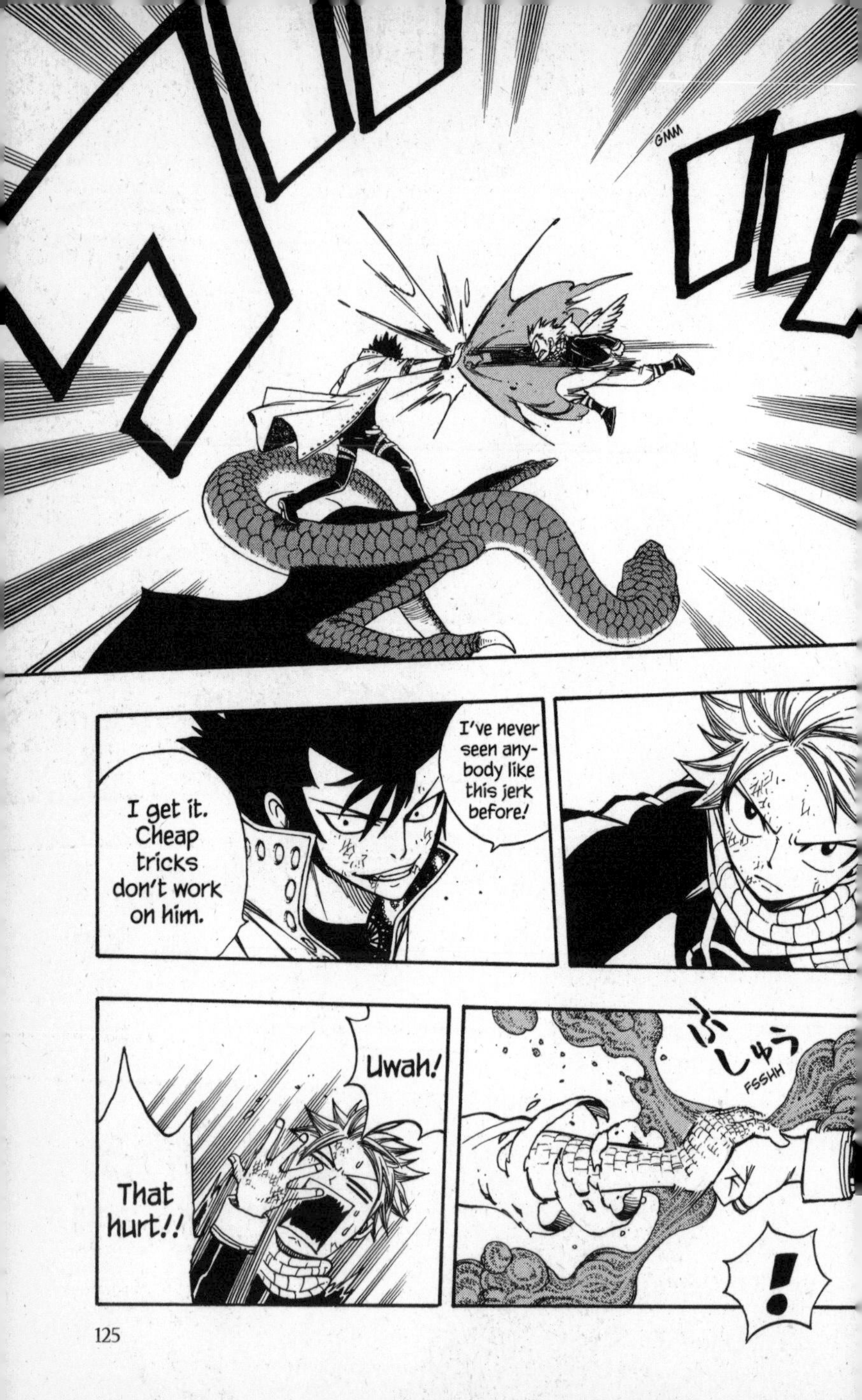
GMM
I've never seen any-body like this jerk before!
I get it. Cheap tricks don't work on him.
ふしゅう
FSSHH
!
Uwah!
That hurt!!

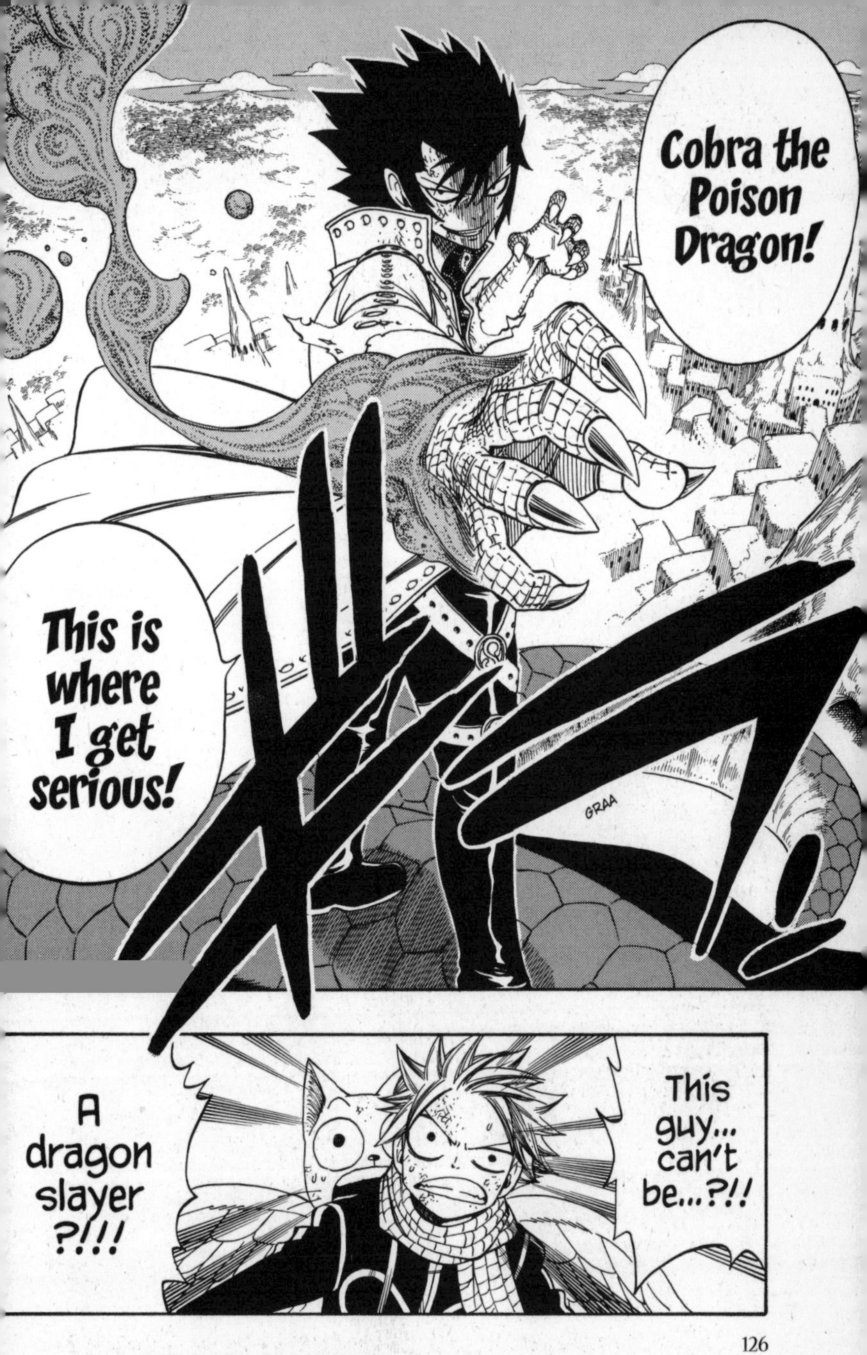
Cobra the Poison Dragon!
This is where I get serious!
GRAA
This guy... can't be...?!!
A dragon slayer?!!!

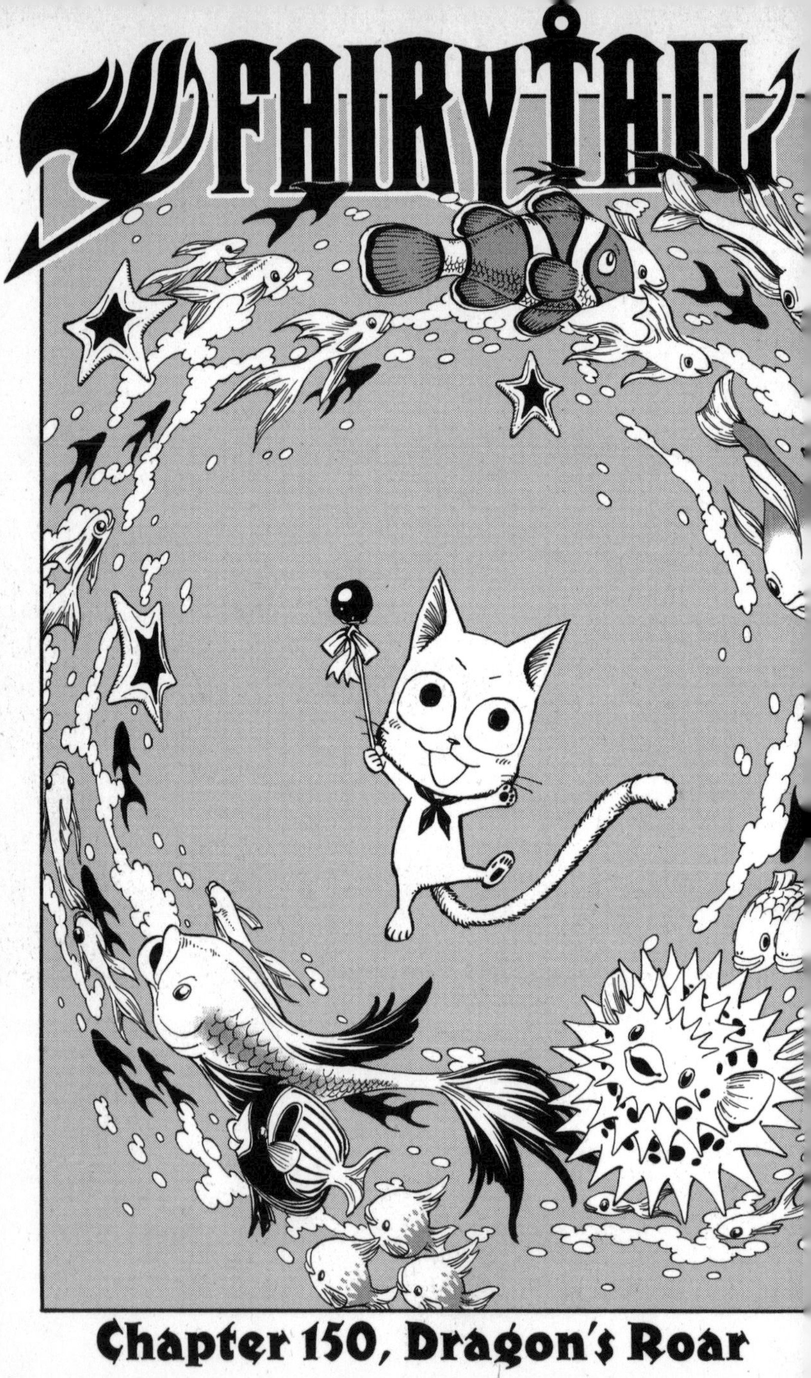

Chapter 150, Dragon's Roar

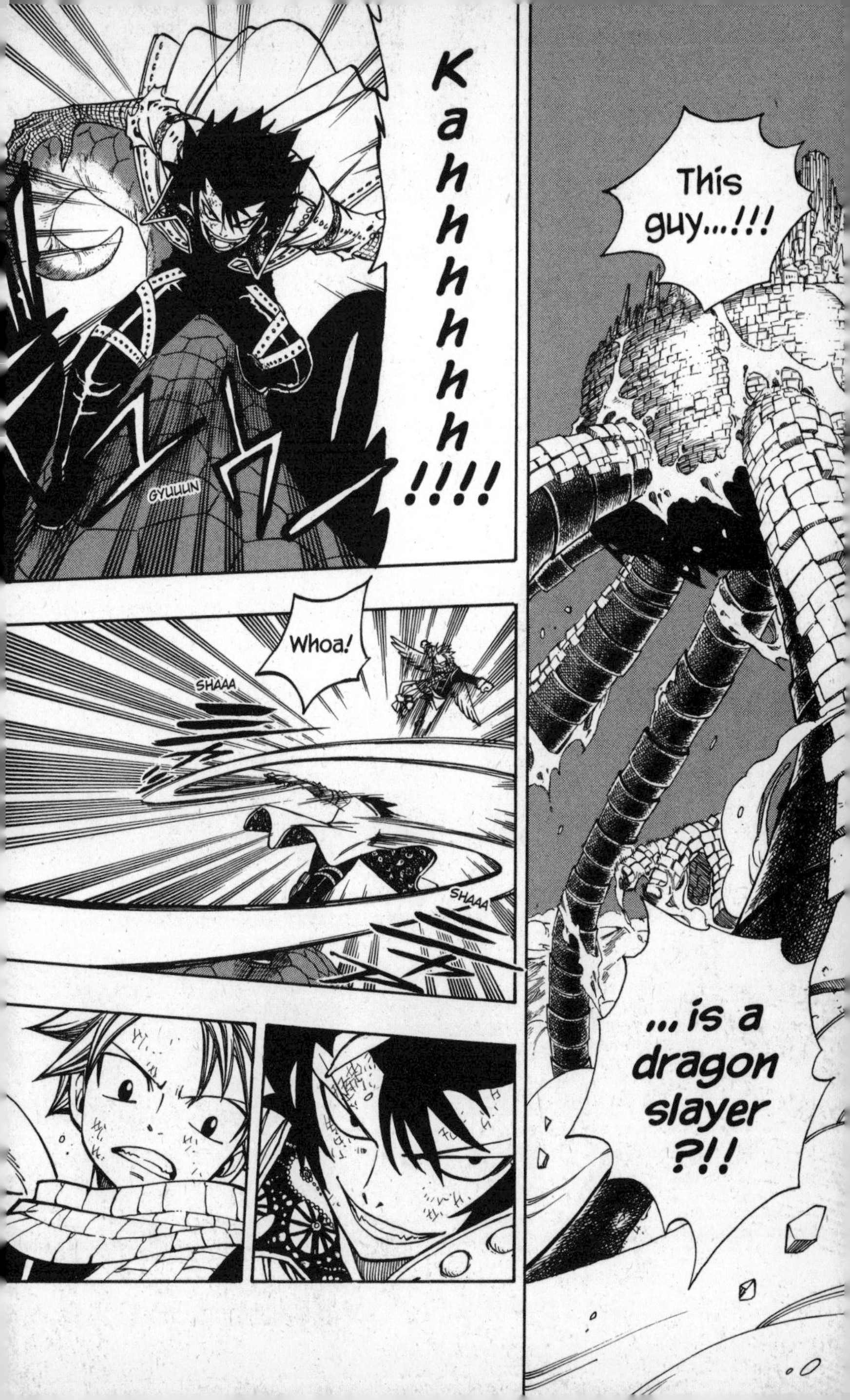
This guy...!!!
...is a dragon slayer?!!
Kahhhhhh!!!!
GYUUUN
Whoa!
SHAAA
SHAAA

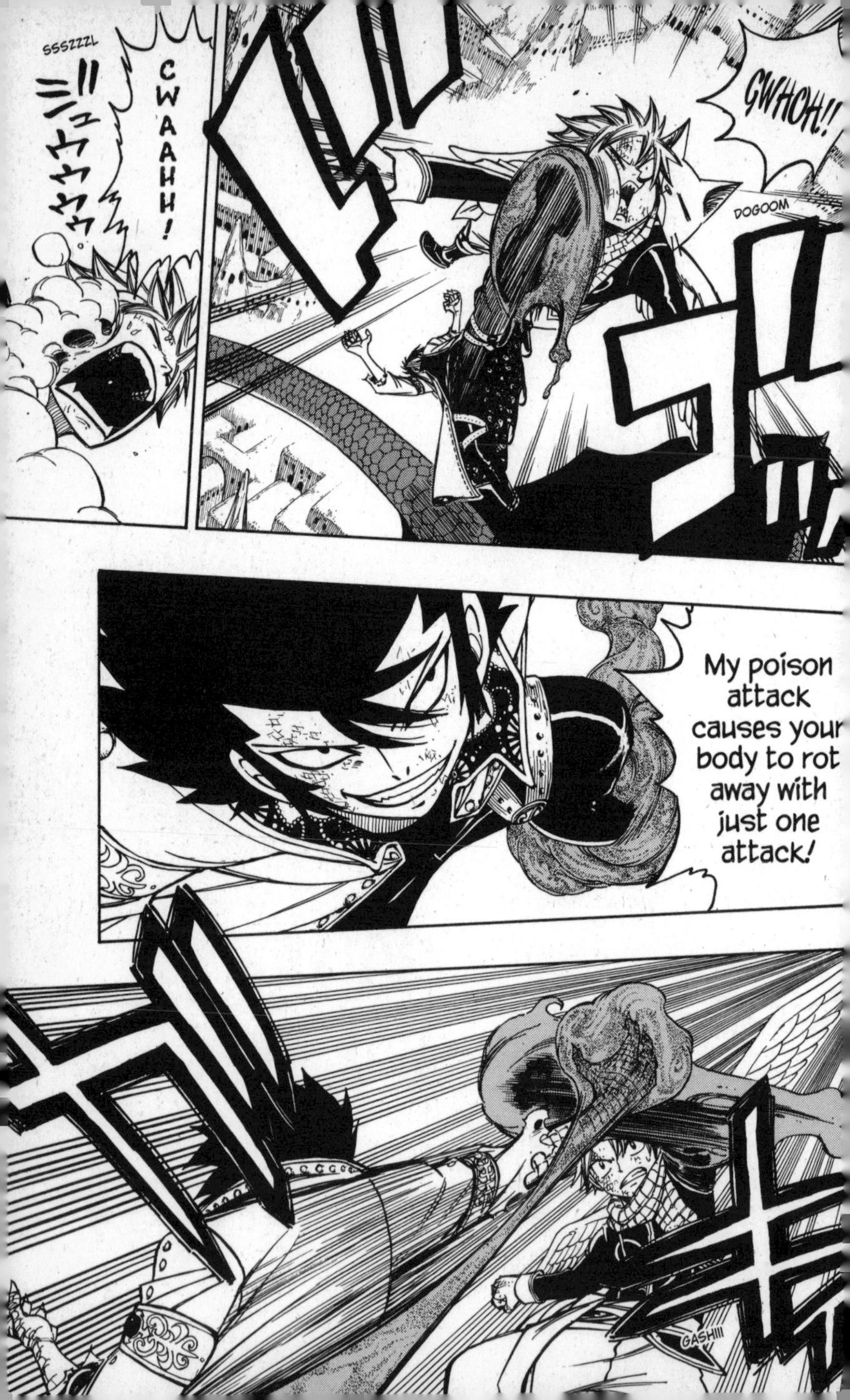
GWHOH!!
DOGOOM
CWAAHH!
SSSZZZL
My poison attack causes your body to rot away with just one attack!
GASHIII

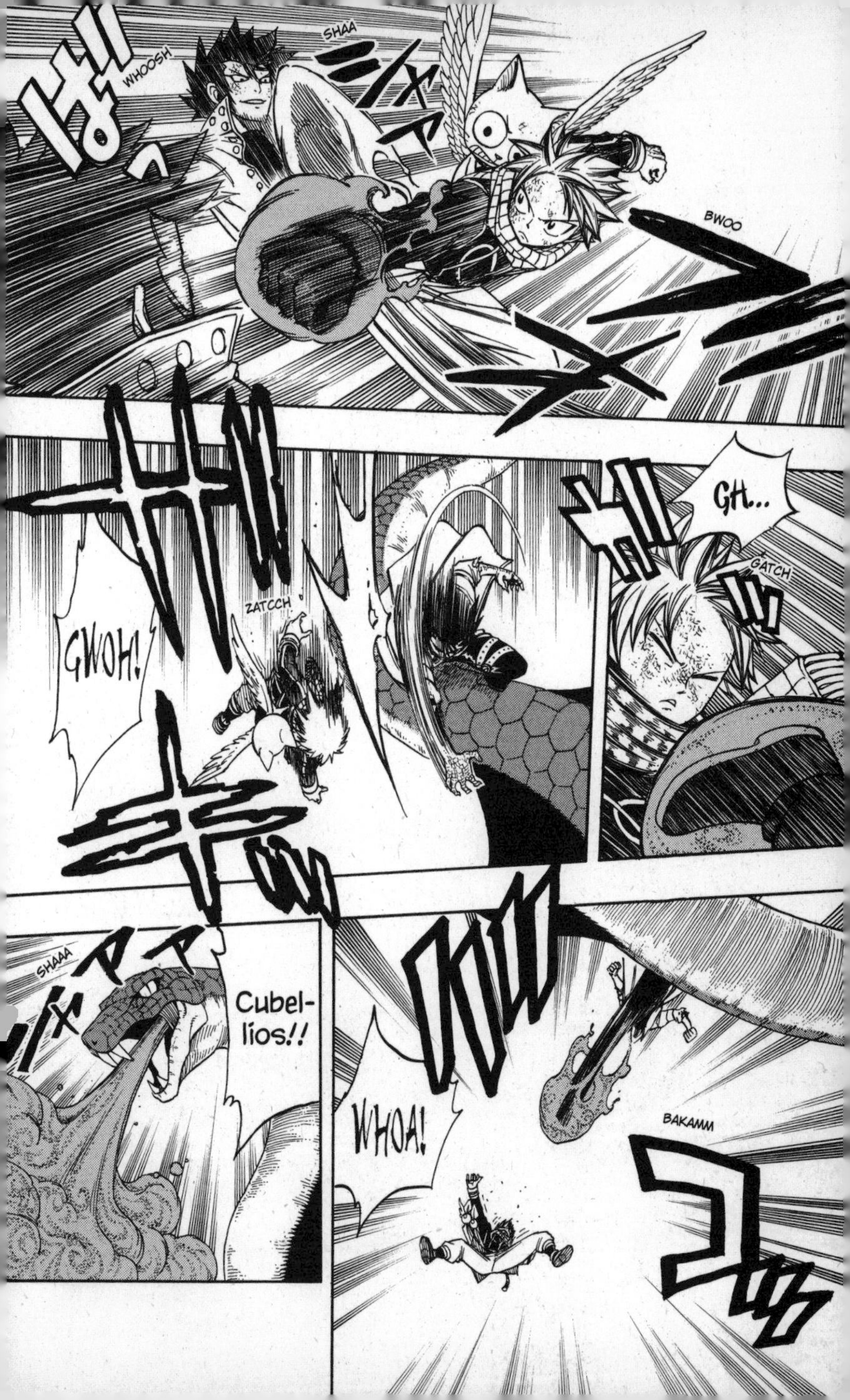
BWOO
SHAA
WHOOSH
GH...
GATCH
ZATCCH
GWOH!
BAKAMM
WHOA!
SHAAA
Cubel-lios!!

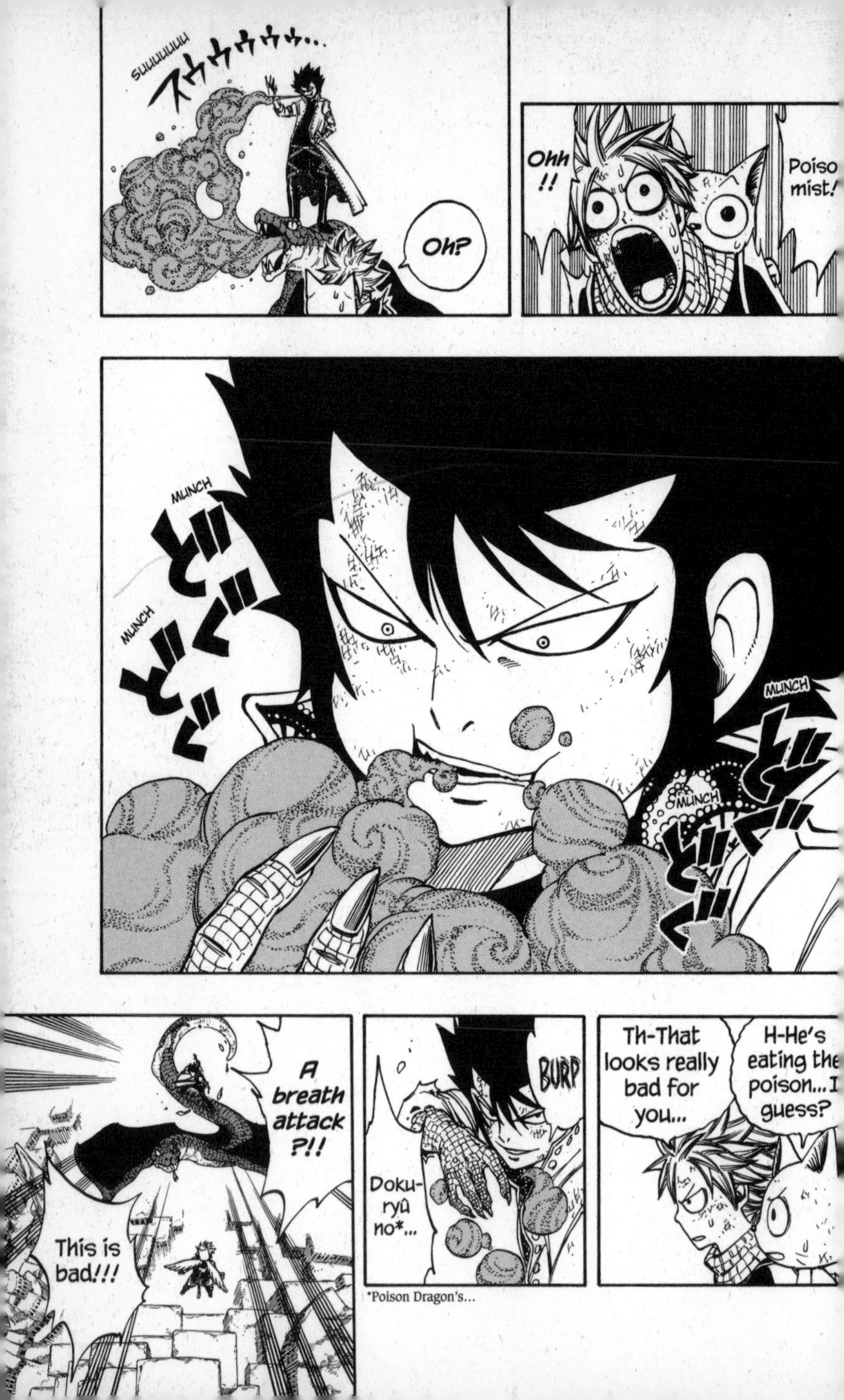
Poiso mist!
Ohh!!
SUUUUUUU
スゥウウウウ…
Oh?
MUNCH
MUNCH
MUNCH
MUNCH
H-He's eating the poison...I guess?
Th-That looks really bad for you...
BURP
Doku-ryû no*...
A breath attack?!!
This is bad!!!
*Poison Dragon's...

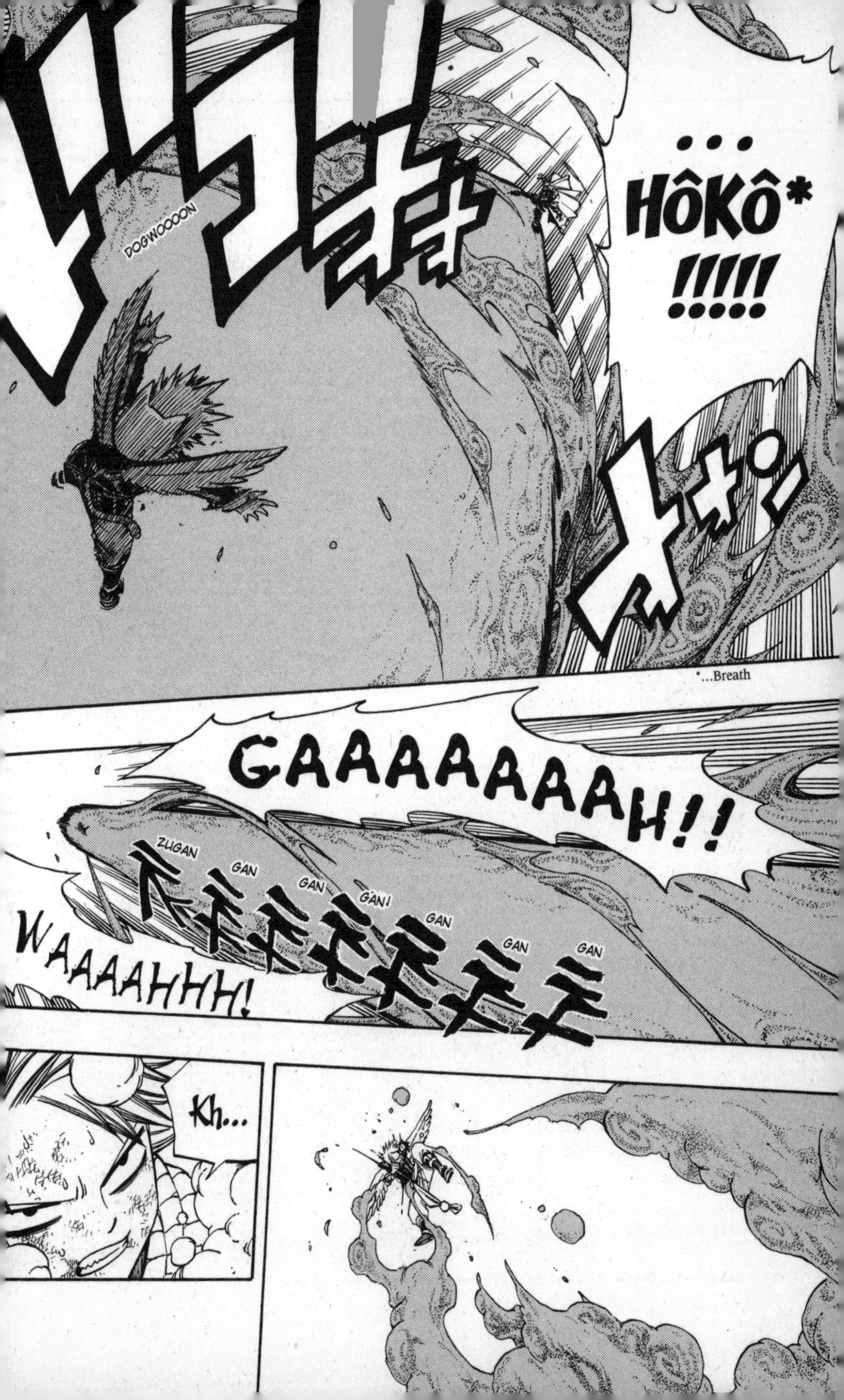
...Hôkô*!!!!!
DOGWOOOON
GAAAAAAAAAH!!
ZUGAN
GAN
GAN
GAN!
GAN
GAN
GAN
WAAAAHHH!
Kh...

*...Breath

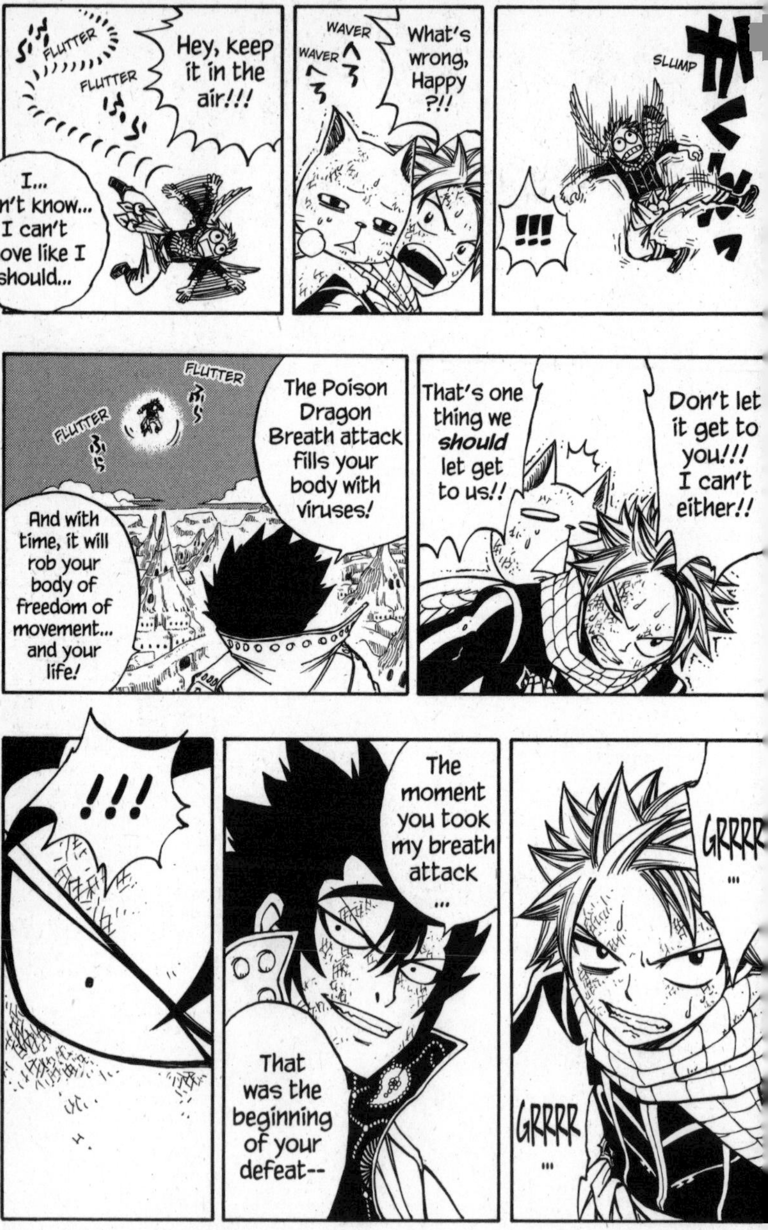
SLUMP
!!!
WAVER
WAVER
What's wrong, Happy?!!
Hey, keep it in the air!!!
FLUTTER
FLUTTER
I... don't know... I can't move like I should...
Don't let it get to you!!! I can't either!!
That's one thing we *should* let get to us!!
FLUTTER
FLUTTER
The Poison Dragon Breath attack fills your body with viruses!
And with time, it will rob your body of freedom of movement... and your life!
GRRRR...
GRRRR...
The moment you took my breath attack...
That was the beginning of your defeat--
!!!

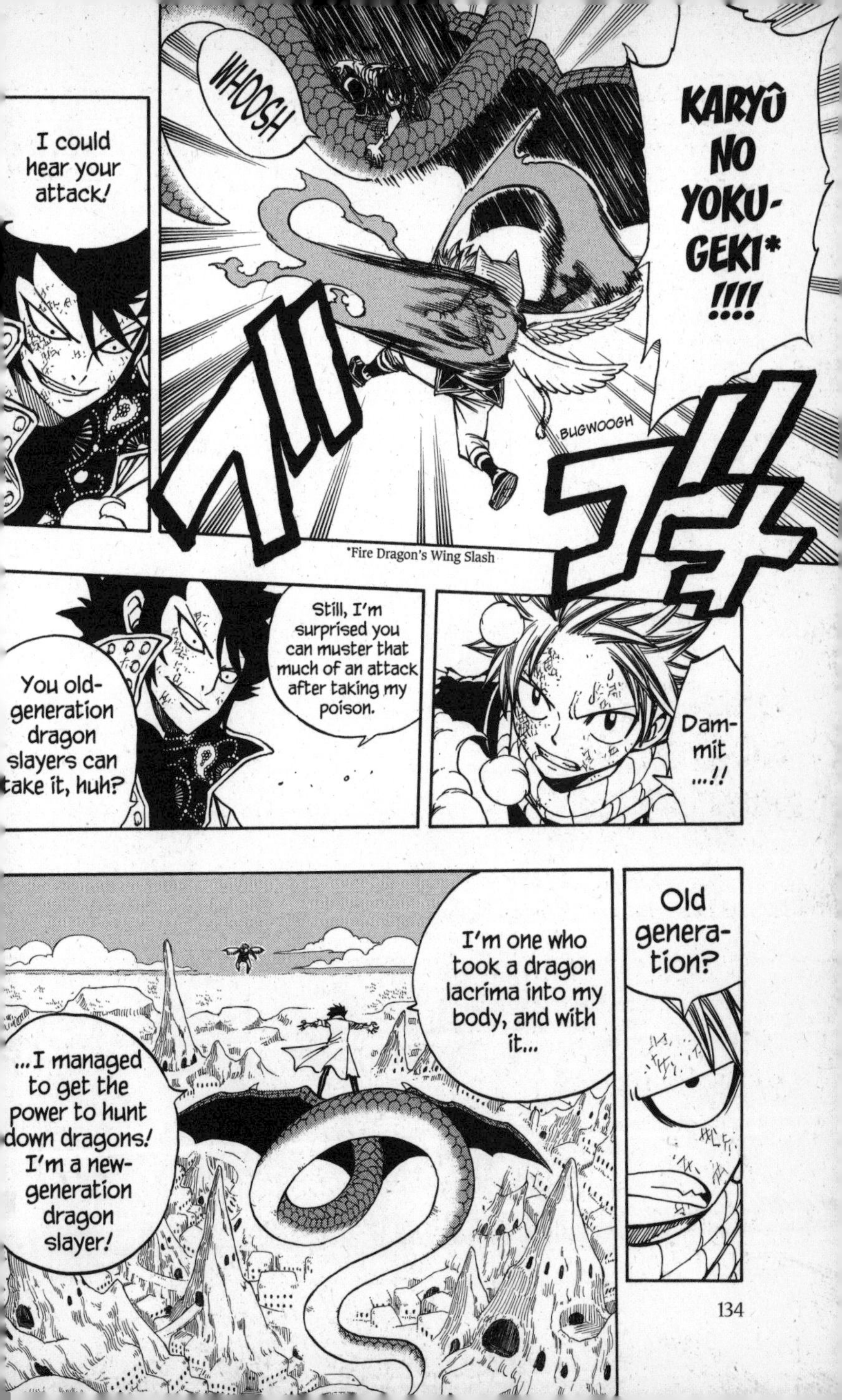
WHOOSH
KARYÛ NO YOKU-GEKI*!!!!
BUGWOOGH
I could hear your attack!
*Fire Dragon's Wing Slash
Dam-mit...!!
Still, I'm surprised you can muster that much of an attack after taking my poison.
You old-generation dragon slayers can take it, huh?
Old generation?
I'm one who took a dragon lacrima into my body, and with it...
...I managed to get the power to hunt down dragons! I'm a new-generation dragon slayer!

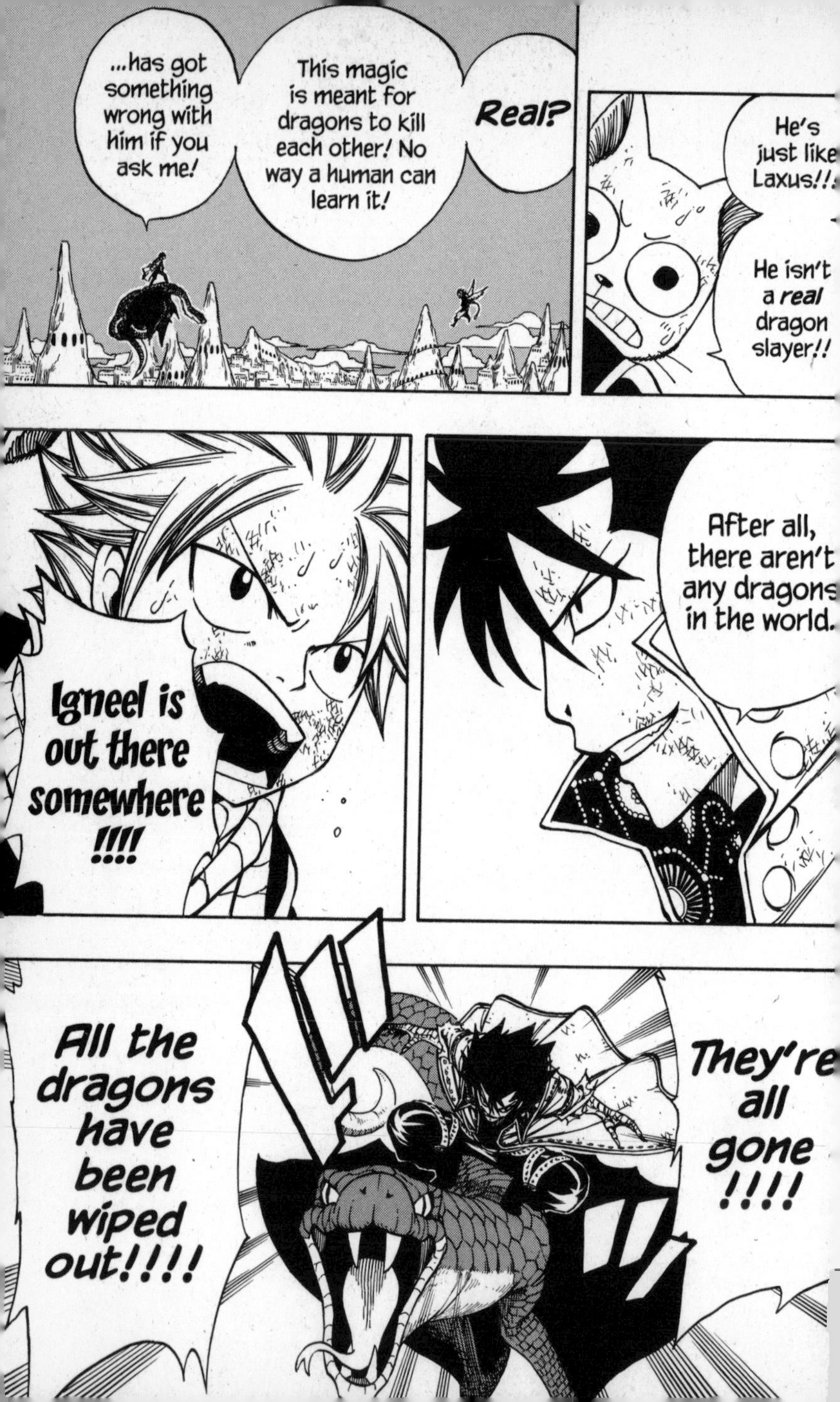
He's just like Laxus!!
He isn't a *real* dragon slayer!!
Real?
This magic is meant for dragons to kill each other! No way a human can learn it!
...has got something wrong with him if you ask me!
After all, there aren't any dragons in the world.
Igneel is out there somewhere!!!!
They're all gone!!!!
All the dragons have been wiped out!!!!

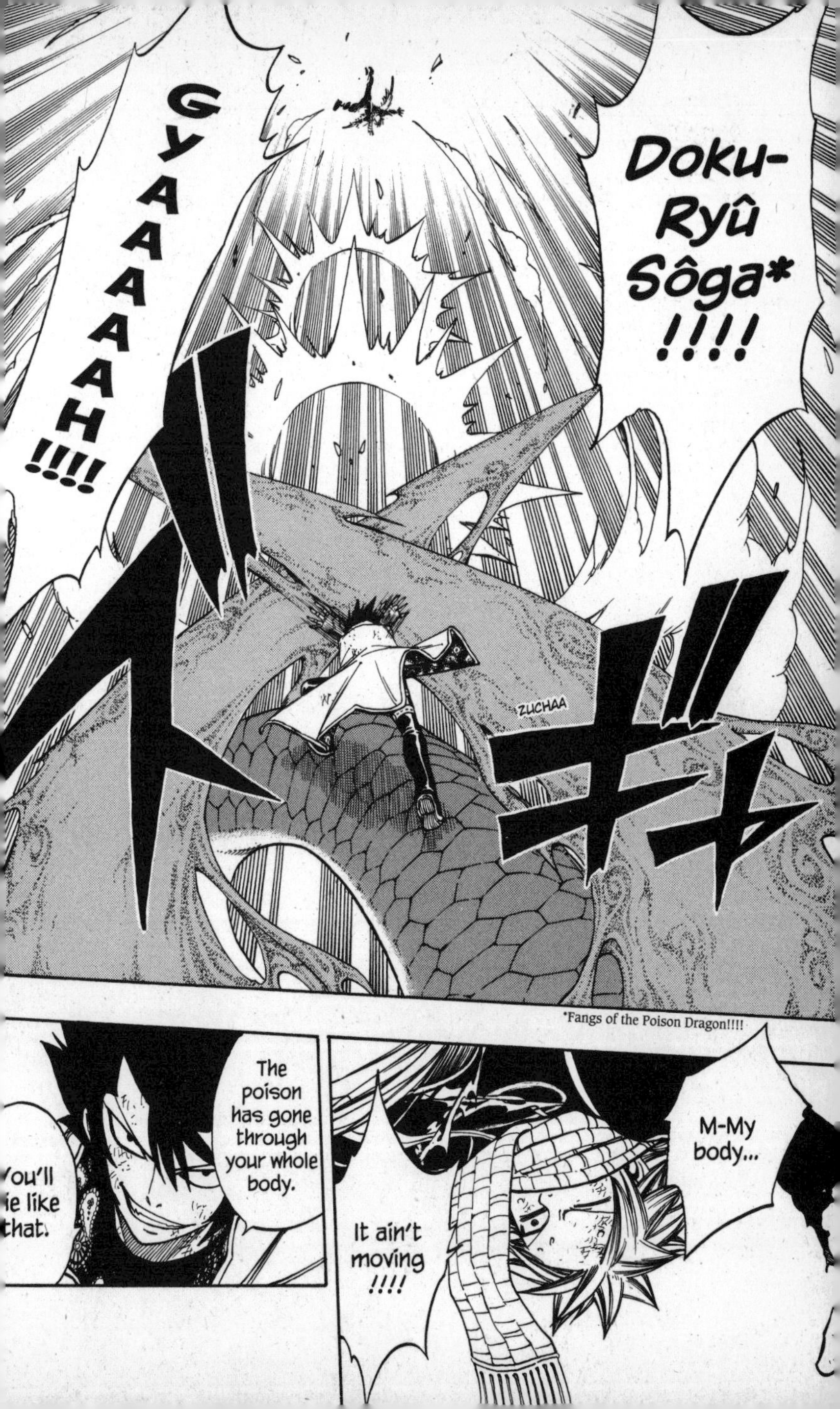
Doku-Ryû Sôga*!!!!
GYAAAAAH!!!!
ZUCHAA
*Fangs of the Poison Dragon!!!!
M-My body...
It ain't moving!!!!
The poison has gone through your whole body.
ou'll ie like that.

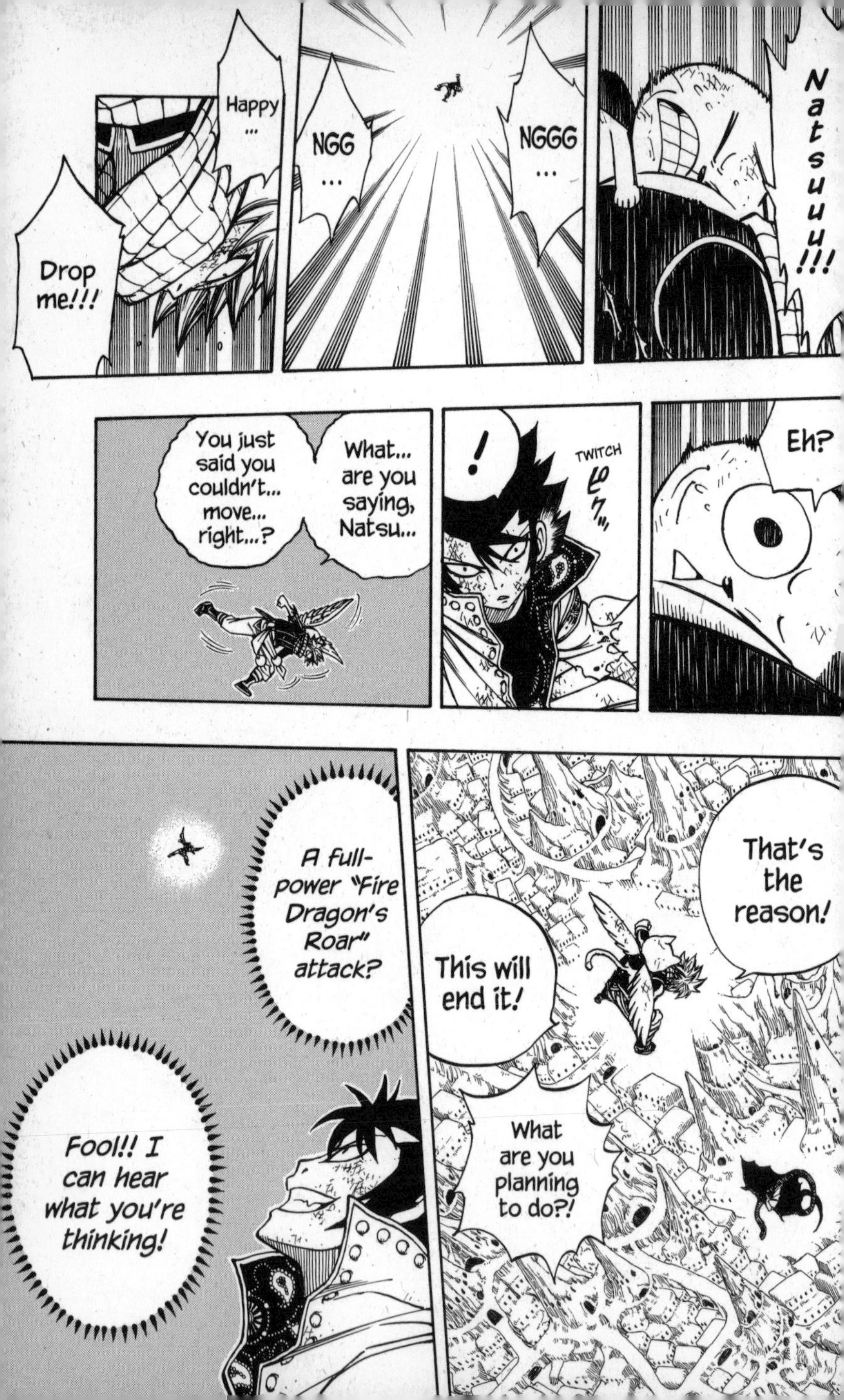
Natsuuuu!!!
NGGG...
NGG...
Happy...
Drop me!!!
Eh?
!
TWITCH
What... are you saying, Natsu...
You just said you couldn't... move... right...?
That's the reason!
This will end it!
What are you planning to do?!
A full-power "Fire Dragon's Roar" attack?
Fool!! I can hear what you're thinking!

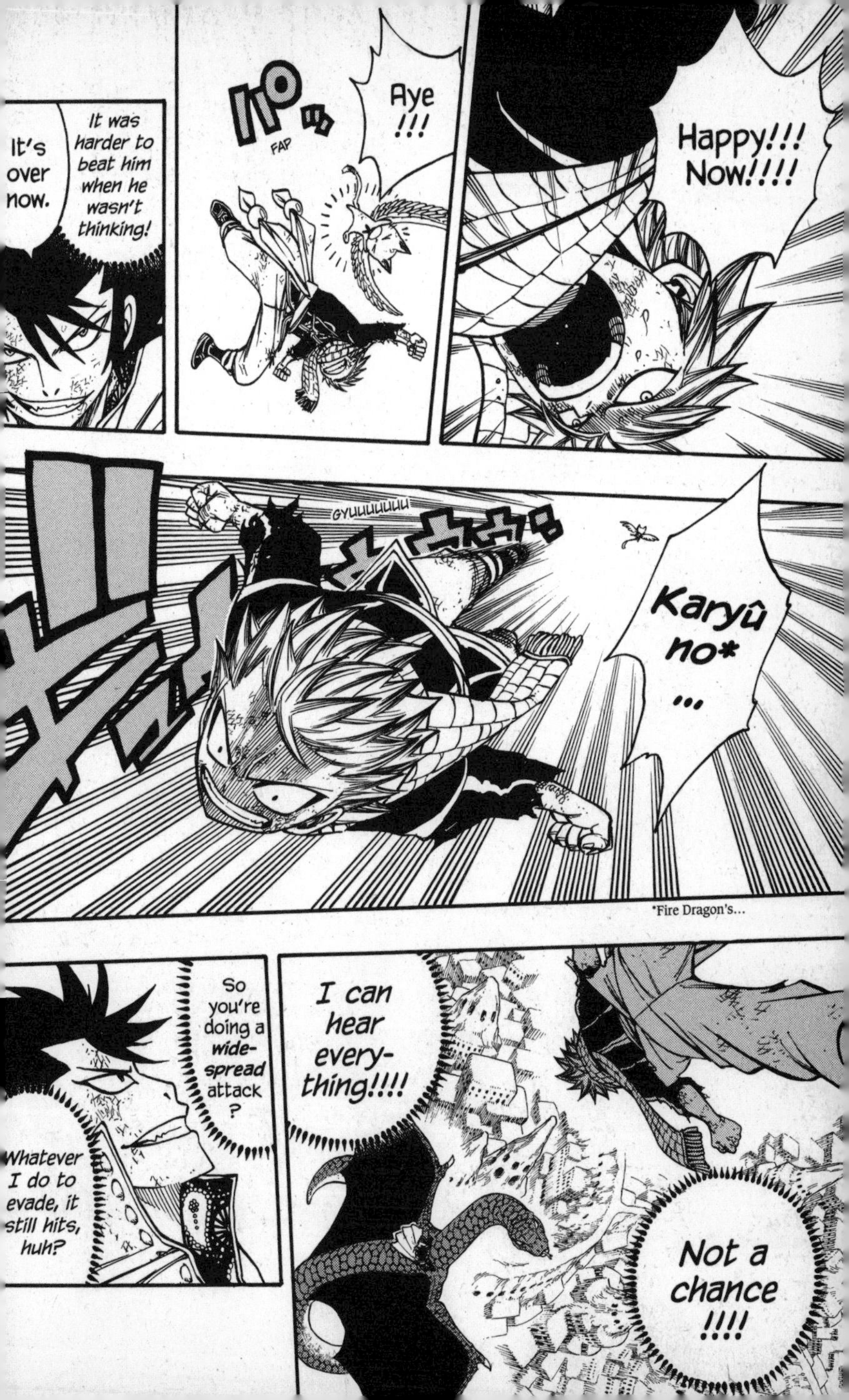
Happy!!! Now!!!!
Aye !!!
FAP
It was harder to beat him when he wasn't thinking!
It's over now.
GYUUUUUUUU
Karyû no* …
I can hear every-thing!!!!
Not a chance !!!!
So you're doing a wide-spread attack?
Whatever I do to evade, it still hits, huh?

*Fire Dragon's…

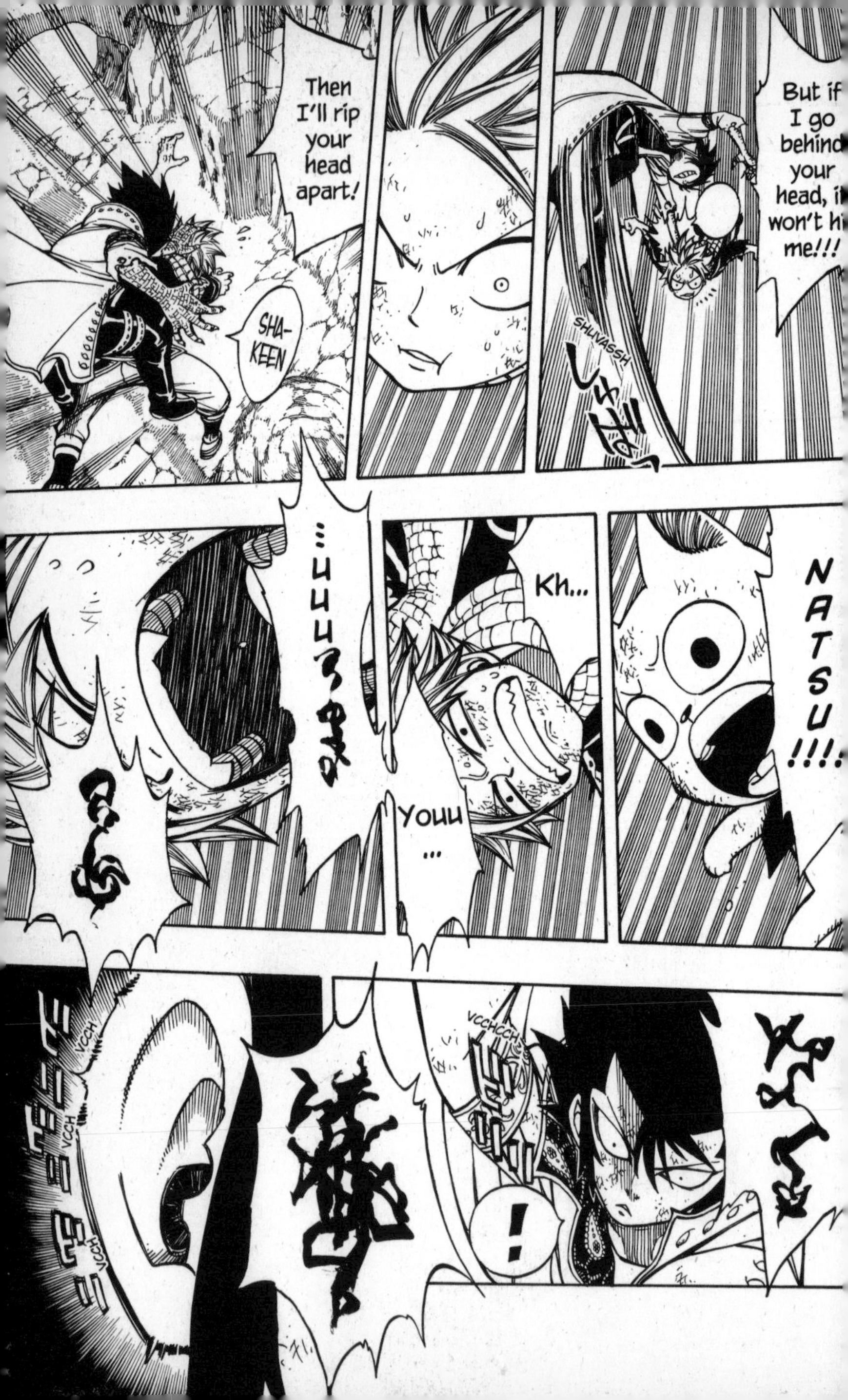

But if I go behind your head, it won't hit me!!!
SHUVASSH
Then I'll rip your head apart!
SHA-KEEN
NATSU!!!!
Kh...
Youu...
VCCHCCH
!
VCCH
VCCH
VCCH

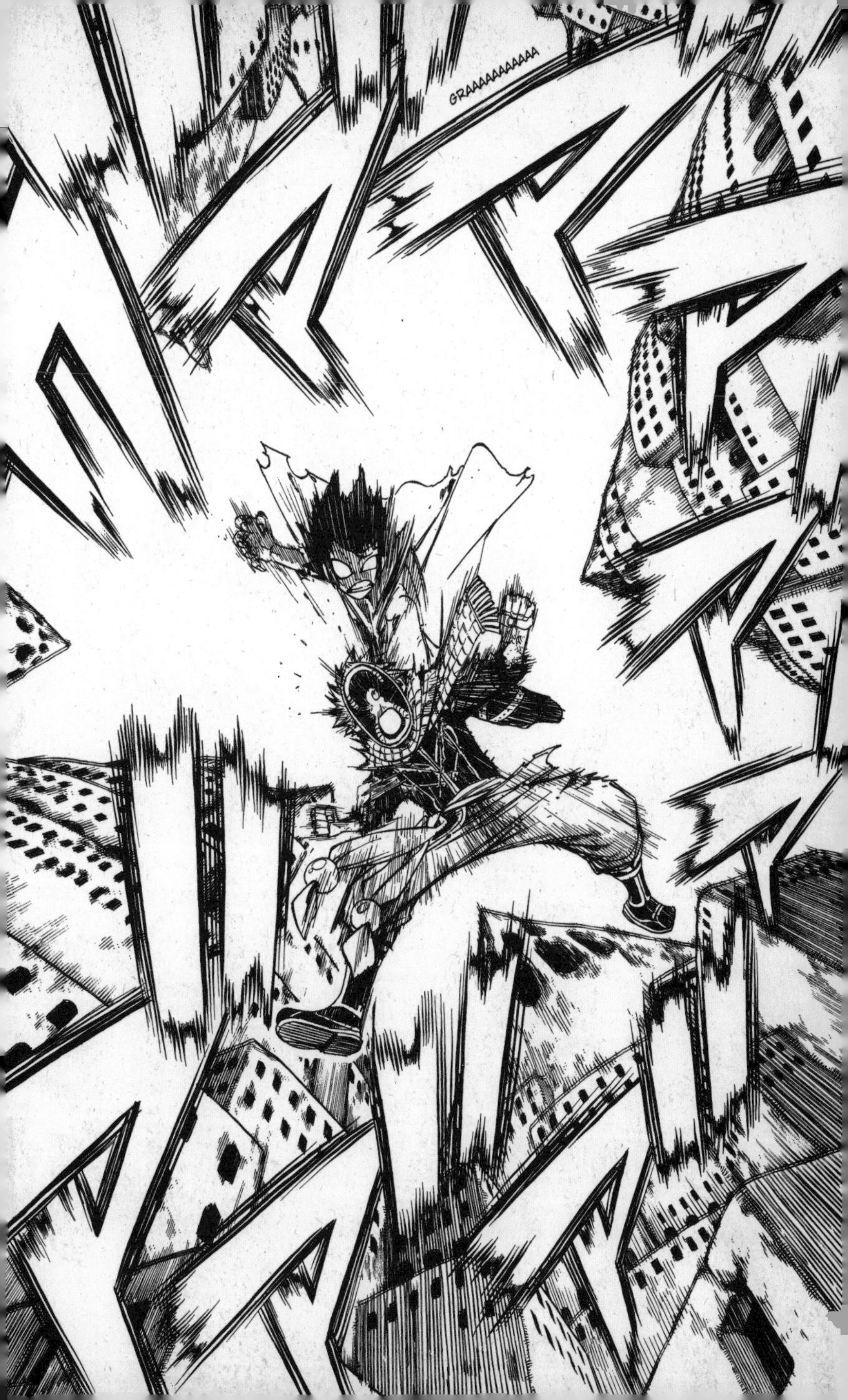
GRAAAAAAAAAAA

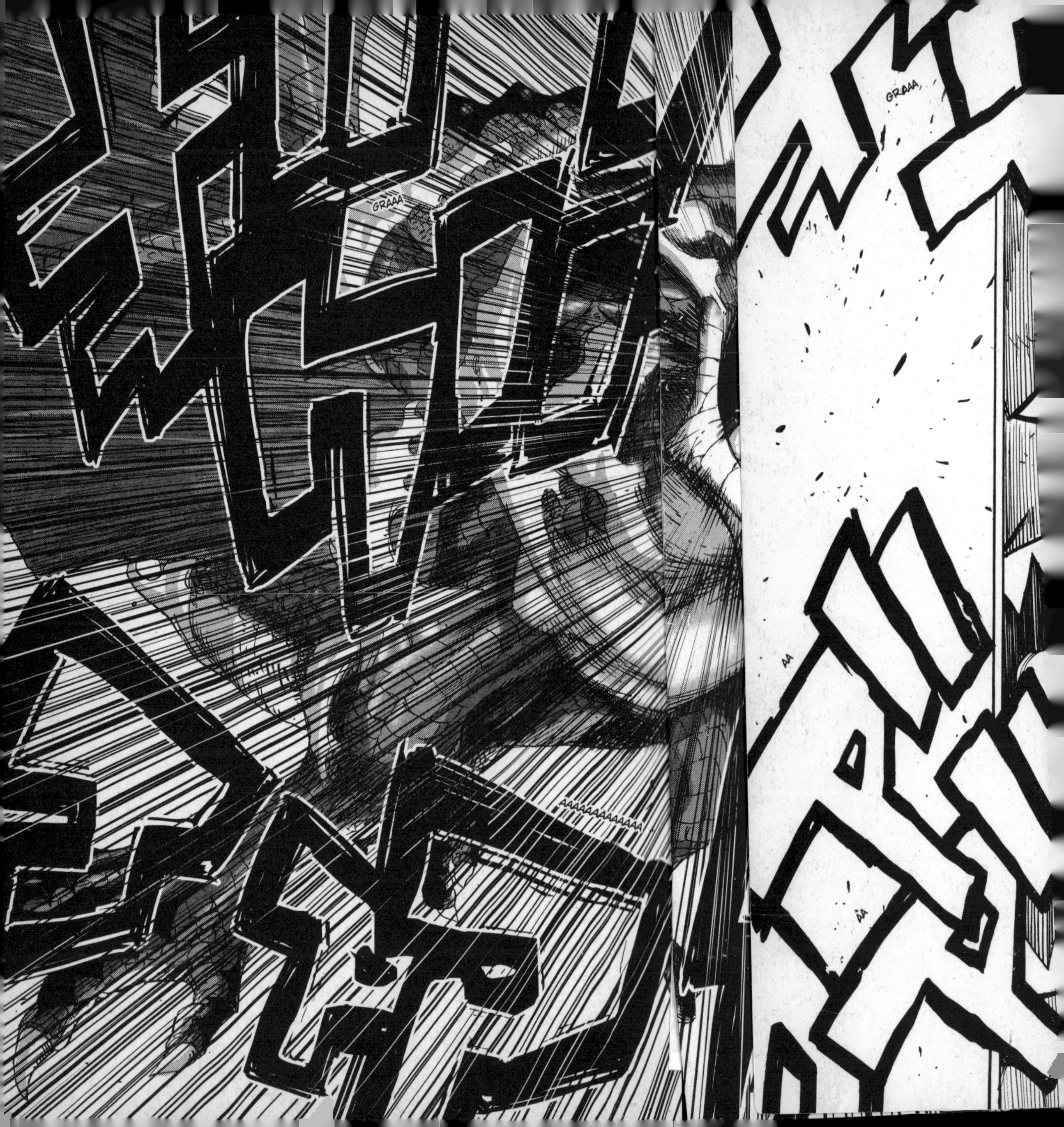
GRAAA
AA
AA
GRAAA
AAAAAAAAAAAAA

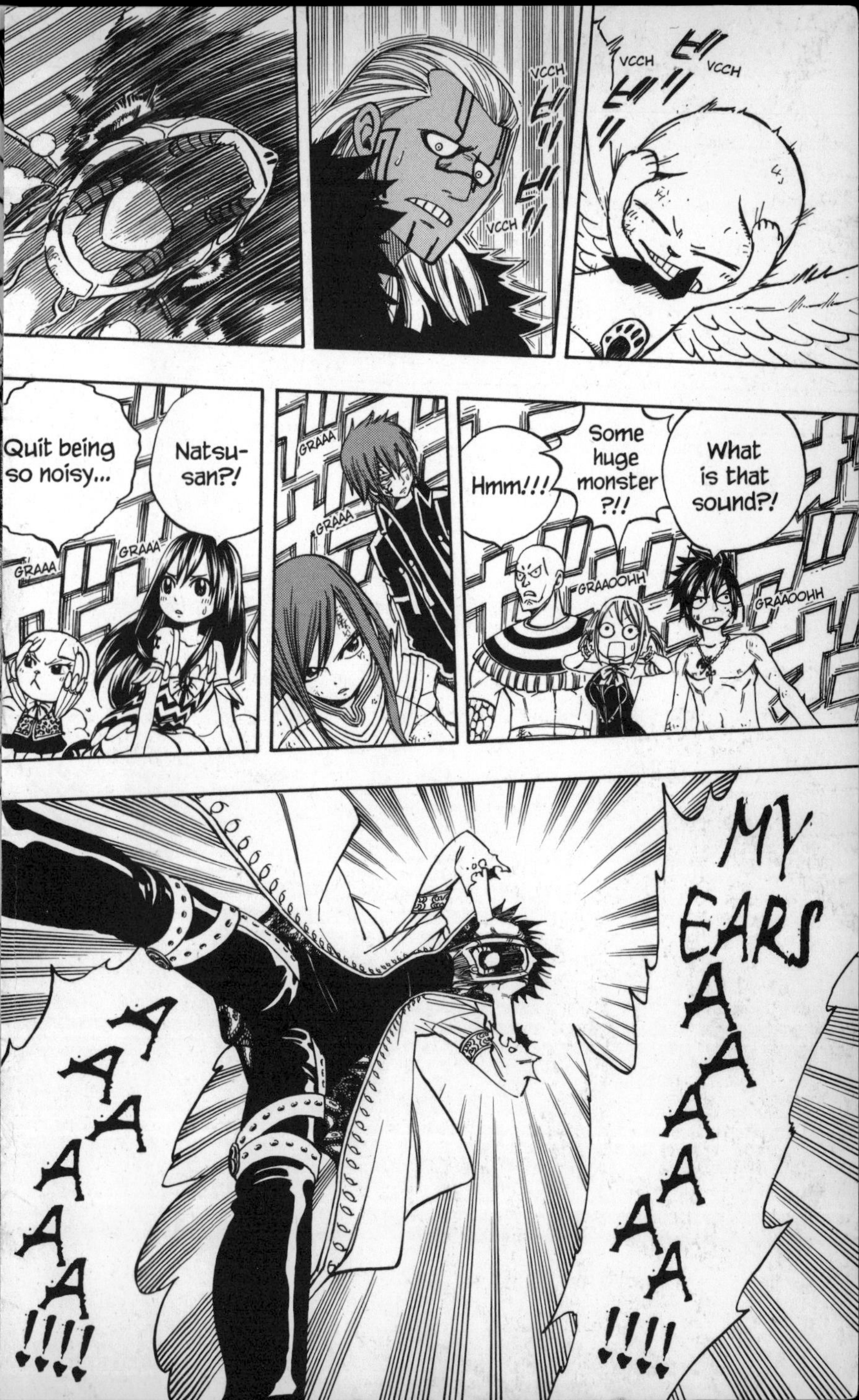
VCCH
VCCH
VCCH
VCCH
What is that sound?!
Some huge monster?!!
Hmm!!!
GRAAOOHH
GRAAOOHH
GRAAA
GRAAA
Natsu-san?!
Quit being so noisy...
GRAAA
GRAAA
MY EARS AAAAAAAA!!!!
AAAAAAA!!!!
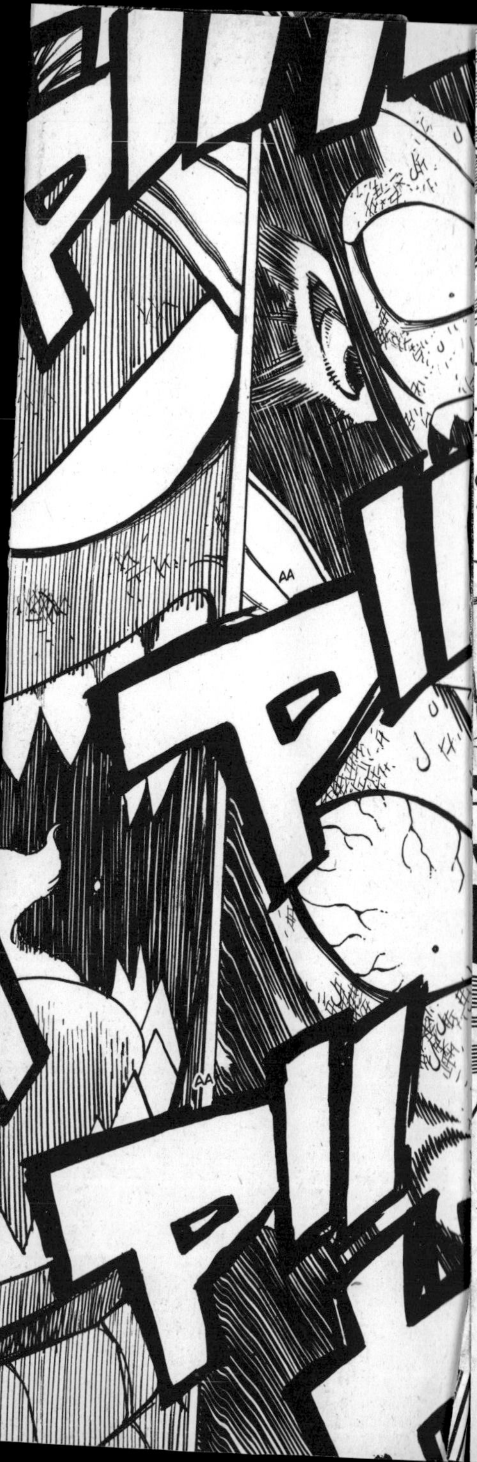
AA
AA

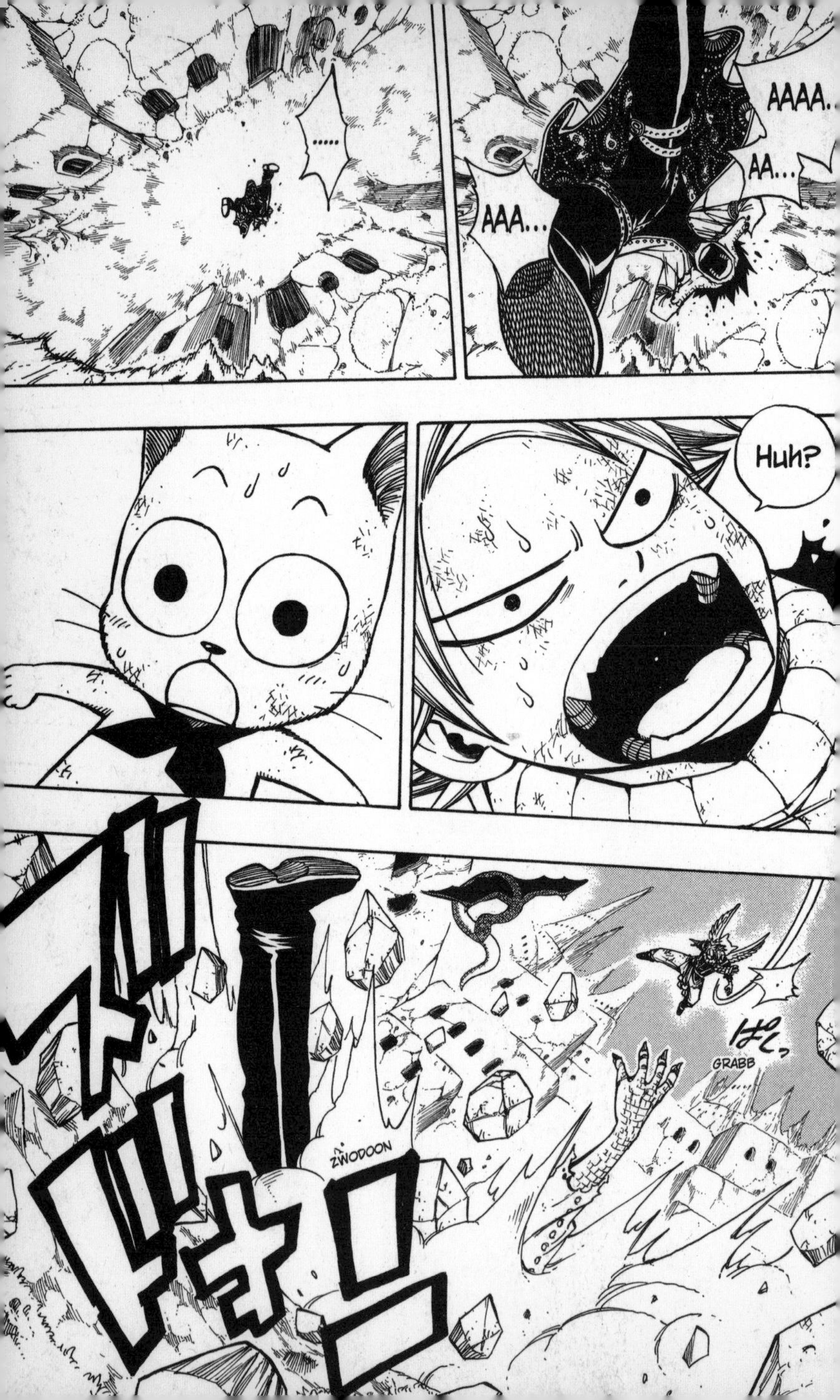
AAAA..
AA...
AAA...
.....
Huh?
ぱしっ
GRABB
ZWODOON

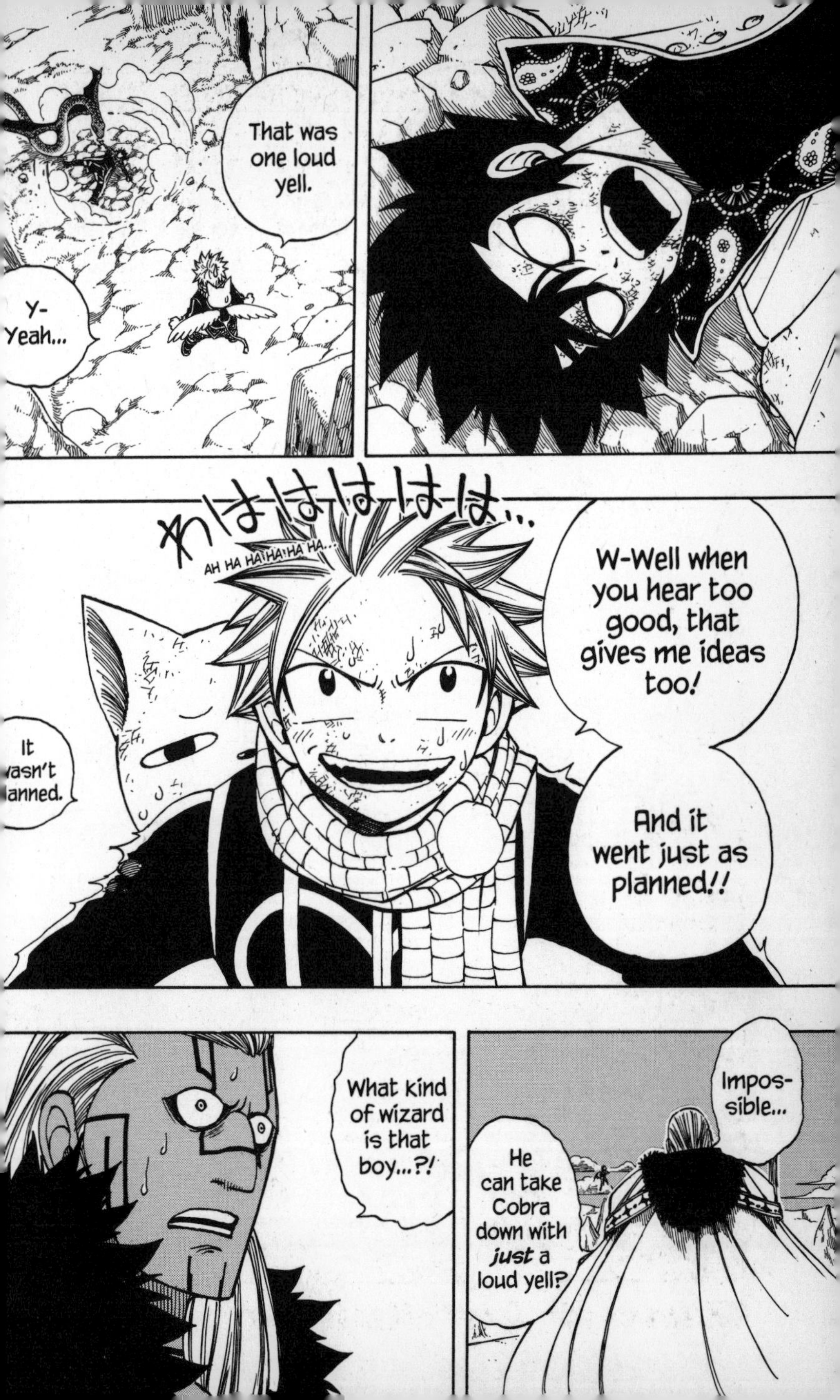
That was one loud yell.
Y- Yeah...
わははははは...
AH HA HA HA HA HA...
W-Well when you hear too good, that gives me ideas too!
And it went just as planned!!
It asn't anned.
Impos- sible...
He can take Cobra down with *just* a loud yell?
What kind of wizard is that boy...?!

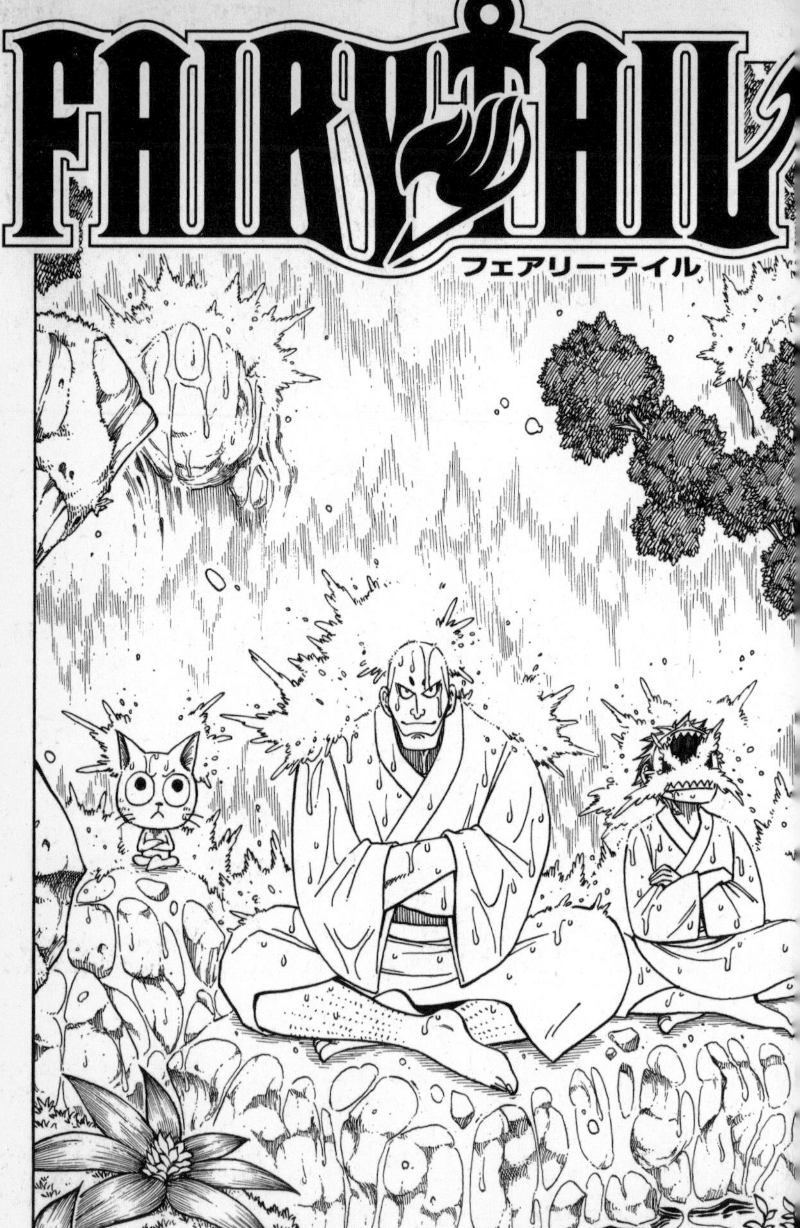
FAIRY TAIL
フェアリーテイル

Chapter 151, Annihilation of Six Demons?!

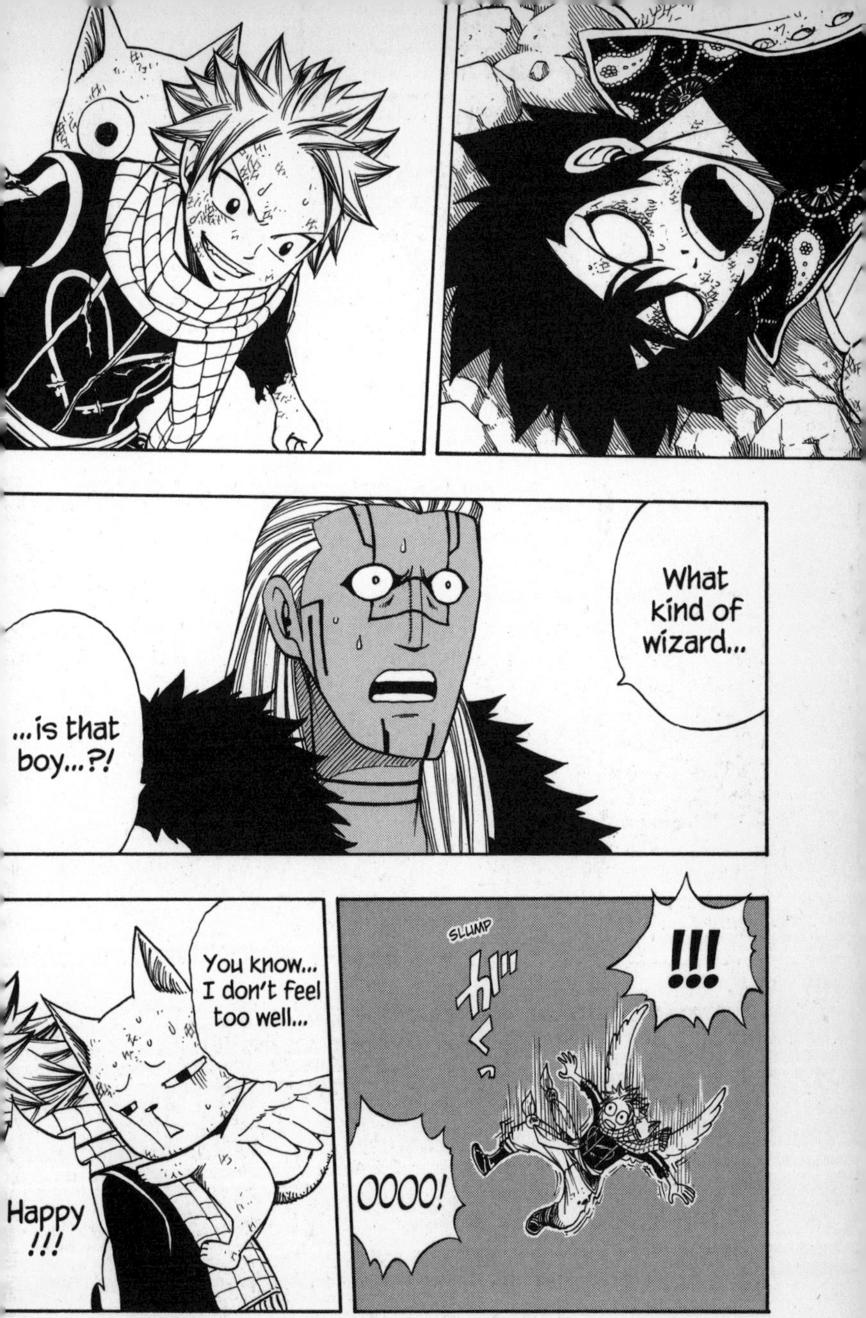
What kind of wizard...
...is that boy...?!
!!!
SLUMP
がくっ
OOOO!
You know... I don't feel too well...
Happy !!!

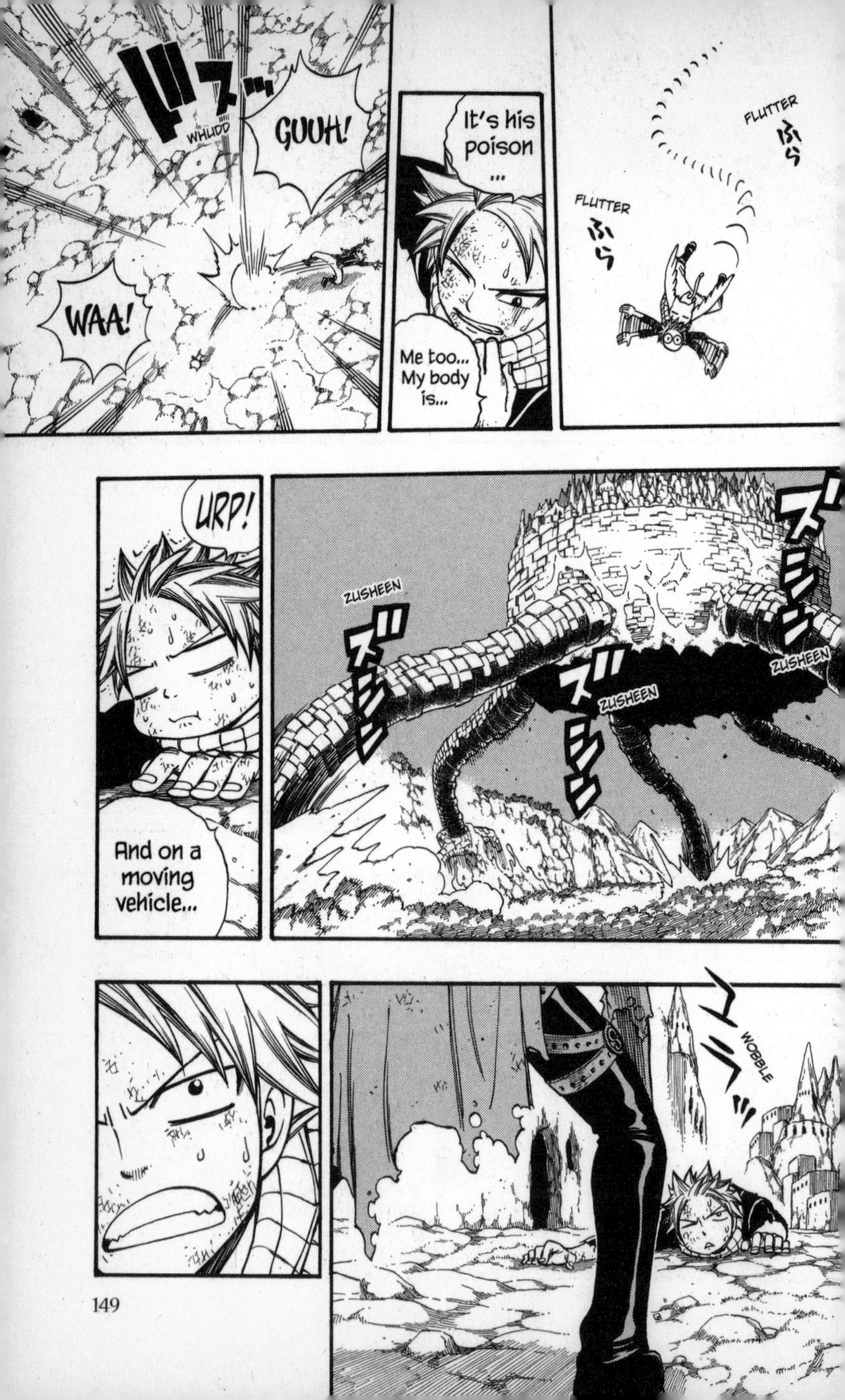
FLUTTER
ふら
FLUTTER
ふら
It's his poison...
Me too... My body is...
WHUDD
GUUH!
WAA!
ZUSHEEN
ZUSHEEN
ZUSHEEN
URP!
And on a moving vehicle...
WOBBLE

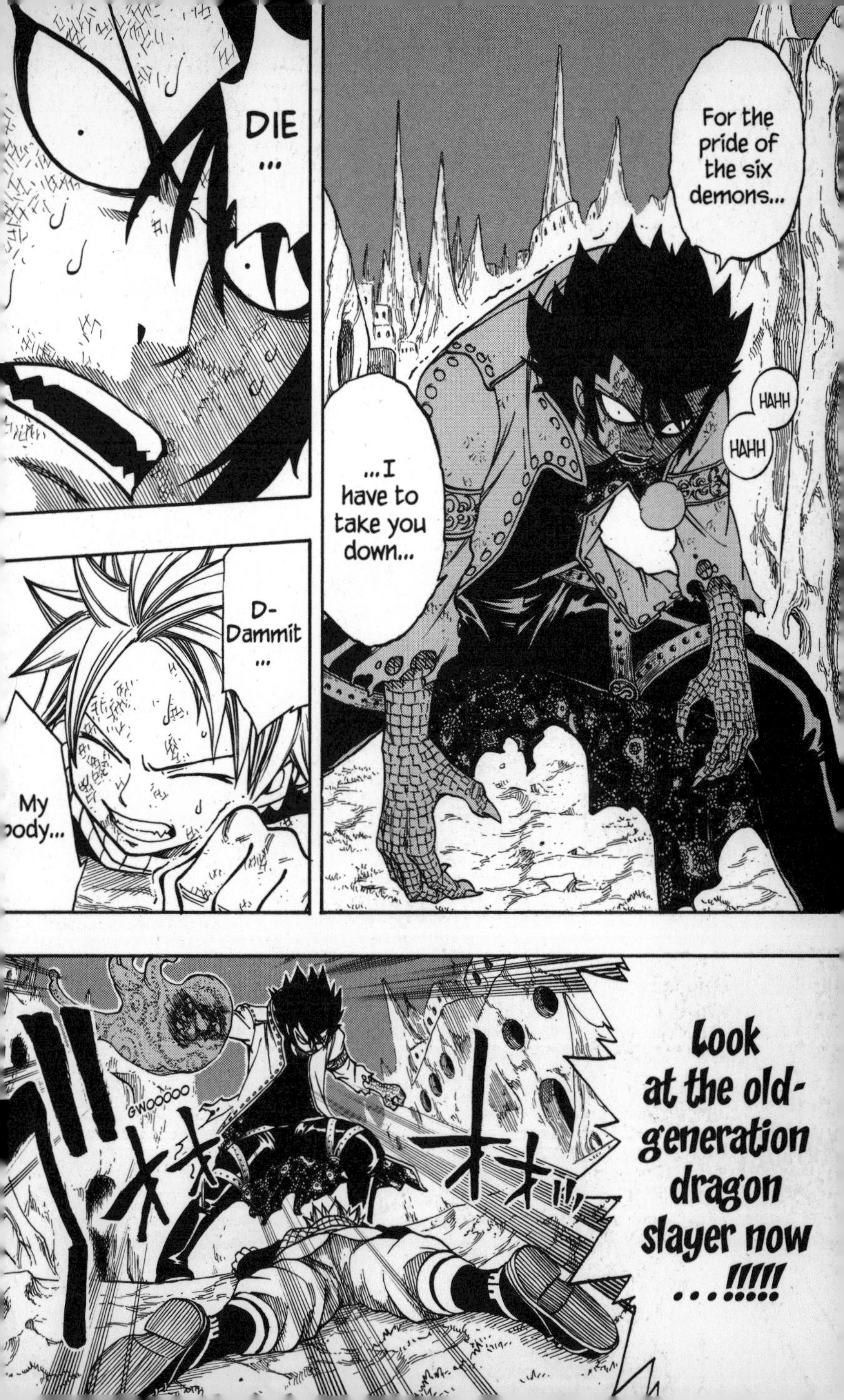
For the pride of the six demons...
HAHH
HAHH
...I have to take you down...
DIE ...
D-Dammit ...
My body...
GWOOOOO
Look at the old-generation dragon slayer now . . . !!!!!

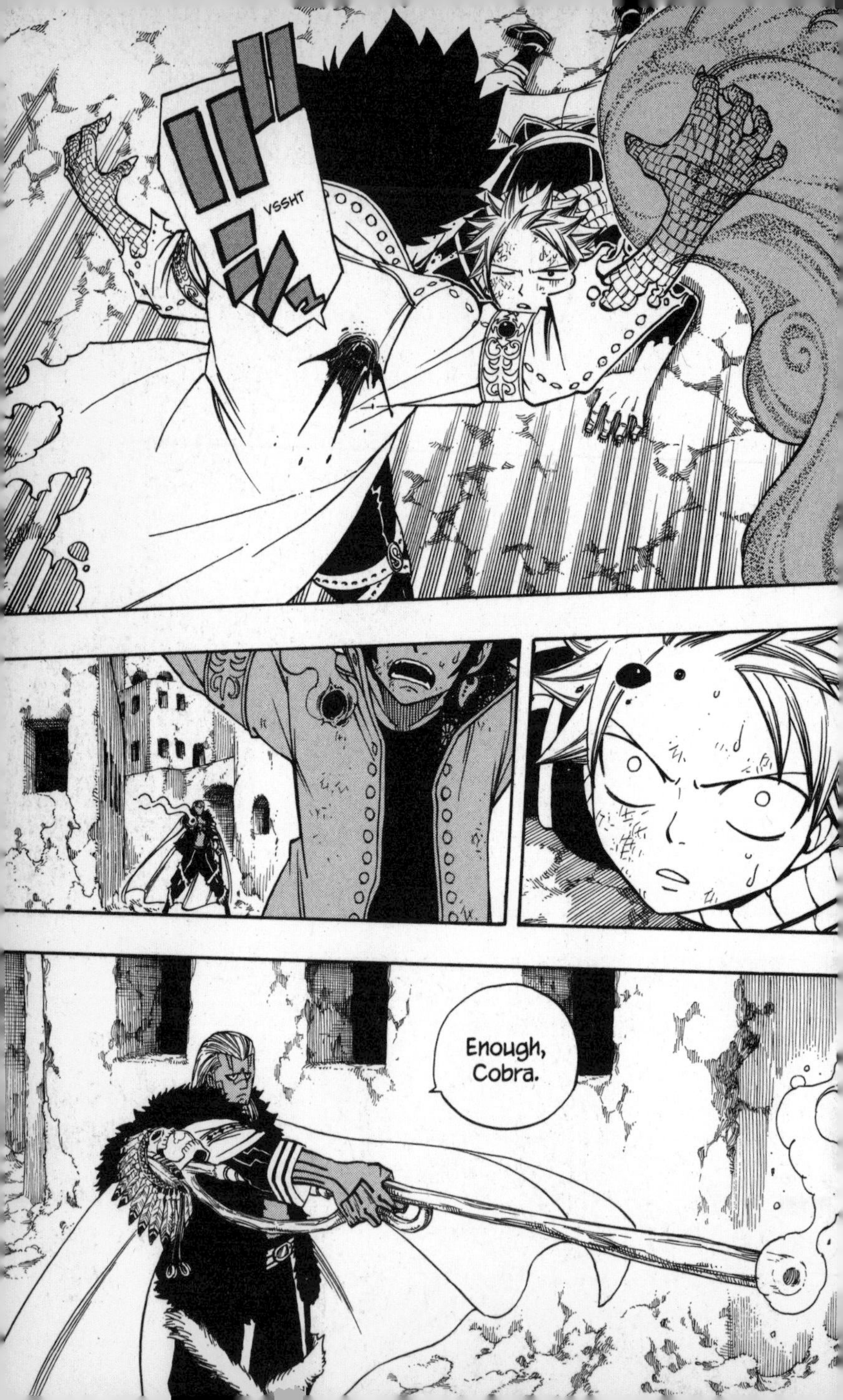
VSSHT
Enough, Cobra.

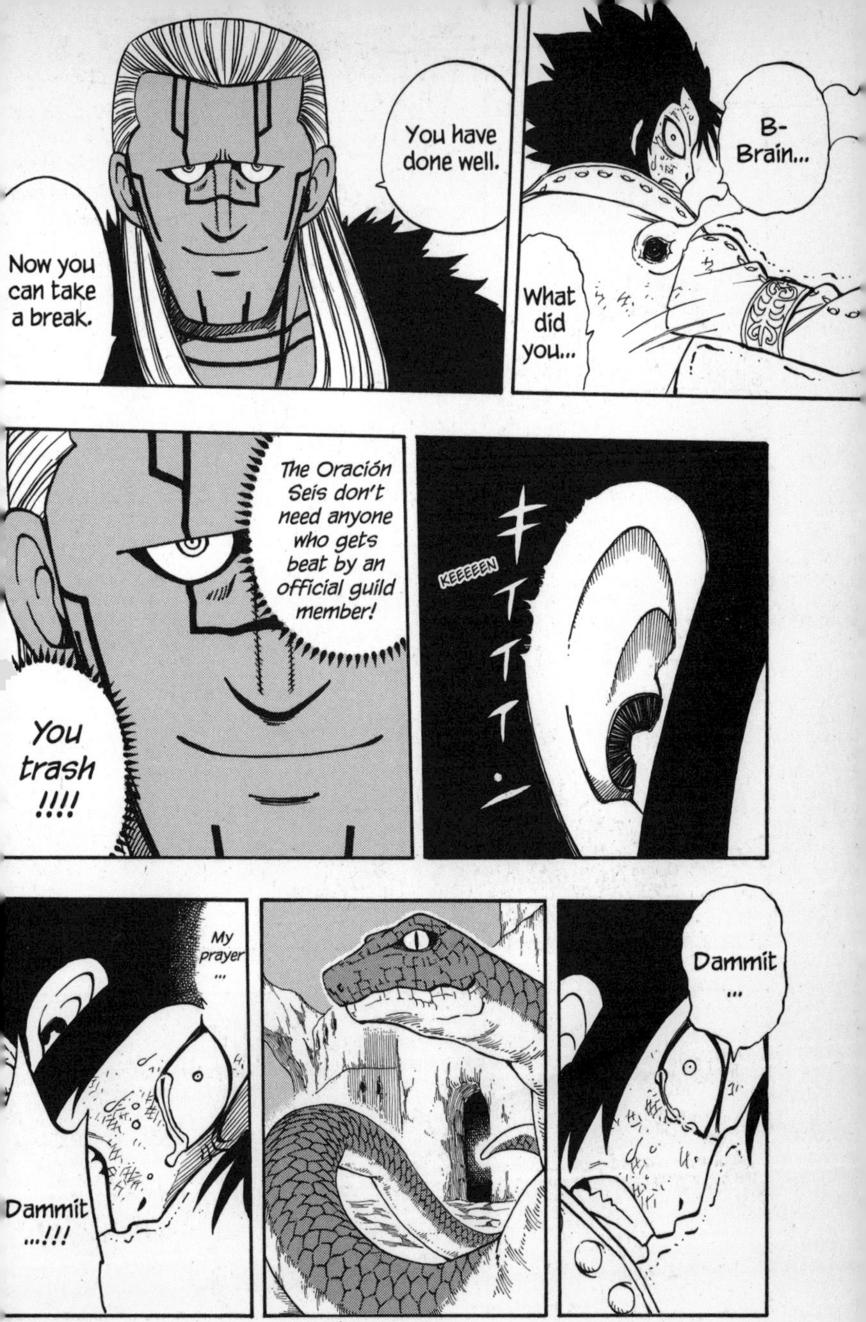
B-Brain...
What did you...
You have done well.
Now you can take a break.
KEEEEEN
The Oración Seis don't need anyone who gets beat by an official guild member!
You trash !!!!
Dammit ...
My prayer ...
Dammit ...!!!

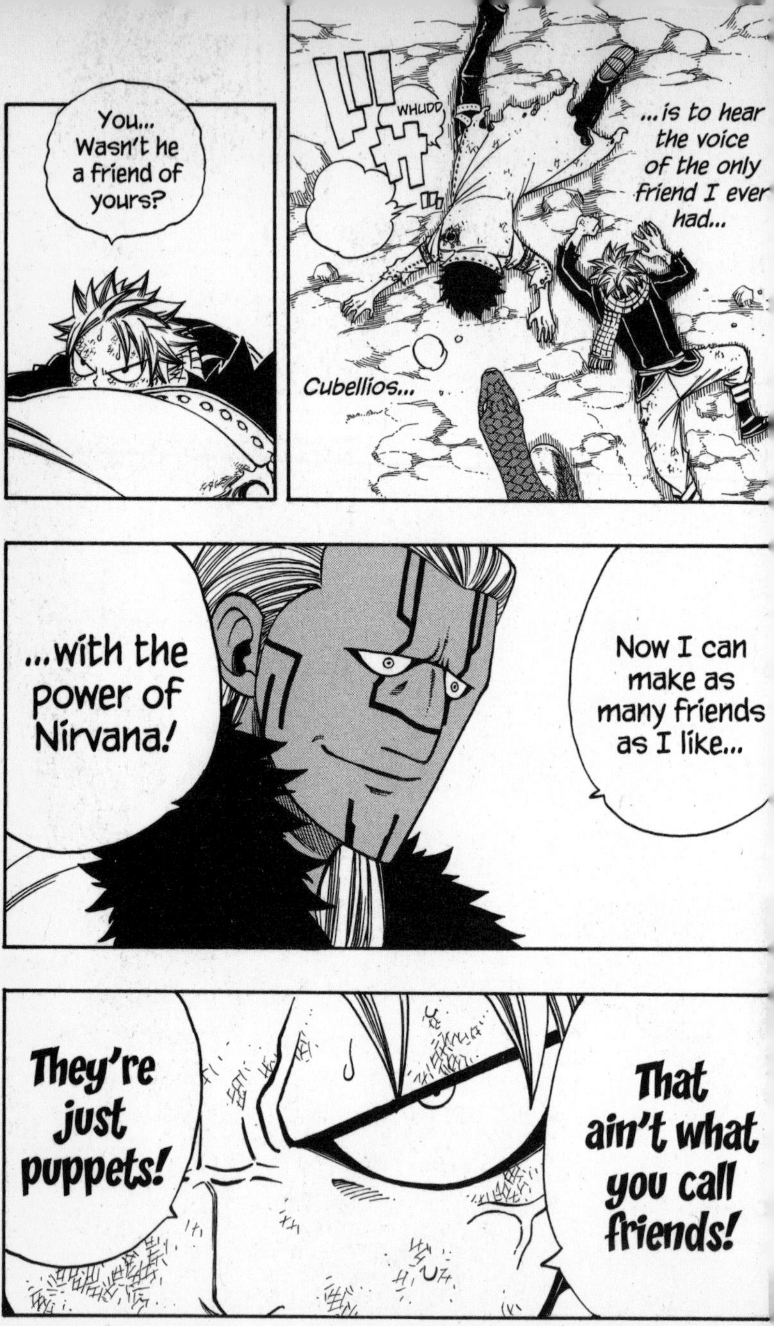
WHUDD
...is to hear the voice of the only friend I ever had...
Cubellios...
You... Wasn't he a friend of yours?
Now I can make as many friends as I like...
...with the power of Nirvana!
That ain't what you call friends!
They're just puppets!

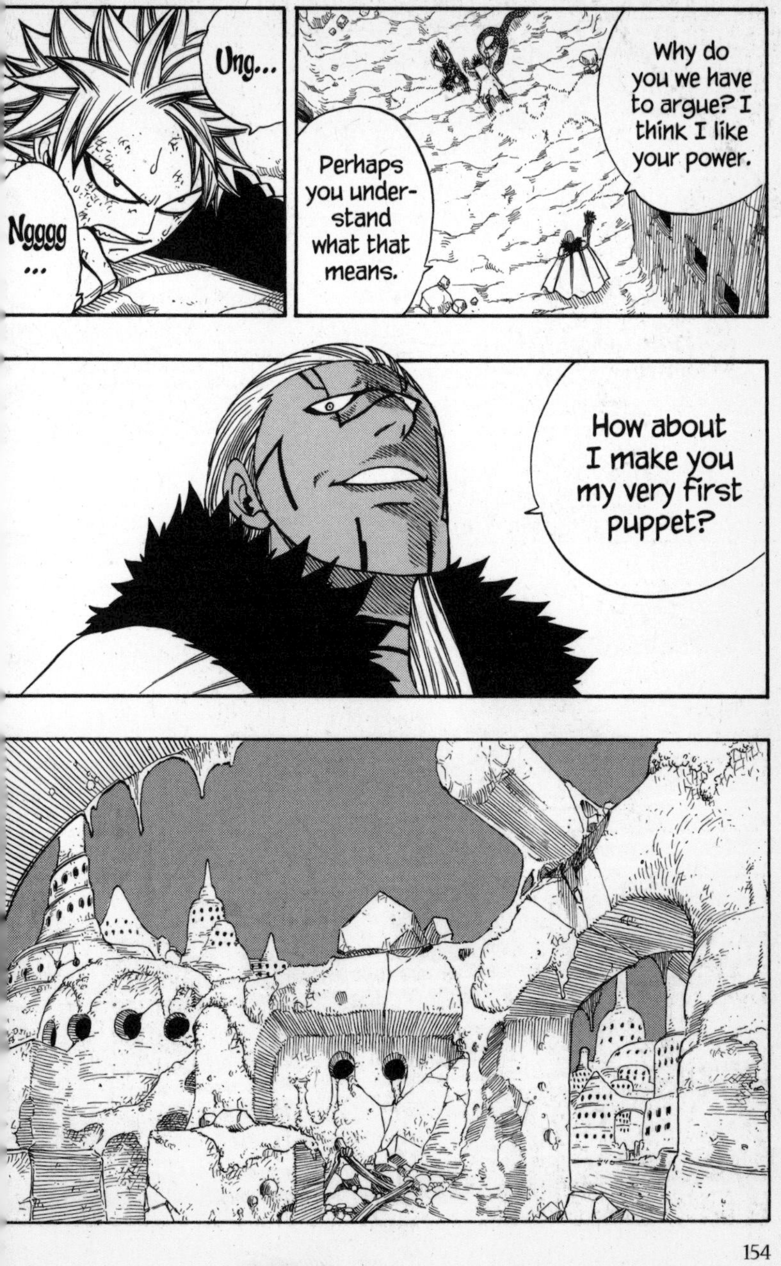
Why do you we have to argue? I think I like your power.
Perhaps you understand what that means.
Ung...
Ngggg ...
How about I make you my very first puppet?

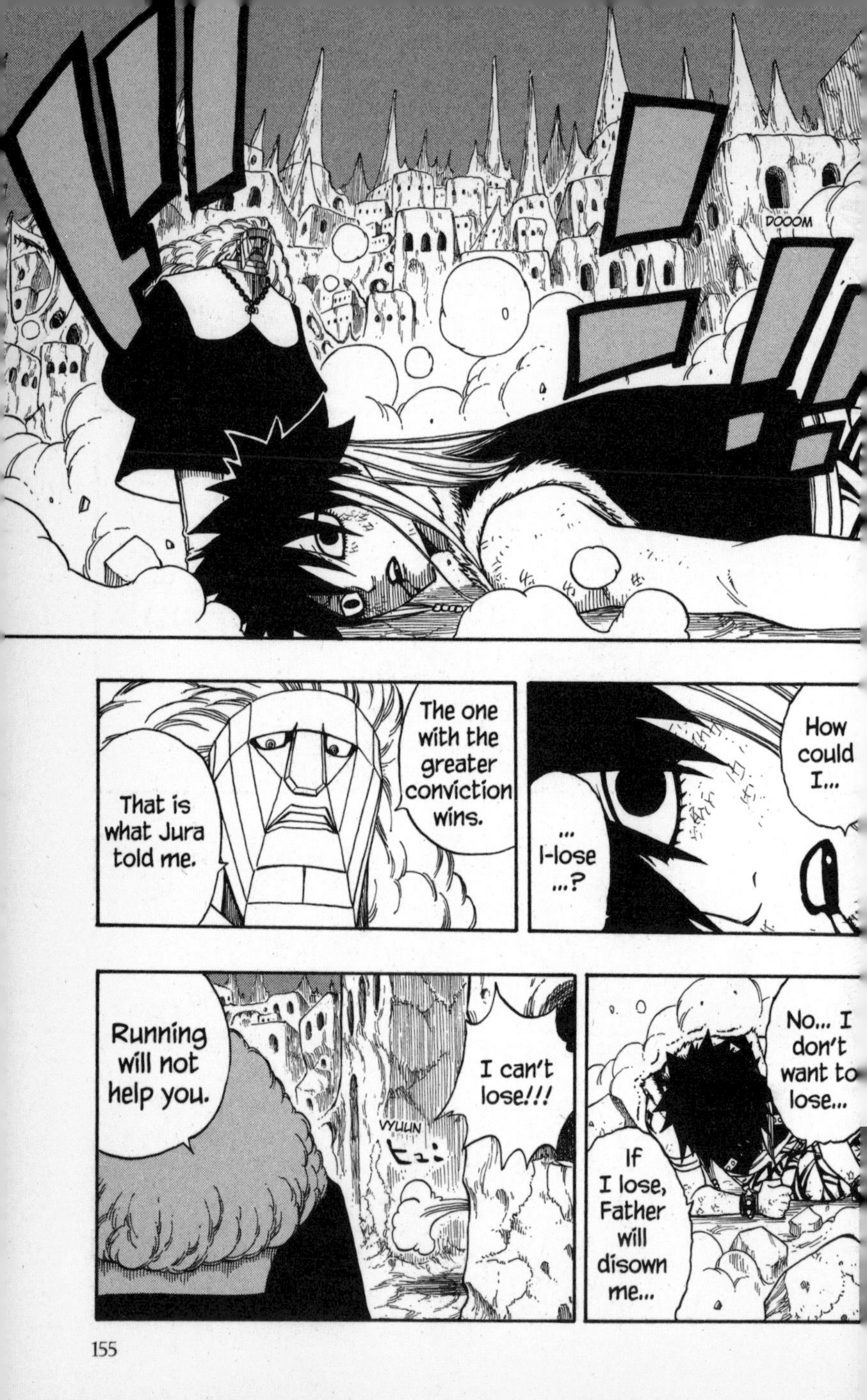
DOOOM
How could I...
... I-lose ...?
The one with the greater conviction wins.
That is what Jura told me.
No... I don't want to lose...
If I lose, Father will disown me...
I can't lose!!!
VYUUN
Running will not help you.

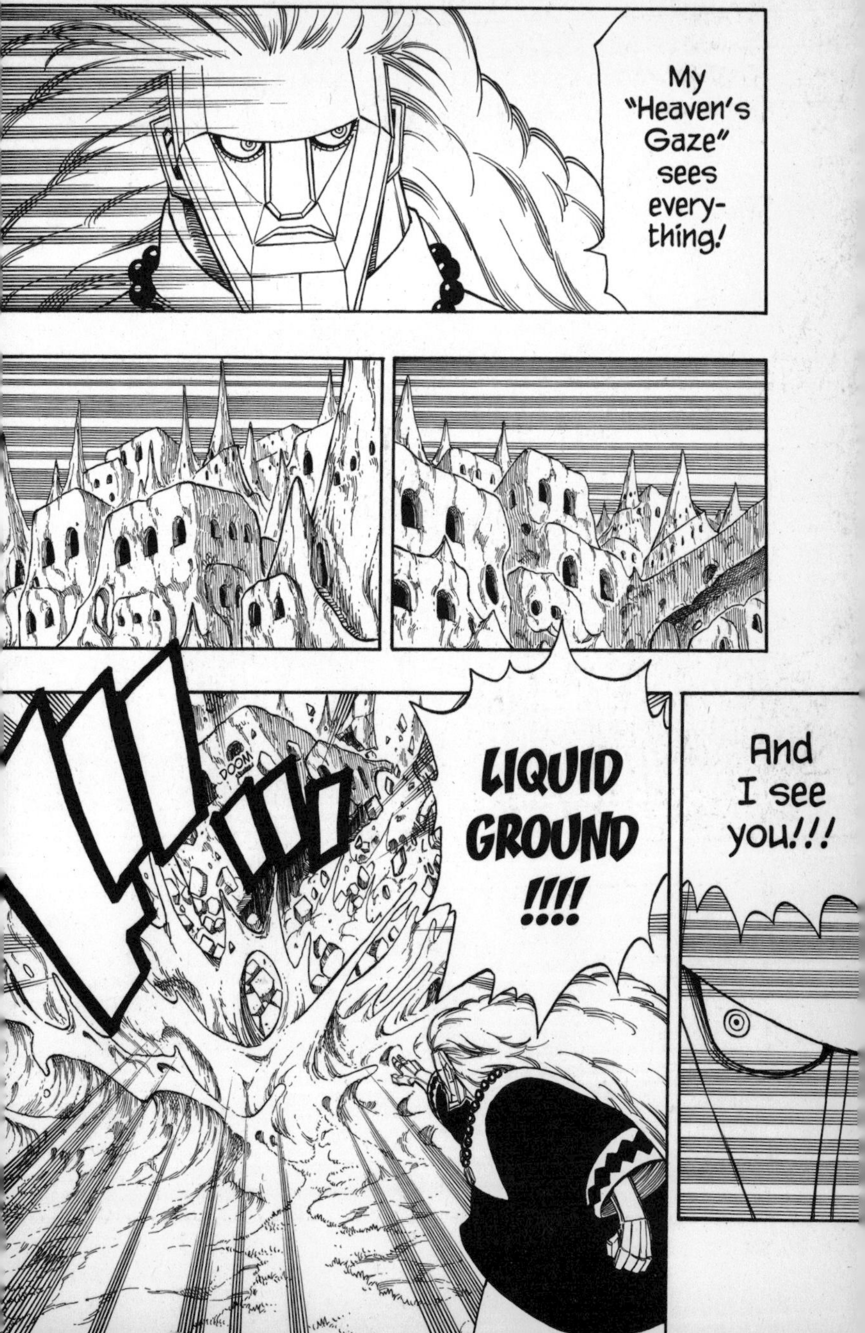
My "Heaven's Gaze" sees every-thing!
And I see you!!!
LIQUID GROUND !!!!
DOOM

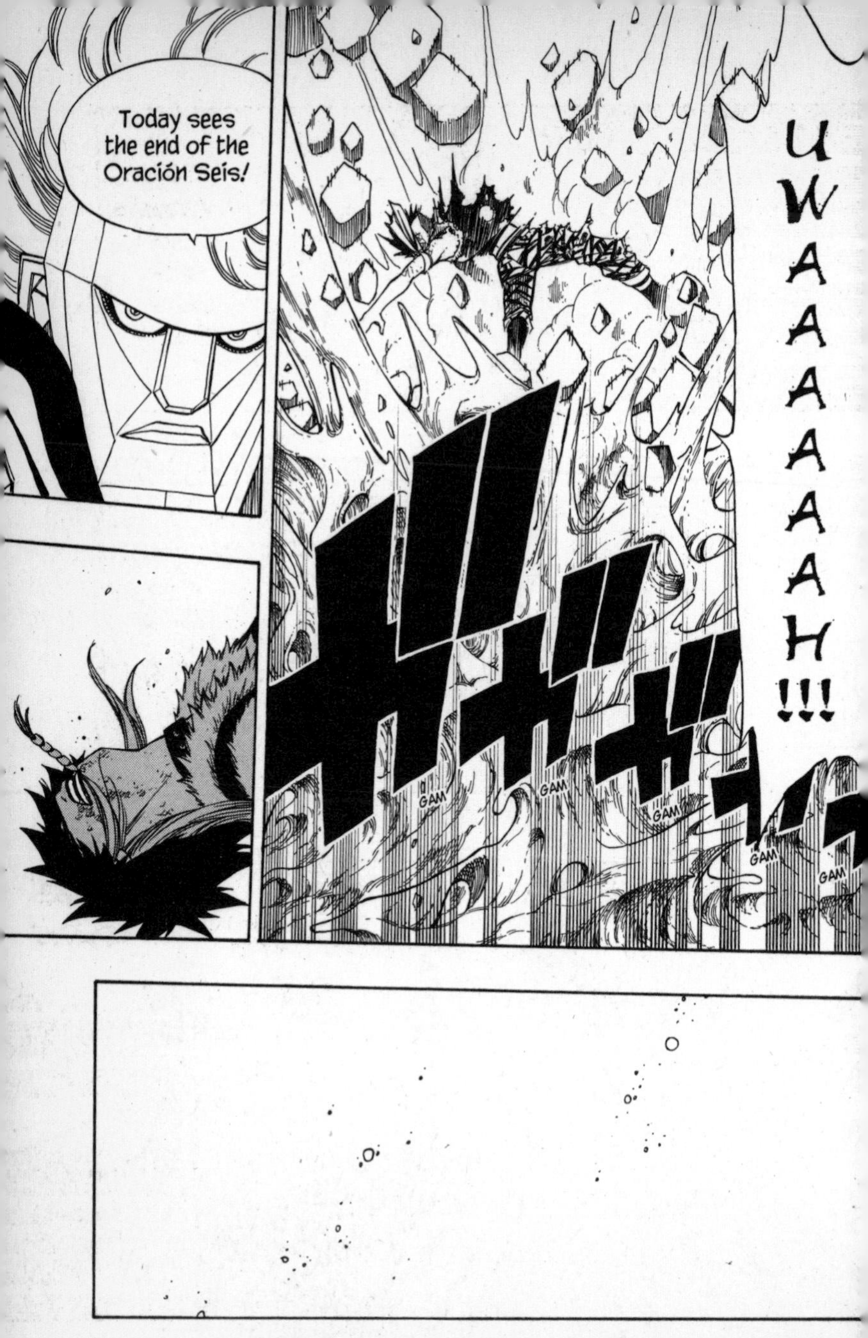
UWAAAAAAH!!!
GAM
GAM
GAM
GAM
GAM
Today sees the end of the Oración Seis!

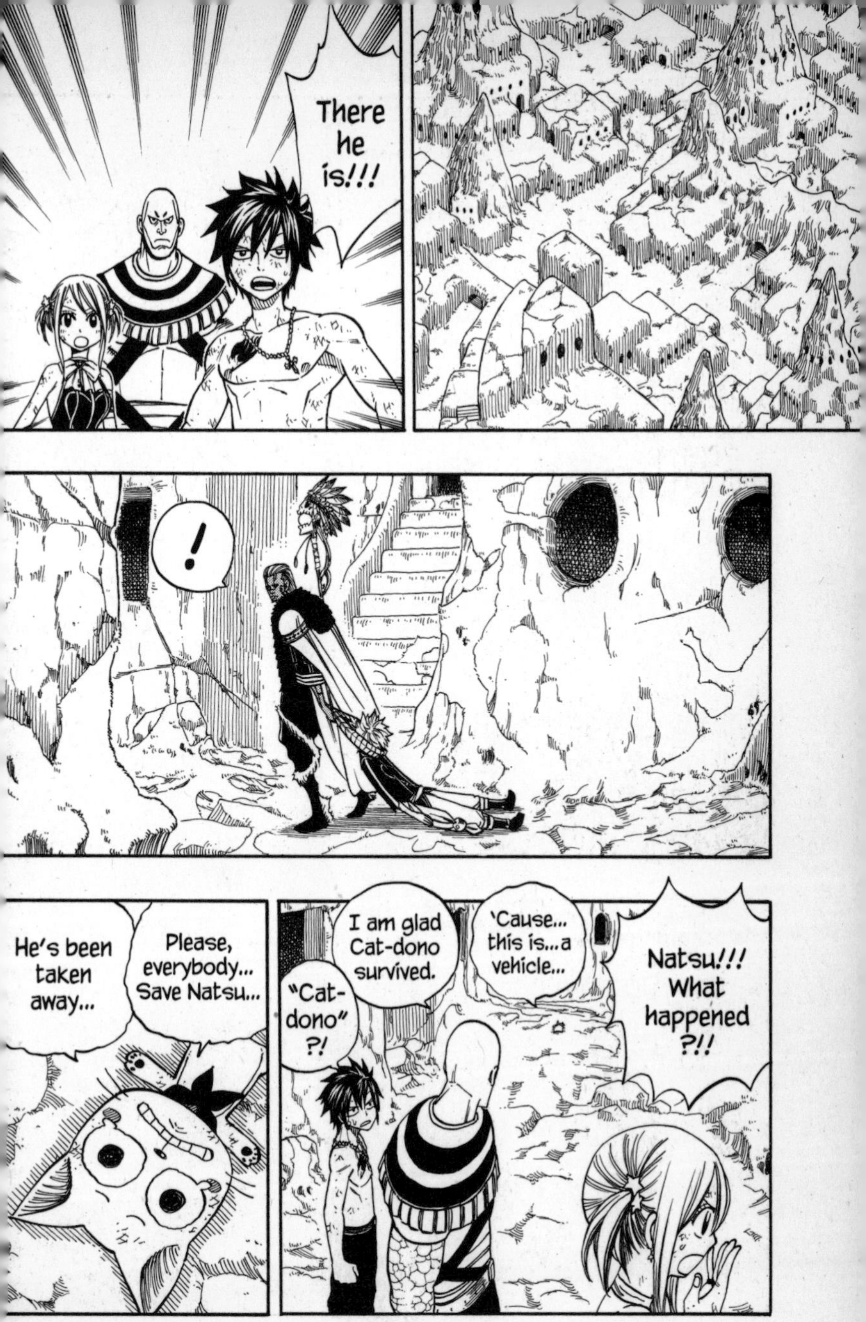
There he is!!!
!
Natsu!!! What happened?!!
'Cause... this is...a vehicle...
I am glad Cat-dono survived.
"Cat-dono"?!
Please, everybody... Save Natsu...
He's been taken away...

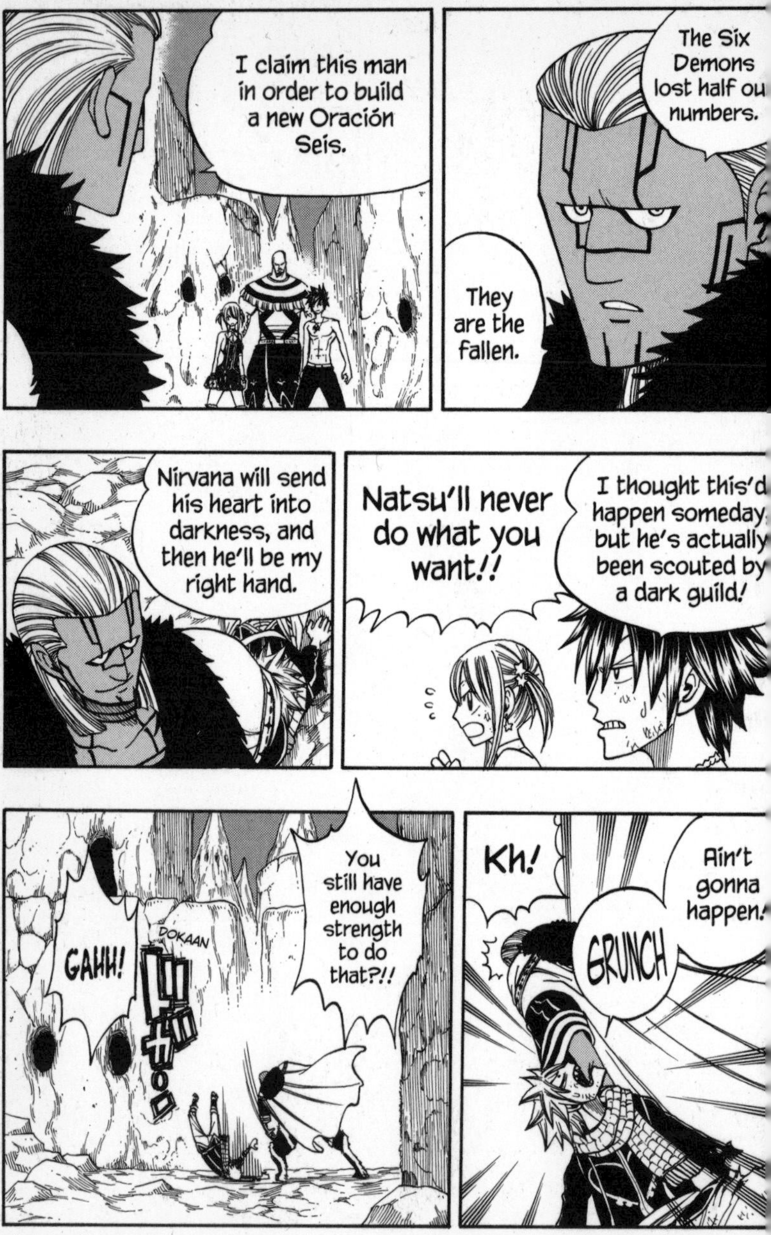

The Six Demons lost half ou numbers.
They are the fallen.
I claim this man in order to build a new Oración Seis.
I thought this'd happen someday, but he's actually been scouted by a dark guild!
Natsu'll never do what you want!!
Nirvana will send his heart into darkness, and then he'll be my right hand.
Ain't gonna happen!
Kh!
GRUNCH
You still have enough strength to do that?!!
DOKAAN
GAHH!

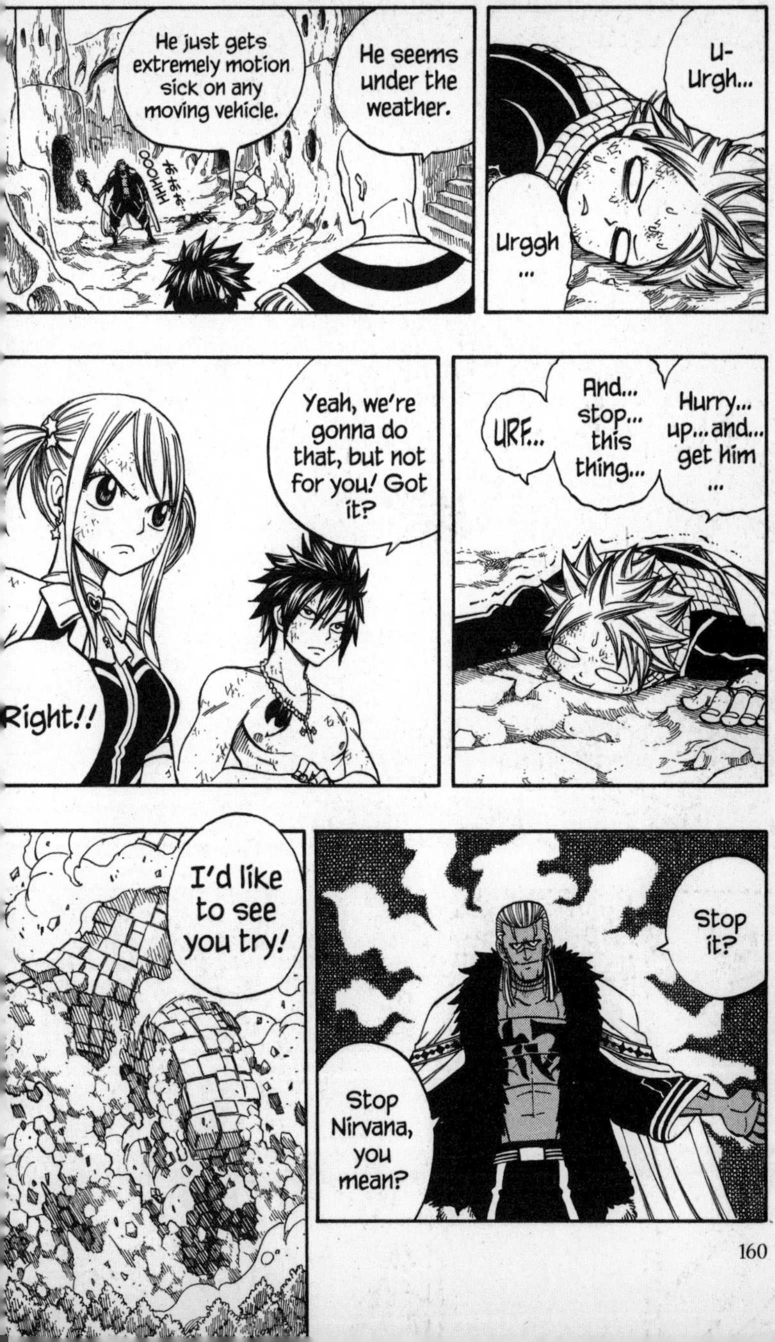
U-
Urgh...
Urggh ...
He seems under the weather.
He just gets extremely motion sick on any moving vehicle.
OOOHHH
Hurry... up...and... get him ...
And... stop... this thing...
URF...
Yeah, we're gonna do that, but not for you! Got it?
Right!!
Stop it?
Stop Nirvana, you mean?
I'd like to see you try!

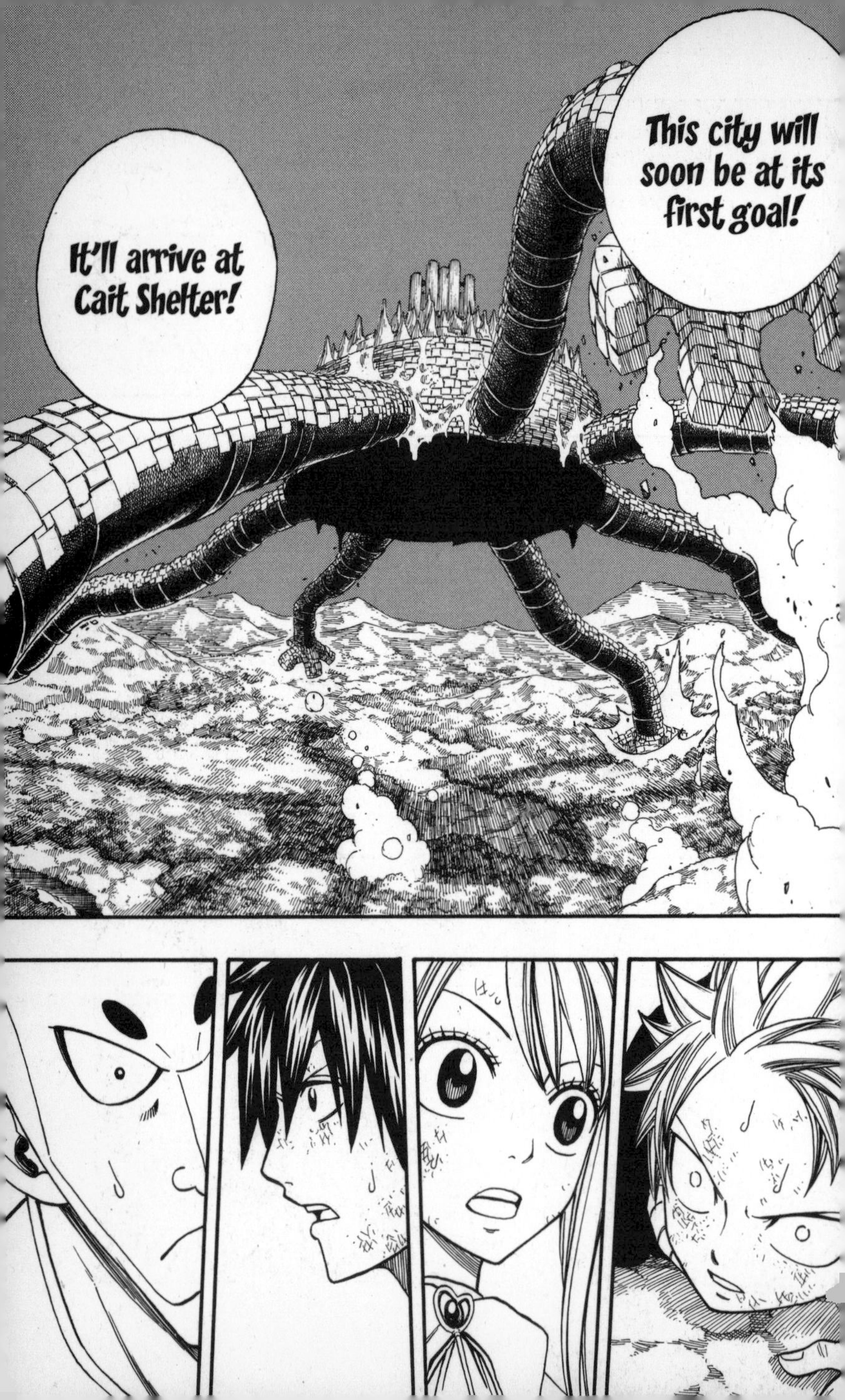
This city will soon be at its first goal!
It'll arrive at Cait Shelter!

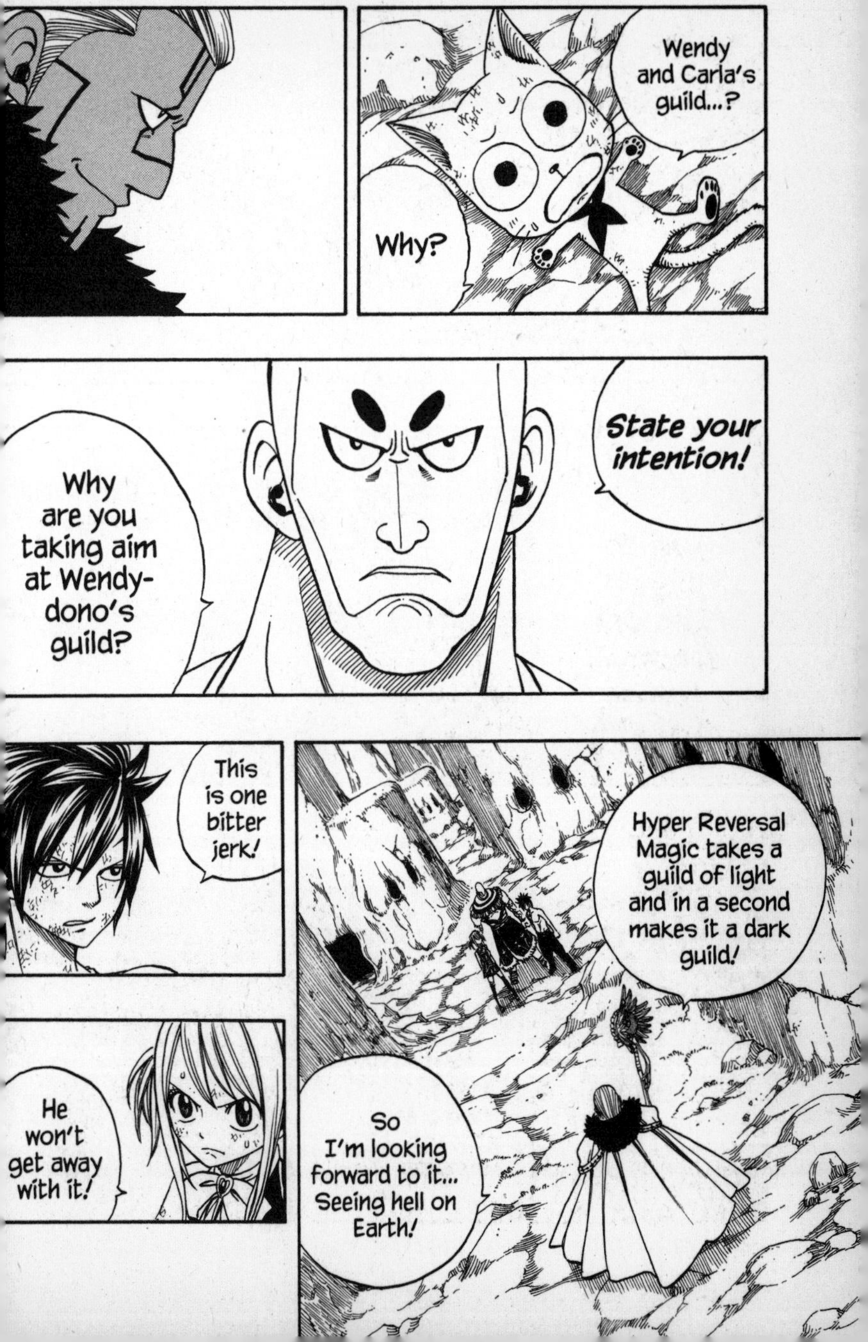
Wendy and Carla's guild...?
Why?
State your intention!
Why are you taking aim at Wendy-dono's guild?
Hyper Reversal Magic takes a guild of light and in a second makes it a dark guild!
So I'm looking forward to it... Seeing hell on Earth!
This is one bitter jerk!
He won't get away with it!

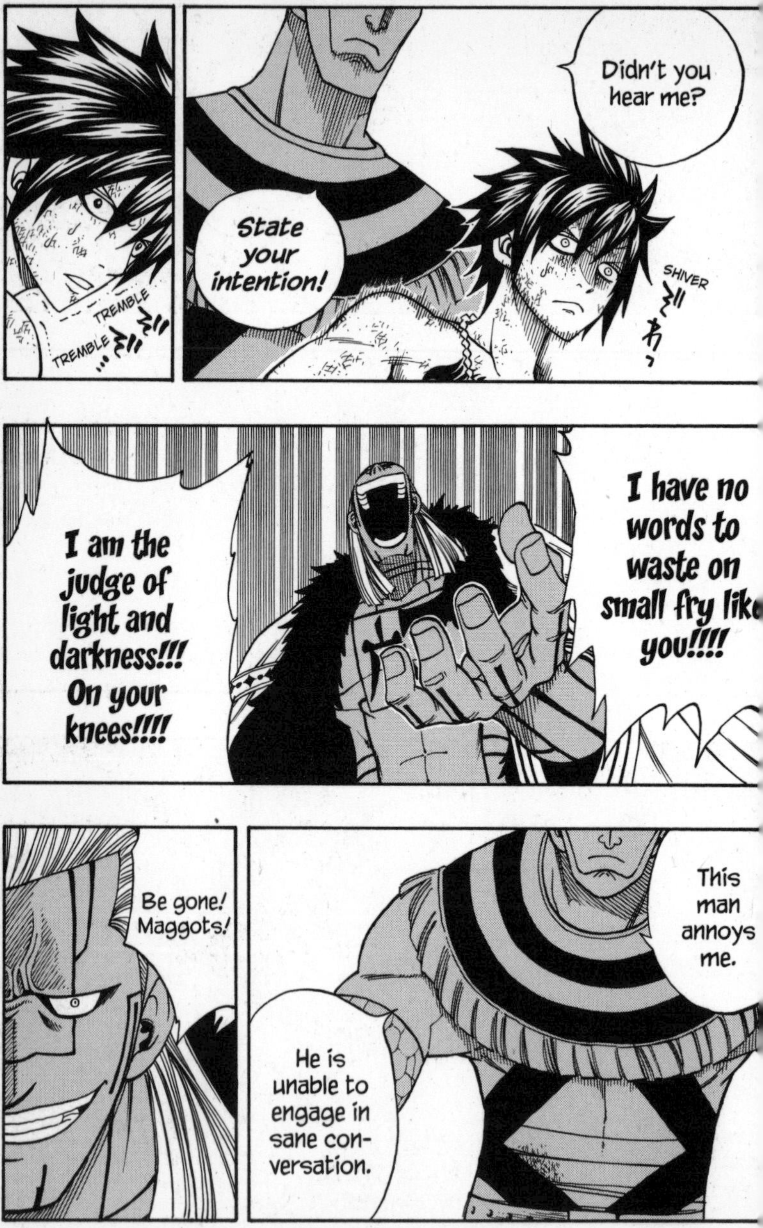

Didn't you hear me?
SHIVER
State your intention!
TREMBLE
TREMBLE
I have no words to waste on small fry like you!!!!
I am the judge of light and darkness!!! On your knees!!!!
This man annoys me.
He is unable to engage in sane conversation.
Be gone! Maggots!

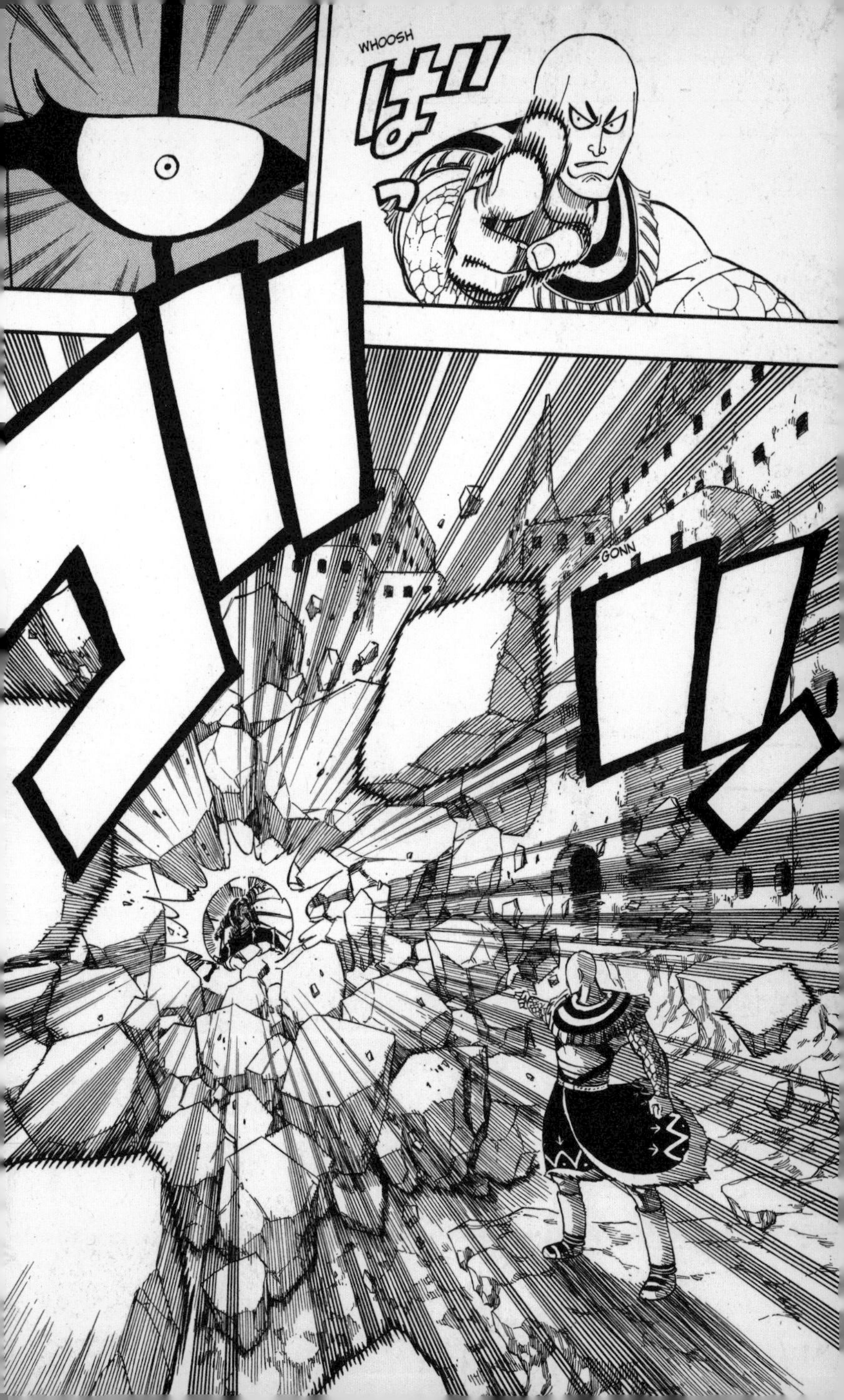
WHOOSH
GONN

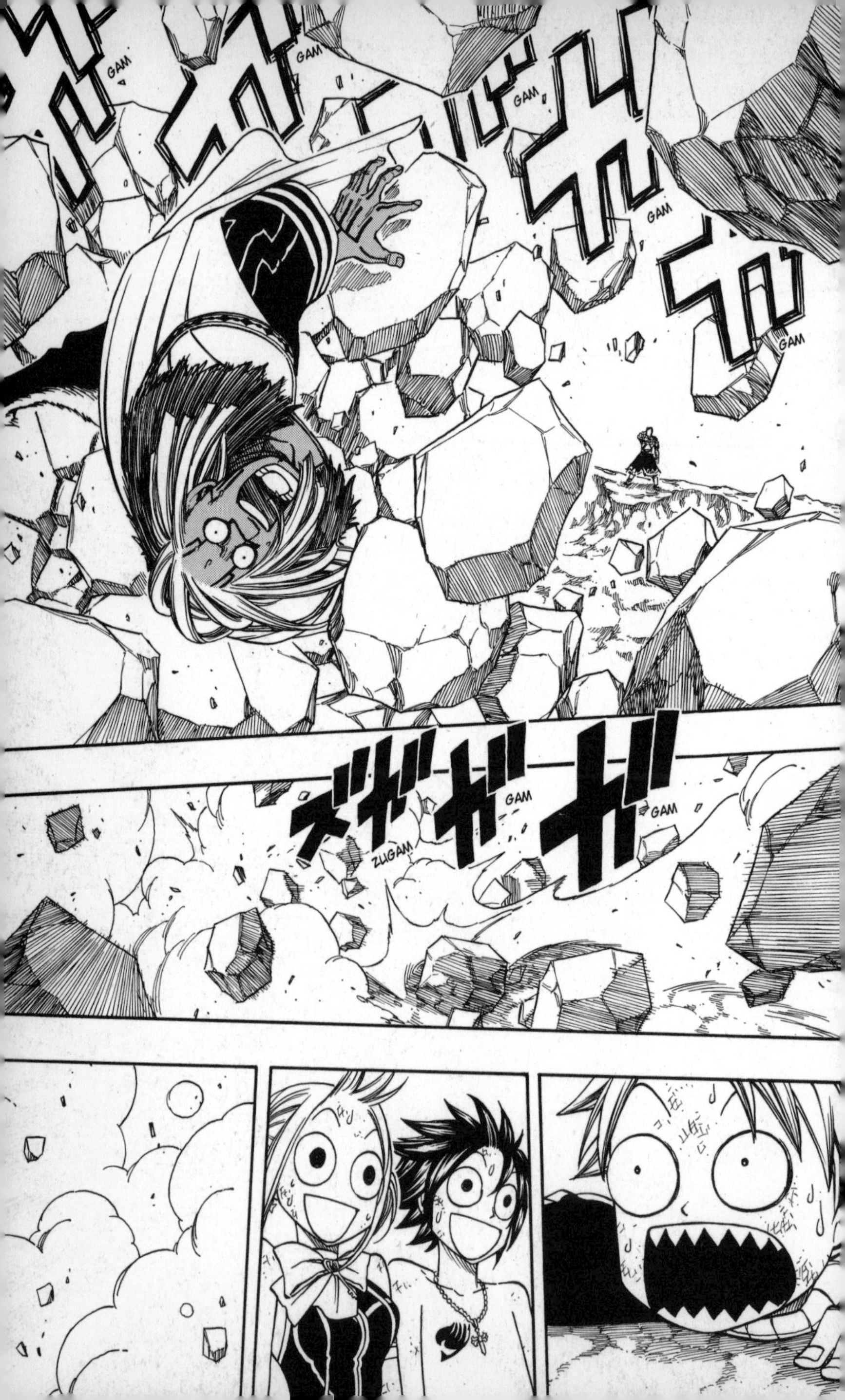
GAM
GAM
GAM
GAM
GAM
ZUGAM
GAM
GAM

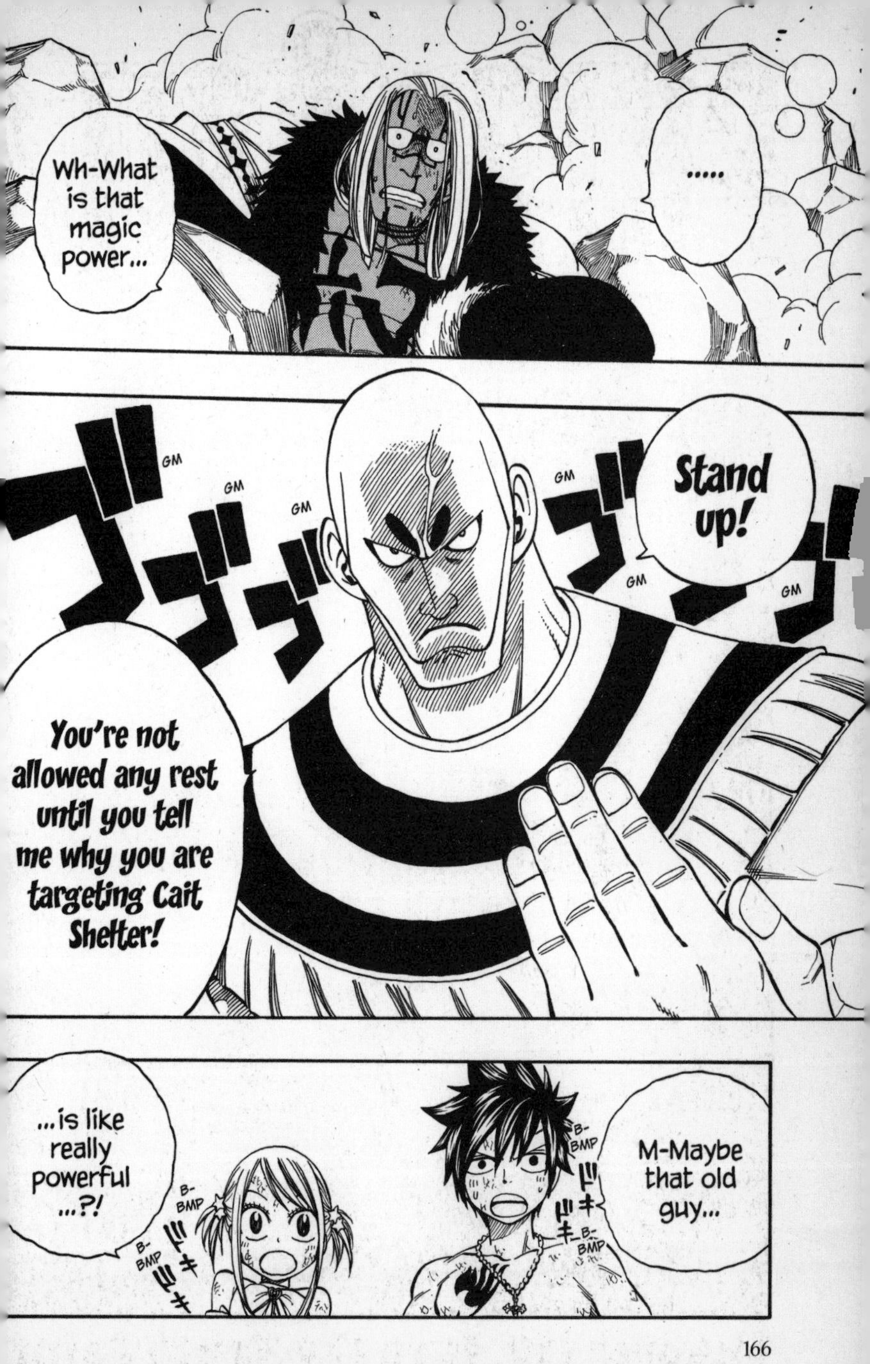
.....
Wh-What is that magic power...
Stand up!
GM GM GM GM GM GM
ゴゴゴゴゴ
You're not allowed any rest until you tell me why you are targeting Cait Shelter!
M-Maybe that old guy...
B-BMP B-BMP
ドキドキ
...is like really powerful ...?!
B-BMP B-BMP
ドキドキ

FAIRY TAIL

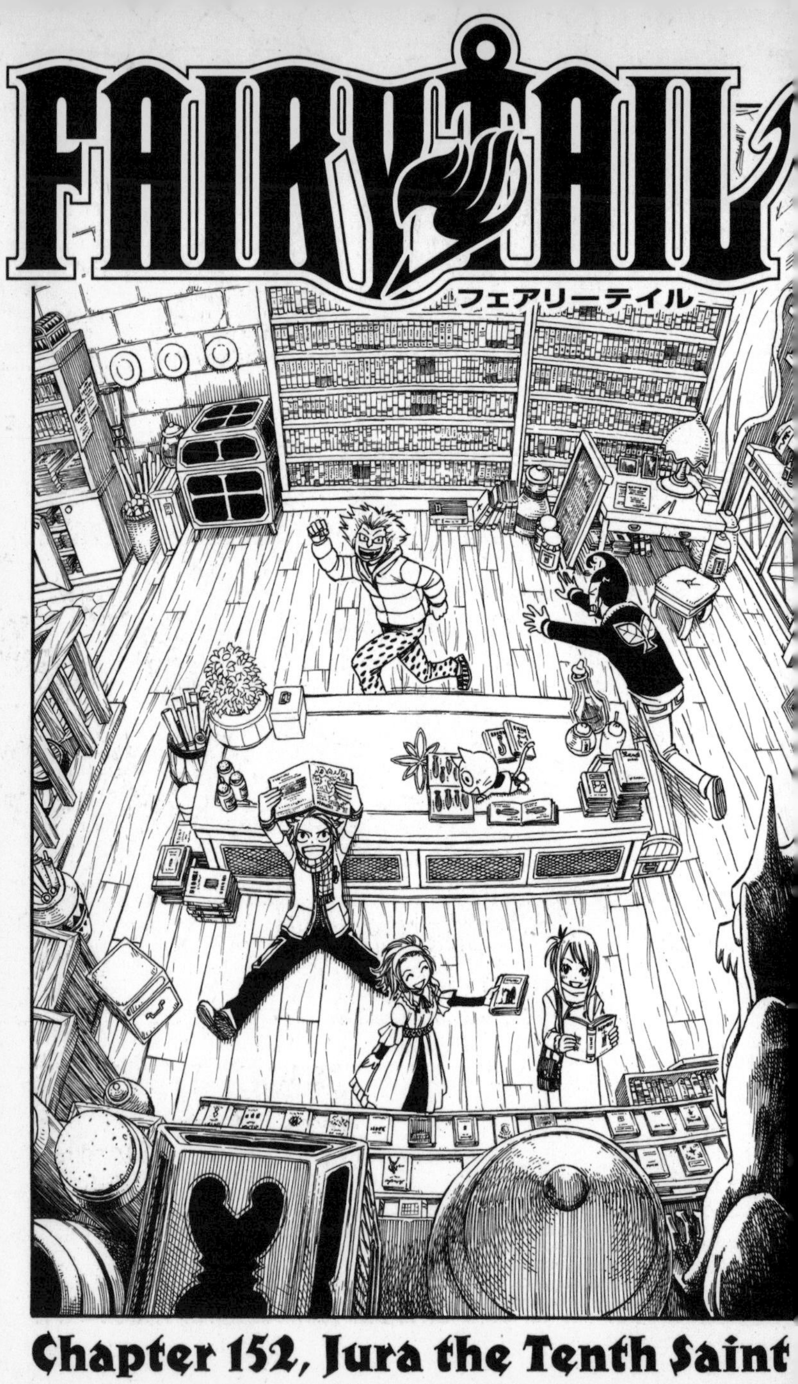

フェアリーテイル

Chapter 152, Jura the Tenth Saint

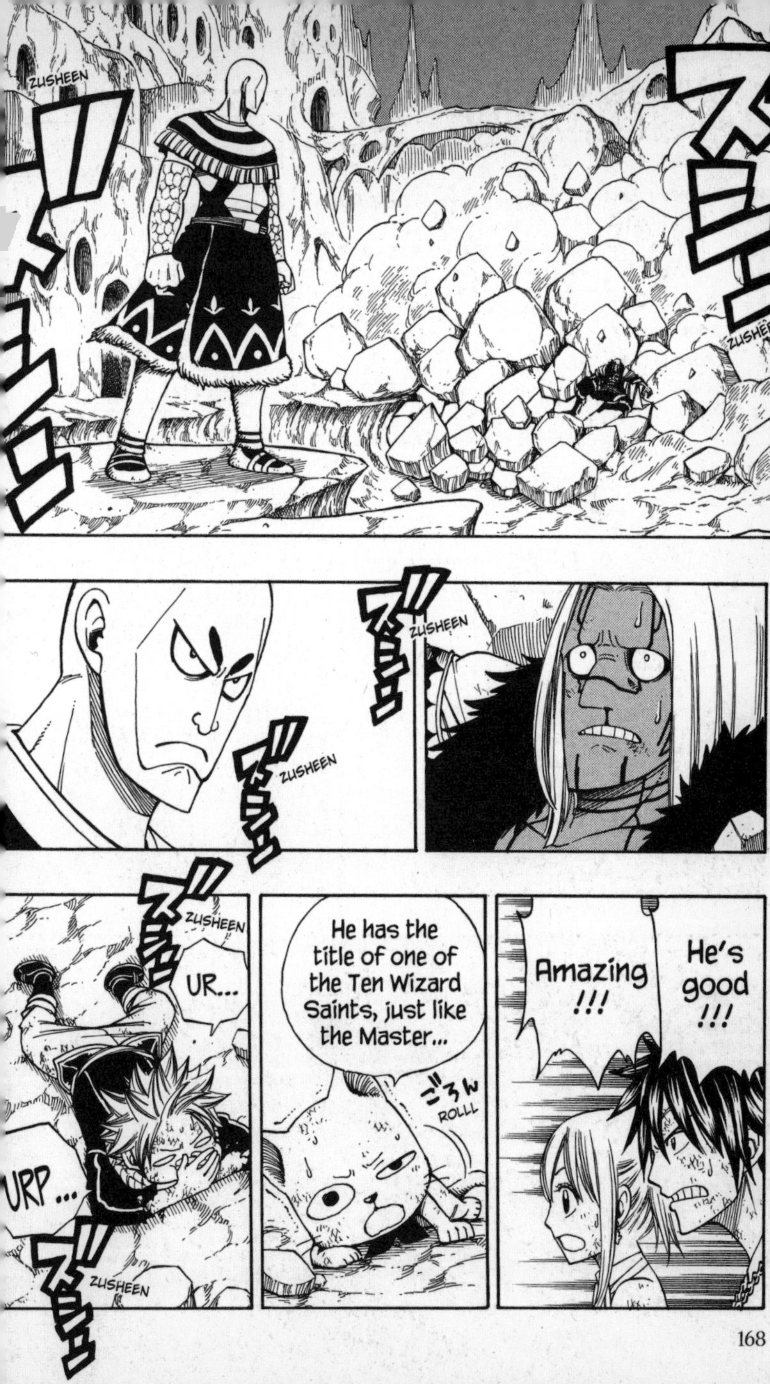
ZUSHEEN
ZUSHEEN
ZUSHEEN
ZUSHEEN
He's good!!!
Amazing!!!
He has the title of one of the Ten Wizard Saints, just like the Master...
ごろん
ROLLL
ZUSHEEN
UR...
URP...
ZUSHEEN

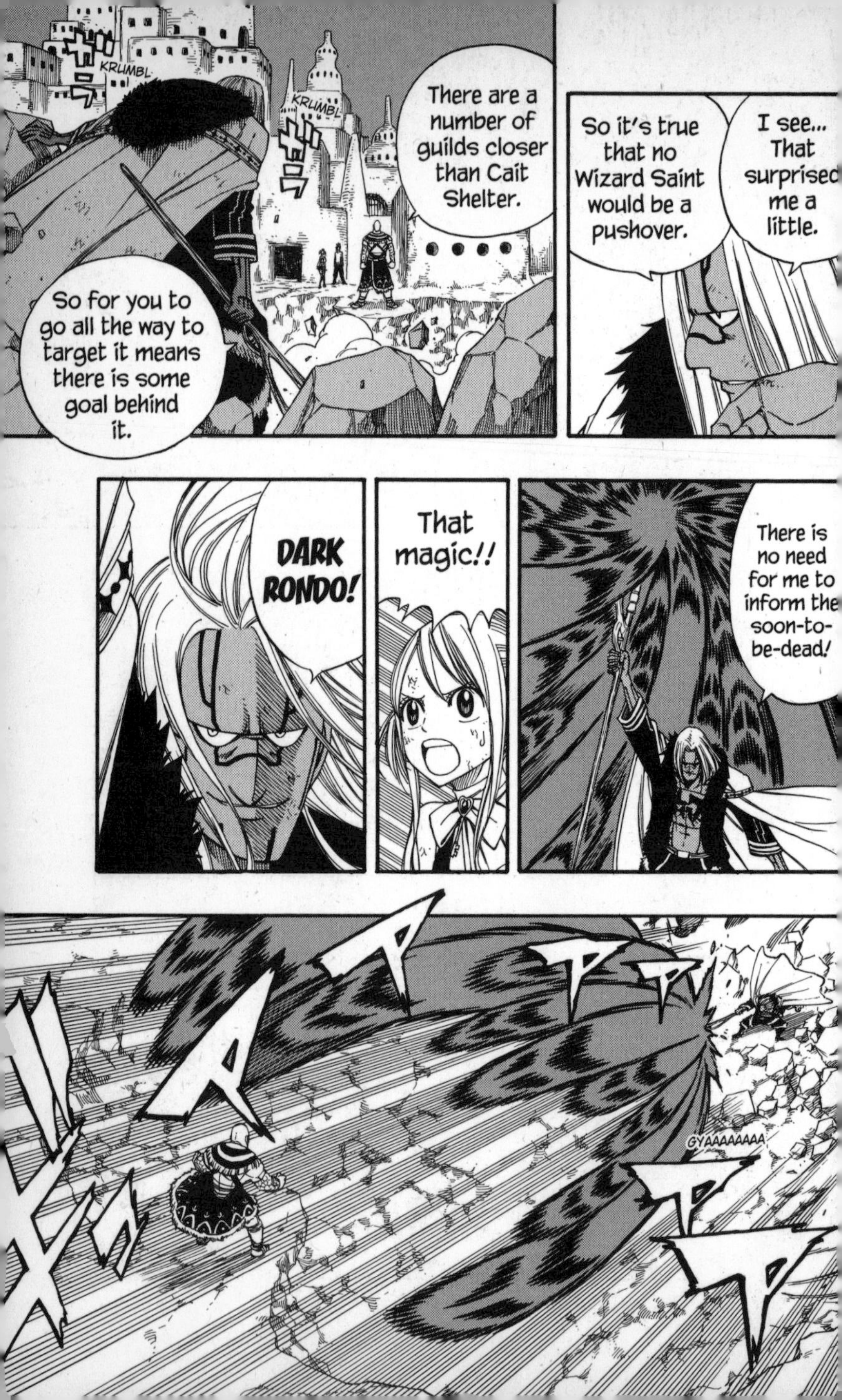
I see... That surprised me a little.
So it's true that no Wizard Saint would be a pushover.
KRUMBL
KRUMBL
There are a number of guilds closer than Cait Shelter.
• • • •
So for you to go all the way to target it means there is some goal behind it.
There is no need for me to inform the soon-to-be-dead!
That magic!!
DARK RONDO!
GYAAAAAAAA

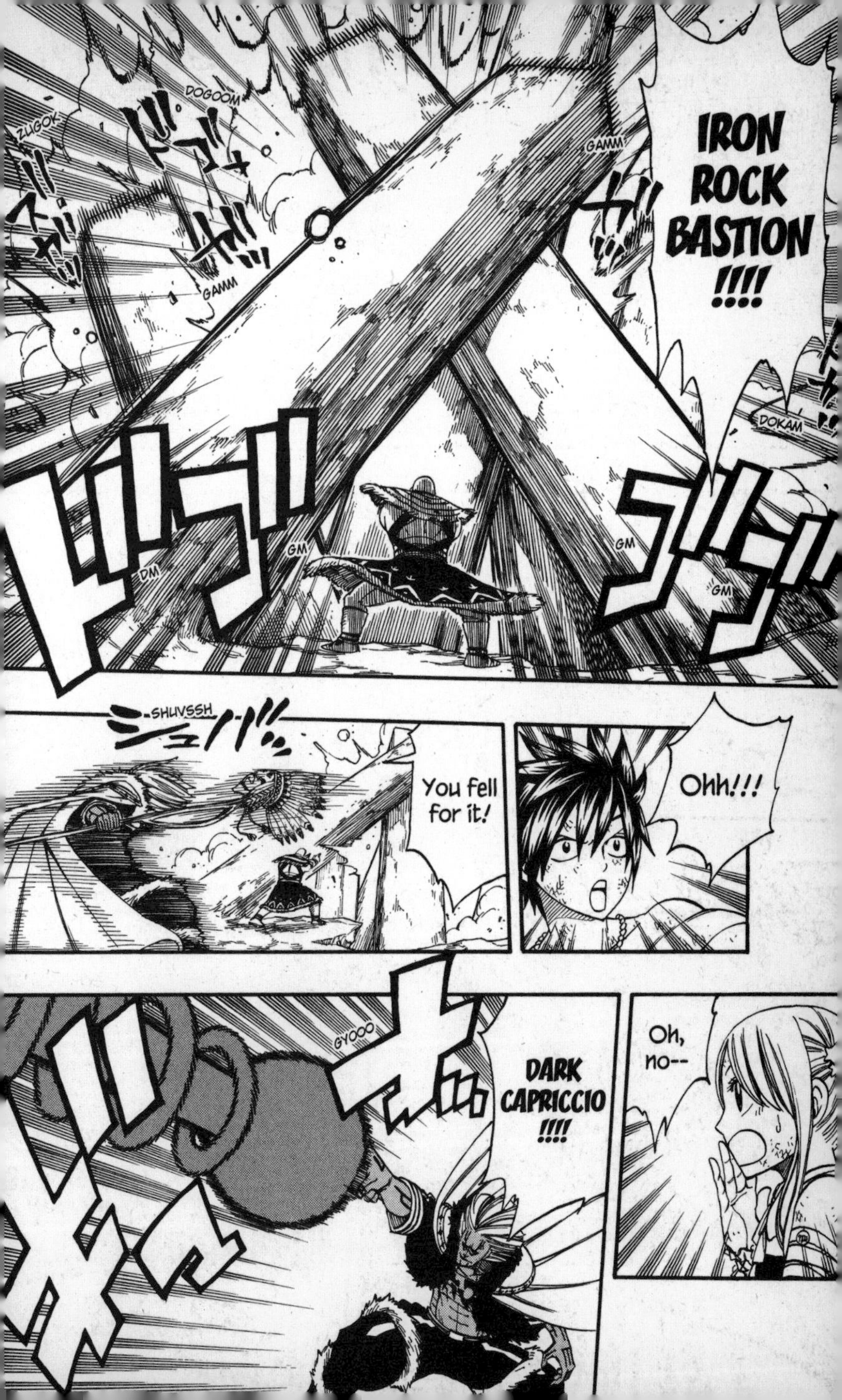
IRON ROCK BASTION!!!!
GAMM
DOKAM
GM
GM
DOGOOM
ZUGOK
GAMM
GM
DM
Ohh!!!
You fell for it!
SHUVSSH
Oh, no--
DARK CAPRICCIO!!!!
GYOOO

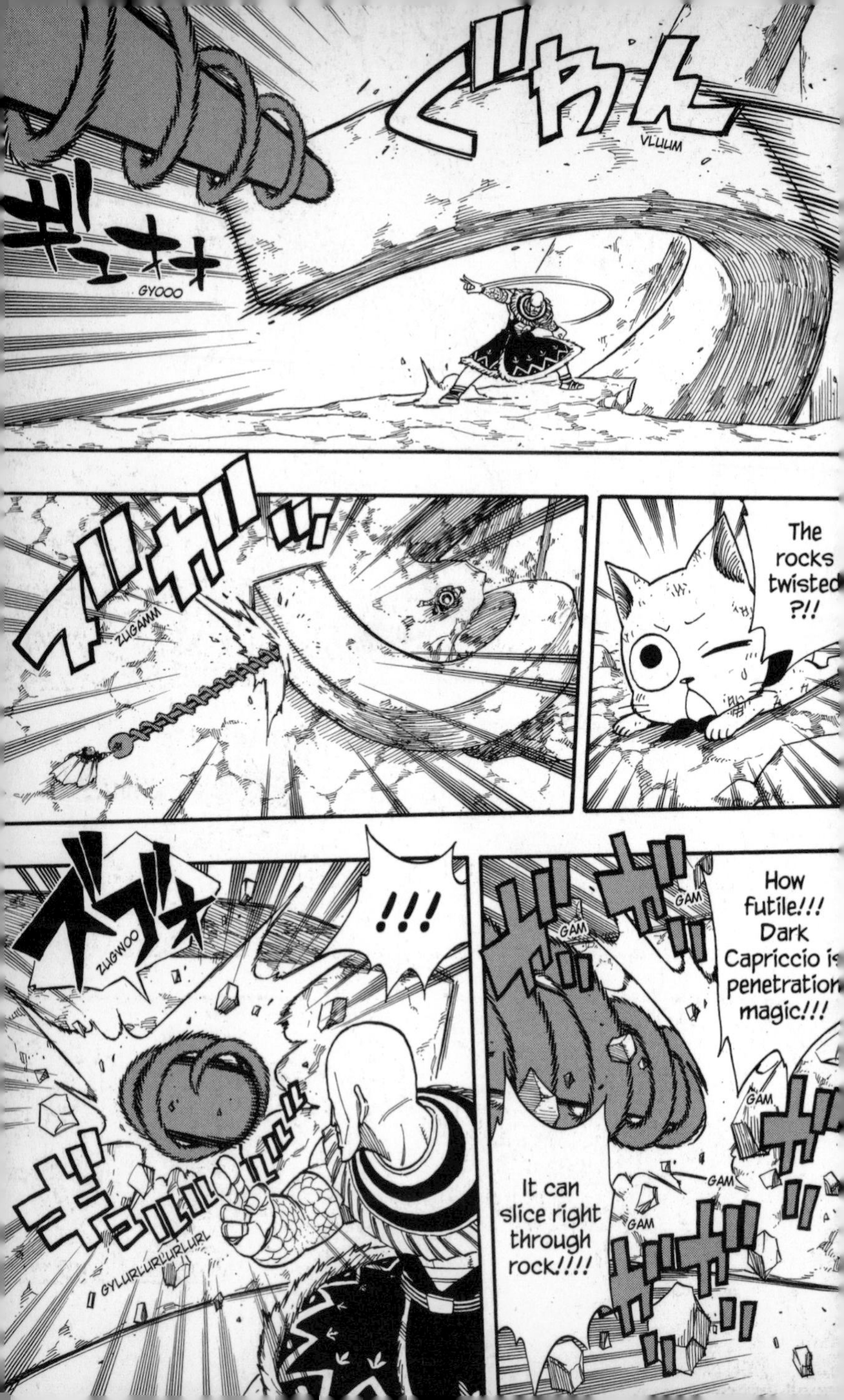

ぐわん
VLUUM
GYOOO
The rocks twisted?!!
ZUGAMM
GAM
GAM
How futile!!! Dark Capriccio is penetration magic!!!
GAM
GAM
GAM
It can slice right through rock!!!!
!!!
ZUGWOO
GYLURLURLURL

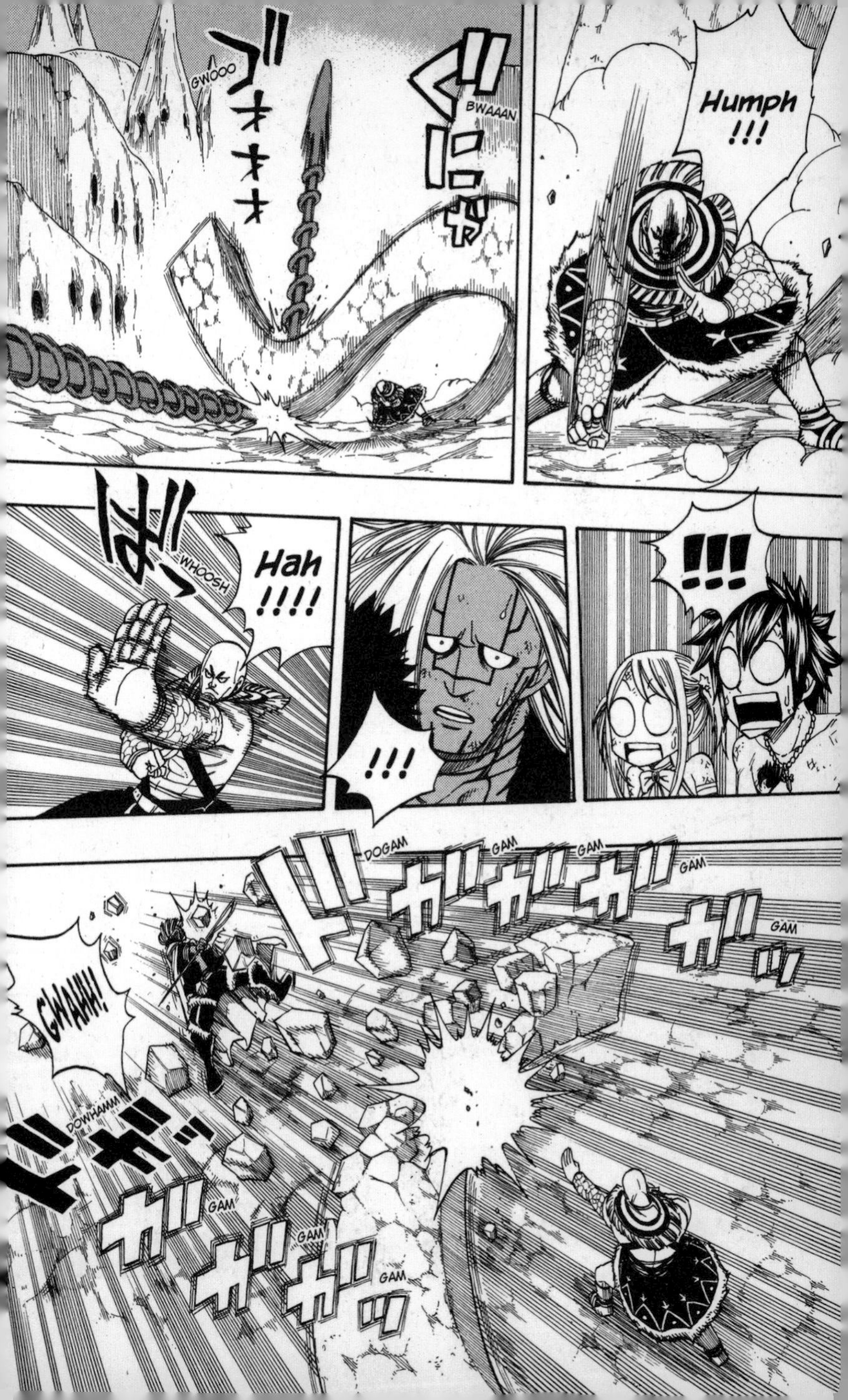
Humph!!!
GWOOO
BWAAAN
!!!
!!!
Hah!!!!
WHOOSH
DOGAM
GAM
GAM
GAM
GAM
GWAHH!
DOWHAMM
GAM
GAM
GAM

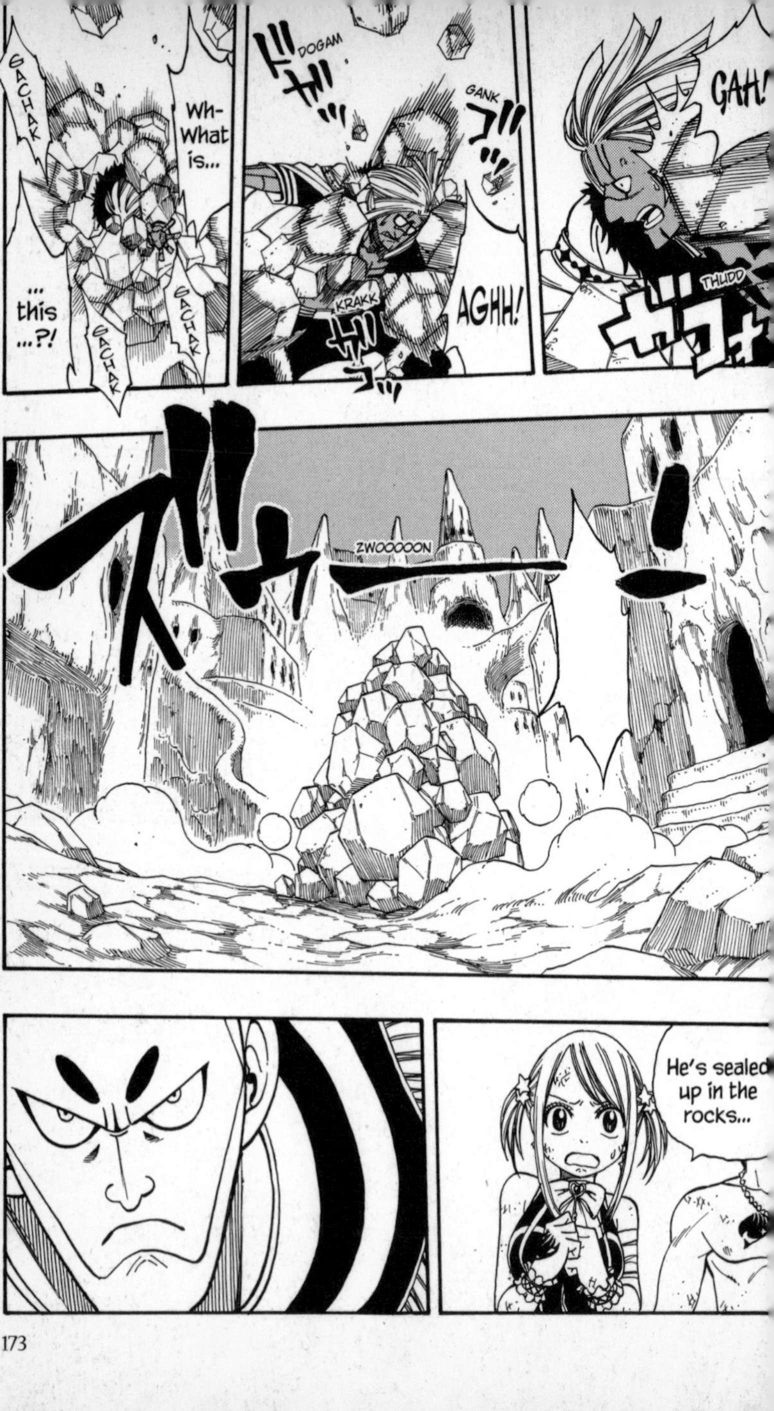
GAH!
THUDD
DOGAM
GANK
KRAKK
AGHH!
GACHAK
Wh- What is...
... this ...?!
GACHAK
GACHAK
ZWOOOOON
He's sealed up in the rocks...

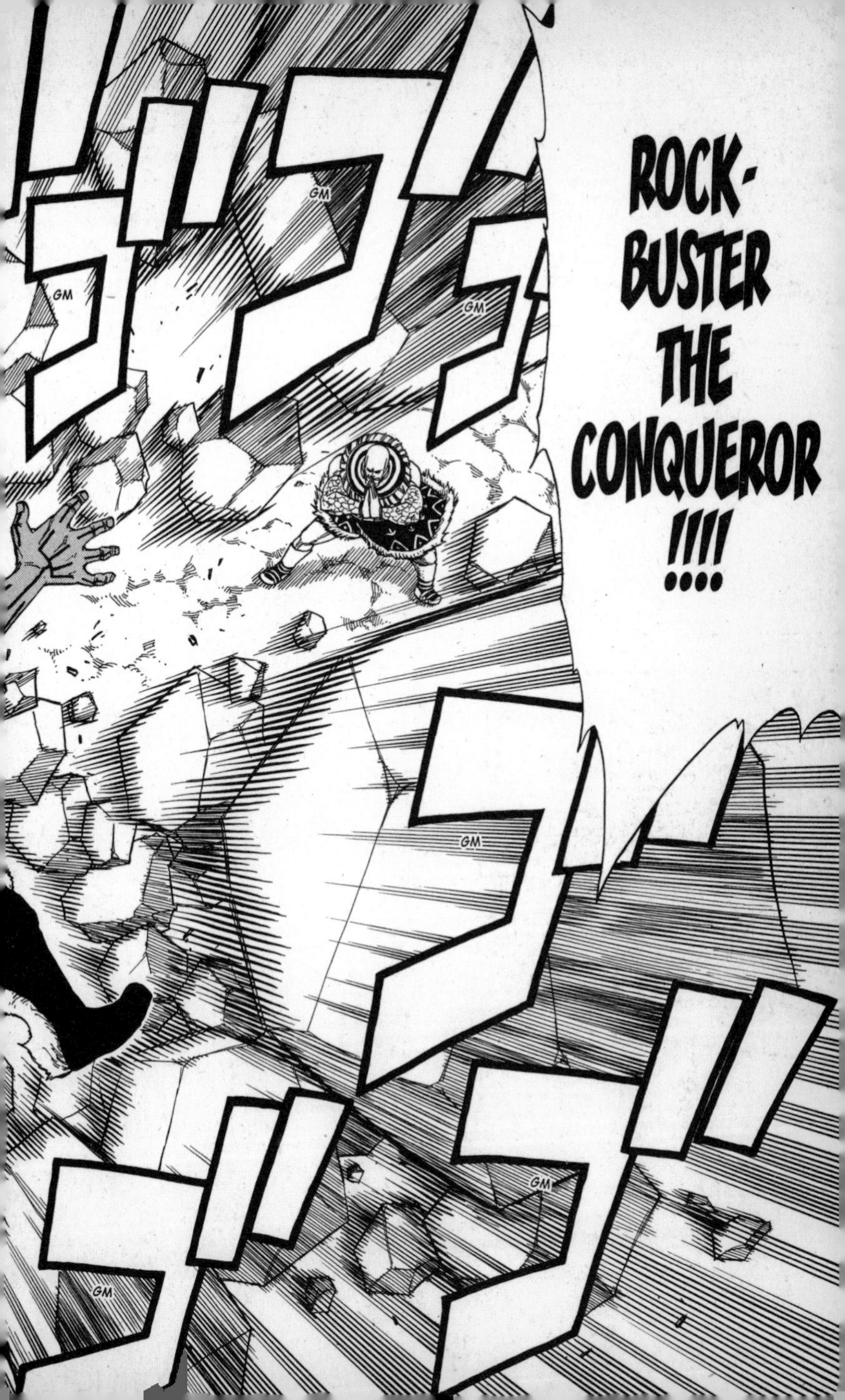
ROCK-BUSTER THE CONQUEROR!!!!
GM
GM
GM
GM
GM
GM

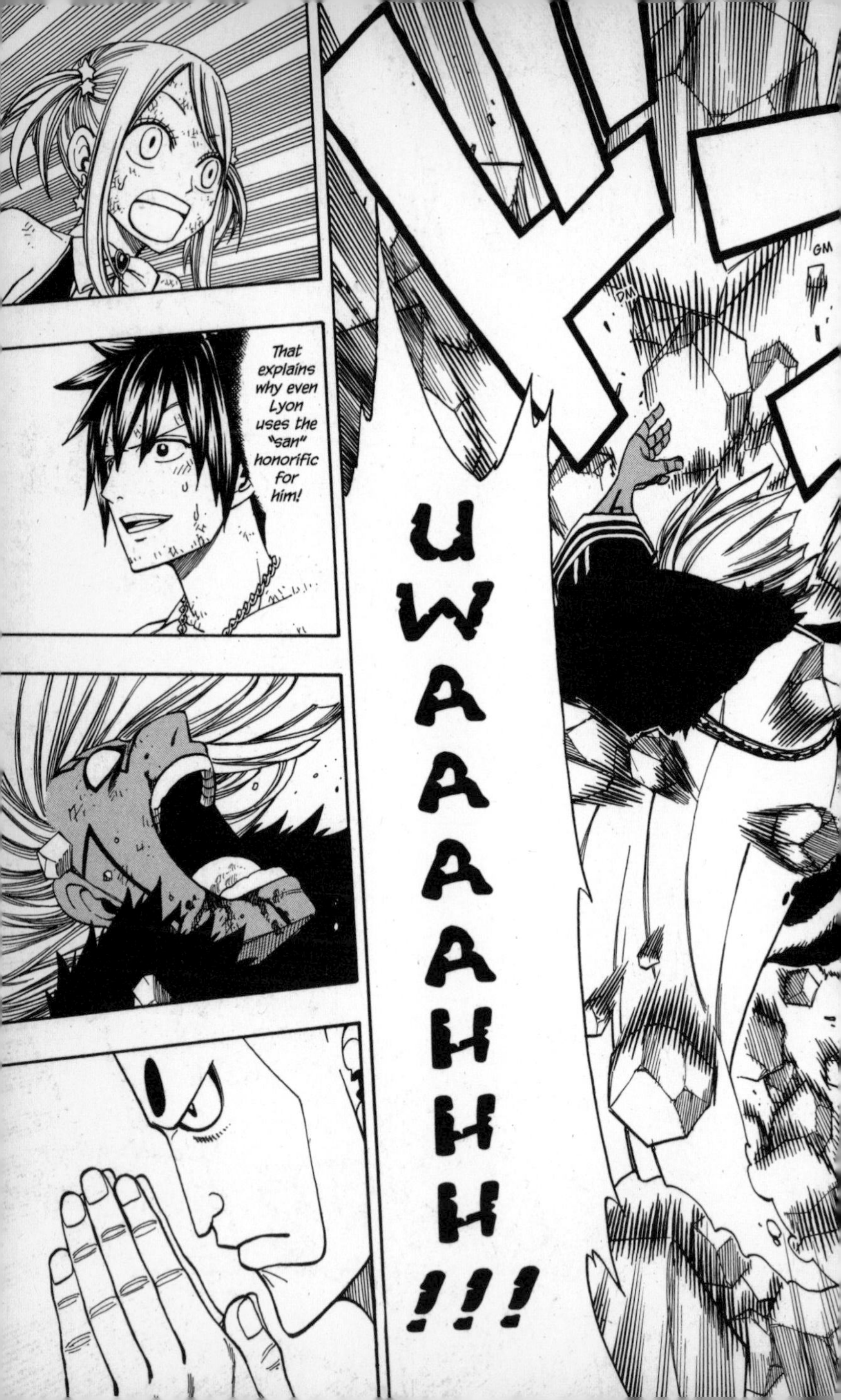
GM
DM
UWAAAAHHH!!!
That explains why even Lyon uses the "san" honorific for him!

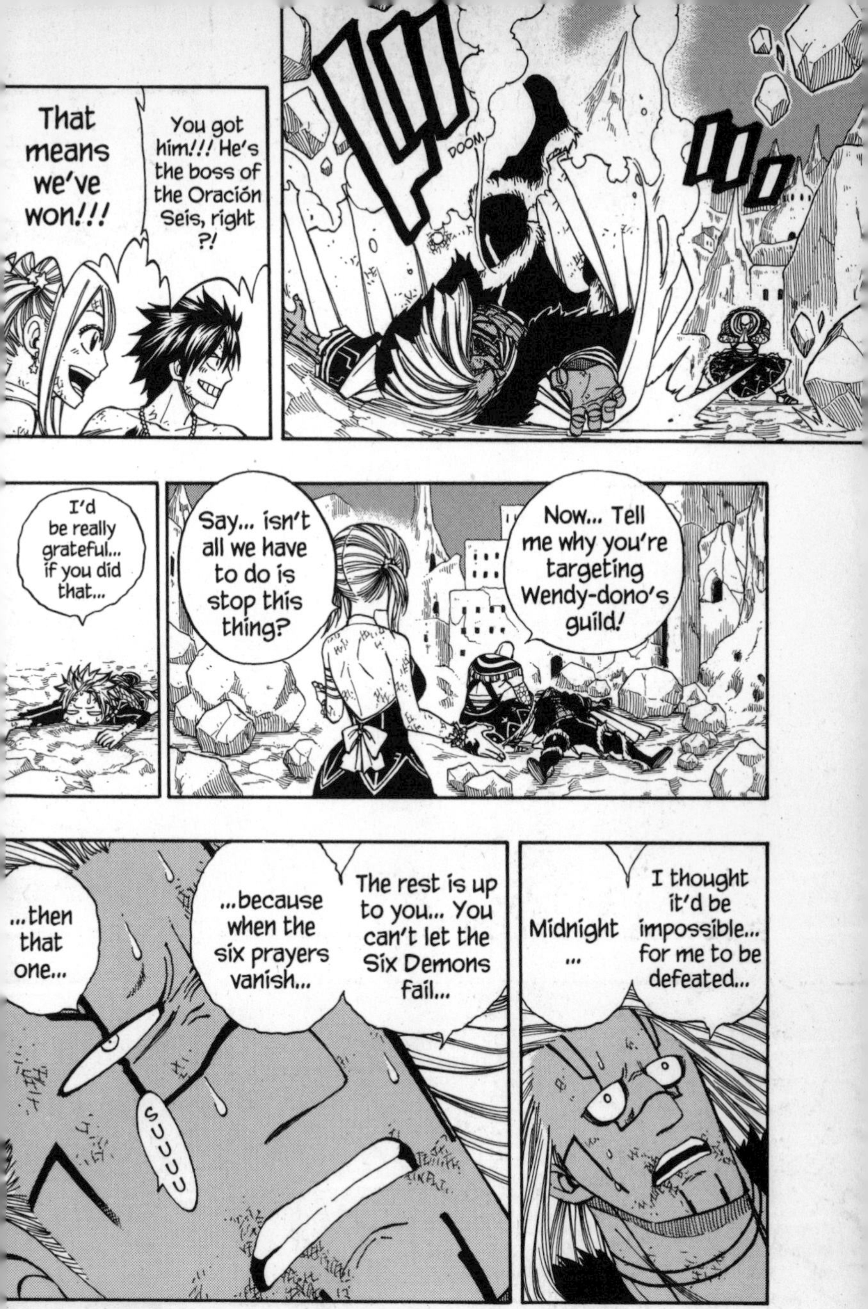
DOOM
You got him!!! He's the boss of the Oración Seis, right ?!
That means we've won!!!
Now... Tell me why you're targeting Wendy-dono's guild!
Say... isn't all we have to do is stop this thing?
I'd be really grateful... if you did that...
I thought it'd be impossible... for me to be defeated...
Midnight ...
The rest is up to you... You can't let the Six Demons fail...
...because when the six prayers vanish...
...then that one...
SUUUU

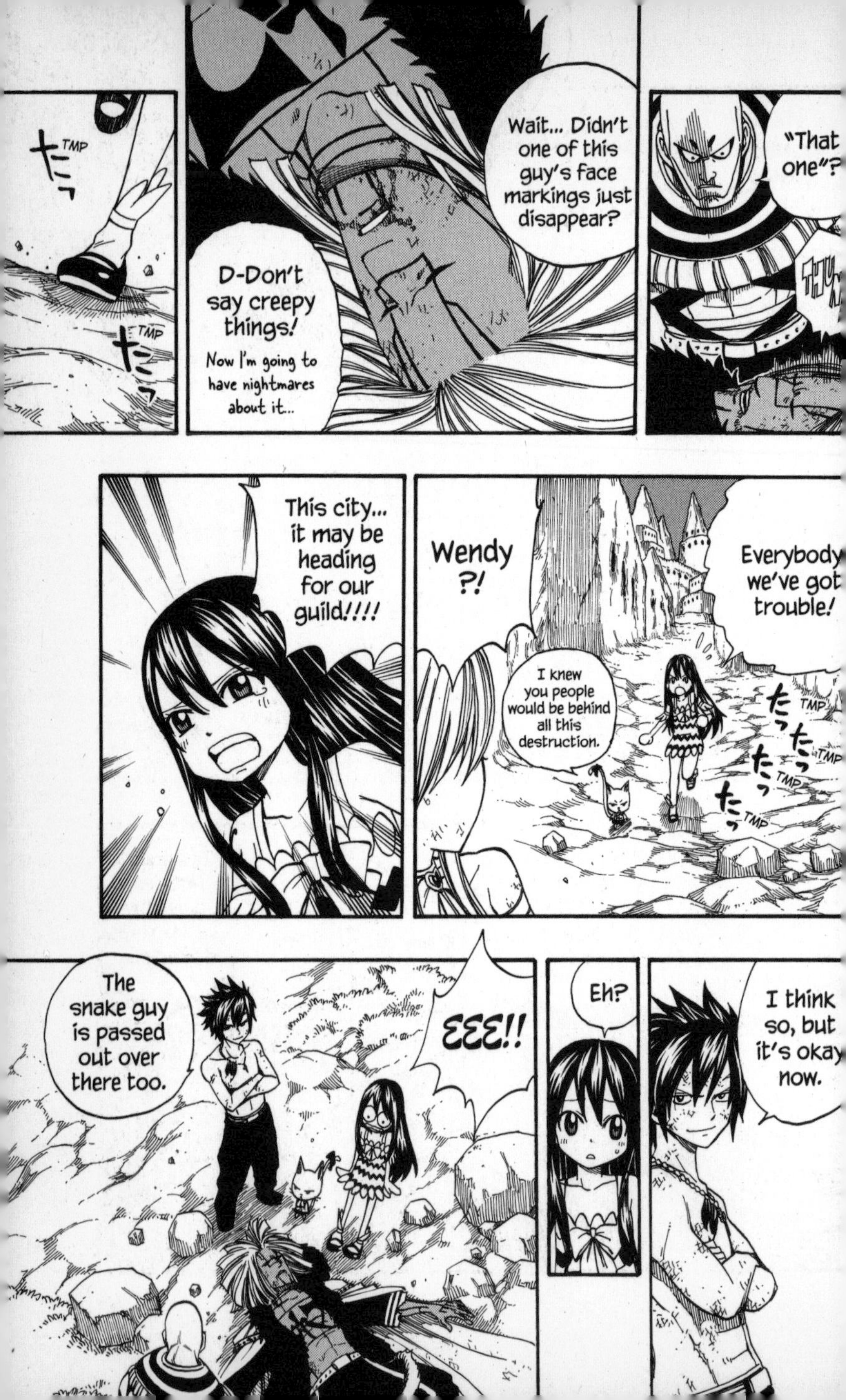
"That one"?
Wait... Didn't one of this guy's face markings just disappear?
D-Don't say creepy things!
Now I'm going to have nightmares about it...
TMP
TMP
Everybody we've got trouble!
Wendy ?!
I knew you people would be behind all this destruction.
TMP
TMP
TMP
TMP
This city... it may be heading for our guild!!!!
I think so, but it's okay now.
Eh?
The snake guy is passed out over there too.
EEE!!

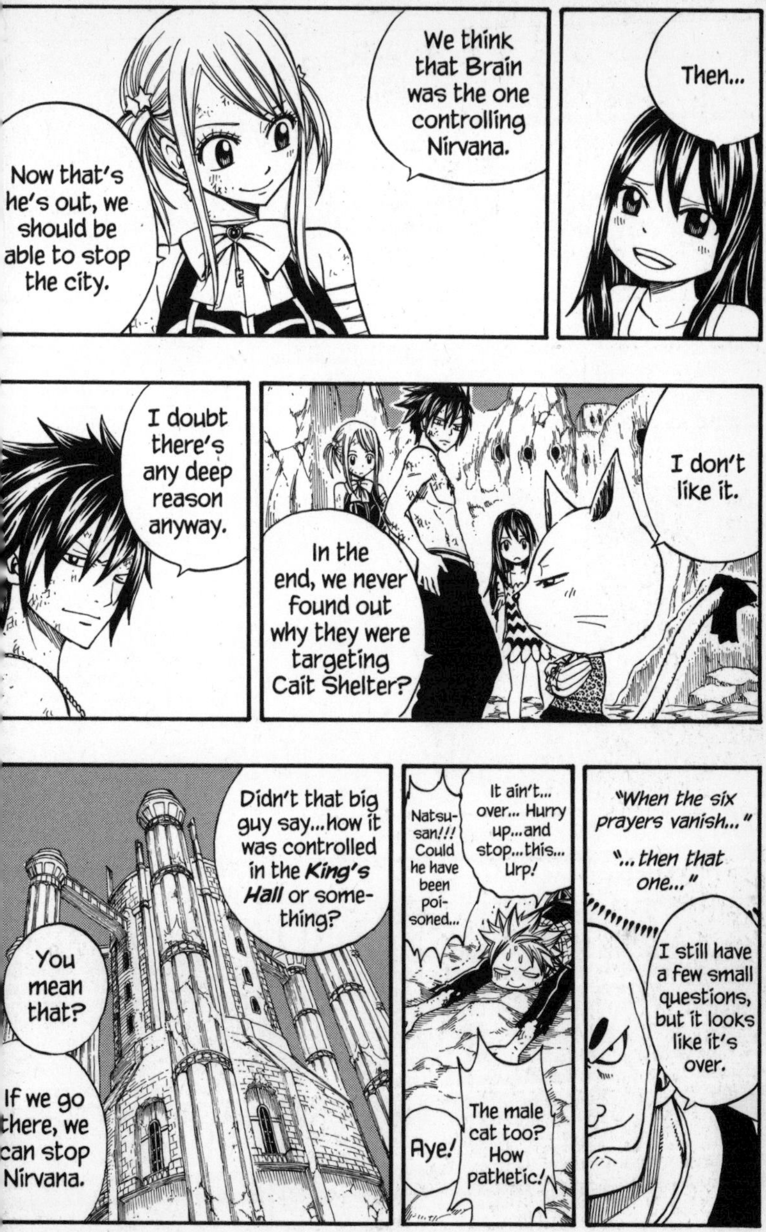

Then...
We think that Brain was the one controlling Nirvana.
Now that's he's out, we should be able to stop the city.
I don't like it.
In the end, we never found out why they were targeting Cait Shelter?
I doubt there's any deep reason anyway.
"When the six prayers vanish..."
"...then that one..."
I still have a few small questions, but it looks like it's over.
It ain't... over... Hurry up...and stop...this... Urp!
Natsu-san!!! Could he have been poi-soned...
The male cat too? How pathetic!
Aye!
Didn't that big guy say...how it was controlled in the *King's Hall* or some-thing?
You mean that?
If we go there, we can stop Nirvana.

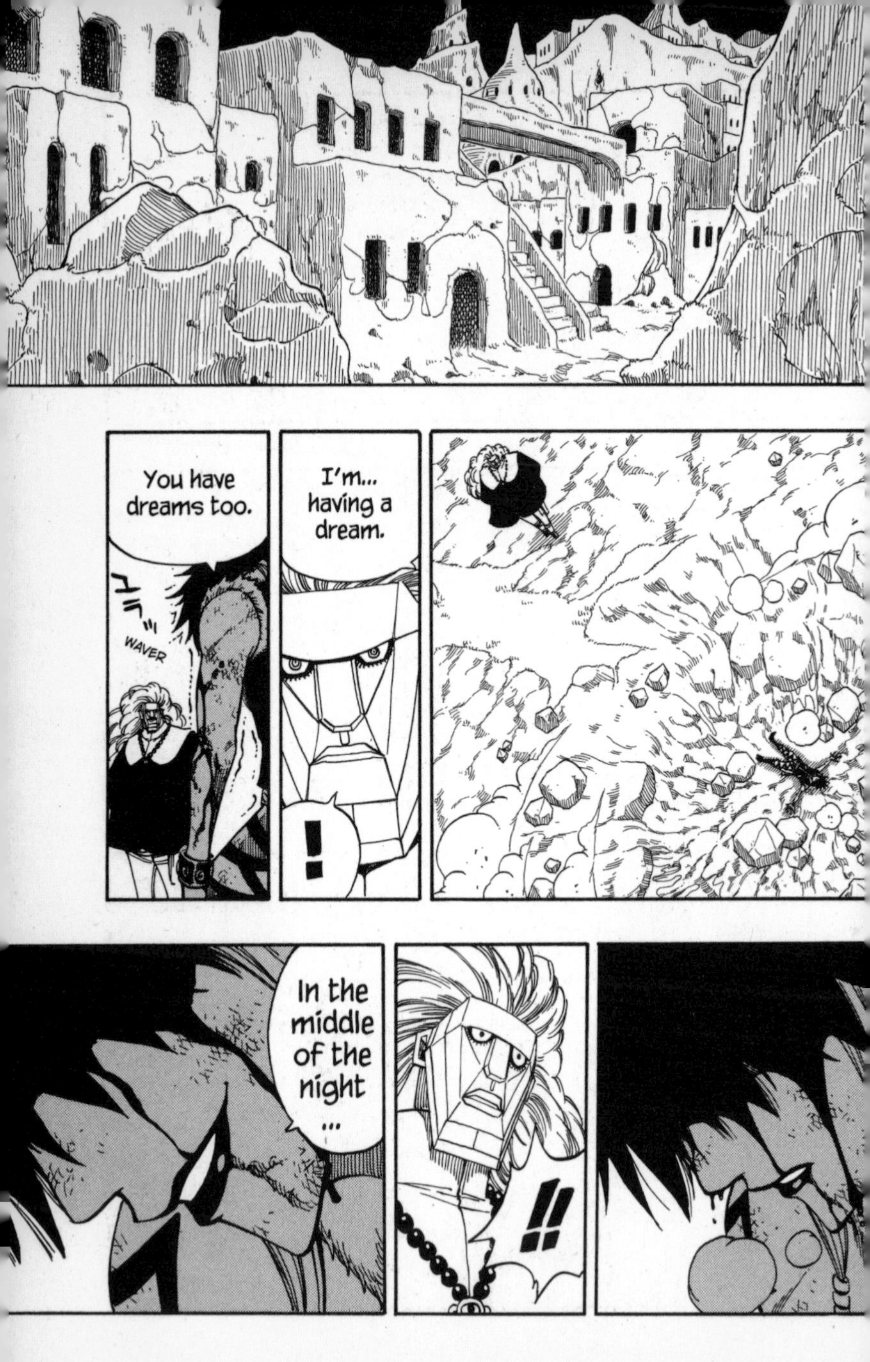
I'm... having a dream.
!
You have dreams too.
WAVER
!!
In the middle of the night ...

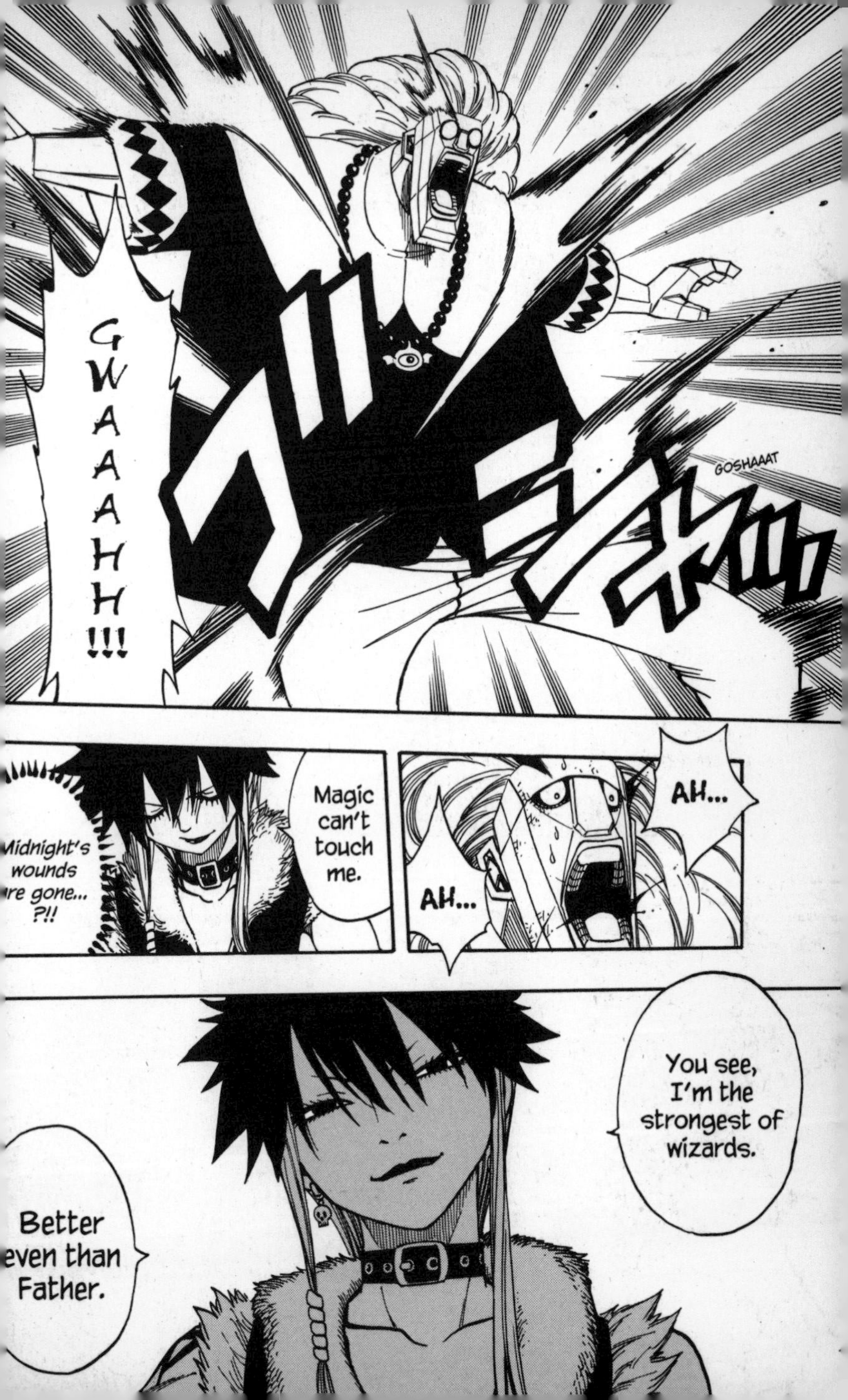
GOSHAAAT
GWAAAAHH!!!
AH...
AH...
Magic can't touch me.
Midnight's wounds re gone... ?!!
You see, I'm the strongest of wizards.
Better even than Father.

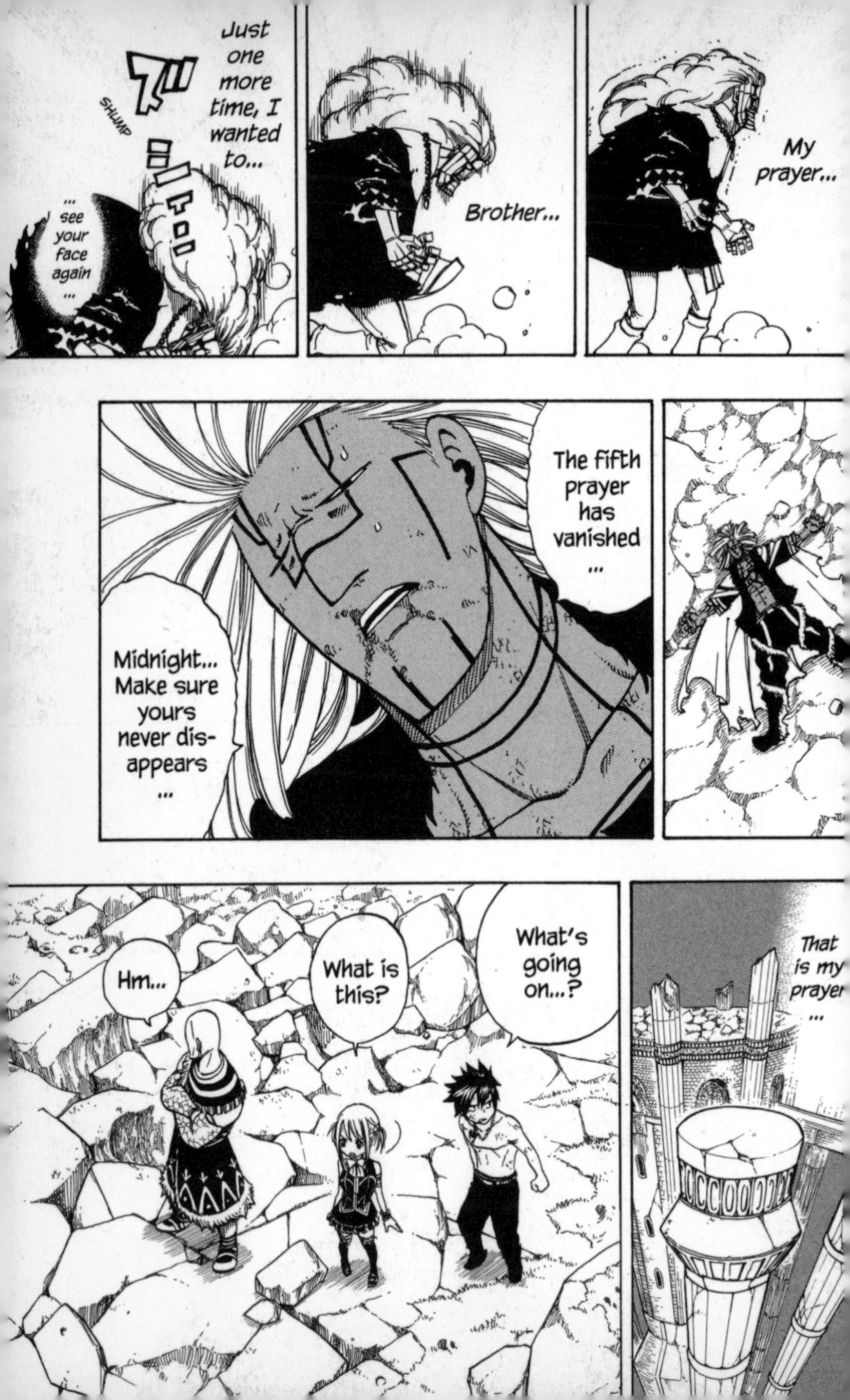
My prayer...
Brother...
Just one more time, I wanted to...
SHUMP
... see your face again ...
The fifth prayer has vanished ...
Midnight... Make sure yours never dis-appears ...
That is my prayer ...
What's going on...?
What is this?
Hm...

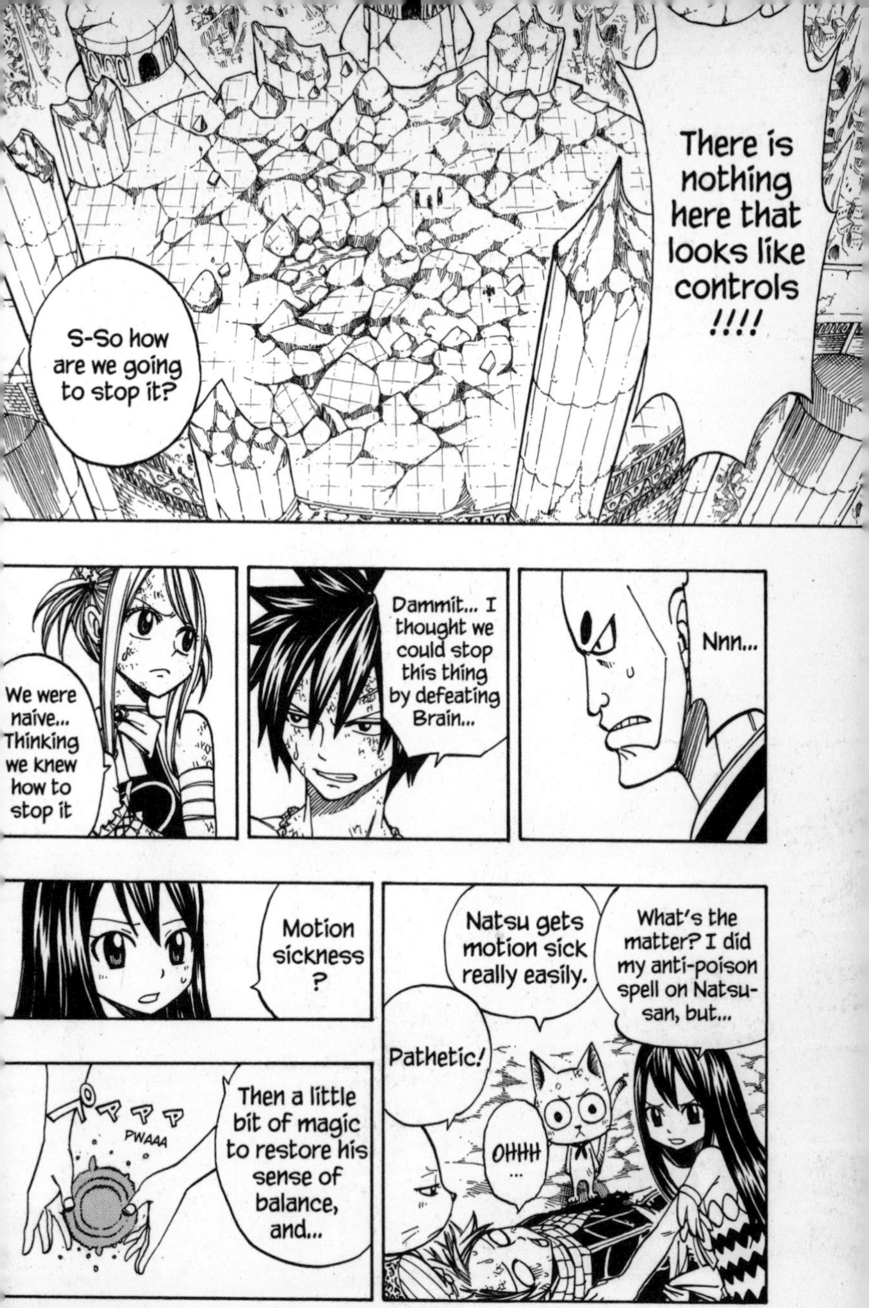
There is nothing here that looks like controls !!!!
S-So how are we going to stop it?
Nnn...
Dammit... I thought we could stop this thing by defeating Brain...
We were naive... Thinking we knew how to stop it
What's the matter? I did my anti-poison spell on Natsu-san, but...
Natsu gets motion sick really easily.
Pathetic!
OHHH ...
Motion sickness ?
Then a little bit of magic to restore his sense of balance, and...
PWAAA

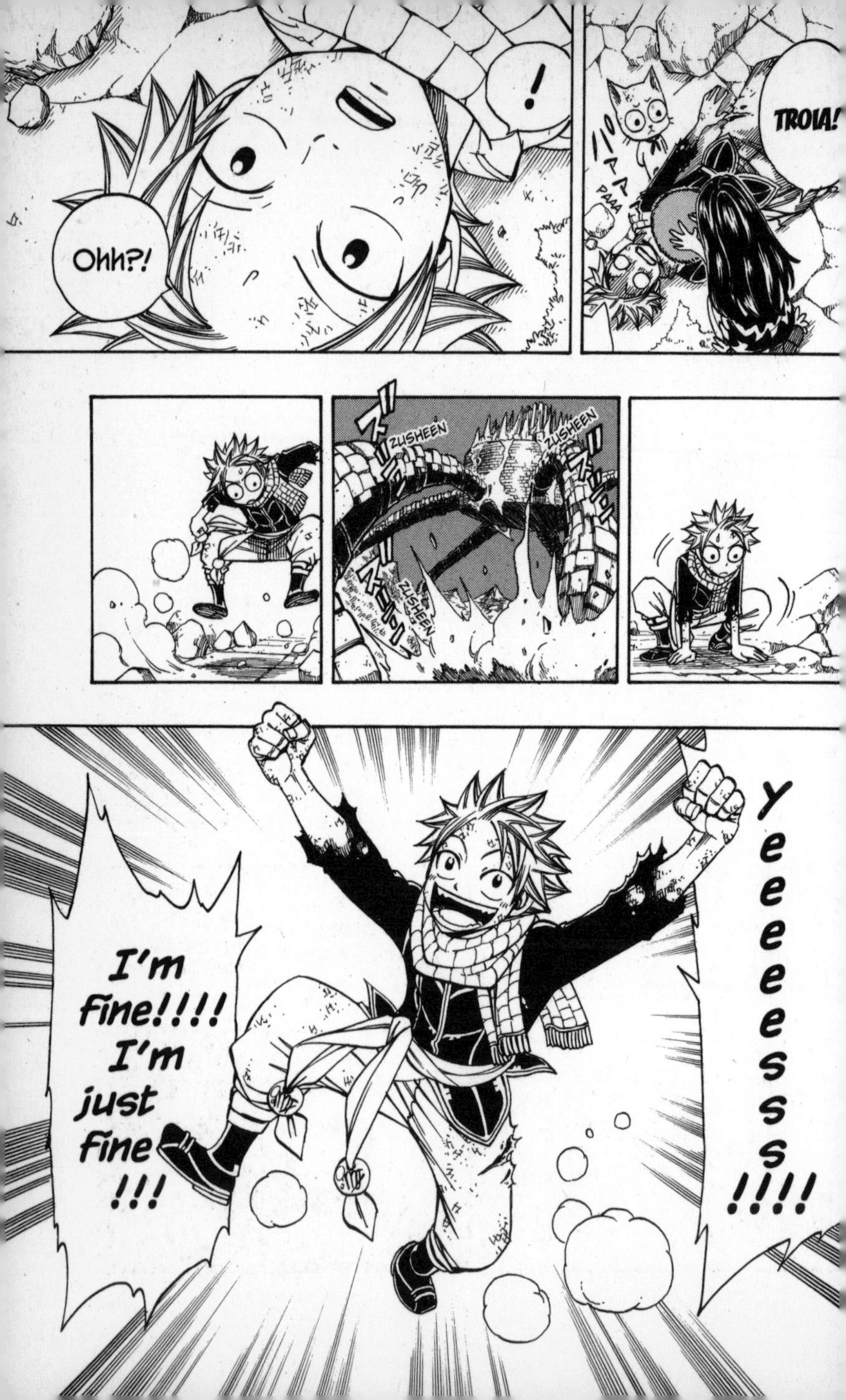
TROIA!
PAAA
!
Ohh?!
ZUSHEEN
ZUSHEEN
ZUSHEEN
Yeeeeesss!!!!
I'm fine!!!! I'm just fine!!!

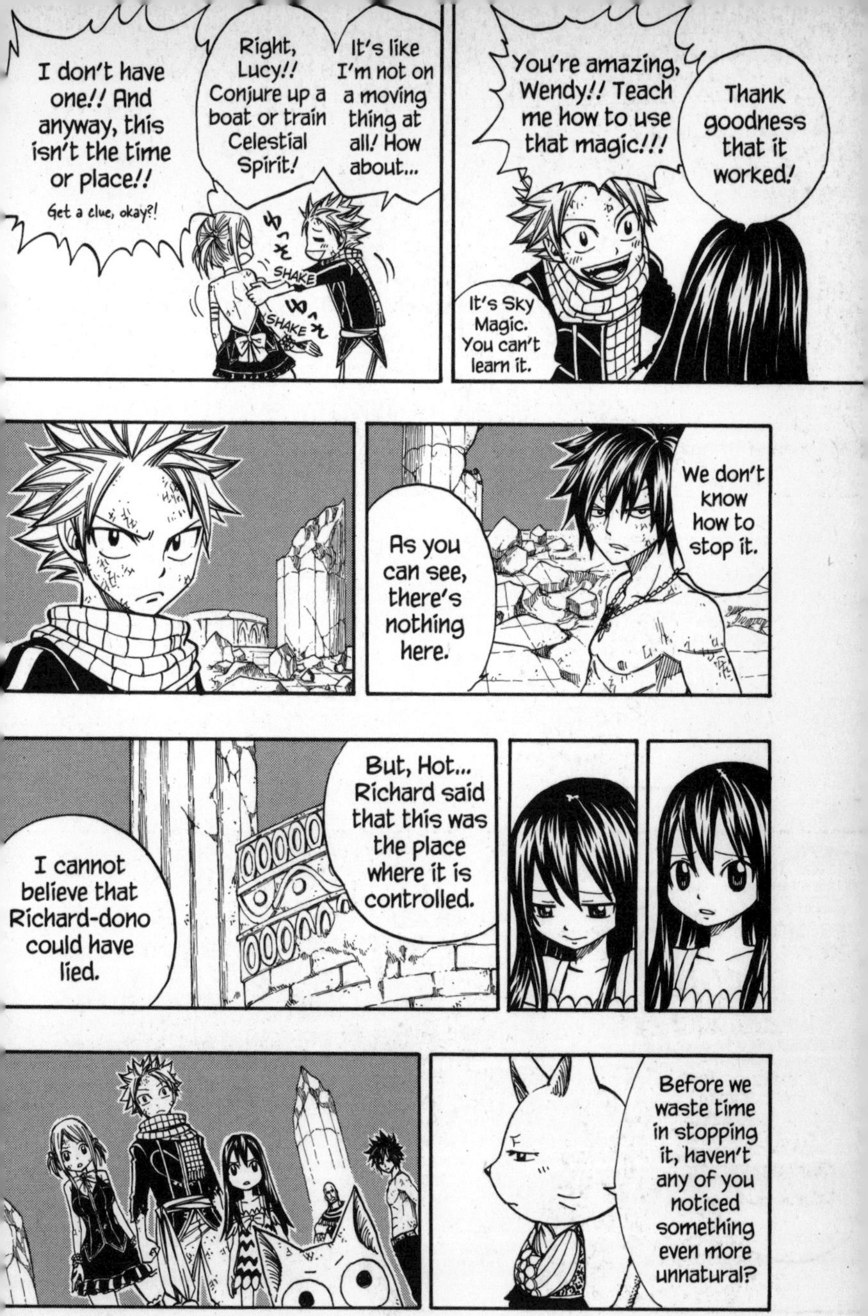
Thank goodness that it worked!
You're amazing, Wendy!! Teach me how to use that magic!!!
It's Sky Magic. You can't learn it.
It's like I'm not on a moving thing at all! How about...
Right, Lucy!! Conjure up a boat or train Celestial Spirit!
SHAKE
SHAKE
I don't have one!! And anyway, this isn't the time or place!!
Get a clue, okay?!
We don't know how to stop it.
As you can see, there's nothing here.
But, Hot... Richard said that this was the place where it is controlled.
I cannot believe that Richard-dono could have lied.
Before we waste time in stopping it, haven't any of you noticed something even more unnatural?

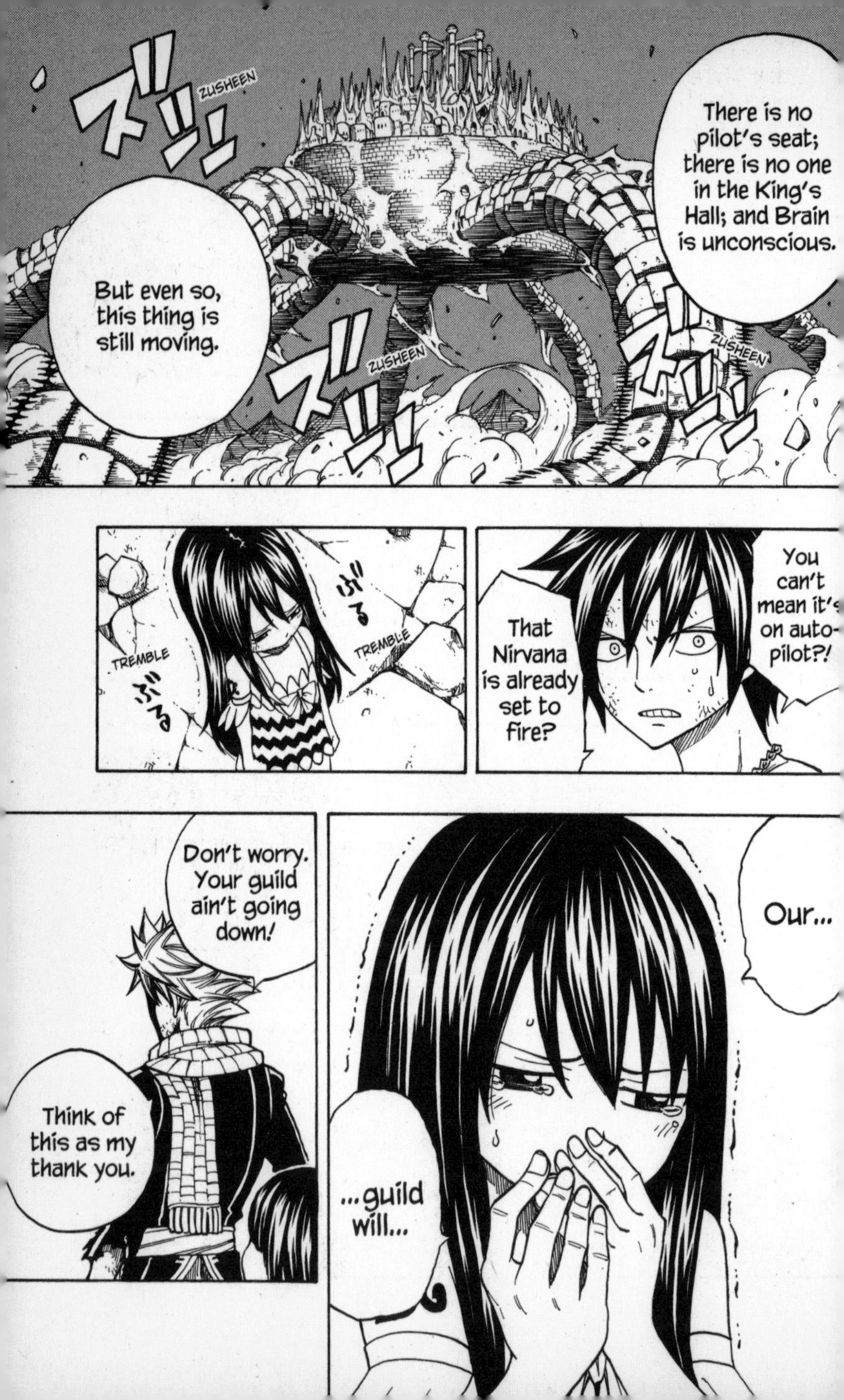
ZUSHEEN
There is no pilot's seat; there is no one in the King's Hall; and Brain is unconscious.
ZUSHEEN
ZUSHEEN
But even so, this thing is still moving.
You can't mean it's on auto-pilot?!
That Nirvana is already set to fire?
ぶる
TREMBLE
ぶる
TREMBLE
Our...
...guild will...
Don't worry. Your guild ain't going down!
Think of this as my thank you.

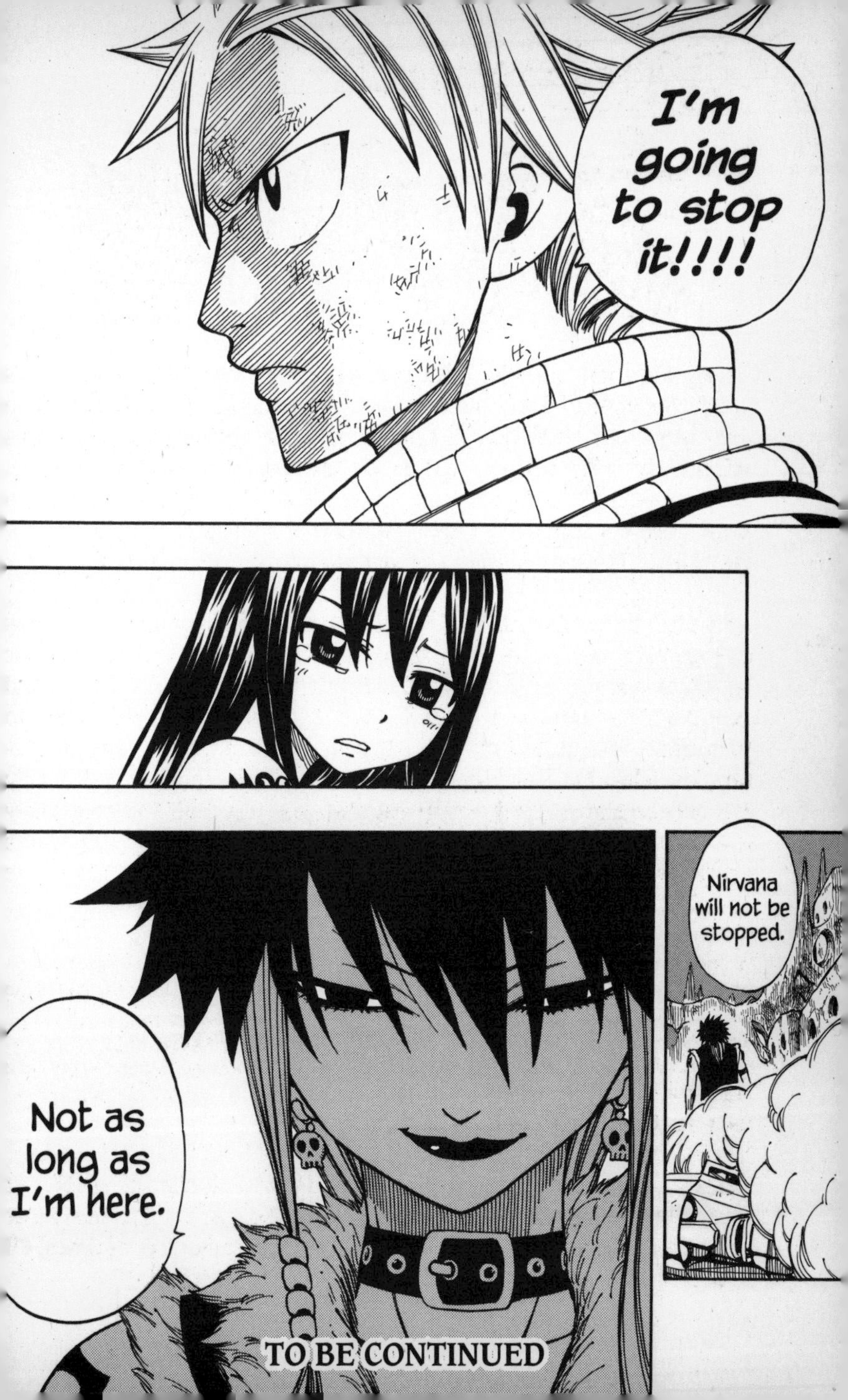
I'm going to stop it!!!!
Nirvana will not be stopped.
Not as long as I'm here.
TO BE CONTINUED

Afterword

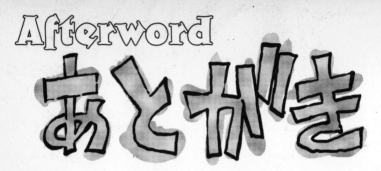

Urano Metoria!! ..... Also, Natsu and Happy's mid-air battle!!! Jura's good!! So, with all that, how was Volume 18 for you? Of it all ,the Natsu and Happy mid-air battle was something I always wanted to do, and this might be the very first time that Happy has taken part directly in a battle. Actually, with the arrival of Carla, my concept of Happy has undergone a huge change. I can't say anything now, but at some point I'd like to draw the "Happy Chapter" (such a pleasant name, huh?). Someday.

Now I never did any calculations to make this happen, but before this one, all of the story arcs have taken about three volumes of the graphic novels to come to an end. But this Oración Seis arc started in 16, and now it's 17 and 18, and it's looks like it's going to continue well into (through?) volume 19. It's probably because there are so many characters, but while I'm drawing, I always seem to forget somebody. Normally it'd only be Happy that I forget! (laughs) And this time, I've completely and fully forgotten Ichiya-sama. That guy... Maybe he'll get to play his part after this... So I'd like to take this opportunity to put up a top-five list of the things I've forgotten.

No. 5: Just as I said above, the existence of Happy. (Sorry! I won't forget again!)
No. 4: Rings and necklaces from a wide variety of characters. (Look for them...On the other hand, you don't have to look.)
No. 3: Scars from a wide variety of characters (especially Gray's big scar).
No. 2: What Erza's armor looks like. (It's a secret that the design changes every time she appears.)
No. 1: People's faces and names. (Really! I'm so sorry!)

Recently, I've been receiving business cards from all sorts of people. At a recent party, in one day, I received some 50 cards. But I'm terrible at remembering who gave them to me. If I meet you a number of times, I'll remember but... I'm just a failure at being a part of society...

continued from the left-hand page.

Lucy: Would you please stop doing that?! You're not planning on beating me up that to cover our shame for the entire column, are you?!

: All of the rules and limitations of Gemini will be explained at a later date.

: Really?

: Maybe.

: .....

Mira: And the next question.

Is Hibiki's magic the Internet?

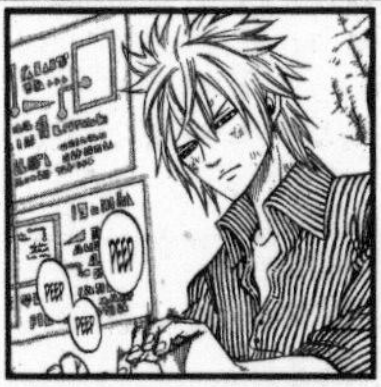

PEEP
PEEP
PEEP
PEEP

Lucy: "Internet"?

Mira: It's something close to what people call the Internet in the reader's world.

Lucy: What is it supposed to be?

Mira: Sorry, I don't know much about it myself.

Lucy: He said it was about compressing data and transferring it to others faster than it would take to tell them.

Mira: Puuunch!!

: Oww!!

: Is that what it means?

: Is that what *what* means?!!

Mira: Then here's the final question.

I really didn't like how Cobra was defea—

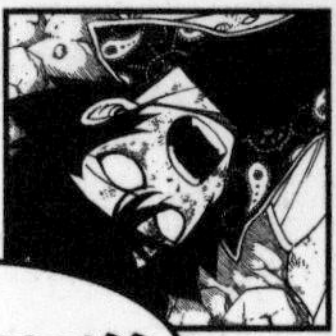

PUUUNCH!!

: W-Wait just a second, Mira-san!! You can't go punching the readers!!

Mira: There are some things that are best left untouched.

Lucy: Well, of the Oración Seis characters, he's pretty popular. And that way of being defeated was disappointin—

SATAN SOUL!

: Nooooo!!!

: Let's be adults about this, Lucy. Sometimes it's good for a wizard to go out that way.

Lucy: R-Right!

Mira: Besides, it's pretty cool! I'm sure he'll go down in legends as

THE GUY WHO WAS DEFEATED BY LOUD YELL!

: For something going unsaid, you just said it pretty loud!!

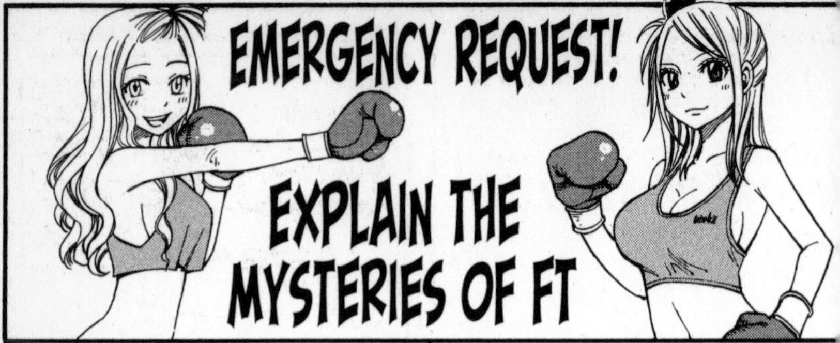

EMERGENCY REQUEST!

EXPLAIN THE MYSTERIES OF FT

At the Fairy Tail Gym

: Hah! Hyaah! Hup!

: Puuunch!!

Lucy: So, as you see, today we're coming to you from the gym inside the guild.

Mira: Puuunch!!

Lucy: First question.

If Racer only slows the rest of the world down, how come Brain praised his speed?

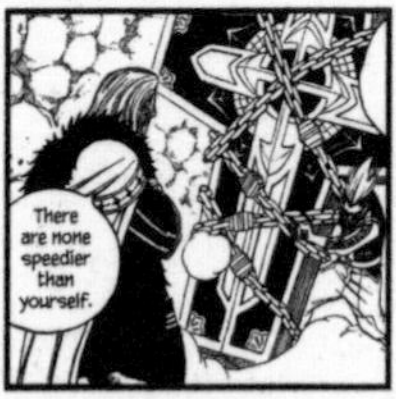
There are none speedier than yourself.

Mira: Simple flattery, perhaps.

: But he did actually deliver the coffin in only one hour, right?

Mira: True. But it just had to be close by to start with.

Lucy: What would it be close for?

: Puuunch!!

: Ow!

Mira: Next question!

Lucy: I've got a bad feeling about our corner this volume...

If Angel had Gemini turn into Erza or Midnight, wouldn't they have made quick work of Lucy?

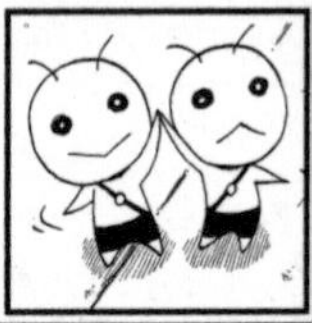

Mira: You lucked out there, Lucy.

Lucy: Th-That's true... I wonder why she didn't.

: Just chance, right?

: If she had used Ichiya's perfume that destroys people's will to fight, it could have been a real problem too.

Mira: I know! Once somebody changes into Ichiya once, they never want to do it again!

Lucy: They changed into Gray and me twice, but they never changed into Erza even once.

: Puuunch!!

: That's exactly the bad feeling I had!!!

Mira: Kiiick!!

Continued on the right-hand page.

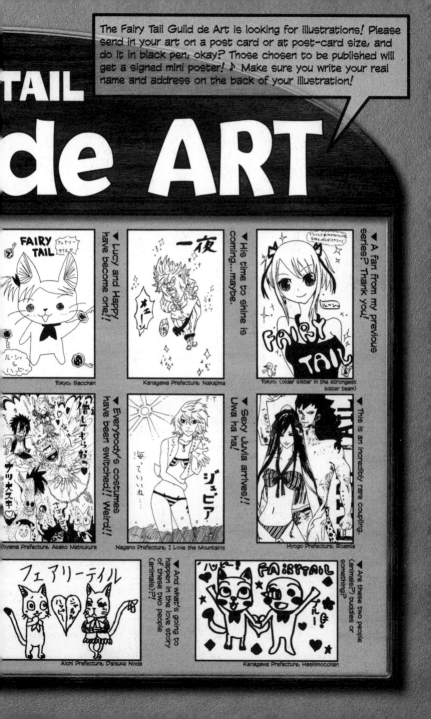

The Fairy Tail Guild de Art is looking for illustrations! Please send in your art on a post card or at post-card size, and do it in black pen, okay? Those chosen to be published will get a signed mini poster! ♪ Make sure you write your real name and address on the back of your illustration!

TAIL de ART

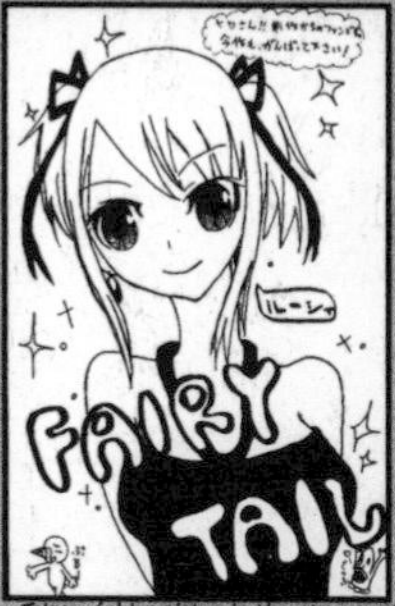

FAIRY TAIL
ルーシィ

Tokyo, (older sister in the strongest sister team)

▼ A fan from my previous series? Thank you!

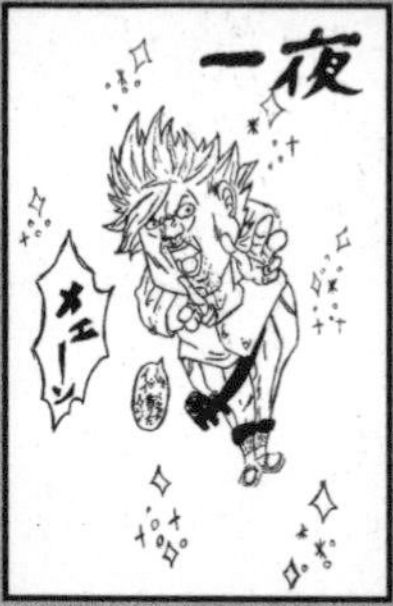

一夜

Kanagawa Prefecture, Nakajima

▼ His time to shine is coming...maybe.

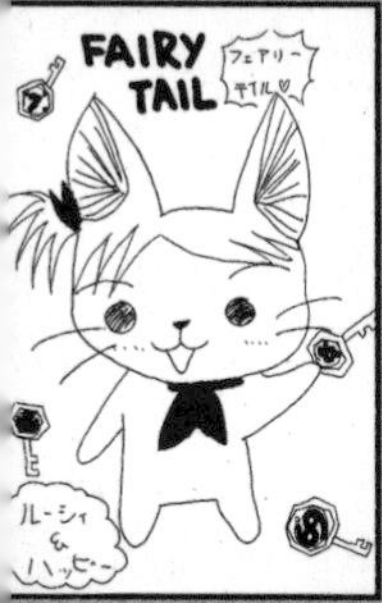

FAIRY TAIL
フェアリーテイル♡
ルーシィ & ハッピー

Tokyo, Sacchan

▼ Lucy and Happy have become one!!

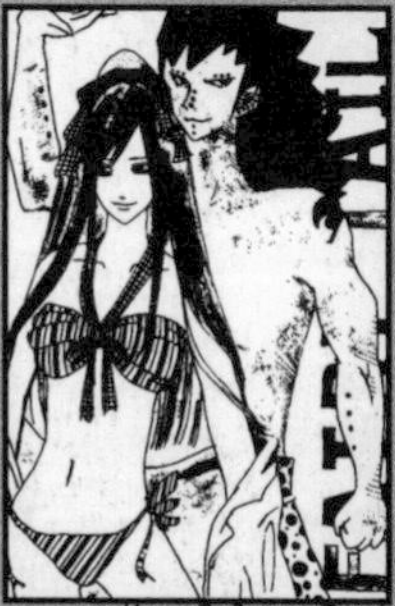
Hyogo Prefecture, Roamia

▼ This is an incredibly rare coupling.

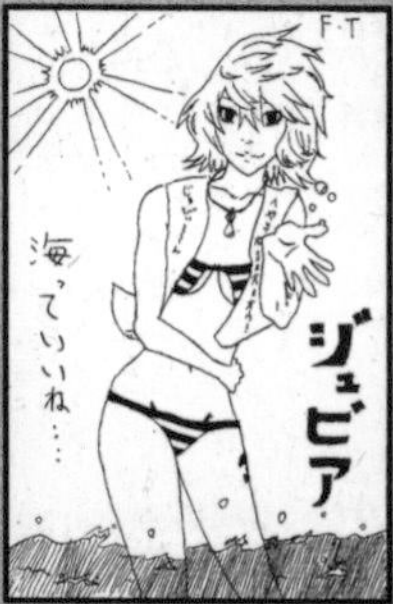

F・T
海っていいね…
ジュビア

Nagano Prefecture, I Love the Mountains

▼ Sexy Juvia arrives!! Uwa ha ha!

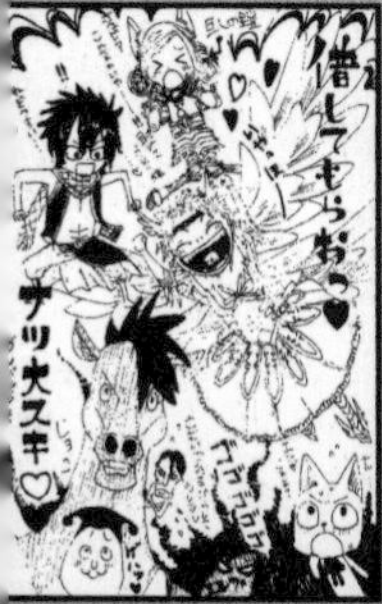

ナツ大スキ♡

Toyama Prefecture, Asako Matsukura

▼ Everybody's costumes have been switched!! Weird!!

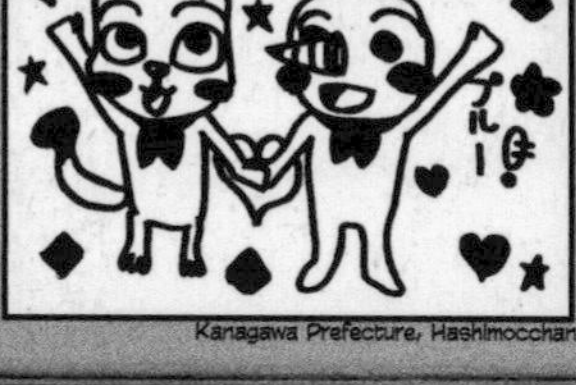

ハッピー!
FAIRYTAIL

Kanagawa Prefecture, Hashimocchan

▼ Are these two people (animals?) buddies or something?

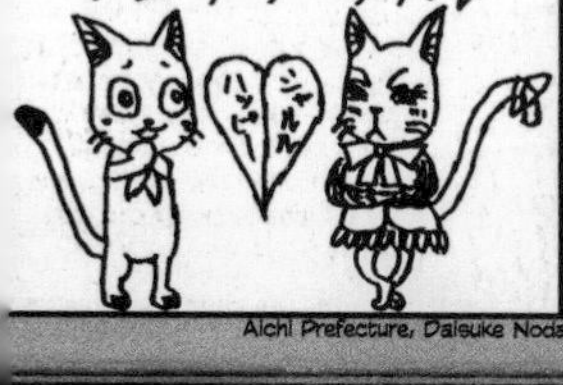

フェアリーテイル
ハッピー
シャルル

Aichi Prefecture, Daisuke Noda

▼ And what's going to happen in the love story of these two people (animals)?!

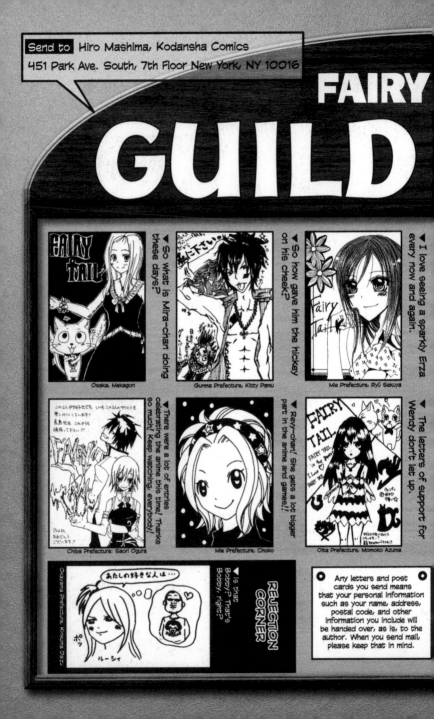

Send to Hiro Mashima, Kodansha Comics
451 Park Ave. South, 7th Floor New York, NY 10016

FAIRY GUILD

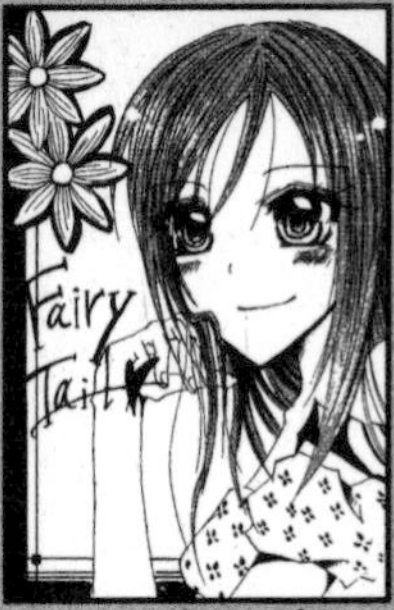
Fairy Tail

Mie Prefecture, Ryū Sakuya

▼I love seeing a sparkly Erza every now and again.

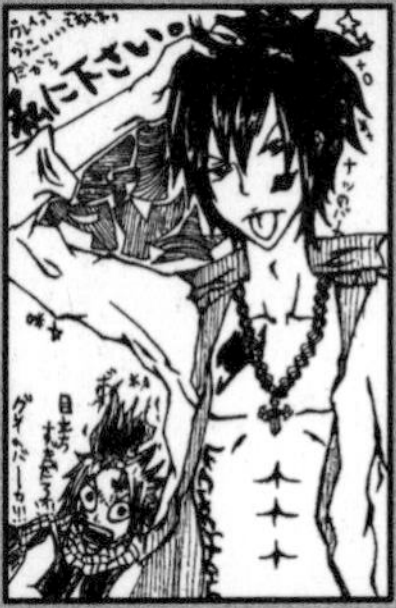

Gunma Prefecture, Kitty Pamu

▼So how gave him the hickey on his cheek?

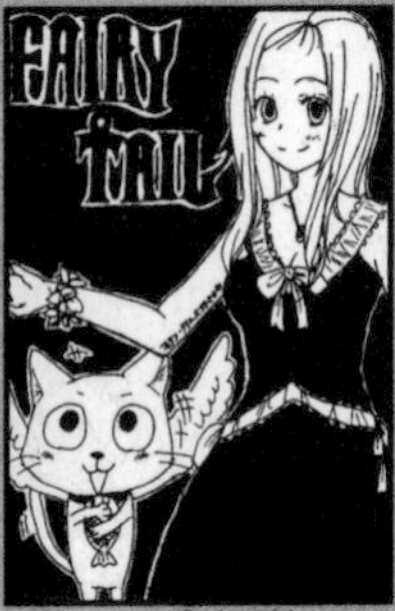
FAIRY TAIL

Osaka, Mekagon

▼So what is Mira-chan doing these days?

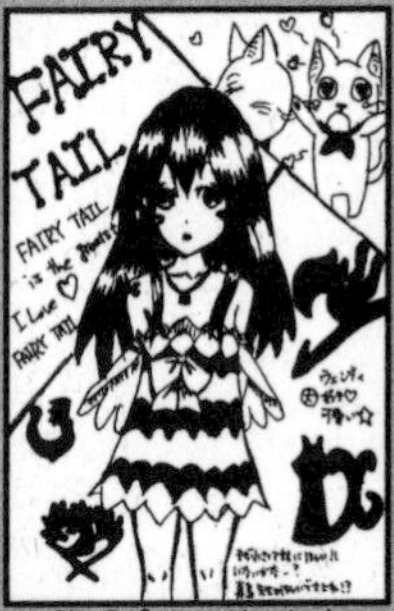
FAIRY TAIL

Oita Prefecture, Momoko Azuma

▼The letters of support for Wendy don't let up.

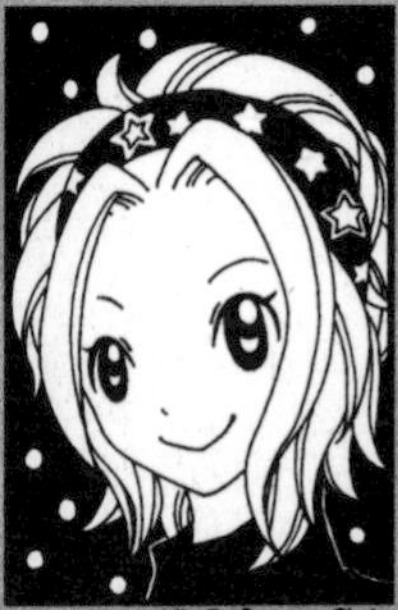

Mie Prefecture, Choko

▼Revy-chan! She gets a lot bigger part in the anime and games!!

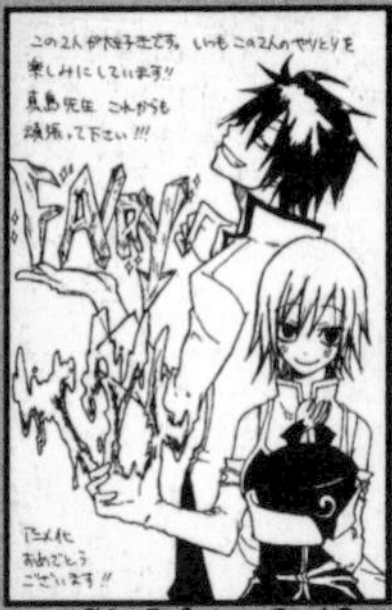
アニメ化
おめでとう
ございます!!

Chiba Prefecture: Saori Ogura

▼There were a lot of entries celebrating the anime this time! Thanks so much! Keep watching, everybody!

Any letters and post cards you send means that your personal information such as your name, address, postal code, and other information you include will be handed over, as is, to the author. When you send mail, please keep that in mind.

REJECTION CORNER

▼Is that Bobby? That's Bobby, right?

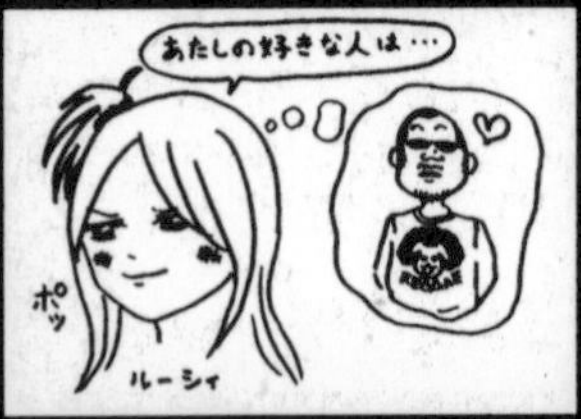
あたしの好きな人は…
ポッ
ルーシィ

Okayama Prefecture, Kinkuma Daizu

Translation Notes:

Japanese is a tricky language for most Westerners, and translation is often more art than science. For your edification and reading pleasure, here are notes on some of the places where we could have gone in a different direction with our translation of the work, or where a Japanese cultural reference is used.

Page 19, Tetrabiblos

The founder of the Ptolemaic system, Claudius Ptolemy, wrote a four-part book series describing the heavens called the Tetrabiblos -- The Four Books. One of the most important works of ancient astrology, the Tetrabiblos describes the constellations of the zodiac and their astrological influence on the world. Within the system, the Earth was a fixed point with the heavens spinning around it in complicated circles-within-circles. Its view of the universe was adopted by the Catholic Church until the time of Galileo and Copernicus some 1500 years after Ptolemy's writings.

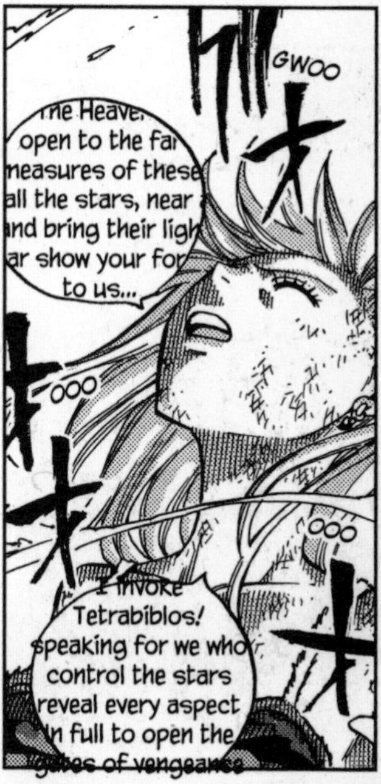
GWOO
The Heave open to the fa measures of these all the stars, near and bring their ligh ar show your fo to us...
OOO
OOO
Tetrabiblos! speaking for we who control the stars reveal every aspect in full to open the

Page 19, 88 Stars of the Heavens

Looking up on a night sky, you'd realize there are far more than 88 stars. What this is referring to is the 88 official constellation that astronomers use to divide and chart the night sky. Each constellation represents a region of the sky and is based on the ancient Greek charts of the heavens.

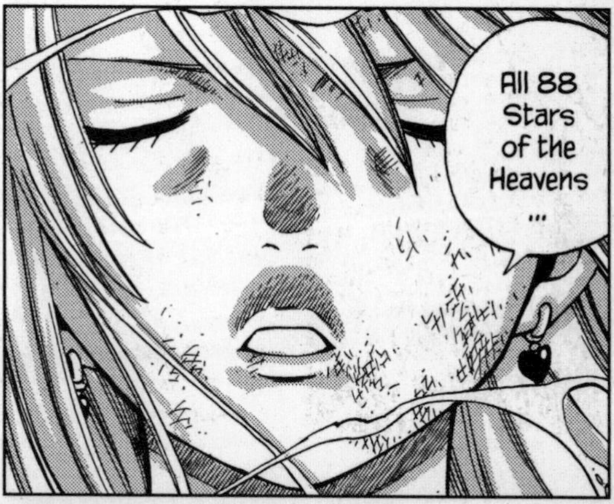
All 88 Stars of the Heavens ...

Page 158, Cat-dono

The honorific, -dono comes from the word tono which means "lord." So calling someone by that honorific is like adding a "my lord" to the name. Like some very polite people add the honorific -sama to every name they utter, Jura adds -dono to names. But still, cats are usually given "cute" honorifics like -chan, and only sometimes jokingly referred to as -san. Adding such a respectful honorific as -dono to a cat's name would surprise any listener.

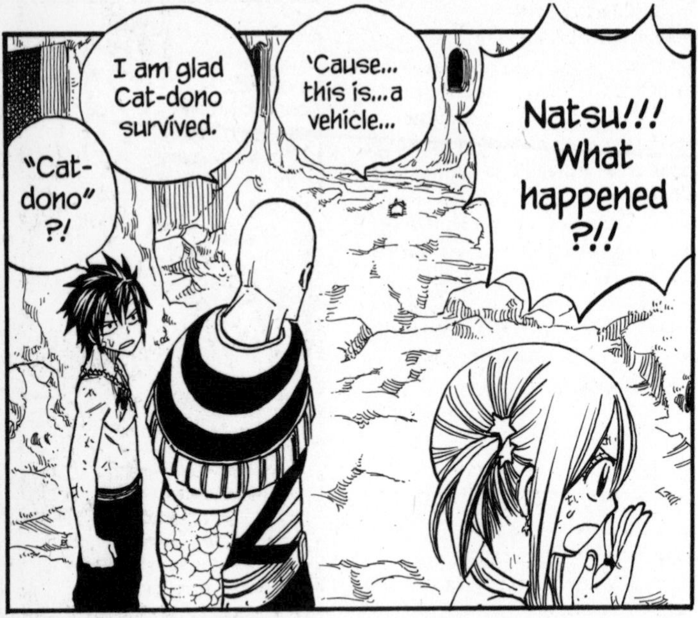
Natsu!!! What happened ?!!
'Cause... this is...a vehicle...
I am glad Cat-dono survived.
"Cat-dono" ?!

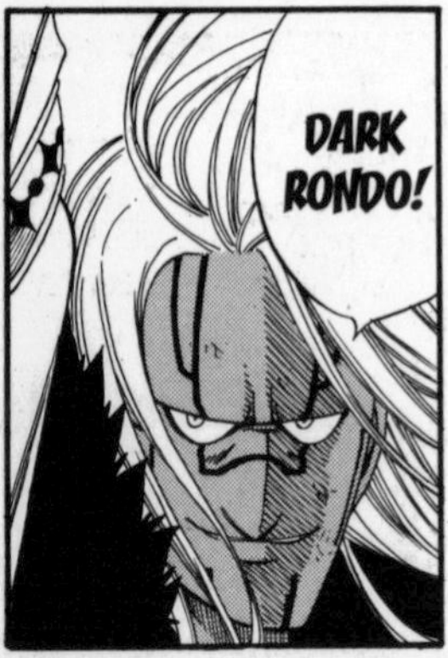
DARK RONDO!

Page 169, Dark Rondo

As described in the notes for Volume 16, "Rondo" means a theme that is repeated many times in music.

Page 169, Dark Capriccio

Like Rondo, Capriccio is a musical term describing a piece of music that is lively, bright, and free-form. It's taken from the same root word as the English word "capricious" comes from, which indicates that it is music performed at the musician's whim. The form was most popular among 17th century keyboard musicians.

Page 175, Lyon uses "san"

As you might note from the portrayal of Lyon in the manga, Lyon doesn't use honorifics very often because he does not think many people are worthy of his honors. So when Lyon uses the honorific, -san, for Jura, it shows more respect than Lyon is likely to give anyone else. For normal people, -san is a normal honorific that can be applied to nearly everyone, but for someone like Lyon, the use of -san is like the use of -sama for anyone else.

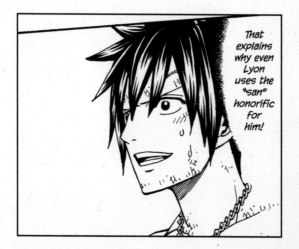

That explains why even Lyon uses the "san" honorific for him!

Preview of Fairy Tail, volume 19

We're pleased to present you a lettered preview from Fairy Tail, volume 19. Please check our website (www.kodanshacomics.com) to see when this volume will be available.

FAIRY TAIL

フェアリーテイル

19

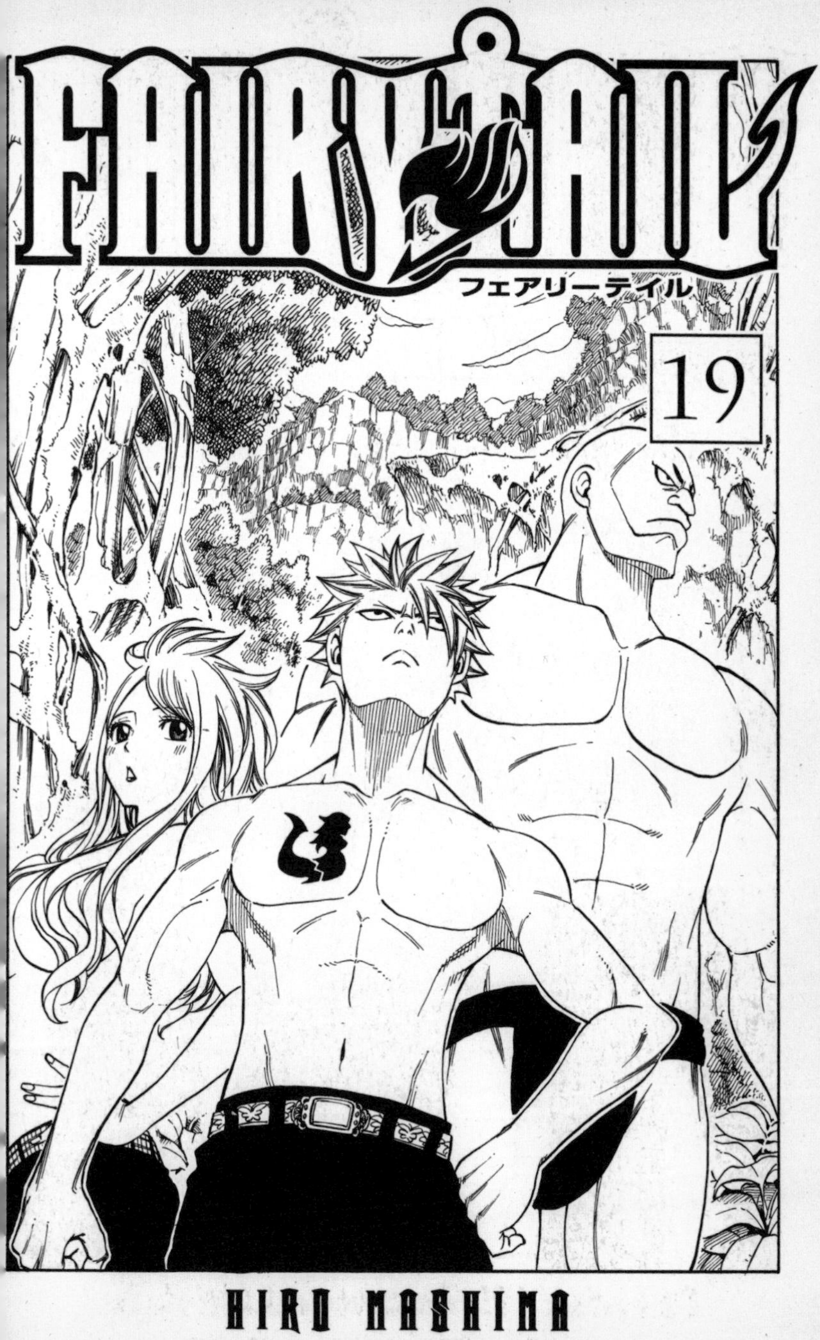

HIRO MASHIMA

FAIRY TAIL

フェアリーテイル

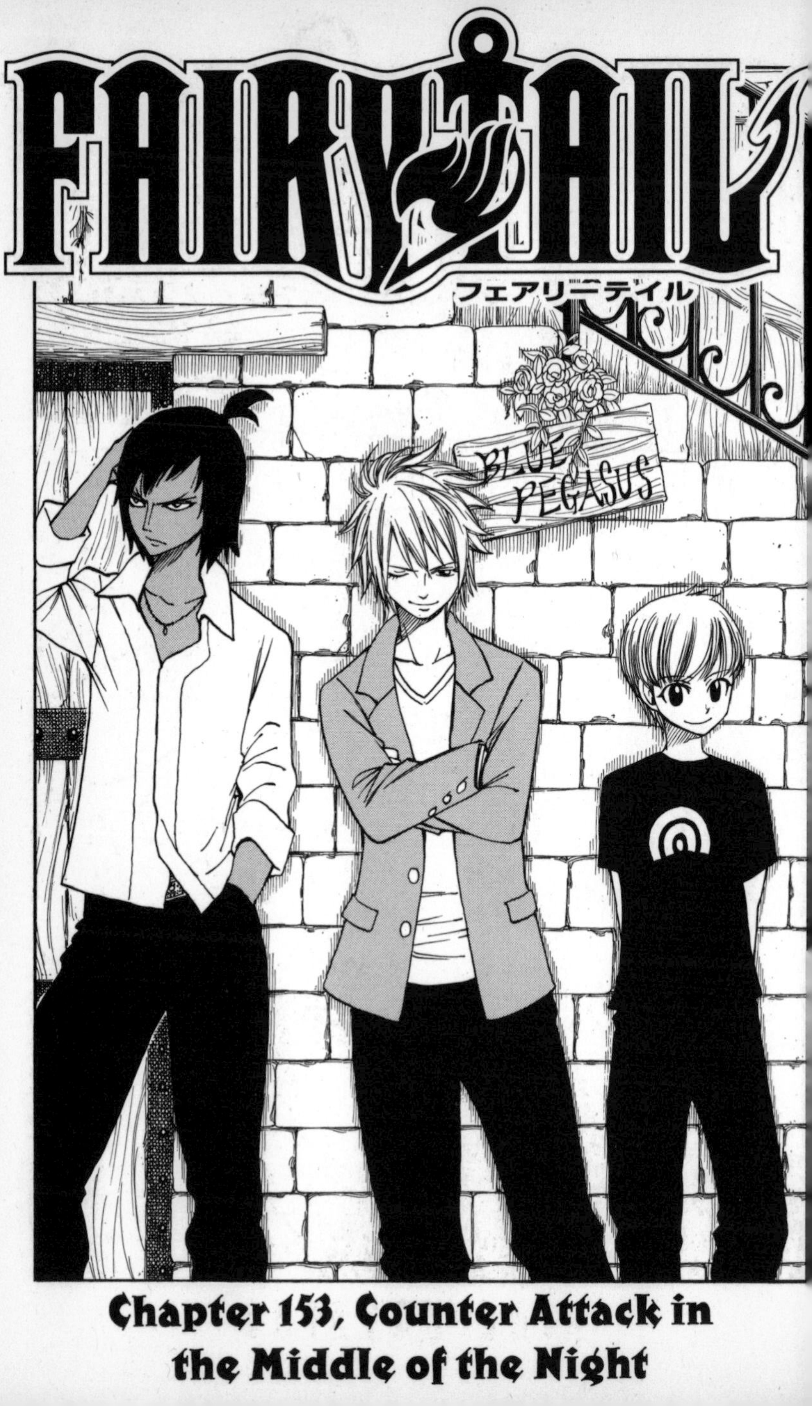
BLUE PEGASUS

Chapter 153, Counter Attack in the Middle of the Night

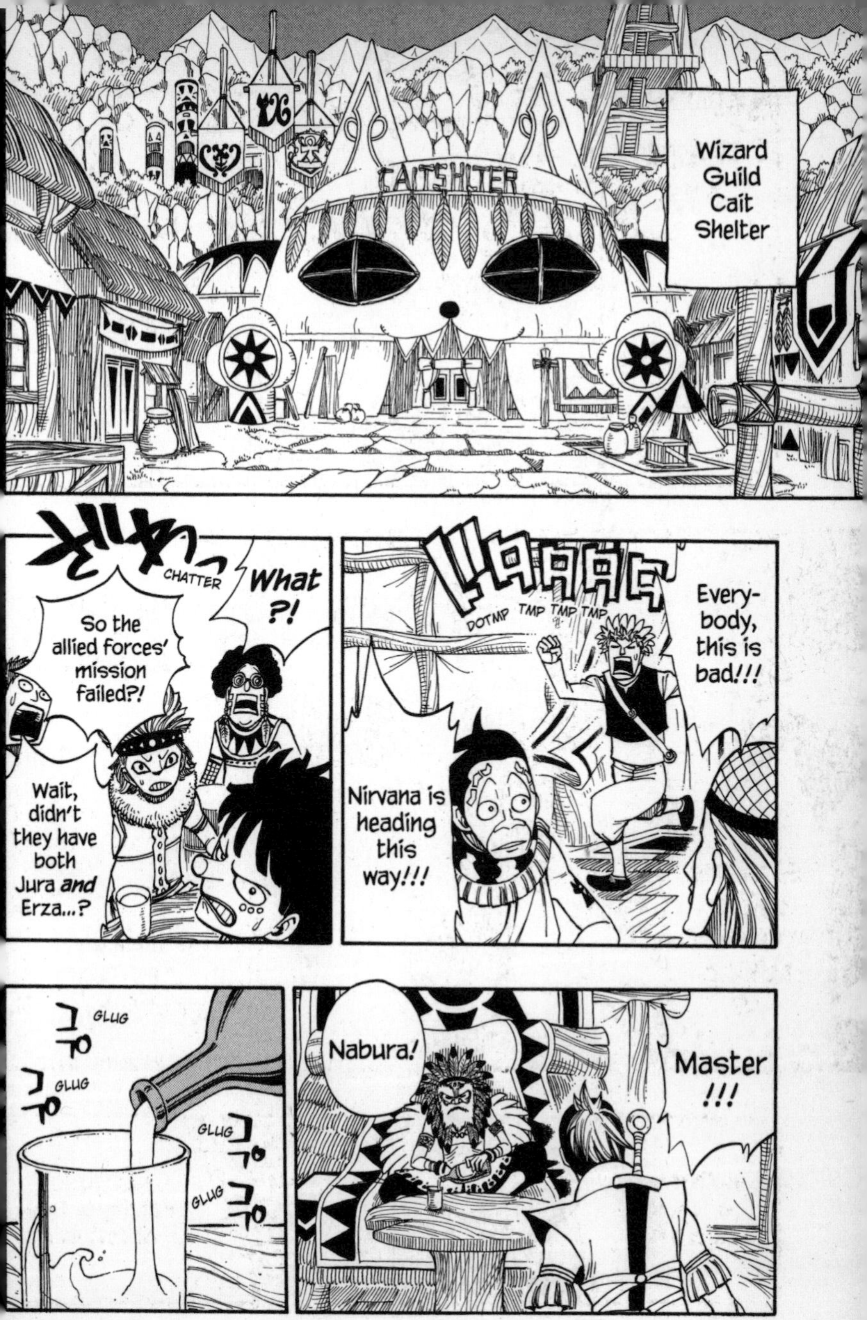

Wizard Guild Cait Shelter
CAITSHLTER
DOTMP TMP TMP TMP
Every-body, this is bad!!!
Nirvana is heading this way!!!
CHATTER
What?!
So the allied forces' mission failed?!
Wait, didn't they have both Jura and Erza...?
Master!!!
Nabura!
GLUG
GLUG
GLUG
GLUG

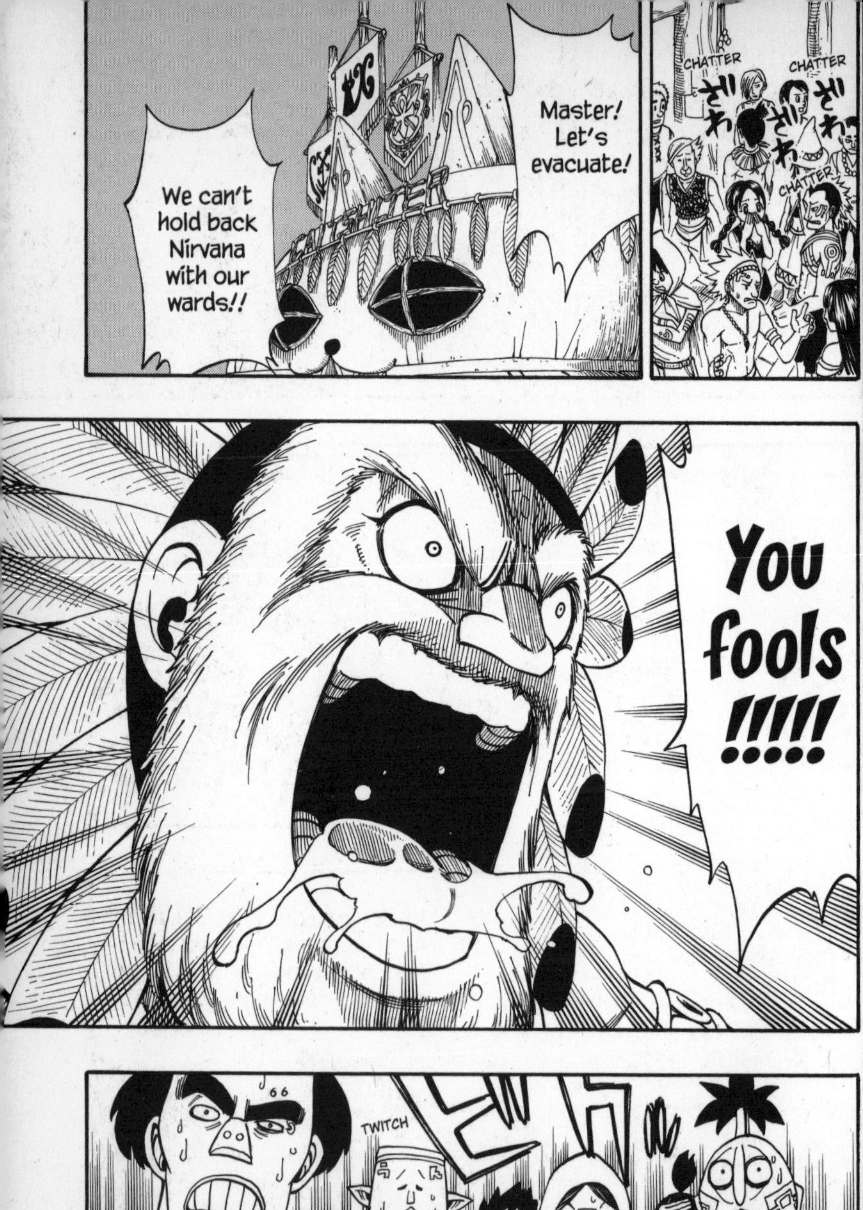
CHATTER
CHATTER
ざわ ざわ ざわ
CHATTER
Master! Let's evacuate!
We can't hold back Nirvana with our wards!!
You fools !!!!!
TWITCH

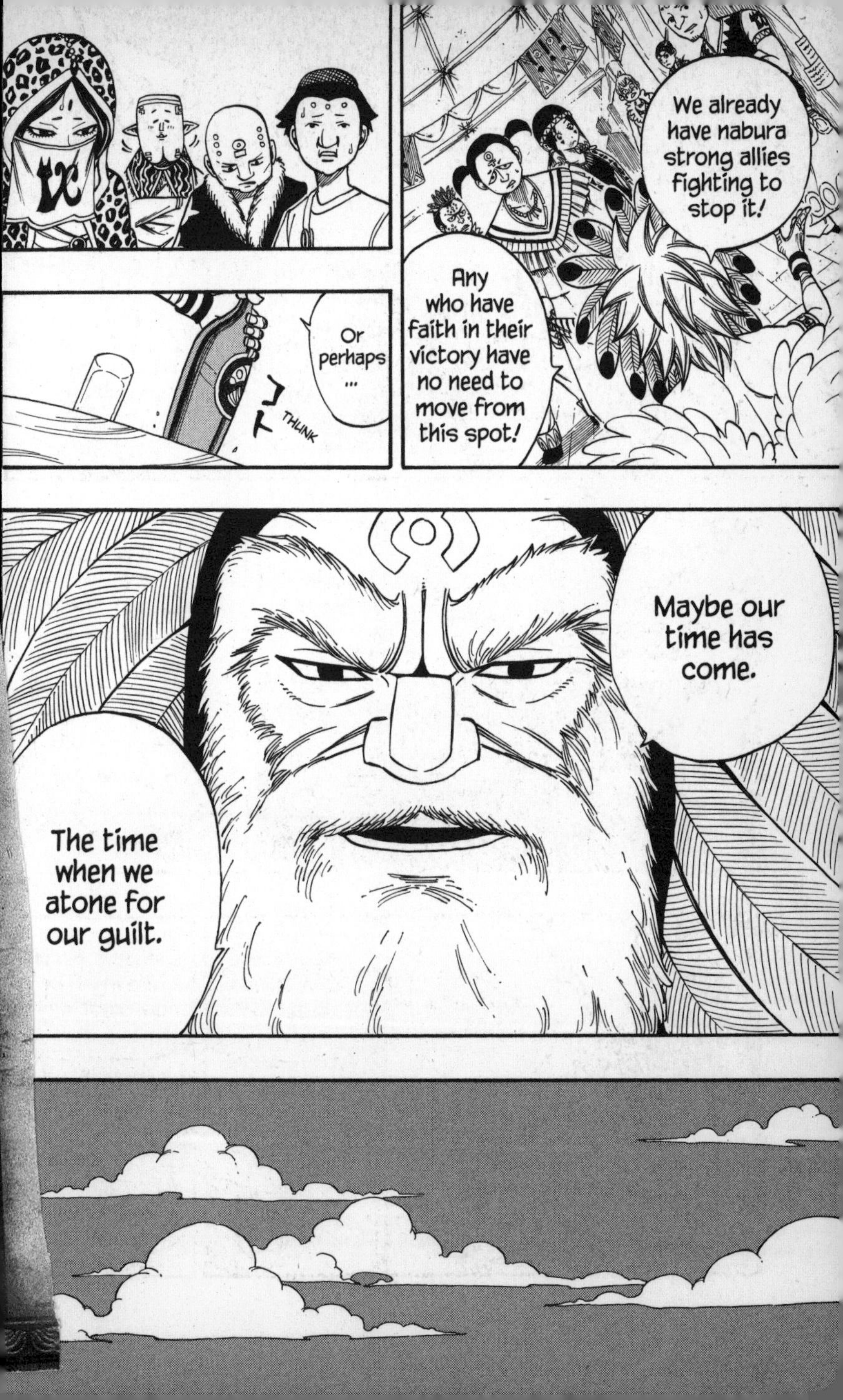
We already have nabura strong allies fighting to stop it!
Any who have faith in their victory have no need to move from this spot!
Or perhaps ...
THUNK
Maybe our time has come.
The time when we atone for our guilt.

Fairy Tail volume 18 is a work of fiction. Names, characters, places, and incidents are the products of the author's imagination or are used fictitiously. Any resemblance to actual events, locales, or persons, living or dead, is entirely coincidental.

A Kodansha Comics Trade Paperback Original

Published in the United States by Kodansha Comics, an imprint of Kodansha USA Publishing, LLC, New York.

Publication rights for this English edition arranged through Kodansha Ltd., Tokyo.

First published in Japan in 2009 by Kodansha Ltd., Tokyo

ISBN 978-1-61262-055-8

Printed in the United States of America

www.kodanshacomics.com

9 8 7 6 5 4 3 2 1

Translator: William Flanagan
Lettering: AndWorld Design

TOMARE!

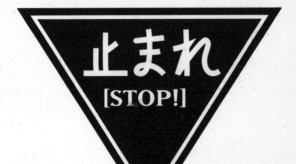

You're going the wrong way!

Manga is a completely different type of reading experience.

To start at the *beginning*, go to the *end*!

That's right! Authentic manga is read the traditional Japanese way—from right to left, exactly the *opposite* of how American books are read. It's easy to follow: Just go to the other end of the book and read each page—and each panel—from right side to left side, starting at the top right. Now y̶̶̶̶̶̶̶̶̶̶ was meant to be!